The Blue-Eyed Enemy

Kamikaze Pilots. Detail of painting by Iwata Sentaro, 1944.

THEODORE FRIEND

The Blue-Eyed Enemy

JAPAN AGAINST THE WEST
IN JAVA AND LUZON,
1942–1945

PRINCETON UNIVERSITY PRESS

Library of Congress Cataloging in Publication Data will be
found on the last printed page of this book

ISBN 0–691–05524–6

This book has been composed in Linotron Trump

Clothbound editions of Princeton University Press books
are printed on acid-free paper, and binding materials are
chosen for strength and durability. Paperbacks, although satisfactory
for personal collections, are not usually suitable for library rebinding

Printed in the United States of America by Princeton University Press,
Princeton, New Jersey

Designed by Laury A. Egan

TO MY TEACHERS

CONTENTS

CONTENTS

CONTENTS

LIST OF ILLUSTRATIONS

Frontispiece. Kamikaze pilots. Detail of painting by Iwata Sentaro, 1944, "Departure of Special Air Attack Corps." RG 331, JWP 127, NARS.

1. Princess Kartini (standing, right) as teacher of school established for children of Indonesian officials (1903). KITLV-G48.
2. Arithmetic, English, and geography: classroom in the Philippines, early twentieth century. Note central photo of George Washington, and review questions on Russo-Japanese War. 350-P-Ca-8-2-7, NARS.
3. Toothbrush drill, La Carlota, Negros Occidental, Philippines, 1928. 350-P-Ca-6-13-5, NARS.
4. Drill with wooden guns. Javanese children under Japanese occupation. From *Djawa Baroe* No. 23, January 12, 1943.
5. Governor General Tjarda's address at the opening of the Volksraad, Jakarta (Batavia), June 15, 1938. KITLV, unnumbered.
6. Ceremonial farewell ride in carabao cart for Secretary of War George H. Dern, Zamboanga, November 19, 1935. U.S. Signal Corps 116395, Dept. of the Army, Washington, D.C.
7. Surrender of British General Percival to General Yamashita, Singapore, 1942; painting by Muyamoto Saburo, 1944 (Yamashita is second from left, gesturing with wristwatch). U.S. Signal Corps B161-301121, Dept. of the Army, Washington, D.C.
8. Surrender of General Yamashita to American troops, Baguio, Luzon, September 3, 1945 (Yamashita is second from right and Gen. Mutō Akira is at far right). U.S. Signal Corps B161-211382, Dept. of the Army, Washington, D.C.
9. Premier Tōjō visits Manila July 10, 1943, and dines with Laurel (dark suit) and other Philippine leaders. Painting by Kawashima Hiichiro, 1943, entitled "Birth of New Philippines." U.S. Signal Corps B161-301123, Dept. of the Army, Washington, D.C.
10. Laurel enjoys merienda in his honor with Filipino cadets in Tokyo, at the time of the Greater East Asia Conference, November 4, 1943. Dept. of Justice, People's Court, Manila.
11. Sukarno leading the Seinendan (youth corps) in banzais for the emperor, responding to the promise of independence. Niels Douwes-Dekker, private collection, Huizen, Netherlands.

LIST OF TABLES

PREFACE

How can one determine the significance of events without first establishing their proportions? I try, in writing history, to establish proportion through comparison. That is particularly hard to do with the parts of Southeast Asia and the West Pacific Rim that I have chosen, but my pleasure in the task has been positively related to its degree of difficulty.

I began this book by trying to understand national development and decolonization in Indonesia and the Philippines during and immediately after Japanese occupation. Proper comprehension of that in turn required a compressed background of American and Dutch styles of imperial management, and full examination of the meaning of the Japanese irruption and its sequel. While Jakarta and Manila are the main points for tuning in, there are repeated signals from Tokyo, as well as from Washington and The Hague.

To produce a tightly woven narrative is a first necessity in Southeast Asian history, where gaps abound. By making my study comparative, at the same time as providing such a weave, I felt I could get beyond local and national patterns of inquiry, test prevailing interpretative values, and grasp the larger meanings of events that begin the present age in Southeast Asia. Comparison sometimes forces one's thoughts into a theoretical mode. I have given in to that necessity when I thought it might prove fertile for the reader.

I have not sought testable hypotheses in social science, which would have required more cases, with thinner understanding of each. But I believe that a primarily humanistic exploration of materials in five cultures has yielded observations and insights with a significance for modern Southeast Asia, and much, perhaps, of the postcolonial world.

Finding a title for the work has not been easy. Comprehensive ones that aimed to embrace all contents would have run on at eighteenth-century length. I have finally settled on a relatively short one, partly for its brevity. The main title aims to evoke something of the enmities and affinities, the bondings and freeings, that these pages describe. Although the epithet, "The Blue-Eyed Enemy," came from a Japanese general, its use here is not meant to suggest that any nation has a monopoly on racist feeling. Nor is it meant to accentuate a strand of ethological reasoning above other lines of analysis that I bring to bear on individual and collective motivations.

The clash of polities and national styles inevitably leads into the conflicted subject of the psychology of colonialism. Here I hope to have offered a helpful angle on the topic. Occasional extrapolations from individual and family psychology to national politics and leadership, however, are meant to be taken in context with discussions of social and economic factors, state structures, and military and strategic considerations, not to mention leaderly actions based on calculations of group and personal interest. So to stress, however, is to draw us back into the irrational and the subrational, and I hope to have accorded just weight to such forces.

The cross-weaving of the narrative—its parallelisms and contrasts, its confluences and divergencies—will, I trust, make events narrated before look fresh. I hope not only to have provided richer understanding of specific happenings, but also new interpretations of the multiple events that are summarized by terms like the Indonesian Revolution, the Philippine Restoration, and the Japanese imperial drive to the South.

Whatever the reader may wish to argue with, I trust he or she will find me consistently eclectic, as the project requires. This is the first book, to my knowledge, to embrace the three large island nations of the West Pacific—Japan, Indonesia, and the Philippines. Together their populations are approaching 350 million people. The world that is emerging requires new historical perspective. And that new focus in turn demands different texture and synthesis. I have tried to reconstruct the evidence and conceive its significance to illuminate part of modern world history as an open system, multivariant and multivalent.

When I first planned this work, Sukarno still had a shred of power, and Marcos had just won his initial presidential election. The debts of thanks I have accumulated while pursuing my inquiries since then are naturally many. An Office of Education (NDFL) grant enabled me to study Bahasa Indonesia intensively at Cornell University in 1966–67, and to work with a stimulating company of scholars. A Guggenheim Foundation grant in 1967–68 supported documentary research and interviews in Indonesia, the Philippines, and Japan. The State University of New York at Buffalo assisted research trips to the Netherlands in 1969 and 1970. My responsibilities as President of Swarthmore College, 1973–82, halted my progress, but the gift of a sabbatical leave in 1982–83 allowed me to resume and completely recast my inquiries. A Fellowship at the Woodrow Wilson International Center for Scholars in 1983–84 gave me excellent colleagueship with which to advance my design. Since then, the Trustees and staff of Eisenhower Exchange Fellowships, Inc. have been understanding of my phases of preoccupation with finishing the book.

In the notes throughout and in the list of interviews in the essay on sources I have tried to indicate most of my personal debts. Some special and substantial ones: to Beth Kodama for editorial work on an earlier stage of the manuscript, to Ōshima Kazuko and Ōshima Shōtarō for copious translations from Japanese, and to Barbara Gifford Shimer and Guy Hobbs for still more such translations, and scholarly teamwork. Evert van den Broek provided the larger part of the translations from the Dutch. Susan Sternglass helped me with books in German; Professor Robert Tucker of Princeton University and an anonymous friend helped with books in Russian.

Guy Hobbs and Susan Sternglass were my assistants at the Wilson Center. They and I found Kohar Rony of the Library of Congress invariably helpful. The same has been true of the staff of the John M. Echols Collection at Cornell. Marie Coleman and Shellie Wilensky Camp typed most of the manuscript. V. R. Boscarino designed the map. Jerry Ordansky, with Sydney Cohen, did the index. Niels Douwes-Dekker supplied me with gin, rare photographs, and moral encouragement.

James Billington, Prosser Gifford, and Ronald Morse led in providing an unforgettably stimulating atmosphere at the Woodrow Wilson Center. Several colleagues in Southeast Asian studies have commented on parts of the work as it evolved. Shlomo Avineri and Samuel Huntington were astute critics of its theoretical aspects. Professor Miwa Kimitada and two anonymous readers gave me still more to think about in the last stages of the work. Margaret Case shepherded the book through publication. My debts to all of these, and to others for silent dialogue with their writings, are only partially expressed here and in the notes that follow. After such help, I regret any errors or insufficiencies of mine that remain in the work.

My wife Elizabeth has been patient and impatient across the years of the effort. I thank her for her sustaining courage in both moods.

Philadelphia
June 1987

ABBREVIATIONS
AND TRANSLITERATIONS

To avoid a polyglot page studded with acronyms, I have generally rendered foreign terms in English. For convenience, however, some Indonesian, Japanese, and Dutch terms are used in the text. A brief list of them, and of abbreviations used in the notes, follows below. For more complete lexicons of wartime Japanese and Indonesian terms, see Anthony Reid and Oki Akira, *The Japanese Experience in Indonesia: Selected Memoirs of 1942–1945* (Athens, Ohio: Ohio University Center for Southeast Asian Studies, 1986), ix–xii; Benedict R. O'G. Anderson, *Java in a Time of Revolution* (Ithaca: Cornell University Press, 1972), 459–70; and Harry J. Benda, James K. Irikura, and Kōichi Kishi, *Japanese Military Administration in Indonesia: Selected Documents*, Yale University Southeast Asia Studies (New Haven, 1965), glossary following p. 279.

I follow Indonesian orthography in its post-1972 form, except for personal names and some place names, preferring to risk anachronism rather than to achieve awkward correctness.

I have used the *Japan Style Sheet* (Tokyo: Society of Writers, Editors, and Translators, 1983) to try to eliminate the inconsistencies of usage that result from combining the work of four different translators from the Japanese. I am sure I have not succeeded, but I hope at least to have shown respect for the problems of transliteration.

AR	Algemene Recherche (General Investigation Service)
ATIS	Allied Translators and Interpreters Service
BB	Binnenlands Bestuur (Interior Administration Department of Netherlands East Indies)
Beppan	Special Task Team
BIA	Bureau of Insular Affairs
Dai Tōa Kyōieken	Greater East Asia Co-Prosperity Sphere
Daitōashō	Japanese Ministry for Greater East Asia
Gaimushō	Japanese Ministry of Foreign Affairs (or documents therefrom)
Gunseikan	Chief of Military Administration

Gunseikanbu	Military Administration Headquarters
IMTFE	International Military Tribunal Far East
JPL	Jose P. Laurel Collection (Lyceum of the Philippines, Manila)
Kenpei	(Japanese) military policeman
Kenpeitai	military police
KITLV	Koninklijk Instituut voor Taal-Land en Volkenkunde
MacA	MacArthur Memorial Archives (Norfolk, Va.)
Malacanang	Wartime records collection in the bodega of the presidential palace, Manila
Nanpō	"Southern Area" as defined by the Japanese (south of Formosa, and north of Port Moresby; east from Burma, but excluding southern China; west of the International Date Line)
NARS	National Archives and Records Service
Partindo	Partai Indonesia
PC/DJ	Records of the People's Court, Department of Justice, Manila
PID	Politieke Inlichtingen Dienst (Political Intelligence Service)
PKI	Partai Komunis Indonesia
PNI	Partai Nasional Indonesia
PPO	Politiek-Politionele Overzichten (Political Police Surveys)
Q	Quezon Collection, National Library of the Philippines
R	Roxas Collection, National Library of the Philippines
RG	Record Group
Rikugunshō	Japanese War Ministry
RVO	Rijksinstituut voor Oorlogsdocumentatie (Royal Institute for War Documentation)
SEATIC	Southeast Asia Translators and Interpreters Corps

Where an abbreviation is used briefly for a series of references, it is specifically identified in that chapter.

In notes, official titles are given in presumptively readable abbreviations (Gov. Gen. = Governor General; Min. Kol. = Minister of Colonies; Lt. Col. = Lieutenant Colonel; Sec. War = Secretary of War; etc.).

The Blue-Eyed Enemy

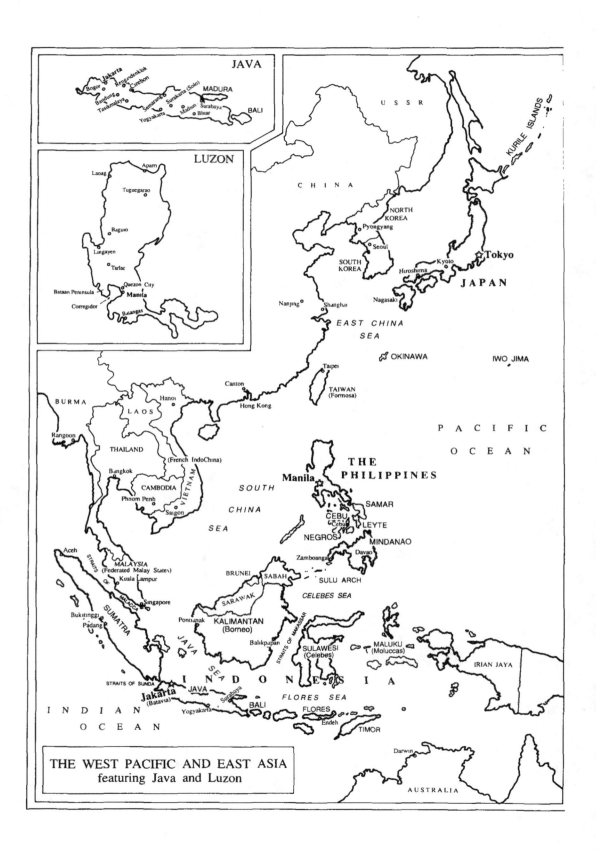

THE WEST PACIFIC AND EAST ASIA
featuring Java and Luzon

INTRODUCTION

LIBERATORS AND OPPRESSORS

IN SOUTHEAST ASIA

THE "HOLY WAR FOR ASIAN LIBERATION"

With Bernard of Clairvaux and Saladin, holy war became an institution. Vasco da Gama's age of exploration made world wars possible; Adam Smith's industrial age made them periodic. Humankind has since lived in jeopardy of world war and holy war converging.

Japan's "Holy War for Asian Liberation," although part of a world war, aimed specifically to establish a "Greater East Asia Co-Prosperity Sphere." The Japanese concept of holy war was not religious as Islam and Christianity suggest religion, and was even nonreligious in the sense that most Japanese do not believe in a supreme deity. But that did not diminish the intensity with which most Japanese saw the war as sacred and just,[1] a struggle that bore analogy to *jihad* in Islam. The Indonesians, however, for whom *perang sutji* conveys a similar meaning, felt less than complete identification with the Greater East Asian war, and reserved their fervor for their own battle for national independence, or even for Islamic separatism. Educated Christian Filipinos, for whom the term "just war" evokes argumentative principles that rationalized the Crusades, found the Japanese holy war as alien as Islamic jihad, and even harder to understand.

In any event, during the global crisis of 1939–45, Japan sought by force and preachment to substitute itself as the superior power in

[1] For Japanese sense of their divine origin, collective purity, "holy task," and the spiritual cleansing of war, see John W. Dower, *War Without Mercy: Race and Power in the Pacific War* (New York: Pantheon, 1986). As a starting point for historical debate on conflicting senses of justice, see C. Hoyosa, N. Andō, Y. Ōnuma, and R. Minear, eds., *The Tokyo War Crimes Trial: An International Symposium* (Tokyo: Kodansha International, 1986).

several long-standing imperial relationships. What happened can be analyzed as the product of capitalist competition, as Asian national liberation, or as a war of colonial reorganization; but none of these rubrics is broad and deep enough to contain all the variables of power, resources, and spirit that arise in imperial-national pairings.

The problem of power is basic to our age. Competitive self-development in an interdependent context raises it every day in many forms. In that perspective, obsession with the "means of production" and economic self-interest leads to reductionist fallacies. We need to see production as no more and no less than one of several key intertwining factors. Effective military force is another; it clearly may be held in restraint where relatively high economic stakes pertain, or deployed where little or minimal economic interest is involved. That is likely to happen when political interests, as such, prevail—when one nation or people or government is determined to have its presence and its will expressed even at the cost of bloodshed. That, in turn, however obtuse it may appear to the idealist or obscure to the analyst, will occur when basic cultural identities and sacred values of the contending national forces are stung and aroused.

Japan's "Holy War" for Greater East Asia raises and focuses all these questions, and with particular pertinence in Southeast Asia. The self-expression of numerous peoples was involved: the national strivings of all the peoples of that region; the imperial identity of the North Atlantic powers governing there; and the conflicted ambitions of the Japanese, whose own self-development expressed itself in the wish to be hailed as liberators at the same time as they installed a surrogate regional empire.

A broad concept of culture may help at this point: culture as embracing all means of self-development—ideas and values as well as force and wealth. Imperial-national conflicts involve contending deployments of all the means of self-development available to each nation—a complex political-cultural tangle. History happens in that very mix, unfolding through resistances and imitations, through oppositional mirrorings with transformative powers, through contrapuntal debasings and ennoblements.

To find a way through the historical mass of symbolic and illusory factors as well as concrete and objective ones, we must borrow freely, but selectively. Mannoni's "Prospero and Caliban" suggests the creative dependence of opposites, but topples into literary fancy.[2] Freudian theory allows searching of deeper sources of psychic energy, but is fraught with cultural narrowness and failed dogmas. Neo-Marxian doctrine suggests some dynamics of exploitation and willed dependence, but tends both to arrogant rigidity and opportune plasticity.[3] Psychopolitical analysis, as advanced by Fanon and promoted by Sartre, demonstrates that outer and inner conflict both may be resolved by force, but does so in a manner that glorifies violence.[4] One may usefully borrow from Hegel's concept of lordship and bondage, with its dialectic of mutual self-discovery, while avoiding the nineteenth-century philosophic baggage with which he loaded it.[5] Along with selected intimations from all the above, one may even lift insights from the nascent field of ethology—particularly regarding pseudo-speciation, the neurological basis for stereotyping—with its explanatory power for the collective ways we tend to treat strangers as dangerous animals.[6]

[2] Mannoni, *Prospero and Caliban: The Psychology of Colonization* (New York: Praeger, 1964).

[3] As for Freudo-Marxianism, Herbert Marcuse, *Eros and Civilization* (New York: Random House, 1955) is seminal. Frederic Jameson takes off from a Marcusean springboard into his own chosen depths: *Marxism and Form: Twentieth Century Dialectical Theories of Literature* (Princeton: Princeton University Press, 1971); *Fables of Aggression* (Berkeley: University of California Press, 1979); *The Political Unconscious* (Ithaca: Cornell University Press, 1981). These critiques of repressive capitalist abundance have implications for imperial projection in a world that is both excolonial in sovereign terms and neocolonial in other terms. They concentrate, however, on the aesthetics of Western metropolitan man.

[4] Frantz Fanon, *The Wretched of the Earth* (New York: Grove Press, 1966).

[5] I have explored the application of Hegelian themes in "Lordship and Bondage: the Philippines, Indonesia, and Japanese Impact, 1942–1945," Woodrow Wilson International Center for Scholars, Asia Program, Occasional Paper no. 19, 1984.

[6] Konrad Lorenz, *On Aggression*, trans. Marjorie Kerr Wilson (New York: Harcourt, Brace and World, 1966), conceives of pseudo-speciation as the tendency in Homo sapiens to treat racially or culturally varying members of the same species as if they were of a different species. That under some conditions humans treat other humans as beasts is not a new discovery. But inquiry into the evolutionary basis for this behavior has given rise to two recent waves of controversy. The first, initiated by the writings of Lorenz and others in the 1960s, may be followed in Ashley Montagu et al., *Man and Aggression*, 2d ed. (New York: Oxford University Press, 1973). The second, provoked by Edward O. Wilson and the sociobiologists, again aroused Montagu and others to rebuttal: *Sociobiology Examined* (New York: Oxford University Press, 1980). Wilson, with Charles J. Lumsden, provides an interesting reply in *Promethean Fire: Reflections on the Origin of Mind* (Cambridge: Harvard University Press, 1983).

To assist interpretation of history I rely more readily on anthropologically derived data than on attempts to elicit laws common to insects, geese, monkeys, and humans. The neurophysiologist Jose Delgado wisely says that to behave is to choose

Eclectically, then, and with that fertile form of focused vision that English and Americans call "common sense," one may explore the emergence of the present age in insular Southeast Asia. The propelling dynamic came from Japan's "Holy War."

SOVEREIGNTY CONTESTS IN SOUTHEAST ASIA

The great Japanese explosion outward raised everywhere it reached the fundamental question of constituted government and of individual identity—From whence flows authority? In most of Southeast Asia that question was answered by reference to Western governmental apparatus and theories of state, varying according to the national histories and colonial styles of the French, Dutch, British, and Americans. During a time of extraordinary turbulence and deprivation, the Japanese displaced all of those with their own idiosyncratic theory and structure.[7]

When the Allies returned, the question—Who rules?—was up for a fresh answer, with new assumptions. The struggles that followed may be seen as ranged upon a heat scale. Thailand, with its many compromises, but with no overt sovereignty contest, stands at the coolest end, at a theoretical absolute zero. Vietnam stands at the other, the superheated, end of the scale. There, revolution occurred that was clearly both national and social. In the midrange, the Philippines, Malaysia, Burma, and Indonesia represent situations where social revolution failed. The Huk revolt, the Malaysian "Emergency," Communist insurrectionary forces in Burma, and the series of differently motivated social actions in Indonesia—at Madiun, in the Tiga Daerah, and on North Sumatra—illustrate efforts to redefine status and redistribute wealth in Southeast Asia in this period. But the very reason for their not approaching revolutionary success was the significance of a still higher priority: to reorder power vis-à-vis the imperial presence. Even Tan Malaka put national revolution over social revolution, and when others tried to reverse the priorities, he was among those who lost their lives.[8]

---

one pattern among many. While agreeing with that—and I write about people choosing and behaving—I will occasionally and pliably allow for the relevance of ethological insights.

[7] Ramon H. Myers and Mark Peattie, eds., *The Japanese Colonial Empire, 1895–1945* (Princeton: Princeton University Press, 1984) is excellent on the Northeast Asian area it covers, and on Micronesia, but its focus on long-term administration requires it to leave out the Japanese occupations in Southeast Asia.

[8] Analyses of the primacy of sovereignty is central in my essay, "Revolution and

Only Ho Chi Minh managed successfully to fuse national liberation with social redefinitions, but terrible costs of atrocity and disappointment accompanied that progress. Far from Ho, close to the
Thai, stand the Philippines, with a devolution of sovereignty so un-
troubled as to be classifiable as a restoration. Malaysia and Burma
hold midpoints on the scale. Indonesia is far from the Thai and
closer to Ho, with a revolutionary contest for national sovereignty
that took four years, and aroused great heat of will and forceful
skill.[9] The primacy of contests for sovereignty throughout the area
testifies to the vital importance in all Southeast Asian political entities, whether conceived as cultures, nations, or powers, of throwing off the imperial critic, censor, and boss.

When the Japanese arrived in the Netherlands East India in 1942,
the Javanese and other Indonesians welcomed them as "liberators."
When the British troops arrived in 1945, as precursors to the Dutch,
it was known as the "reoccupation." The Philippine vocabulary for
the analagous periods is the very opposite. There, the Japanese "occupation" was finally undone by American forces in the period
1944–45, which was known as the "liberation." In between, the Japanese, who saw themselves as supersovereign throughout Greater
East Asia, revealed themselves as countersovereign in the eyes of
Indonesians and Filipinos alike. Contests for sovereignty in the two
countries, as throughout the region, illustrate the Hegelian paradigm of the struggle of bondsman and lord.

IMAGES OF BONDED IDENTITY AND CONFLICT

Understanding imperial motives and endurance, as well as national
uprisings in response to them, requires comprehension of naked
power and shrouded will; of what can be done by force and what
can not; of what is imaginable by way of counterforce, and what is
not; of a clash of images, of other and self; and, inescapably, of a
linkage of images, of self and other.

Language thrives on antinomies. Imperial-national situations are

---

Restoration: Indonesia and the Philippines as Paired Opposites, 1945–1949," a paper
presented to the Ninth Conference of the International Association of Historians of
Asia, Manila, November 1983.

[9] Some of the international diplomatic phenomena are expertly treated in Evelyn
Colbert, *Southeast Asia in International Politics* (Ithaca: Cornell University Press,
1977); and Robert J. McMahon, *Colonialism and the Cold War: The United States
and the Struggle for Indonesian Independence, 1945–1949* (Ithaca: Cornell University Press, 1981).

inescapably bipolar and oppositional. Naturally one looks for antithetical images that can contain as much meaning as possible, and
that allow supple and suggestive discourse. The "dominator" and
the "dependent" is not a clear antinomy, but has the contrived
sound of sociological jargon. "Master" and "slave" is clear in its
opposition, and humanly evocative; but it refers too clearly to past
institutions of servitude, while implying judgment from that context.

"Lord" and 'bondsman" have an antique ring to them, but the
terms have advantages as well.[10] They clearly suggest superordinate
and subordinate status. They imply synergy, working together even
when understanding is incomplete and emotions not fully shared.
They specifically denote bonding, the mental and spiritual impression that two beings make upon each other, with the connotation
that there is no rift without a calculus of pain and loss in both parties.

The fact that Hegel used the terms "lordship and bondage" may
be a disadvantage, but not an insuperable one. He did not set out to
explain imperialism, but in trying to explain the phenomena of the
spirit he did show how self-consciousness is both independent and

[10] The basic source is G.W.F. Hegel, *The Phenomenology of Mind*, trans. and ed.
J. B. Baillie (New York: Harper and Row, 1967), 228–40. The German for lordship and
bondage is "Herrschaft und Knechtschaft" (Hegel, *Phänomenologie des Geistes*
[Leipzig: Felix Meiner, 1921], 123–31). Baillie's 1910 translation allows the reader, if
he wishes, to introduce connotations of Edwardian imperialism into the choice of
terms. It would be hard to find a precise equivalent in modern American speech.
There is little help from the influential French neo-Hegelian, Alexandre Kojève, "assembled" by Raymond Queneau, translated by James H. Nichols, Jr., and edited by
Alan Bloom, *Introduction to the Reading of Hegel* (Ithaca: Cornell University Press,
1980). His abstruse ratiocinations on "the end of history" include the observation
that "in the extreme every Japanese is in principle capable of committing, from pure
snobbery, a perfectly gratuitous *suicide* . . . which has nothing to do with the *risk* of
life in a fight waged for the sake of 'historical' values that have social or political
content" (159–62n; quotation, 162n). Had Kojève grounded himself in Japanese so-
ciology and history, he might not have gone into such an erroneous Gallic spin.
For sounder interpretations of Hegel I have benefited from George Kelly, *Hegel's
Retreat From Eleusis* (Princeton: Princeton University Press, 1978), with its understanding of Hegel's view of "history and politics as a sequence of ennoblements, not
of submissions" (247). Also: Judith Shklar, *Freedom and Independence: A Study of
Hegel's Phenomenology of Mind* (Cambridge: Harvard University Press, 1976); Stanley Rosen, *G.W.F. Hegel: An Introduction to the Science of Wisdom* (New Haven:
Yale University Press, 1974); and George Dennis O'Brien, *Hegel on Reason and History* (Chicago: University of Chicago Press, 1975). While making grateful use of Hegel's dialectic between lord and bondsman, I frankly do not wish to carry the burden
of the rest of his thought, or to be charged with importing it into this study.

dependent at the same time. He offered as illustrative metaphor the master and servant (not "slave"; not "serf").

In each, the plane of action must be distinguished from the levels of awareness that accompany the act. The master orders, and is conscious of being superordinate as he does so. But he is also conscious of his dependence on the servant. The servant obeys, and is conscious of being subordinate as he does so. But as he obeys he is also conscious of his independence of his master.[11] That independence is only partial, and certainly not pronounced; but it has the potential to prevail. In analysis of the conflict between lord and bondsman, Hegel moves to the dramatic statement that "Each aims at the destruction and death of the other. . . . The relationship of both self-consciousness is . . . so constituted that they prove themselves and each other through a life-and-death struggle. . . . And it is solely by risking life that freedom is obtained."[12]

For modern usage, the focus on the ultimate confrontation between lord and bondsman is valuable. For "the reflexion of self into self" essential to growth, both fear and service are necessary. "Without the discipline of service and obedience," fear does not spread throughout one's existence. But that discipline shakes natural consciousness, pushes anxiety toward "absolute fear," and makes possible a new freedom and mastery. The bondsman discovers a "mind of his own," a reaching for objective consciousness beyond a determinate mode of being. By grappling with particulars across the span of objective reality he realizes a self.[13] Always, of course, the "other" was required for the "self" to be revealed. Hegel's translator summarizes the argument: "The equality of selves is the truth, or complete realization, of self in another self; the affinity is higher and more ultimate than the disparity."[14]

Thus a late Edwardian, in summarizing, modifies a pre-Victorian argument. He helps us by prefiguring modern thinking on questions of individual personality and growth, as well as on questions of identity in cultures and development of nations. Lord and bondsman exist within the psychology of single individuals, and between different individuals. They also exist between groups within a given culture, as well as between whole cultures. In the last case, the phenomena frequently become focused upon representative groups and individuals. Four levels entailed in this discussion must be distin-

[11] Hegel, *Phenomenology of Mind*, 37.
[12] Ibid., 232–33.
[13] Ibid., 239–40.
[14] Ibid., 228.

guished and kept in mind: the intrapsychic and interpsychic, the intracultural and intercultural. I ask for the freedom to use metaphorical language pliably across all four: to suggest what may be sharply sensed but hard to describe, and to try imaginatively to picture what would be foolish to put in binding definitions.

SUKARNO AND QUEZON AS BONDSMEN AND LORDS

Two individuals, Sukarno and Manuel Quezon, exemplify the workings of "lord" and "bondsman" at various levels. Each had roughly fifteen years of significant apprenticeship before rising to twenty years of national political primacy. Quezon was second behind Sergio Osmena among young Filipino constitutional nationalists, until defeating him to become Nacionalista party leader in 1922 and president of the Commonwealth from 1935 to 1943. Sukarno began to get control of the Indonesian stage as the years of Quezon's Philippine leadership concluded. After many years in detention during the period 1926–42, he made use of the Japanese era to rise to the presidency of the Indonesian Republic. His formal power began in 1945, and lasted until the events following the attempted coup of 1965 initiated his decline.

Sukarno's extraordinary power of projected ego was only latent in the 1920s and 1930s,[15] but he was already using "Indonesia" as a collective noun. He attracted Dutch surveillance with his daring subjective tonality in first-person singular and plural. Then they put him under lock and key. His lowest recorded moment was in September 1933, when he pleaded in four letters to the Dutch colonial attorney general to be released from prison, and promised that he would never again enter political activity. The self-abasement of that correspondence won him nothing. Not freedom, certainly. To the continuing distrust of Indies officials was now added lasting contempt. They shipped Sukarno off to detention in Boven Digul.[16]

When the Japanese released Sukarno in 1942, they easily extracted a promise of cooperation from him. He later exuberantly re-

[15] J. D. Legge's work—*Sukarno, a Political Biography*, 2d ed. (Sydney: Allen and Unwin, 1986)—is basic, as is Bernhard Dahm, *Sukarno and the Struggle for Indonesian Independence*, trans. Mary F. Somers Heidhues (Ithaca: Cornell University Press, 1969).

[16] John Ingleson, *Road to Exile: The Indonesian Nationalist Movement, 1927–1934* (Singapore: Heinemann, 1979), 216–22. Key documents are published in R. C. Kwantes, *De Ontwikkeling van de Nationalistische Beweging in Nederlandsch-Indië* (Development of the nationalist movement in the Netherlands Indies) (Groningen: Bouma's Boekhuis, 1982), 4: 37–50.

called, "For the first time in my life I saw myself reflected in an Asian mirror."[17] From the Dutch his reflected image had been on cracked glass without silver backing. Among the Japanese he felt complemented: whole. Sukarno's career flourished in the service of Dai Nippon, which he saw as identical with service to Indonesia *merdeka*—free Indonesia. He exhorted his people in September 1942, in language strikingly Hegelian, even if his inspiration was more likely Marxian. Throw off the *sklavengeest*—"slave spirit"— he said, and adopt the *heerengeest*—"lord spirit." If he were still making the point in Dutch, he also made it in Bahasa Indonesia: in each Indonesian soul the *jiwa ksatriya* must prevail over the *jiwa budak*—the warrior over the servant.[18] He told his people that the Japanese were models of warrior spirit; and as he climbed out of his prison of subordination and isolation, he not only used the samurai to inspire his people, but submitted himself to that ethic, like a *rōnin* freshly bonded to a newfound lord.

Twenty years later, in the voice of the Sukarno who clamored for Indonesia Raya, who took West Irian (1962), and who cried for the "crushing" of Malaysia (1962–64), were the strident tones of the overlord, the new imperialist who may lurk in every colonized subordinate. Sukarno played in his own time the roles of abject bondsman under the Dutch, fighting feudal serf allied with Japanese lords, master at last in his own house of state, and eventually would-be lord over unwilling others.

Quezon's trajectory is less dramatic than Sukarno's, but it illuminates the range of modern Philippine history. As a young guerrilla officer, after two years in the hills he surrendered, unpunished, to the Americans in 1901.[19] He never forgot that the war for independence, which could have been won against Spain, was lost against the Americans. Even though the new regime propelled the Philippines rapidly toward autonomy, he cherished his anger: "I keep remembering it was done by force of arms."[20]

[17] *Tjahaja* (Bandung) November 9, 1944, cited in Theodore Friend, " 'Menjadi Banteng': Sukarno's Wartime Rhetoric and its Aims, 1943–45," a paper presented to the Middle Atlantic Regional Meeting, Association of Asian Studies, Philadelphia, October 1983.

[18] *Asia Raya: Memperingati Enam Boelan Balatentara Dai Nippon Melindoengi Indonesia* (Greater Asia: commemorating six months of Japanese army protecting Indonesia) (Jakarta: n.p., September 1942?).

[19] Manuel Quezon, *The Good Fight*, 2d ed. (New York: AMS Press, 1974), pp. xi–xii, 42–80.

[20] Theodore Friend, *Between Two Empires: The Ordeal of the Philippines* (New Haven: Yale University Press, 1954), 64.

Sometimes he wished the lords would still show naked steel. "Damn the Americans! Why don't they tyrannize us more?"[21] They did not supply the oppressive target that could have facilitated nationalist politics. They no longer offered a life-and-death struggle, but a relatively easy and comradely tutorial relationship. So comfortable and secure was the bondsman, in fact, that Quezon scrambled twice—before passing of the Jones Act in 1916 and during the congressional independence debates of 1929–33—to avoid having his country cut loose by the United States. Only the pressure of American anti-Philippine lobbies and anti-imperialist principle, combined with Quezon's tactical vulnerability to internal opponents, made him move finally, in 1934, to take the banner of independence determinedly in his own hand.

When the Japanese overlords came, Quezon was reluctant to go, but he yielded to MacArthur and to exile. From Washington, before his death, he wrote in 1943 a "last political testament" that entreated his people to see an even closer relationship with America as their destiny.[22] For national security and for a share in American prosperity he was willing to accept a relationship that could only be subordinate in power.

If internationally Quezon was willing to be a semibondsman ad infinitum, he was not so intraculturally. Within the framework of the Commonwealth autonomy, he advocated one-party government, practiced considerable executive fiat, and advocated an authoritarian ethos (even a social *Bushido*!) in the affairs of the anticipated sovereign Philippine state. But the cries of tyranny that he produced he also mollified, with exemplary support of freedom of speech and assembly, civil rights, and due process of law. An American high commissioner looked over Quezon's shoulder, and American political and educational values continued in the ascendent.[23]

The histories of Indonesia and the Philippines converged with regard to indigenous authoritarian rule in the 1970s. But they were widely different in the 1930s. Quezon, during his only trip to the Netherlands East Indies, in 1934, was brought by Indonesian na-

[21] Ibid., 4.

[22] Quezon to Franklin D. Roosevelt, October 26, 1943, Q. Quezon's request that this "testament" be published to his people was apparently overlooked after his death and under the pressures of war. Its spirit was realized in any case.

[23] For clear distinctions between Quezon's authoritarianism and the martial law rule of Ferdinand Marcos, see Theodore Friend, "The 'Yellow Revolution': its Mixed Historical Legacy," in Carl Landé, ed., *Rebuilding a Nation: Philippine Challenges and American Policy* (The Washington Institute Press, 1987), 69–86.

tionalists to a secluded darkened room in Surabaya. They asked how to go about getting independence. "Open all the windows and shutters," Quezon urged them, and "make a hell of a lot of noise." He did not appreciate that throwing open windows in Java had led to Sukarno's being thrown in jail.[24]

Forty years and martial law made a great difference. When the American ambassador to the United Nations, Andrew Young, visited Manila, he met with the opposition to President Marcos and gave them a strangely Quezonian message: tell the police beforehand about the meeting you are planning—when, where, who is speaking, who is coming. That is how the civil rights movement dispelled hostility and suspicion in the south, and eventually won. The Filipino opposition leaders were polite, but shocked to incredulity at the black American leader's lack of understanding. Young's counter-response, not verbally expressed to them, was implicitly critical of their relying on the United States to restore democracy instead of doing the job themselves.[25]

What worked in Manila in the 1930s would not work in Surabaya. What worked in Atlanta by the 1970s would not then work either in Manila or Surabaya. The appearance of indigenous lordship in repressive strength carries us back to an analysis of its preceding imperial forms.[26]

[24] Friend, *Between Two Empires*, 185.

[25] Evelyn Colbert (former deputy assistant secretary of state) to the author, May 1, 1984.

[26] Although Marcuse and his followers fantasize about societies without repression, to me it seems more plausible and fertile to treat repression as inescapable, and to consider its forms and phases, its intensities and laxities. As a definition of repression in colonial context, I offer this: objective denial of accustomed or desired rights, producing, as felt subjective results, constraint, subordination, diminishment, or fear.

Filipino wartime and restoration leaders are represented and defended in: Teodoro A. Agoncillo, *The Burden of Proof: the Vargas-Laurel Collaboration Case; with Jorge B. Vargas' 'Sugamo Diary'* (Quezon City: University of the Philippines Press, 1984); [Jose Lansang, ed.] *War Memoirs of Dr. Jose P. Laurel* (Manila: Laurel Memorial Foundation, 1962); Armando J. Malay, *Occupied Philippines: The Role of Jorge B. Vargas During the Japanese Occupation* (Manila: Filipiniana Book Guild, 1967); and in Malay's introduction to *Memoirs of General Artemio Ricarte* (Manila: National Heroes Commission, 1963); Claro M. Recto, *Three Years of Enemy Occupation: The Issue of Political Collaboration* (Manila: People's Publishers, 1946); and Marcial Lichauco, *Roxas* (Manila: n.p., 1952).

Japanese Expansion, Imperial Policy, and Their Consequences

Kawashima Shin'ichi has compiled *Tōnan Ajia Hōbun Shiryō Mokuroku* (Bibliography on Southeast Asian materials in the Japanese language, 1946–1983) (Tokyo: Japan Orientalist Librarians Group, 1985), an excellent starting point. Harry Wray and Hilary Conroy, eds., *Japan Examined: Perspectives on Modern Japanese History* (Honolulu: University of Hawaii Press, 1983) contains numerous relevant contributions and bibliographic leads on important themes. Akira Iriye, *Power and Culture: The Japanese–American War, 1941–1945* (Cambridge: Harvard University Press, 1981) is a lucid study of war objectives, concrete and symbolic, with a valuable bibliography. John W. Dower, *War Without Mercy: Race and Power in the Pacific War* (New York: Pantheon Books, 1986) is excellent on ethnopsychological demonism. Christopher Thorne brings earlier studies to comprehensive focus in *The Issue of War: States, Societies and the Far Eastern Conflict of 1941–1945* (New York: Oxford University Press, 1985).

Of a number of books justifying Japan's motives and conduct in the Second World War, Hattori Takushirō, *Dai Tōa senso zenshi* (Complete history of the Greater East Asian War) (Tokyo: Masu Shobō, 1953) is a detailed account of military courage. Tsunoda Jun, *Taiheiyō sensō e no michi* (The Road to the Pacific War), 8 vols. (Tokyo: Asahi Shinbunsha, 1962–63) contains contributions that seek to shift guilt and responsibility from Japan; and Ueyama Shumpei, *Dai Tōa sensō no imi* (The meaning of the Greater East Asian War) (Tokyo: Chūō Kōronsha, 1964), sorts interpretations under a prevailing tone of nostalgia. Kojima Noboru's biography of

1

DEPENDENCE AND DEVELOPMENT

UNDER DUTCH AND

AMERICAN RULE

Why did Indonesians revolt against the Dutch in 1945, while Filipinos were reembracing an American semicolonial system? If we put aside the disposition of imperial forces in that year, and examine the underlying historical causes, differences of scale immediately loom up. Gross realities are important truths. In a colonial relationship, as in other things, small relies on large, and large may ignore small.

The land area of the Indies was sixty times that of the Netherlands, and the population seven times as great. Government revenues, according to the 1930 budget, were 30 percent larger in the colony than in the mother country. At the same time, the Philippines had a land area one-thirtieth that of the United States, a population one-tenth as great, and a government revenue of the same dollar magnitude as the twelfth largest American city.[1]

The Netherlands was heavily dependent on its colony economically, and deeply involved with it, both constitutionally and emotionally. In the Philippine-American situation, however, the colony was economically dependent on and emotionally attached to the mother country. That power found it an encumbrance and sought in the 1930s to be rid of it. Differences in economic and educational practices, and in levels of political participation and repression in the two colonies, follow from the consequences of scale. These dif-

[1] Figures on the Netherlands, Gov. Gen. Davis to Sec. War Hurley, July 15, 1931, confidential memo, p. 13, BIA 18868-w-55. Figures on the Philippines computed from standard almanacs.

ferences, in turn, help explain the contrasting responses to Japanese conquest and to Western reoccupation.

INDONESIA AND THE PHILIPPINES IN 1931:
AN OVERVIEW

Governor General Dwight Davis of the Philippines made a six-week tour of the Netherlands East Indies, French Indochina, and the Federated Malay States in 1931, a trip unique in American imperial history and in the impressions reported. The Philippines derived a larger proportion of its income from taxation than other Southeast Asian colonies, which all used government monopolies—including opium—as a source of income. In 1930, opium sales raised almost $11 million for the Dutch.[2] In the Philippines the Americans tolerated an illegal trade, and thus both abjured opium revenue and avoided subsequent blame. The United States, by not taxing heavily, and by not developing government monopolies, had come to be appreciated by most Filipinos as relatively nonexploitative.

Dutch developmental priorities, to Davis's eye, however, made the Netherlands East Indies stand out—in public buildings, public utilities, and roads, and in telephone, telegraph, and shipping facilities—as "the most complete and most efficiently managed colonial development that I have yet observed."[3] In scientific knowledge of agriculture, Java led the Philippines by "30 or 40 years." The single salvation of Philippine sugar was its preferential treatment in the United States market, without which it could not survive world competition.[4]

In the light of history, however, the Dutch had their own deficiencies of vision. They apparently planned roads and harbor facilities with military as well as economic objectives in mind, and 26 percent of Indies government expenditures went to maintain military forces stationed there.[5] Had the United States made the Filipinos bear all local military costs in the Philippines, this would have

[2] Davis to Hurley, July 15, 1931, 14–15. For the origins of the Dutch system, see James R. Rush, "Social Control and Influence in Nineteenth Century Indonesia: Opium Farms and the Chinese of Java," *Indonesia* 35 (1983): 53–64.

[3] Davis to Hurley, re French Indochina, Federated Malay States, Netherlands East Indies (hereafter abbreviated FIC, FMS, NEI), 3, 8, 10, 15, 9–10. Also manuscript report of the Governor General of the Philippine Islands, 1931, 24–25 (BIA).

[4] MS report Gov. Gen., 1931, 24, 64, 67.

[5] Davis to Hurley, tabular enclosure, "Estimated Expenditures for 1931 (General Ordinary Budget)."

consumed 37 percent of the insular budget. As it was, the American taxpayer bore the entire expense.[6]

The Dutch spent a particularly large amount of money on their executive branch of government—eight times as much, relatively, as the Philippines—of which amount over $16 million went to what the Americans saw as "local princes, grandees, and . . . local government bodies."[7] In practice this meant perpetuating elaborate and impressive courts and a hollow advisory apparatus at high cost.

Davis and his party did not articulate any reasons for the greater incidence of communism they found in other colonies, but the Philippine secretary of agriculture believed that the Filipino farm laborer was the highest paid in the area. He reported that in Java, particularly, housing standards were "noticeably lower" than in the Philippines. Overall, the governor general concluded: "Nowhere . . . did we find that the laboring man is better cared for, better paid, better protected from outside competition or by accident, insurance, and labor legislation than in our own country."[8] His report implicitly attributed the relative lack of anti-imperial nationalism in the Philippines to the high proportion of the budget devoted to the direct benefit of Filipinos. The Philippine government spent, proportionately, nearly three times as much on education and social services, including public works, as the Indies. Lower administrative costs and the absence of a defense item in the Philippine budget both accented this relative generosity, American style.[9]

In the figures, however, lies a pattern not noted by Davis: the per capita expenditures of the insular government of the Philippines were lower than those of any other colony he visited except Indochina.[10] The expenditures of the municipal government of the city of Buffalo, New York, exceeded those of the government of the Philippines, which served thirty times as many people.[11] Filipinos generally, however, did not have a way of perceiving or judging the stinginess of their government. Instead, they apparently viewed the relatively strong internal budgetary accent on education and health as evidence of the good intentions of the colonial power, and that view survived in the Philippines long after independence.

[6] Sec. War Hurley, transcript of press conference, January 18, 1932, BIA 364-897.
[7] Quotation, Davis to Hurley, 11; computation from "Estimated Expenditures for 1931."
[8] MS report Gov. Gen., 1931, 25.
[9] Davis to Hurley, 14–15.
[10] From table, "Estimated Expenditures for 1931."
[11] Figures for Buffalo, 1931, courtesy of former Councilman William B. Hoyt.

Dutch imperial accent on infrastructure, support of obedient native princes, and financing a military presence on the basis of native revenues all appeared, in the long run, to create indigenous skepticism. Relatively high American expenditures on education and health, even if absolutely small, tended to create local trust.

Economic Dependence and Development

To understand the events of 1942–45, it helps not only to know how the colonial governments were spending money in the Indies and Philippines, but how the imperial powers were deriving national revenue from their colonies. When the question arose after the war, two prominent Dutch economists attempted a compilation of all sources of income the Netherlands would lack if it did not have its Indonesian possessions and connections.[12] These sources—dividends and interest derived from investments in plantations, mines, and businesses; income from trade and shipping; salaries, wages, and pensions of Dutch in private enterprise; salaries, pensions, and furlough payments of Dutch in the Indies civil service; currency transfers to families in the Netherlands; and undisbursed profits of companies active in the Indies—constituted primary revenues. On the assumption that possession of the Indies constituted a general stimulant to the Netherlands economy, and that their loss would be a depressant, the economists calculated secondary revenues as 70 percent of primary revenues, and added them to complete the economic picture. The results showed that the interwar Dutch economy relied upon its major colony for one-seventh of its national income (see Table 1.1), probably the highest ratio in any country in the world.[13]

By contrast, the income derived from the Philippines was a negligible factor in American national income—so small that no one ever bothered to compute it. The American population in the Philippines in 1938 was only 8,700, compared with 40,000 Dutch proper

[12] J.B.D. Derksen and J. Tinbergen, "Berekeningen over de economische beteekenis von Nederlandsch Indie voor Nederland" (Calculation of the economic significance of the Netherlands Indies for the Netherlands), *Maandschrift van het Centraal Bureau voor de Statistiek*, 40 (1945): 210–16.

[13] Prof. Dr. Jan Tinbergen, interview, November 19, 1970. Only the Belgian Congo, where 5 percent of total Belgian capital was invested before independence, could compare among modern colonial situations; see Alan P. Merriam, *Congo: Background of Conflict* (Evanston, Ill.: Northwestern University Press, 1961), 275–76. For prewar figures on trade, industry, and finance, see chap. 14 of [British] Naval Intelligence, *The Belgian Congo*, B.R. 522, 1944, restricted.

TABLE 1.1
Dutch Income, Indies-Derived, in Millions of Gulden

Category of Income	1925–34	1938
1. Dividends and interest[a]	179	155
2. Salaries, wages, pensions (private enterprise)	36	29
3. Salaries, pensions, etc. (civil service)	26	26
4. Currency transfers to families	9	5
5. Shipping	67	63
6. Exports, 75% of total value[b]	81	75
7. Trade in colonial products; misc.[c]	60	35
8. Undisbursed profits[d]	30	40
Total primary income	488	428
Total secondary income (70% of 1–7, excluding 8)	321	272
Total Indies-derived income	810	700
Total Netherlands national income	5,500	5,100
Indies-derived income as a percentage of national income	14.7%	13.7%

SOURCE: Adapted from Derksen and Tinbergen, "Berekeningen over de econo-mische beteekenis."

[a] Consisting of: dividends from Dutch companies working in the Netherlands East Indies (G117 million); interest on government bonds received from NEI (G29 million); interest, private companies (G4 million); and interest on loans made by the Dutch government and the Nederlands Bank to the NEI government (G5 million).

[b] To allow for imported raw materials, 25% has been deducted.

[c] Revenues from international trade, conducted in the Netherlands, in products such as tobacco, teak, chinchona, and sugar; consequences of noncontrol of large oil companies; and some minor sources of revenue.

[d] Very rough estimate.

in Indonesia, and another 200,000 "Europeans," mostly Dutch citizens of Eurasian blood. American investment in the Philippines in the 1930s was about $200 million, or only 1 percent of total American foreign investment. The American share of total Philippine trade reached a high of 77 percent in 1940, when the Philippines was America's sixth best customer.[14] Taking the whole pattern of

[14] Catherine Porter, *Crisis in the Philippines* (New York: Knopf, 1942), 23–24, sup-

settlement, investment, and trade together, of which only the last was of any significant size, one may estimate that Philippine-derived income as a proportion of American national income was at most a very small fraction of 1 percent.

From many vantage points the Philippines was not an economic asset but a liability. While the insular treasury met nearly all civil expenditures, the United States government regularly paid for defense, the Coast and Geodetic Survey, the census, and some aspects of public health. Over a forty-year period, American government expenditures in the Philippines totaled about a billion dollars, including over $900 million for military expenses.[15] In view of strategic jeopardy from Japan, these military expenditures were so pathetically small that they endangered the whole Philippine-American achievement. The Netherlands, with its enormous economic dependence on its colony, understandably clung to the Indies. But what kept the United States in the Philippines under conditions of strategic danger without clear economic gain? Spain had endured in the Philippines for the glory of God; America, perhaps, for the sake of "democratic mission." Financially, both were losing propositions.

The Great Depression threw Philippine-American relations into crisis. Complaints arose over economic competition from the colony; American beet sugar, dairy, and labor interests all felt and exaggerated the effect of free entry of Philippine sugar and coconut oil, and free immigration of Filipino laborers.[16] Give them independence, the argument went, so we can shut out their products and their people. The reasoning was tawdry. Any relief to American farmers and laborers would have been so gradual as to be unfelt. The lobbyists' success nonetheless illustrates a polar difference from the Dutch-Indonesian situation, where imperial power and colony were economically and emotionally welded together.

Although actual prewar Dutch income dependence on the Indies was around 14 percent, influential businessmen, government officials, and decision makers uniformly thought the percentage of In-

plies these figures, against which may be compared those of G. Gonggrijp, "De sociaal-economische betekenis van Nederlands-Indie voor Nederland" (The socio-economic significance of the Netherlands-Indies for the Netherlands) (Utrecht: Het Spectrum, n.d.), esp. 6–7, tables, 1, 2.

[15] Porter, *Crisis in the Philippines*, 24–25.

[16] Theodore Friend, *Between Two Empires: The Ordeal of the Philippines* (New Haven: Yale University Press, 1965), 81–85.

dies-derived national income was as much as 40 to 50 percent.[17] The slogan of the postwar years ran, *Indië verloren, rampspoed geboren* ("Indies lost, disastrous cost"). What a contrast to the depression-born American psychology, which might have expressed itself in sloganistic exaggeration as "American needs the Philippines freed."

Debates of the immediate predepression years on the *poenale sanctie* in Indonesia and the corporation law in the Philippines illustrate, if a trifle overdramatically, the two different styles of economic development. The controversial "penal sanction" was part of an ordinance affecting coolie labor, chiefly on the East Coast of Sumatra.[18] The law defined sanctions against both employer and employee for violation of contracts, but coolies, who generally signed the contract out of sheer need and ignorant of its conditions, were the only ones who had cause to break it. The Ethical Movement at the turn of the century had first brought the penal sanction under criticism for its exploitation and cruelty.[19] The number of coolies sentenced because of offenses against the ordinance—for each year from 1922 to 1930 constantly in the neighborhood of 5 percent of the daily average of hands[20]—brought about renewed debate in the Volksraad. The sharpest remarks came from Haji Agus Salim, a prominent Muslim leader, who called the penal sanction "this stain on civilization, this blow in the face of humanity," as bad as pre–Civil War American slavery, and worse than anything in twentieth-century Islamic countries. Despite such criticism, the Netherlands parliament voted a renewal of the penal sanction in 1924, while trying to soften opposition by expressing "the intention of coming to a gradual abolition."[21]

[17] Tinbergen, interview, November 19, 1970.

[18] The general description following is from *Encyclopedie van Nederlandsch-Indië*, 8 vols. (The Hague: Nijhoff; Leiden: Brill, 1917–39), vols. 5, 7, and supp., under the heading "Poenale Sanctie." Ann Laura Stoler, *Capitalism and Confrontation in Sumatra's Plantation Belt* (New Haven: Yale University Press, 1985) has subsequently appeared as an ethnographic history.

[19] Particularly in the pamphlet by a lawyer from Medan, J. van den Brand, *De Millioenen uit Deli* (The millions from Deli) (Amsterdam: 1902).

[20] Calculated from *Statistisch Jaaroverzicht voor Nederlandsch-Indie* (Statistical abstract for the Netherlands East Indies) (Weltevreden: Statistisch Kantuor van het Department van Landbouw, nijverheid en handel, 1922–29), 1922–23, table 36; 1926, 1927, table 128; 1928, table 161; 1929, table 166; and *Indisch Verslag* (Indies report), *1931–1941* (The Hague: Algemene Landsdrukkerij, 1932–42), 1931, pt. 2, table 166.

[21] *Handelingen van de Volksraad. Eerste gewone zitting* (Proceedings of the Volksraad, first regular session) (1923), appendixes, topic 7. Hereafter the style of citation will be: HV 1e gew z 1923, Bijl, 7 (and/or page numbers). Quotation from *Handelin-*

Not Dutch intentions, but the Great Depression and American legislation against importing articles made by indentured labor finally changed the situation. Contract coolie employment hit its peak in 1929 and declined rapidly thereafter.[22] The half century of legal sanctions behind indentured labor, however, showed the willingness of the Netherlands parliament and of the Indies government to protect and support Dutch business interests despite strong evidence of exploitation and injustice.

In the Philippines, a contemporaneous debate over the corporation law illustrates the difficulty American business interests experienced in obtaining the governmental cooperation and investment conditions they desired. Henry Stimson, arriving as governor general in 1928 with the perspective of a Wall Street lawyer, noted that all the Philippines generated no more electric power than Havana, Cuba. To correct what he considered general economic underdevelopment, Stimson attempted revisions in the land law and the corporation law in order to attract American capital.[23]

Both statutes had originated early in the century. The land law prohibited purchase of public lands in excess of 16 hectares by individuals, or 1,024 hectares by corporations. The corporation law limited the life of corporations to fifty years and prohibited investors from holding an interest in more than one agricultural corporation. The first law was the work of American beet sugar interests, anti-imperialists, and conservationists, and the second the result of the antitrust atmosphere of the Progressive era. The Philippine legislature, from its inception in 1907, defended this American legal handiwork because it coincided with Filipino desires to "preserve

---

gen der Staten Generaal—Tweede Kamer, 1923–24, Bijl, 97, and debate of June 12, 1924.

[22] Indentured Coolies and Free Coolies on the East Coast of Sumatra

Year	Indentured	Free
1920	238,336	12,126
1929	261,124	40,812
1934	6,059	153,671
1940	53	215,670

Sources: Statistisch Jaaroverzicht, 1922–23, table 36, and 1929, table 164, Indisch Verslag, pt. 2 1935, 1941, table 164.

[23] Stimson, "Future Philippine Policy under the Jones Act," Foreign Affairs 5 (1927): 459–71; MS report Gov. Gen., 1928, 4–7; and Lyman P. Hammond, "Report on Economic Conditions of the Philippines" (Manila: Bureau of Printing, 1928), Stimson papers, Sterling Memorial Library, Yale University.

the patrimony" against foreign plantation development and imperial capital.[24] Filipino convictions about landholding and the success of the sugar industry in adapting to small plots eventually persuaded Stimson to forget about land law revision.[25] As for the corporation law, the legislature revised Stimson's proposals so that it remained nearly impossible for a holding company to obtain centralized control of two or more corporations.[26]

Unlike the Indonesian Volksraad debate on the penal sanction, the Filipino debate concluded with a native legislature checking the intentions of a foreign executive, and defending native political and economic autonomy at the cost of decelerated economic development. Not until Philippine weakness coincided with American expansionism in 1945–46 would American business lobbies achieve some of the inroads they desired against the restraints erected by turn-of-the century Progressives and anti-imperialists.

EDUCATIONAL DEVELOPMENT

As colonial political systems are characterized by foreign dominance, and such social systems by foreign eminence, so are colonial educational systems distinguished by foreign preference. Imperial power projects its own educational system abroad, with adjustments for scale, resources, and long-term policy.

In the United States in 1938, 70 percent of youths aged twelve to nineteen were in school, while in the Netherlands only 30 percent were enrolled in secondary and vocational schools.[27] An even larger

[24] Sister Mary Elizabeth, "Agriculture Credit and Banking in the Philippines, 1913–1917: An Administrative Study" (Ph.d. diss., University of Chicago, 1962), and Juan G. Collas, Jr., "The Philippine Law on Corporate Combination" (Ph.D. diss., Yale University, 1959).

[25] Stimson Diary, September–October 1928, Stimson papers.

[26] *Diario de Sessiones de la Legislatura Filipina*, November 1928; Frederick Fisher, *The Philippine Law of Stock Corporations* (1929), 260. Glenn May argues cogently that the Philippines was a site for testing conservative formulas: *Social Engineering in the Philippines: The Aims, Execution, and Impact of American Colonial Policy, 1900–1913* (Westport, Conn.: Greenwood Press, 1980). But the 1920s show that the Progressives' design for the laboratory had prevailed.

[27] American figures computed from *The U.S. Book of Facts, Statistics and Information for 1966*, 109, citing *U.S. Census of Population, 1950*, vol. 2, pt. 1; Dutch figures from *Zeventig Jaren statistiek in tijdreeksen, 1899–1969* (Seventy years of statistics in time charts), Centraal Bureau voor de Statistiek (The Hague: Staatsuitgeverij, 1970), 37ff. The American and Dutch tables are not perfectly comparable, since the American does not clearly distinguish between levels of education. Higher

imbalance existed between those going on to higher education in the two countries. The American system was clearly oriented toward the mass, while the structure of education in the Netherlands, like that in most of Europe, "had the effect of reinforcing class distinctions and reducing the flow of social mobility. . . . The upper levels of education were the preserve of the upper classes."[28] Those who squeezed through all the filters of the system to graduate from Dutch universities, however, were usually grounded in the classics, fluent in two or more Western languages, well-spoken in their own tongue, and familiar with other subjects of consequence.

Administrators carried to their respective colonies these sharply different educational philosophies—the mass orientation of the Americans and the elitism of the Dutch. Comparative literacy figures and enrollment statistics at primary, secondary, and university levels illuminate the systems; the employability of graduates reveals still more; and considerations of cultural gain and loss are also part of an ideal reckoning of value.

The prewar Filipino literacy rate was five times as high as that of the Javanese.[29] Immediately before the war, Western-style school enrollment in the Philippines as a proportion of total population was more than three times as great as that of the Netherlands Indies (Table 1.2). In public high schools (the eighth through eleventh years of academic and vocational education) the Philippines in 1938 had 76,000 students enrolled. The Netherlands Indies had a more rigorous and complex secondary system that included: HBS (Higher Civil School) and lyceum schools comparable in curriculum to those in Holland; MULO (More Extended Lower Instruction) and AMS (General Middle School) levels, whose curricula were partially adapted to the need for Malay language and Asian subject matter; and vocational, commercial, and technical schools. Taken together their total enrollment was 15,000. Thus the Netherlands East Indies, with four times the population of the Philippines, enrolled

education: Johan Goudsblom, *Dutch Society* (New York: Random House, 1967), 99; UNESCO, *Statistical Yearbook, 1970*, 300ff.

The essays in Philip G. Altbach and Gail Kelly, eds., *Education and Colonialism* (New York: Longman, 1978) deliver little beyond naive discoveries of inequality and cultural imperialism, except for Remi Clignet's analysis of colonial dilemmas, 122–48.

[28] John E. Talbott, "The History of Education," *Daedalus* 100, no.1 (1971): 136.

[29] H. A. Wyndham, *Native Education: Ceylon, Java, Formosa, the Philippines, French Indo-China, and British Malaya*, 91, cited in Joseph R. Hayden, *The Philippines: A Study in National Development* (New York: Macmillan, 1942), 597.

TABLE 1.2
School Enrollment as a Percentage of Total Population,
1938–40

Netherlands East Indies	3.2
Philippines	10.7
Netherlands	17.9
United States	21.0
Japan	21.0

SOURCES: Calculation for the Netherlands, 1938, based on *Ze-
ventig jaren statistiek*, 14. Other figures from Joseph R. Hayden,
The Philippines: A Study in National Development (New York:
Macmillan, 1942), 470.

one-fifth as many students in secondary education.[30] The Philippines, however, had no alternative school systems comparable to
the Islamic *pesantrèn* and *madrasah* in Java, which offered significant opportunities for non-Western learning.

In higher education, differences of quality apparent at the secondary level remained, and differences of quantity became still more
pronounced. In 1938–39, there were about 7,500 students at the
University of the Philippines, the apex of public education in that
country, and another 3,600 in normal and technical schools at a col-
legiate level.[31] In the same year, at all institutes of advanced education in the Indies, there were only 128 Indonesians.

In both colonies university degrees from abroad were a prized distinction. Between 1924 and 1940 there averaged annually twenty
Indonesian and twenty-one Chinese from the Indies studying in
Dutch universities,[32] with an uncertain career future on return. In
the United States, the government-operated *pensionado* program

[30] Figures compiled from Hayden, *Philippines*, 472, and Paul W. van der Veur, *Education and Social Change in Indonesia* (I), Ohio University Southeast Asia Program
(Athens, Ohio, 1969), 11, 11a. George McT. Kahin, *Nationalism and Revolution in
Indonesia* (Ithaca: Cornell University Press, 1952), 31, says that only 240 Indonesians graduated from high schools in 1940. Van der Veur's figures (pp. 14, 14a) indicate
that 220 graduated from HBS5, Lyceum, and AMS schools and another 1,969 from
vocational, commercial, and technical schools, suggesting a problem of categories
and tallies.

[31] Hayden, *Philippines*, 472, 537.

[32] Calculations based on S. L. van der Wal, *Some Information on Education in Indonesia up to 1942* (The Hague, 1960), 12–13.

provided an American university education for Filipinos, in return for their obligating themselves to a period of service in the insular government. During the twenty-seven years of the program's operation, an average of twenty-one Filipinos a year were graduated at American public expense.[33] Filipinos educated in American universities at family expense were a large multiple of that number.

All figures illustrate the fact that Americans concentrated on "education for citizenship" and made sacrifices for the sake of quantity, whereas the Dutch considered a few persons "educated to perfection" to be a significant and satisfactory achievement. The sociopolitical context, however, makes one wonder if even these latter were not "educated to discontent."[34] Where could highly educated Indonesians go? Into the civil service, mainly; but Western-style education expanded at a rate of 7 percent per year, while openings for Indonesians in the Western-style government service increased at a rate of only 2 percent.[35] Industrialization proceeded far too modestly to provide managerial jobs for Indonesians, so that the effect of educating even a few of them to the pinnacle of available learning was to leave a significant number crucially dissatisfied.[36] Men like Soedjono and Subardjo could not earn a sufficient living as lawyers; they became moonlighters, intellectual adventurers, sojourners in Japan, aggravated nationalists.[37]

A Dutch educator in the Indies made a careful study of the Philippine system in 1923 and found great vitality in it, much of which he attributed to the cumulative influence of the Spanish who had

[33] Calculations from "Education" section, unpublished BIA MS, "American Stewardship in the Philippines," Leila M. Pool Collection, author's possession.

[34] Interviews with BB officials 1969–70; Leslie H. Palmier, *Indonesia and the Dutch* (London: Oxford University Press, 1962), chap. 4; Hayden, *Philippines,* chap. 18.

[35] Palmier, *Indonesia and the Dutch;* 28. Van der Veur, *Education and Social Change,* 22–49, contains his translation of one of the reports of the Dutch-Indonesian Education Commission: "The Social and Geographic Origins of Dutch-Educated Indonesians." J. S. Furnivall, *Netherlands India* (London: Cambridge University Press, 1967), 374–75, defined part of the problem of employability in prewar perspective.

[36] A thorough study of such education and political careers is Robert Van Niel, *The Emergence of the Modern Indonesian Elite* (The Hague and Bandung: W. van Hoeve, 1960). For the picture in the early twentieth century, see Heather Sutherland, *The Making of a Bureaucratic Elite* (Singapore: Heinemann Educational Books, 1979), 45–55; for retrospective interviews and surveys (1969), see Donald K. Emmerson, *Indonesia's Elite: Political Culture and Cultural Policies* (Ithaca: Cornell University Press, 1976), 147–57.

[37] Interviews, March–April 1968.

created the University of Santo Tomas in 1611. He criticized the Americans for using English too early as a medium of instruction: popular education based on a foreign culture would be a failure for the many who broke off their education at an early age and spent most of their lives in vernacular contexts. He faulted his own Dutch countrymen, however, for paucity of effort, for excessive complexity of system, for concentration on knowledge to the exclusion of practice, and on repetition to the detriment of knowledge. He criticized them for spending too much on buildings and too little on books; for lack of social, vocational, and athletic content in learning; and for an educational process so extended that it killed the idealism in the very youths bright enough to complete it.[38]

If most Dutch thought such opinions idiosyncratic, the appearance a decade later of the so-called wild schools, with registration estimated at 142,000,[39] was proof of considerable dissatisfaction. The most distinguished experiment was Ki Hadjar Dewantoro's Taman Siswa schools. Devised to preserve native character against the distractions and debilitations of Dutch education, they attracted many students who wished to escape the West through native thought and arts, and others who wished to prepare for an assault on it through politics.[40]

As for the quality of Philippine education, a former vice–governor general, whose major responsibility it was, wrote: "The Philippine Government has had to choose between enrolling a relatively large number of pupils, more than half of whom would not remain in school long enough to benefit fully and lastingly from the experience, and teaching a smaller number enough to quality them as first rate citizens in the kind of state that the Philippines is seeking to become. The choice was made in favor of the former alternative."[41]

The Philippine system conceded the production of a great many persons with less than a first-rate education, as a corollary of a policy of political autonomy followed by eventual independence. The unanswered question was: How can one be a first-rate citizen with

[38] G. J. Nieuwenhuis, *Opvoeding tot Autonomie: Een sociaal-paedagogische studie van het Philippijnsch onderwijsstelsel, vergeleken met het Nederlands-Indische* (Education for autonomy: a social-pedagogical study of the Philippine educational system, compared with that of the Netherlands Indies) (Groningen: Wolters, 1923).

[39] Van der Veur, *Education and Social Change*, 8.

[40] The best short account is Ruth T. McVey, "Taman Siswa and the Indonesian National Awakening," *Indonesia* 4 (1967): 128–49. For contrast see Edilberto N. Alegre and Doreen G. Fernandez, *The Writer and His Milieu: An Oral History of First Generation Writers in English* (Manila: De La Salle University Press, 1984).

[41] Hayden, *Philippines*, 471.

a second- or third-rate education, or worse? Was this better than the Indonesian system, which created a handful of top-flight subjects, whose erudition made more galling their pronounced subordination? If so, the achievement involved serious costs.

One cost was the suffocation of Spanish culture. Claro Recto and others have suggested that American impact cut off a Spanish cultural fluorescence, the culmination of a nineteenth-century growth that included the novels of Jose Rizal. After twenty years of American occupation, Spanish culture in the Philippines relied on a small number of Hispanic families carrying on cloistered traditions. A generation later, a few nostalgic voices gave this tradition spiritual expression, but even the most eloquent of them, Nick Joaquin, wrote chiefly in English in order to be read. The prevailing culture for Filipinos above the peasant level was a kind of hothouse Americanism, a forced bloom with a certain radiance, but artificial and vulnerable. Meanwhile their Indonesian contemporaries, however politically alienated, could innovate upon traditional cultural themes, playing, like a gamelan musician, with dignity, composure, and unselfconscious resonance.

In sum, the twentieth-century Philippine system consisted of quantity-oriented education for citizenship, with an initially high percentage of American teachers, emphasis upon instruction in English wherever possible, and rapid and overwhelming Filipinization of the teaching force after the second decade. The ultimate purpose was to leave a sovereign state in Filipino hands, with Filipinos conducting public business on American foundations and in the English language.

The Indonesian system emphasized quality-oriented education for a few in Dutch, with a large force of Dutch teachers.[42] For the rest of the population, a brief vernacular education was sometimes available. The intent of the system was protection of indigenous culture and production of a manageable native official elite during a protracted period of preparation for autonomy—in short, minimal disturbance of both native tradition and Dutch sovereignty. The Dutch system and the American each produced psychic disorientations. The one erupted in violent postwar revolution; the other persisted in frustrate simmer.

[42] Figures for Dutch teachers, 1916, in *Jaarcijfers voor het Koninkrijk der Nederlanden Kolonien* (Statistical annual of the Kingdom of the Netherlands, the colonies) (The Hague: Centraal Bureau voor de statistiek, 1888–1923), 1917, 23–40, and for 1940 in van der Wal, *Some Information*, table 2, may be compared with American figures for the same years in Hayden, *Philippines*, 493–94.

CHAPTER ONE

Political and Administrative Development

Twenty years after independence a traveling scholar found a serious disjuncture between national policymaking and administrative operations everywhere in Southeast Asia except Malaysia and the Philippines.[43] In ascertaining why, the Dutch rubric "divide and rule," and the American "educate and depart," provide a good beginning.

Under the Netherlands Indies system, the main administrative division of the forty-one million people in Java and Madura (1930 census) was the regency, of which there were seventy-six. There was also four "autonomous" principalities in Yogyakarta and Surakarta, whose noble rulers—the sultan, *susuhunan, mangkunegoro,* and *pakualam*—presided over a total of four million people. Of the eighteen million people of the "outer" islands more recently under Dutch sway, about eight million belonged to 265 native states whose rulers had signed pacts with the Dutch; the rest were under a variety of other forms of government.[44]

The two most distinct kinds of native authority were regents and rulers, of whom the latter were recognized rather than appointed by the Dutch and presumably had a more traditional and organic connection with their peoples. Regents became more hereditary under the Dutch, who for most of the nineteenth century favored predictable lineage as a way of ensuring support and loyalty. Both rulers and regents were vulnerable to Dutch displeasure and selective sanctions, but the rulers far less so. Dutch residents, in any case, ruled while the regent merely reigned.

The Dutch built up an administrative policy by accrual, led by the professedly apolitical Binnenlands Bestuur (Interior Administration Department, or "BB"). After 1918 the BB tolerated in connection to it the quasi-representative Volksraad (People's Council). Although the regencies, units of indigenous authority from which representatives arose and through which the whole system operated, had their origins in precolonial Java, they were increasingly adjunct to the Western bureaucratic apparatus.[45]

Native administrative hierarchy, then, was part of a dualistic

[43] Lucian Pye, *Southeast Asia's Political Systems* (Englewood Cliffs, N.J.: Prentice-Hall, 1967), 75, 81.

[44] Rupert Emerson, *Malaysia: A Study in Direct and Indirect Rule* (New York: Macmillan, 1937), 420, 460.

[45] Of various descriptions of the system I follow most closely that of Henry J. Benda in "The Pattern of Administrative Reforms in the Closing Years of Dutch Rule in Indonesia," *The Journal of Asian Studies* 25 (1966): 589–605.

structure in which the Dutch element was superordinate and separate. For Indonesian civil servants there was no means of transfer into European service. The total system operated according to hereditary, aristocratic, and appointive principles, and admitted the elective principle only with rigorous qualifications, indirect processes of choice, and racially distinguished constituencies.

By contrast, the American system in the Philippines moved immediately toward representative principles and a joint civil service with a diminishing American component. In the first municipal elections, held in 1903, only 2.44 percent of the population qualified, a proportion not vastly larger than the class known as the *principales* in Spanish times. These elections, however, established the electoral principle and process in a country still recovering from the traumas of revolution and war.[46] By the election of 1941, the abolition of property requirements, liberalization of literacy requirements, enfranchisement of women, and lowering of the voting age from twenty-three to twenty-one had increased the number of registered voters to about 14 percent of the population.[47] The first election of a House of Representatives took place in 1907, of a Senate in 1916, and of a president and vice-president in 1935.

In the executive branch of government, Americans practiced rapid Filipinization. By 1903, 99 percent of municipal officials were Filipinos, and by 1917 provincial government was also fully in Filipino hands.[48] Only the national government was not. In 1916, however, the Jones Act replaced the Philippine Commission (roughly analagous to the Raad van Indië as an "upper chamber" and body advisory to the governor general) with an elective Senate of Filipino membership, thus giving Filipinos complete control of both legislative houses. Furthermore, the legislature had genuine powers: if it chose to override a governor general's veto, only the president of the United States could reinvoke it.

Regency councils were introduced to Java in the 1920s to give a more democratic cast to the system, while the residents were simultaneously trying to transform their tutelary relationship with the regents into a more cooperative one. In the regency council elections of 1928 and 1929, the electorate was approximately 15 percent of the total Javanese population, closely comparable with the Philippine electorate figures for the same period, but its influence was

[46] Hayden, *Philippines*, 267–68.
[47] O. D. Corpuz, *The Philippines* (Englewood Cliffs, N.J.: Prentice-Hall, 1966), 133.
[48] Hayden, *Philippines*, 268, 270–72.

indirect only. Voters chose electors, who in turn elected a bare majority of the council membership. Report for 1931 show that an average regency council consisted of twenty members, of whom fifteen were Indonesian, three Dutch, and two "other Asian." Among the Indonesians were an occasional peasant, four or five "professionals," and an average of eleven civil servants, two or three of whom were appointed rather than elected. The high proportion of Indonesian membership thus did not necessarily imply a nationalistic character. Although the number of regencies and council members changed for administrative reasons across the next decade, the proportion of Indonesians, of officials among them, and of electees among the officials did not significantly change.[49] Whatever modest increases occurred in the numbers of Indonesian representatives, a conservative Dutch trend from 1926 to 1942 made relationships increasingly tutelary again.

At the summit of the system of political participation was the Volksraad. After 1929, its membership of twenty-five Europeans, thirty Indonesians, and five "other Asians" gave it an Indonesian majority, but the practical importance of this majority was partially limited by the appointive principle and conditioned by a very small electorate—about two thousand persons, consisting of members of regency, municipal, and local councils. Limits in powers more seriously diluted its significance. The Volksraad had the right of free expression, of petitioning, of questioning, and, after 1925, of consent to the budget. But any deadlock between the Volksraad and the governor general on the budget was referred to the States General at The Hague. The Volksraad's legislative work applied only to internal affairs, and not to the imperial framework itself. The Dutch parliament could always negate the Volksraad's decisions, but the Volksraad could not negate decisions of the Indies government.[50] In such circumstances, many nationalists chose to stay aloof from the Volksraad. Those who participated adopted stances that many Dutch considered "irresponsible," but the colonial government did not seriously consider improving the level of criticism by yielding more responsibility.

In addition to politics both executive and legislative, careers in government opened up through the civil service. As early as 1919

[49] Based on computations from *Indisch Verslag*, 1931, pt. 2, table 432, and 1941, pt. 2, table 431. *Indisch Verslag*, 1941, pt. 2, table 431, 540–41, shows that as for municipal councils in Java all of the thirty reported in 1941 had a European majority, and all the municipalities had European mayors.

[50] *Encyclopaedie von Nederlandsch-Indië* 6 (1932): 438–72; 8 (1939): 464–68.

the top 1,100 positions of the Philippine Civil Service, short of the level of secretaries of departments, were 94.9 percent Filipino, whereas in 1938, at the level of "higher personnel," the Indies Civil Service was still only 6.4 percent Indonesian.[51] Indonesians outnumbered Dutch at lower strata of the Indies Civil Service, but the Dutch clearly prevailed in positions of higher responsibility.

In such a system, the educated Indonesian had a choice of becoming a civil servant or a politician. The former meant maturing to honorable but subordinate responsibility under Dutch authorities; the latter allowed no clear career trajectory for an independent mind and hence entailed an eventual insubordination that was, by Dutch definition, immature. The choice, in retrospect, appears to have been between clerk and agitator.

In the 1930s, nonetheless, the civil service was the pride of the Dutch colonial system, for its competence, efficiency, and attention to detail. For many educated Indonesians the civil service was more than a career—it was a benign destiny: to nestle under the wing of the Dutch superior, to mind his hints, and to carry out his plans for the sake of development of one's own people, leaving determination of the rate of that development to faith, or to the Dutch as better informed.

IF, IN SUM, the Philippine governmental system was a simple inverted cone in which native talent strove up from the bottom and was drafted toward the top, the Indonesian system was a baroque castle, in which Indonesians were promoted not in the main hall but in one wing. The Philippine-American system stressed Filipinization, democratization, local autonomy, and good government. That is the order in which it achieved its major ends. Autocratic and oligarchic tendencies remained strong; a bias toward centralization inherited from the Spanish was never overcome; and good government in the Anglo-American sense reached at best a temporary draw with comfortable government in a Malay-Hispanic sense. By the mid-1930s, there were extremely few Americans left in positions of significant governing power. Whatever losses that meant in efficiency and honesty, there were clear gains in Filipino experience and responsibility.

The Dutch system, by comparison, accented peace and order, pro-

[51] W. Cameron Forbes, *The Philippine Islands* (Boston: Houghton Mifflin, 1928), 2: 230; *Verslag van de commissie tot bestudering van staatsrechteligjke hervormingen* (Report of the Commission for the Study of Constitutional Reforms) (Batavia, 1941), vol. 1, chap. 3, "Enkele gegevens van sociale aard" (Some data of social nature), 56.

cedural impeccability, and leisurely ripening to autonomy. In all these goals, considered from year to year, the Dutch could satisfy themselves that they had achieved a modest increment of progress, but its pace implied considerable Indonesian distress.

In fostering a complex form of government, the Dutch were making understandable concessions to a staggered chronology of conquest and varied patterns of culture. Although they were also consciously trying not to make a nation, they would fashion one more by inhibition than design. They dreaded, in succession and to some degree concurrently, an aroused Islam, an insurgent communism, and a subversive secular nationalism. All three would one day burst through in revolution to contend for primacy.

American developmental policy in the Philippines applied with radical speed and scope a presumption not nearly so deeply felt by other North Atlantic powers: that education leads to moral and political progress. Even in its most cautious form, American policy expressed the belief that the best government was representative government, which required educated public opinion to sustain it. Testing and proving the belief involved demonstrations of quantity: a high percentage of indigenous peoples in elective and appointive office, and a high percentage of literate persons qualified to elect those in such positions, or fill them themselves. The Netherlands, however, had neither the motive nor the means to carry out such policies in Indonesia, and it satisfied its own conscience with demonstrations of quality. In an era of rising national will, however, exactions of quality would prove more explosive than concessions to quantity.

2

EXPRESSION AND REPRESSION

UNDER DUTCH AND

AMERICAN RULE

Secretary of State Henry Stimson, hoping to retain the Philippines under a dominion rule, told Congress in 1929: "We have gotten beyond the caveman age in regard to colonial development. We do not and cannot now hold colonies by force."[1] Congress treated Stimson as the caveman, and in 1934 passed an independence act on a twelve-year schedule. Two years later, Governor General B. C. de Jonge of Indonesia, taking pains to avoid the term "nationalist movement," countenanced only nonpolitical striving for prosperity based on order and labor: "Now we have worked here in the Indies for three hundred years. We should expect another three hundred years before the Indies will, perhaps, be mature for a form of autonomy."[2]

Sharply different expectations regarding the future of their colonies not only led the United States and the Netherlands to introduce different types of civil administrations and educational systems, but also to exercise different kinds of control and degrees of restraint over their colonial subjects. The methods of control available to both governments were those known universally—surveillance, search, arrest, internment, deportation, and execution. The last of these was the least used by both: the Dutch, between 1909 and 1940, executed only 125 persons for all crimes, of which crimes

[1] United States Congress, *House Committee on Commerce, Hearings*, 70:2 (1929), 685.

[2] Prof. S. L. van der Wal, in *Tijdschrift voor Geschiedenis* (1967), 498–99, traces this remark to a press interview given by de Jonge; quotation from *Deli-Courant*, 4 April 1936.

against the state were only one category. The Americans, after the atrocities of the war of subjugation, cannot readily be said to have executed anyone for political cause, although there were political elements in the convictions for murder in some famous cases.[3] The Dutch resorted to political internment frequently—1,145 people between 1855 and 1920, 4,500 after the Communist uprisings of 1926–27, and various nationalist leaders in the 1930s.[4] The Americans used deportation early and sparingly, and their "political" trials arose more frequently out of magico-messianic social protest than out of organized modern dissent.

In the long run, routine systems of political surveillance and reportage in both colonies were far more significant than the controversial punishments that were occasionally their consequence. The Dutch style provoked, even as it suppressed, Islamic, Marxist, and nationalist opposition, and radicalism among the young. Most radical nationalism in the Philippines, however, might be said to have died in infancy; it had relatively little to feed on and was over-wrapped in swaddling.

THE DUTCH: PID, SURVEILLANCE, AND INTERNMENT

"In . . . every domain I am insufficiently informed. Also about what's going on among the natives, we don't know a tenth part."[5] With that complaint, the governor general of the Indies had moved to establish the Politieke Inlichtingen Dienst (PID), or Political Intelligence Service.[6] In 1918, only weeks after creation of the Volksraad two years later, critics rose there to challenge the budget of the PID as unnecessarily large, to complain of its specific surveillance

---

[3] *Jaarcijfers* (see chap. 1, note 42), 1913, 55, 1916, 67, 1921, 51; *Statistisch Jaaroverzicht* (see chap. 1, note 20), 1924, table CVIII, 1928, table 87c, *Indisch Verslag* (see chap. 1, note 20), 1941, pt. 2, *Statistisch Jaaroverzicht*, 1940, table 97. For the cases of Felipe Salvador, Macario Sakay, and Mariano Noriel, see W. Cameron Forbes, *The Philippine Islands* (Boston: Houghton Mifflin, 1928), 1: 229–31; David R. Sturtevant, *Popular Uprisings in the Philippines, 1840–1940* (Ithaca: Cornell University Press, 1976), 132–38, 199; and Historical Conservation Society, *General History of the Philippines*, pt. 5, 1 (Manila: 1984): xxii–v, 474–80.

[4] P.H.C. Jongmans, *De Exorbitante Rechten van den Gouverneur-General in de Praktijk* (Amsterdam, 1921), app. 1, 176–88, is the source for the years 1855–1920; for subsequent years, Bernhard Dahm, *History of Indonesia in the Twentieth Century* (London and New York: Praeger, 1971), 59–60, 66–70.

[5] Gov. Gen. J. P. van Limburg Stirum to Min. Kol. Th. B. Pleyte, May 20, 22, 1916 (Algemeen Rijksarchief, Den Haag, Collectie Pleyte); Pleyte to von Limburg Stirum, August 18, 1916 (Algemeen Rijksarchief, Den Haag, Collectie van Limburg Stirum).

[6] Gov't. decree (Jav. Ct. no. 38), May 6, 1916.

of the Insulinde and Budi Utomo parties, and to allege violation of the privacy of letters, telephone, and telegraph. The PID chief, one Muurling, offered the engaging reply that the elaborate kind of secret service described in Kipling's *Kim* would have been too expensive, with too many underemployed special agents; that a service relying only "for its information on the help of all order-loving people" would have been flooded with much useless data; and that therefore the PID relied on officials of the existing administration. The Volksraad upheld the PID by a vote of 24 to 10.[7]

Muurling proclaimed the sanctity of all private communication in the Indies, but his personal correspondence six months later clearly reveals the monitoring of telephone calls for certain communists and socialists.[8] The Indies government putatively abolished the PID in 1919, but in the following year, as part of a general reorganization of police on Java and Madura, they reintroduced it under the name Algemene Recherche, or General Investigation Service.[9] Thus they dodged the word "political" and tried to avoid the imputation that there was a "political police."

Following earlier police reforms of 1897 and 1911, the reorganization of 1920 had among its major aims to make effective the control of the attorney general over the police, which he had previously commanded only in theory, and to fill a security gap in the countryside, where police coverage was thin, and varied according to regent's tastes. Within a few years the attorney general stood at the apex of a system of reportage and responsibility that included the field police (*veldpolitie*), ninety garrisons strong on Java alone by 1924; the city police (*stadspolitie*), long established; and the armed

[7] *Handelingen van de Volkstaad* (see chap. 1, note 21), 1918, le gew z, June 18, 48f.; June 20, 183f., 221, 230f.; June 22, 286ff., 305f. The Insulinde had a heritage of Eurasian membership and perspective. The Budi Utomo went through several phases after its founding as a cultural association, but could only be thought of as radical in a Dutch imperial context. See Nagazumi, Akira, *The Dawn of Indonesian Nationalism: The Early Years of Budi Utomo, 1908–1918* (Tokyo: Institute of Developing Economies, 1972).

[8] W. Muurling to J. Hulshoff Pol, November 19, 1918 (Algemeen Rijksarchief, Collectie van Limburg Stirum). Muurling was no mere reactionary policeman; he was at the same time trying to persuade the socialist J. E. Stokvis to edit a newspaper to be bought by the government to defend government policies against rising conservative opposition. Muurling to Stokvis, January 11, 18, 31, 1918 (International Instituut voor Sociale Geschiedenis, Amsterdam, Collectie Stokvis).

[9] HV le gew z 1919, Bijl, 1, II, 3, p. 2, and Bijl, 48, 8ff. Its full title was: "Dienst der Algemene Recherche bij het Parket van de Procureur Generaal in Nederlandsch-Indië (General Investigation Service of the Office of the Attorney General in the Netherlands Indies).

police (*gewapende politie*), strengthened after 1912 as the "mailed fist" of the Binnenlands Bestuur (BB) and after 1920 phased into the field units. The police system was thus centralized: no authority was conceded to provincial and regency councils; every policeman received the same training and could move from city to field and vice versa. The police were semimilitary in character, ubiquitous in location, and omnicompetent in function, even to helping fill out people's tax forms.

The field police had its own investigation service, and the city police an analogue even busier, because large cities were the centers of political action. The Algemene Recherche, however, was the central intelligence gatherer. Attached to the attorney general's office, it handled political intelligence on a supralocal level, as well as problems involving foreigners, counterfeiters, and opium, and assisted the attorney general in planning action in these areas. Residents and assistant residents, in their capacities as local heads of police, were responsible to the attorney general, and so were the village heads—not formal officials but "acknowledged chiefs"—useful for countless purposes and indispensable to the police system. Although official language dropped the term "PID," it continued in general usage to mean the whole apparatus of political surveillance leading to prosecution.[10] While technically incorrect, this habit was a convenient way of acknowledging a major truth: that under whatever shelter, or with whatever innocuous coloring, political investigation was central to the aim and style of Dutch colonial practice.

The budgets of the Algemene Recherche tended to provoke criticism of political investigation, but these central staff budgets were in fact small compared with expenditures on "secret police, rewards for the catching of criminals," and other special purposes,[11] not to

[10] C.G.E. de Jong, *De organisatie der politie in Nederlandsch-Indie* (Leiden, 1933), esp. 9, 51ff., 86ff.; M. Oudang, *Perkembangan kepolisian di Indonesia* (Development of the Indonesian police) (Jakarta: Mahabarata, 1952), 8–32; interviews, E. H. van den Broek with P. A. van der Poel, January 18, February 16, 1972.

[11] Central staff budgets ranged from an introductory f.10,000 (1920) to a high of f.92,750 (1932), back to f.25,850 (1936). For 1920, they may be found in HV le gew z 1919, Bijl, 1, 48, 126A; for the years 1921–27, in HV le gew z 1920–26, Bijl, 1, II, 3; after that in HV 1927/28, 1928/29, etc., Bijl, 1, II, 2 (or 3B), for each year concerned. Secret police funds, 1916–36, fluctuated between f.500,000 and f.1,000,000. They may be found in the so-called seven years' comparisons of NEI budgets, HV le gew z 1920, 1923, Bijl, 1, L for the years 1916–21, and HV 1927/28–1938/39, Bijl, 1, IV, for the years 1922/36. In the Manila Police Department, a Secret Service Force was es-

mention the far greater cost of regular salaries paid to police and other officials doing routine political intelligence work.

The communist uprisings of 1926–27 in West Java and West Sumatra, largely anticipated by the PID, made it difficult for critics of the political police to press a case without appearing to wish to undermine the foundations of the government. In all, there followed 13,000 arrests, 4,500 imprisonments, 1,300 deportations, and some hangings on conviction of conspiracy to murder. Most of the detainees obtained release in a short time, but an investigator writing two years later said that 3,000 in West Java and 2,000 in West Sumatra were still under arrest.[12]

To a significant number of those arrested the Dutch applied the power of *exorbitante rechten.* In the interests of "public peace and order," the governor general could deny residence in the Indies to persons not born there and could assign or deny residence in specific places to Indies-born persons. After the First World War, such action required proper summoning and interrogation of the person in question, followed by consent of the Council of the Indies, notice to the minister of colonies in cases involving Europeans, and notice to the Volksraad in all cases, European and Indonesian.[13] Because this power of deportation and relocation was not technically a law but an administrative right, the Indies government was wont to say that the detainee-exiles affected by it were not criminals but simply persons removed from certain areas for the sake of peace and order. The parliamentary opposition argued that exile, involving as it did certain fundamental rights, should not be a matter of executive determination, but of strict juridical finding.

After the communist uprisings, the Dutch established a special camp in New Guinea—Boven Digul—to contain the expected influx of cases. The number of political internees, not including family members, rose to a high that for two years exceeded the total

---

tablished in 1901, and operated initially at about $2,000 per month (BIA, RG 350, 2552, National Archives).

[12] Dahm, *History of Indonesia in the Twentieth Century,* 59; J. Th. P. Blumberger, *De Communistische beweging in Nederlandsch-Indië* (The Communist movement in the Netherlands Indies) (Haarlem, Tjeenk Willink en Zoon, 1928), 111.

[13] The constitutional basis for these procedures is found in the Regeerings Reglement of 1854, articles 45–48, and the Indische Staatsregeling of 1925, articles 35–38, of which the texts are nearly identical, P.H.C. Jongmans, *De Exorbitante Rechten van den Gouverneur-Generaal in de Praktijk* (The deportation right of the governor general in practice) (Amsterdam, 1921), pp. vii–ix, quotes the first; Blumberger, *Communistiche beweging,* 142–43, quotes the second.

affected by exorbitante rechten from 1855 to 1920. Several hundred remained there in 1941.[14]

After the squelching of the communist uprisings, the Indonesian opposition in the Volksraad revived its attack on the AR. Koesoemo Oetoyo, a conservative regent leader, objected that the Indonesian section of the BB must "spy on its own countrymen . . . and . . . put people in jail" instead of acting as their "natural protectors." The sons of the elite took jobs in the BB "from sheer necessity" and then were forced to "debase themselves to perform spy services." The AR should hire native lawyers so as to evaluate information correctly, he argued, complaining of "Judas wages" paid false informants. Sukardjo Wirjopranoto, a leader of the Parindra party, asked for a separation of functions in the procureur general's office, so that political police work, "nowhere described in the law," would be separated from ordinary police work.[15] Far from accepting these criticisms, many Dutch believed that the AR needed more European and native officials who had a "deep understanding of native society, which is absolutely necessary for understanding and fighting communism." Nothing less than a "department of internal war" would suffice.[16]

The communist uprisings did result in a tightening of the surveillance and reporting system, without either nativizing it or putting it on a level of "internal war." The crux of the system became the Politiek-Politionele Overzichten (Police Political Surveys)— summaries of political tendencies, composed by the AR from Indieswide sources and sent by the procureur general to the governor general. These had the effect of further suffusing the whole administration with surveillance psychology and police-oriented evaluations. Whereas the governor general had yearly conferences with residents and regents treating topical matters, the PPOS were monthly in frequency and Indies-wide in circulation at high levels. In any lack of regular policy instruction from the government, constantly avail-

[14] "Overzicht van den Inwendigen Politieken Toestand" (April 1928–May 1929), 2–5, in *Mededeelingen der Regeering omtrent enkele onderwerpen van algemeen belang* (Government announcements about a few topics of general interest) (Weltevreden: Landsdrukkerij, 1929). Blumberger, *Communistische beweging*, 112–13, 115, gives figures for 1927 and 1928 somewhat at variance with the foregoing. R. Moenander, in Moenander et al, *Indonesian Nationalism and Revolution. Six First-Hand Accounts* (Melbourne: Monash University, 1969) gives a figure of 886 in 1941, whereas *Indisch Verslag*, pt. 2, 1936–41, table 108A, indicates only 379 remaining in 1940.

[15] HV le gew z, 1928–29, p. 1545, 1929–30, p. 1692, 1930–31, p. 159, 1931–32, p. 226.

[16] HV le gew z, 1927–28, pp. 32, 510.

able police information and perspective filled the vacuum. In the very last years the government tried to correct the imbalance with instructions more oriented to civil administration, but this was "never executed entirely, because of lack of time." A prominent BB officer conceded that those who followed the political police surveys "can only recall with esteem the solidarity with which the data were worked out and the sobriety of the explanation. However, the police could not come out of its own skin: their considerations originated naturally from a world of thoughts that was typically police-oriented."[17]

Especially after the communist uprisings, this thought-world saw Moscow as the center of evil, and the Partai Nasional Indonesia (PNI), because influenced by Marxism, as the most dangerous movement in the Indies. The AR broke the PPOs into five categories (Table 2.1). The "Chinese movement" was mainly concerned with reactions of Indies Chinese (on the whole "loyal and order loving"[18]) to events in their homeland. "Extremist movements" dealt with millenarian and messianic movements, especially those affected by expectation of a *Ratu Adil*, or "righteous king." Investigators of extremists, however, often found it difficult to distinguish among religious movements, banditry, and communism. "Trade unionism" was a self-explanatory category, sensitive because of communist probing there, and later because of nationalist efforts among unions. "Foreign movements" took as it concerns the organization of Indonesian students in Holland, the Dutch Communist Party, and the international communist movement.

The category "nationalist and Mohammedan movement," however, considerably exceeded all the others combined in quantity of reports for the period 1931–36, with nationalist behavior of much greater interest than Muslim. The prevailing picture is one of overwhelming obsession with nationalism, and the anxious association of it with international communism, theoretical Marxism, trade unionism, modernized Islam, and, occasionally, regional millenarian movements.

Sukarno, who was laboring to devise a politically potent synthesis of just such elements, was the perfect target of suspicious surveillance; of arrest, trial, and imprisonment; and, after release, of rearrest and exorbitante rechten. Governor General de Jonge wrote

---

[17] P.J.A. Idenburg, "Het Nederlandse antwoord op het Indonesisch nationalisme" (The Netherlands' answer to Indonesian nationalism) in H. Baudet and I. J. Brugmans, *Balans van Beleid* (Assen: Van Gorcum, 1961), 143–45.

[18] Mailrapport, 1934, PPO August–September (Min. Kol.).

TABLE 2.1
Emphasis in Political Intelligence,
Netherlands Indies, 1931–36

Total PPO Pages Devoted to:	1931	1932	1933	1934	1935	1936	Total
Chinese movement	49	25	17	13	7	10	121
Extremist movements	5	11	5	10	15	13	59
Trade unionism	47	35	27	20	16	29	174
Foreign movements	67	16	30	40	27	45	225
Nationalist-Mohammedan movement	144	154	132	67	95	105	697
Total	312	241	211	150	160	202	1,276

SOURCE: Mailrapporten 1931–37, Politiek Politionele Overzichten (Archief Voormalig Ministerie van Kolonien, Den Haag).

of him in his diary early in 1933: "In view of the tense crisis situation, we were in no position to put up with the fanning of political mischief." "Extremist organizations" had developed a system of assembly that held more and more meetings at the same hour in different places, "which made it impossible for the police to carry out the necessary supervision. Consequently the only solution was to limit the right of assembly of the worst faction, the Partindo . . . and the P.N.I., and to arrest Partindo's leader, Engineer Sukarno."[19]

After two years in prison on conviction under the so-called hate-sowing article,[20] Sukarno had been released on December 31, 1931.

[19] Quotations from *Herinneringen van Jhr. Mr. B.C. de Jonge*, ed. S. L. van der Wal (Groningen: Wolters-Noordhoff, 1968), 191–92; translations from this volume prepared by Margaret Broekhuysen.

[20] Ruth McVey, *The Rise of Indonesian Communism* (Ithaca: Cornell University Press, 1965), 258, 454 n. 6, gives a brief account of these articles of the Criminal Code. Roger Paget, ed., *Indonesia Accuses! Sukarno's Defence Oration in the Political Trial of 1930* (Kuala Lumpur: Oxford University Press, 1975) contains Sukarno's views on the Dutch political police, 136–37.

Nineteen months later[21] he was banished to Flores, far away from the chance to influence other exiles. Even there the Dutch kept him under steady watch, tailing him on bicycle or foot. When he grew ill with malaria, the Dutch moved him to South Sumatra and a healthier climate, lest he should die on their hands.[22]

Fellow nationalist Thamrin, in front of whose house Sukarno's arrest took place, presented the government with thirteen questions and a motion of disapproval; the government rejected the motion, and de Jonge began looking for a chance to catch Thamrin.[23] Hatta and Sjahrir tried to clothe the wolf of nationalism in the sheepskin of education by forming the Pendidikan Nasional Indonesia—a study group that interested itself in training cadres to spread ideas among the masses. Its reading lists were the literature of plot and revolt. One member, then a teenager, recalls translating Curzio Malaparte's *Coup d'Etat* from a French version into Dutch, so that another could translate it into Indonesian. Before they could render this revolutionary cookbook into native recipes, Dutch police searched the house, slashed the pillows, and confiscated all subversive materials.[24]

The activities of Hatta, Sjahrir, and other PNI members brought the attorney general to the point of submitting a twenty-seven-page request of the governor general to arrest and intern them. He cited a document found in Hatta's luggage, argued laboriously the Hatta-Sjahrir connection with Marxism and communism, harked back to the uprisings, and asked that "criminal subversion" be ended lest more extensive intervention be required later. On the question of preventive action, the adviser for native affairs strongly demurred. Hatta and the others were dangerous, but banning the party and warning its leaders was sufficient; 1926–27 would not recur, be-

---

[21] *Sukarno: An Autobiography*, as told to Cindy Adams (Indianapolis: Bobbs-Merrill, 1965), 123–24, contains several chronological errors concerning this period. John Ingleson, *Road to Exile The Indonesian Nationalist Movement, 1927–1934* (Singapore: Heinemann Educational Books, 1979), is a carefully detailed study; see especially 176–228. For the immediate prewar period, Susan Abeyesekere, *One Hand Clapping: Indonesian Nationalists and the Dutch, 1939–1942* (Melbourne: Monash Centre of Southeast Asian Studies, 1976).

[22] *Sukarno: An Autobiography*, 127–47.

[23] *Herinneringen . . . de Jonge*, 192; see also R. C. Kwantes, *De Ontwikkeling van de Nationalistiche Beweging in Nederlandsch-Indië* (Development of the nationalist movement in the Netherlands Indies) (Groningen: Wolters-Nordhoff/Bouma's Boekhuis, 1982), 4· 714–18.

[24] Drs. Hazil, interview, February, 1968.

cause "the *politieke recherche* is now so completely up to its task that history will not repeat itself in that respect."

The Council of the Indies, however, supported the attorney general. Though the PNI was "walking along the barbed wire which is stretched by the law," the council was "quite sure that the game of purely intellectual activities will end in serious trouble, even if the people concerned do not desire it." Internment was warranted lest "the foundations of the state be undermined." The executive secretary to the governor general concluded with the consummate argument of bureaucratic caution and self-justification: "The advantage of the *inlichtingsdienst* consists precisely in the fact that one can intervene before much harm has been done."[25] There must be no breach in the colonial dike. The PID identified thought-crimes early; then the BB could plug up any trickle lest it become a political torrent. De Jonge concurred in the recommendation of the Council of the Indies: "Times were quiet," he wrote the minister for colonies, "but one could not allow these leaders to continue their work. . . . In these times, peace and order are necessary above all."[26]

Years later, responding thoughtfully to a question regarding the influence of the Algemene Recherche, its former vice-chief opined that it had been strong because it had "the facts."[27] But the success of the AR-PID depended on more than police initiative, thoroughness, persistence, and "factuality" as construed in an antisubversive framework. It depended on native assistance. A former regent who aspired to high power under the Dutch recalls: "When somebody like Sukarno or Semaun or Darsono was seen in a village at 7:30 in the morning, I would know it at 8:30, and the governor general at 9:30."[28] The Dutch system of political intelligence and surveillance worked not only directly by limiting the activities of nationalists and communists, but indirectly by pitting Indonesian against Indonesian.

[25] Quotations in two previous paragraphs from Procureur Gen. to Gov. Gen., December 22, 1933; advice of Adviseur voor Inlandse Zaken, January 24, 1934; advice of the Raad van Nederlandsch-Indië, February 22, 1934; Secretarie Nota, January 31, 1934; all from Mailrapport 287 geheim (secret)/34, (Min. Kol.); see also Kwantes, *Nationalistisch Beweging*, 4: 189–221, and the published documentary trail subsequent to internment.

[26] *Herinneringen . . . de Jonge*, 236.

[27] Interview, E. H. van den Broek with Mr. H.J.A. Vermijs, vice-chief of the Algemene Recherche, 1929–42, July 12, 1971.

[28] Interview, Abdul Kadir Widjojoatmodjo, May 25, 1969. Semaun and Darsono were prominent communist leaders of the 1920s. Compare American practice, note 49 below.

The Americans and the "Argus-Eyed Constabulary"

American practices in the Philippines were neither innocent of political repression nor addicted to it. In the decades following pacification, the Americans were involved in putting down several provincial outbreaks of a millenarian nature.[29] At the level of modern national politics, however, the major acts of repression by the United States may be enumerated: the brief deportation of forty-three prominent nationalists in 1902, and the subsequent exile of Artemio Ricarte; the deportation of Tan Malaka; the imprisonment of twenty communists involved in the May Day demonstration of 1931; and the imprisonments of Luis Taruc.

When the Americans completed their takeover of the Philippines in 1901, they were asserting foreign sovereignty over a people that had declared independence from another foreign power, fought a revolution, and written a constitution. Anticipating further resistance, some Americans recommended sending to Guam every hostile Filipino military or civil leader who had survived the war, but the McKinley administration chose to deport only forty-three men.[30] A year and a half later, following President Theodore Roosevelt's July 4, 1902, Proclamation of Amnesty, Secretary of War Elihu Root made clear that all deportees were free to return to Manila if they signed an oath of allegiance to the United States, as General Emilio Aguinaldo, commander of the contending army, had done after capture.[31] Soon all the deportees had taken the oath and returned but two: Apolinario Mabini, the revolutionary ideologist, and General Artemio Ricarte.

A Senate resolution sponsored by Senator Carl Hoar, the anti-imperialist leader from Massachusetts, called upon the president to explain the continued detention of Mabini without trial, in apparent violation of his now applicable constitutional rights.[32] In the administration's reply, Root maintained that authority for continued detention was traceable to regulations governing prisoners of war.[33] Root and Roosevelt shared Governor General Taft's view of

[29] Sturtevant, *Popular Uprisings*.

[30] For example, Adm. Ramey to Sec. Nav., November 27, 1900, enclosures, BIA 2376, advocating general deportation; HQ, Division of the Philippines, General Orders no. 4, January 7, 1901 (first 32 deportees), no. 10, January 15, 1901 (last 11 deportees).

[31] Sec. War. to Sec. Nav. July 18, 1902, referred to in Sec. Nav. to Sec. War, July 26, 1902, BIA 2376-13.

[32] Senate Resolution 333, 57:2, January 15, 1903.

[33] Senate Document 111, 57:2.

Mabini: "His consistent course of opposition to the Government, in prison and out of prison, his physical condition as a hopeless paralytic, and his gentle and courteous manner, have all served to place him in the attitude of a martyr and to give him . . . influence and popularity." If released, Taft observed, he would form a nucleus for "plots" and would continue "unjust accusations."[34]

Taft soon had to ask Root that these words not be published, for Mabini, to everyone's surprise, finally signed the oath and came back to Manila, where he died soon after. Only Ricarte did not sign. Taking up Root's offer of passage anywhere in the world touched by a United States transport—except the Philippines—Ricarte went to Hong Kong.[35] This last "irreconcilable" secretly reentered the Philippines in December 1903 but was captured six months later, tried for sedition, convicted, and sentenced to six years of solitary confinement. After deportation to Hong Kong again in 1910, he continued fomenting agitation in Manila, which concluded in the pathetic "Christmas Eve Rebellion" of 1914, little more than a badly organized demonstration stimulated from abroad. American authorities asked for Ricarte's extradition, but he fled to Shanghai and thence Japan, into the embrace of Japanese superpatriots.[36] He eventually returned to Manila in 1942 on a Japanese transport, a political Rip Van Winkle, incongruous, poignant, and nearly powerless.

As the postrevolutionary phase of political repression relaxed, many young revolutionaries, like Manuel Quezon, became lawyer-politicians in the American-established political system. Constitutional gradualists themselves, their earlier radicalism and their legal training made them sympathize with the plight of Tan Malaka, the Indonesian communist, arrested in the Philippines in 1927. Banished from Indonesia by the Dutch in 1922, Tan became Comintern representative for Southeast Asia in 1923 and thereafter enjoyed the role of itinerant romantic revolutionary.[37] Tan visited Manila

[34] Taft, endorsement of War Dept. document, January 12, 1903, BIA 2376-21; Root to President Roosevelt, February 14, 1903, BIA 2376-21; see also Root to Roosevelt, December 29, 1902 in Senate Document 111, 57:2.

[35] Gov. Gen. to Sec. War, February 28, 1903, BIA 2376-23.

[36] Sturtevant, *Popular Uprisings*, 195–204; Grant K. Goodman, "General Artemio Ricarte and Japan," *Journal of Southeast Asian History* 7 (1966): 50–53; Armando J. Malay, introduction, *Memoirs of General Artemio Ricarte* (Manila: National Heroes Commission, 1963).

[37] His autobiography, *Dari pendjara ke pendjara* (From jail to jail), 3 vols. (Bukit Tinggi, n.d.) is an engrossing if often unreliable account of his life. McVey, *Rise of Communism*, 114–120, 220ff., describes Tan's early sympathies and activities; Benedict R. O'G. Anderson, *Java in a Time of Revolution: Occupation and Resistance,*

briefly in 1925, after being denied readmission to Java; then he traveled to Singapore, where he stayed throughout the abortive communist uprisings in Indonesia. Some months later, Indonesian communist agents arrested in Singapore told the British that Tan was in Manila. The news, conveyed to the Philippines through international channels, was probably untrue at the time, but it started local police sniffing the wind. The chief of police in Manila, an American, began a process of photograph matching, house watching, and club and bar checking. That made it easier to net Tan when he actually arrived, equipped with eight aliases, nine languages (or parts of them), ten Singapore dollars, and two Philippine pesos.[38]

Publicity about the case brought Tan the express sympathy of Quezon, speaking on the floor as president of the Senate; of Claro Recto, Jose P. Laurel, Juan Sumulong, and Jose Abad Santos, who acted as his lawyer. The students of the University of the Philippines voted resolutions in his favor, and its president, Apolinario de los Santos, was involved in his behalf. Ramon Fernandez, a wealthy and popular Nacionalista senator, posted a bond of six thousand pesos for Tan, and the entrepreneur Vicente Madrigal eventually offered him free passage on one of his ships. Left labor groups were at first cautious about Tan, but mass meetings were soon planned in his behalf. Muslims sought him out. Filipino newspapers portrayed Tan as a heroic fellow Malay nationalist. Only Americans opposed him, particularly the business community, whose newspaper, the *Bulletin*, published police transcripts and a good deal of damaging supposition and insinuation.[39]

The issue for Acting Governor General Eugene Gilmore was sensitive, heated, and complicated. He could hardly prosecute Tan as a communist when an American economist had recently been in

1944–46 (Ithaca: Cornell University Press, 1972), 270–77, gives an account of his activities up to 1945 and takes a sympathetic view. Rudolf Mrazek, "Tan Malaka: A Political Personality's Structure of Experience," *Indonesia* 14 (1972): 1–48, is a psychological and intellectual assessment.

[38] "Tan Malaka's Manila Memoirs," trans. Willy Pantouw, *Solidarity* 1, no. 1 (1966): 15–22; Tan Malaka to China League for Civil Rights, February 1933, 5–7 (differing in no essential from his later memoirs in Indonesian); Verbaal September 14, 1933, E 22 (Min. Kol.); Proc. Gen. to Cons. Gen. Nederlands, Manila, February 7, 1927, Verbaal November 19, 1927, S 18 (Min. Kol.); Sec. State to Sec. War, October 14, 1927, BIA 18868-26; and BIA 18868-25B, 18868, and 26854.

[39] "Tan Malaka's Manila Memoirs"; Manila *Daily Bulletin*, August 15, 16, 17, 18, 19, 20, 22, 23, 1927; Philippines *Free Press*, August 20, p. 36, August 27, pp. 2, 4, 34, September 3, p. 2, September 10, pp. 12, 57, 60. Jane Ragsdale very generously did this newspaper research for me.

Manila passing out Soviet literature; yet he did not wish to grant Tan asylum. Tan's rights were presumably clear to Gilmore the legal scholar, but "Army, Navy, and merchants" beset Gilmore the administrator. Finally he called up Tan's lawyer and implied prosecution of prominent Filipinos for having connived in the falsification of credentials for Tan. His supporters thus checked, Tan was deported only two weeks after his arrival.[40]

Still looking for asylum six years later, Tan complained to Madame Sun Yat-sen and the China League for Civil Rights that three different imperialistic governments in Asia had imprisoned and banished him. Without mentioning his forged credentials, he asserted that none of them found "sufficient legal grounds to summon me before a Court and . . . try my case in a proper and ordinary way. I was simply persecuted for my 'outlook,' or my 'supposed state of mind.' " America and England, Tan said, broke with their own traditions in refusing asylum and dishonored their own reputations as havens for political refugees.[41]

Tan's criticism points to the nervousness of all colonial administrations before the communism of the 1920s and 1930s. Even the normally relaxed American system tightened up in confrontation with it. In the Philippines, a new generation of dissenters began to take as their model the Russian Revolution rather than the French or American. The Great Depression nourished their influence and made them increasingly bold in attacking the colonial government. Worries over communism reached such a point in 1931 that Governor General Dwight Davis suggested formal cooperation among colonial capitals to find out "if the whole movement is headed up in one place." He learned that Secretary of State Stimson had already agreed to such a request from the Algemene Recherche in the Indies.[42]

During Davis's trip abroad in the same year, a crackdown was begun: the secretaries of justice and the interior were to start suits

[40] "Tan Malaka's Manila Memoirs"; Gov. Gen. PI to Gov. Gen. NEI, September 9, 1927, Verbaal November 19, 1927, S 18 (Min. Kol.).

[41] Tan to China League for Civil Rights, February 1933, p. 9 (Min. Kol.). The Dutch had failed to get Hong Kong to extradite Tan, but there is no evidence of their trying with the Philippine government (A. E. van der Lely, head of AR, to Gov. Gen., March 30, 1927, p. 9 [Min. Kol.]; M. J. Quist, Cons. Gen. So. China to Proc. Gen., November 2, 1932, Verbaal January 27, 1933, N 1 [Min. Kol.]).

[42] Stimson to Sec. War. Hurley, February 13, Hurley to Stimson, February 19, 1931, BIA 28342-15; Davis to Hurley, March 19, BIA 28342-19. A subsequent memo from the State Department distinguishes American from European colonial policies, and is "aloof" to a cooperative "special police regime" (BIA 28342-25).

against communists. Both officials were Filipino, so the issue of racial prejudice was avoided.[43] Two weeks after Davis's return, a May Day mass meeting resulted in a confrontation between the Constabulary and the Philippine Communist Party and the arrest of twenty-seven party members.[44]

In subsequent testimony the party leader, Crisanto Evangelista, declared that Philippine government was the direct product of American revolution against England, and Philippine revolution against Spain and America. At the same time his movement was fighting an inevitable revolution born of the weaknesses of finance imperialism. The truly guilty were at large, while they, the defendants, represented the innocent workers and peasants of the Philippines, "reduced to dumb animals and dumb slaves because of this loss of fundamental freedom." Such eloquence may have moved but did not persuade the Supreme Court, which upheld the trial court convictions of twenty of the accused and declared the Communist Party an "illegal association."[45] Evangelista faced nine years and six months in jail.

During the Commonwealth period, however, President Quezon used his powers in response to a request from an American communist, James Allen: he pardoned the convicts. Evengelista, the last of the internees, obtained his "full civil and political rights" at the end of 1938, and in 1939 legality was restored to Communist Party membership and to its activities, short of sedition.[46]

The career of Luis Taruc carries the story of American repression into the period of independence. In the years 1937–41 Taruc suffered imprisonment four times for leading strikes in Pampanga. As Huk leader during and after the war, he eluded the Japanese but was

[43] Gov. Gen. Davis to Gen. F. LeJ. Parker, Chief, BIA, February 6, 1931, BIA 28342-16; Davis to Sec. War. Patrick J. Hurley, March 19, 1931, BIA 28342-19.

[44] Alvin H. Scaff, *The Philippine Answer to Communism* (Stanford: Stanford University Press, 1955), 12–13. For the Partido Komunista ng Pilipinas in the 1930s, see Benedict J. Kerkvliet, *The Huk Rebellion* (Berkeley: University of California Press, 1977), 49–53.

[45] Transcript, *Crisanto Evangelista et al.; Guillermo Capadocia et al. vs. the People of the Philippine Islands, on Petition for Writ of Certiorari to the Supreme Court of the Philippine Islands*, esp. 128–90, BIA, Evangelista, personnel file.

[46] Scaff, *Philippine Answer*, 20. Quezon publicly praised the motivations of Evangelista and Guillermo Capadocia, in contradistinction to plutocrat landlords (undated draft transcript [41 pp., of which 1–5 are missing], esp. pp. 6–7, and "Conference Between His Excellency the President and Mr. Wilkins of the Bulletin, February 9, 1939," 7–9, 12–15, Q).

imprisoned by the Americans twice in 1945.[47] The arc of Huk military rebellion rose in 1946; Taruc's surrender to the authorities in 1954 was a sign of its having waned. On a series of convictions for "rebellion complexed with murder" he spent fourteen years in jail.

All things considered, the routine level of political surveillance under the Americans was inexact and unsystematic compared with that of the Dutch. The Constabulary had a secret service, later an intelligence branch. One of its agents shadowed a Manila officer of Ricarte's "Revolutionary Army" for four years and issued monthly reports.[48] Others watched suspected "Bolsheviks" and the Philippine equivalents of Ratu Adil types. The testimony of a respected officer suggests the tension in the areas where the Colorum movement arose, compounding social discontent with devotion to the Sacred Heart of Jesus, the Immaculate Heart of Mary, and the imminent return to life of Jose Rizal as the righteous king: "If I heard there was a popular faith healer in my district, I kept him under close surveillance. If I heard that a village prophet was predicting natural disasters, I either arrested him or shipped him to another island."[49] In the cases of the Colorum outbreaks of 1923–25, the "empire" of Florencio Entrencherado in 1927, the Tangulan movement in 1931, and the Sakdal movement in 1935, some powerful Filipinos might see ignorant delusion as the cause, but clearer sighted Filipinos and many Americans saw bossism and agrarian oppression as chief stimuli. The Constabulary itself was a contributing cause: "Argus-eyed,"[50] perhaps, but with the additional reputation of being light-fingered with others' possessions, heavy-handed with their liberties, and sometimes trigger-happy.

Compared with the Dutch-Indonesian system, Philippine-American surveillance concerned itself relatively little with Chinese, or with unionists as such. Christian or syncretistic millenarians were a cause for police alarm. Although a racially mixed Supreme Court made the Communist Party illegal from 1932 to 1938, communist reading never became a "thought-crime" deserving internment. As for nationalism, it was not cause for surveillance at all, but throve

[47] Luis Taruc, *Born of the People* (New York: International Publishers, 1953), 45, 196, 202.

[48] Sturtevant, *Popular Uprisings*, 202 n. 14, citing BIA 4865-106C.

[49] Sturtevant, "The Last Shall Be First," MS, 255 n. 50. I have been unable to find this quotation in his subsequently published *Popular Uprisings*, and so I rely on the earlier MS. Compare practice in Java, note 28 above.

[50] Hayden, *Philippines*, 382, is the source for the quoted phrase.

on the public rhetoric of "immediate, absolute, and complete independence," a Nacionalista slogan since early in the century.

IMPERIAL STYLE IN THE GREAT DEPRESSION

As the Great Depression deepened in the 1930s, the United States saw the Philippines as an economic and strategic liability and scheduled independence for 1946. The Netherlands, however, like other European powers, took economic crisis as occasion for expense-reducing rather than colony-ridding. Governor General de Jonge cut the Indies budget by almost 25 percent, but even this was not sufficient to satisfy Dutch Prime Minister Hendrik Colijn, who suggested also cutting "all western education for the natives."[51] In 1936, to his profound chagrin, Colijn was forced to devalue the guilder. Meanwhile, de Jonge ruled the Indies to ensure that there would be no diminution of Dutch official authority. The challenges to his government seem mild in retrospect; one came from native civil servants, another from a group of young Dutch officials.

In 1932 the Alliance of Native Government Officials asked to replace the word "native" (Inlander) in government documents with the word "Indonesian" (Indonesiër). De Jonge and his administration refused on the grounds of the juridical validity of certain legal precepts implied by the term "native," as well as the geographic and ethnographic unsuitability of the term "Indonesian," and its political inappropriateness. The Dutch were trying to prevent the spread of a national identity through use of symbolic terms, even if it meant continued use of demeaning language. They forgot, perhaps, that Malays and mestizos in the Philippines had objected to being called by the Spanish term "Indios," one matter among others resolved by violent rebellion.[52]

The other challenge to de Jonge came from a group formed in 1930 as the Association for the Furtherance of the Social and Political Development of the Netherlands Indies, but soon known as the Stuw-group, *stuw* suggesting an accumulation of energy behind a dam, and protection against inundation. The original thirteen sign-

[51] *Herinneringen . . . de Jonge*, 430, 435.

[52] De Jonge's rationale appears in his *Herinneringen*, 189; See also Kwantes, *Nationalistische Beweging*, 3: 817–19, 4: 651–58. The epithets American soldiers called Filipinos during the Philippine-American war, 1898–1901, were no improvement on the Spanish. Stewart Creighton Miller has documented their racial attitudes in an essay in Peter W. Stanley, ed., *Reappraising an Empire: New Perspectives on Philippine-American History* (Cambridge: Harvard University Press, 1984), 13–34.

ers of the first Stuw circular were all of some official or professorial eminence in the Indies. Only one, Hubertus van Mook, was a member of the BB, and he later achieved appointment to the Volksraad as sole Stuw member. Most of them had studied at Leiden, where the ideas of Islamicist and humanist Snouck Hurgronje prevailed, in contrast with the "oil faculty" of Utrecht, financed by capitalists with interests in the Indies.[53]

Membership in the consciously "apolitical" group was open only to Dutchmen. Though its members had closer touch with Indonesians than the average Dutch official, the group as a whole had no contact with Indonesian groups or parties. Trying to further "social and political development" while remaining apolitical meant that the Stuwers were in fact a study and discussion group. Their publication, *De Stuw*, had an average circulation of only 275 and relied increasingly on articles by van Mook under various pseudonyms. By later 1933, the activities of the group were negligible.

De Jonge, who considered there to be more danger in the Indies from the Europeans than from natives, rejoiced at the demise of *De Stuw*. "A few measures in the area of internment and the right of assembly were enough to quiet the extreme nationalism," he wrote, but it was harder to bring "impertinent teachers" to reason. The end of *De Stuw* "delivered us from the pedantic, supercilious, denigrating writings by a few professors against a Government which . . . was incapable of sharing their broad vision and deep insights."[54]

That a group with so few members and such brief vigor should have exercised the Dutch community so greatly is the more extraordinary in view of the mildness of their ideas. They never published the word "Indonesian" in a political context referring to a nation, and they maintained silence on the subject of tempo. They considered the nationalist slogan *Indië-los van-Nederland-nu* ("The Indies free from the Netherlands now") dangerous, and talked of an "Indian" commonwealth, eventually able to protect the interests of nonindigenous inhabitants and to fulfill international obligations.[55] In short the Stuw-group had a predictably high Dutch mixture of paternalism and legalism, but they dared to focus their ideas on the

---

[53] These and subsequent summaries and assessments are based on Drs. Elsbeth Scholten, "De Stuw, Tijdstekening en Teken des Tijds" (The Stuw, holding back the tide and a sign of the times) (MS, Leiden, 1969), on author's interview with Drs. Locher-Scholten, 25 November 1970, and on interviews with original and later Stuwers, Netherlands, May 1969, November 1970.

[54] *Herinneringen . . . de Jonge*, 316–18.

[55] Scholten, "De Stuw."

term "emancipation": by furthering prosperity and education, the Dutch could help the natives find their own identity.

The tragedy of the Stuw-group is not complete in their impotence of the 1930s but in their power of the 1940s. Several of them, including van Mook as lieutenant–governor general, rose to prominent offices after the war and thus found themselves in the ironic position of having to reassert Dutch sovereignty over the self-proclaimed Indonesian republic. Instead of harnessing energy, they acted out in authority the other meaning of stuw, trying (unsuccessfully) to protect against inundation.

The colonial policy of the 1930s, questioned by the Stuwers, consisted in more than repressive hauteur toward nationalism. Indifferent to competing social and economic demands and the play of political forces, the government was characterized by centralized indirect rule and aspects of a "nightwatchman state."[56] The combination of efficient administration and efficacious policing gave the illusion that a perfect hygienic sanity was in control against corrosive irrationality. But this "apolitical" system was successful only in the short term; its policies would contribute to a violent postwar reaction.

One Stuwer, looking back a quarter century after the revolution, observed that the statement " 'You will be independent some day' is neither inspiring or satisfying."[57] Setting a specific target date— as the Americans did in the Philippines—would have eased the agony of transition after the war. The last chance was the Soetardjo petition of 1936. A group of Indonesians in the Volksraad proposed a conference of Dutch and Indonesian representatives to work out, on a basis of equality, a plan for autonomy for the Indies within the framework of the Dutch constitution and over a ten-year period.[58] Soetardjo himself, the head of the Alliance of Native Administrative Officials, declared that they did not contemplate independence, or a severance of ties with the motherland, but sought freedom of initiative and responsibility in order to dispel dissatisfaction, and to

[56] Harry J. Benda, "The Pattern of Administrative Reforms in the Closing Years of Dutch Rule in Indonesia," *Journal of Asian Studies* 25 (1966): 589–605, esp. 590–91, 603–5.

[57] Interview, J. A. Jonkman, November 1970. Jonkman, as minister of the colonies, authorized the Dutch police actions of 1947 and 1949.

[58] The following account is based on J. M. Pluvier, *Overzicht van de ontwikkeling der nationalistische beweging in Indonesie in de jaren 1930 tot 1942* (Survey of the development of the nationalist movement in Indonesia, 1930–1942) (The Hague: W. van Hoeve,1953), 118–29, and on Kwantes, *Nationalistische Beweging*, 4: 361–66, 531–35.

restore enthusiasm to working relations between Indonesians and Dutch. Though the more radical nationalists opposed the petition as "treason to the people," enough Dutch and Eurasians voted with most of the Indonesians in the Volksraad to carry it, 26 to 20.[59]

The conference idea took general hold among Indonesians, but they might have detected its eventual fate in the words of Colijn: "One should not say that all 65 million crave extending the autonomy of the Netherlands Indies just because a hundred thousand or fifty thousand, or however many there may be, exert a certain active pressure."[60] In November 1938, more than two years after the petition passed, the Dutch government issued its official no. One faction of the Volksraad, anticipating rejection, had already ceased to speak Dutch in the chamber, and were using Malay instead. By undermining the moderates and refusing to speak on equal terms, the Netherlands government had opened up the symbolic gap of language. Initiative would pass to the radicals, not only speaking a different tongue, but using the political vocabulary of irreconcilability.

A meeting of Soetardjo with de Jonge just before the latter's departure from office and the passage of the petition suggest the flavor of the decade. In his memoirs, de Jonge recalls how he had at first declined to receive Soetardjo, but made time for a meeting with him and two other nationalists when told that they wished not to plead for the petition but to say goodbye.

> When they came in, Soetardjo, Prawoto and Datoek Toemenggoeng, I asked them to sit down on the chairs that had been put ready for them at my desk. But they remained standing in front of it and Soetardjo pulled a large sheet of paper from his pocket and started to read a beautiful address. The quintessence of it was: Although you have not always conducted the administration according to our insights and our wishes, we have always known what to expect from you and that makes it easy for us to appreciate the many good things that have come into being during your administration. We want to give expression to that appreciation and thank you before your departure.—These words, from that side, were surely remarkable and I cannot deny that I was moved by them. . . . In a cordial and confidential discussion I pointed out that . . . they . . . should not overestimate themselves, something which Soetardjo had recently

[59] Pluvier, *Nationalistische beweging in Indonesie*, 124–25.
[60] Ibid., 125.

done in the Volksraad by reproaching the Government that the leading functions were still in the hands of Europeans; ... or did he really believe himself to be the equal of Van den Bussche, de Kat Angelino, Van Buuren, Hart? And also, if he realized that he was not, even then there was no reason for discouragement, because without doubt he would get that far. ... If only they did their duty in the place that had been assigned them, they would contribute, to their own advantage, to the ever increasing autonomy of their country.

With great attention and true or pretended approval they listened to my words; when leaving they thanked me for the reception and bowed deeply over the hand I extended them.[61]

De Jonge's voicing the assertion that they were not the equals of his staff, the nationalists bowing deeply over his extended hand: here is the perfect image of the suffocating symbiosis between the ruling Dutch and the cooperating Javanese, difference buried in ritual, dissent domesticated to the point where it gratifies the conscience of the petitioner to speak and the executive to hear, but nothing is done. De Jonge did not rule with "the whip and the club," as Sjahrir once said of him,[62] but with a confident assumption of superiority, with police surveillance, with the right to rusticate dissenters, and with glittering regalia. His hand was not doubled in a fist but extended for obeisance.

Manuel Quezon visited Java in September 1934, having obtained from the United States Congress an act scheduling independence by 1946. Some nationalists in Surabaya sought him out and took him to a secluded, darkened, and guarded house. When they asked how to go about getting independence, Quezon said, "Open all these windows and shutters, then take away your guards. Hold your meetings in the open, and in front of the Dutch themselves ... make a hell of a lot of noise! And if you do that long enough, you'll eventually get what you want."[63] What the Indonesians replied or thought is not recorded. Sukarno had made a hell of a lot of noise and the Dutch had banished him to Flores. When Soetardjo later tried pleading noises, de Jonge treated him like an adolescent.

---

[61] *Herinneringen ... de Jonge*, 387–88.

[62] Soetan Sjahrir, *Out of Exile* (New York: John Day, 1949), 112, quoted subsequently in other works, such as Leslie Palmier, *Indonesia and the Dutch* (London: Oxford University Press, 1962), 35.

[63] Sukardjo Wirjopranoto, *Philippine Magazine* 32 (1935): 640; Carlos Quirino, *Quezon: Man of Destiny* (Manila: McCullough, 1935), 35–36; and *Quezon: Paladin of Philippine Freedom* (Manila: Filipiniana Book Guild, 1971), 269.

3

JAPAN AS SUCCESSOR EMPIRE

The intrusion of Western power into East Asia and the western Pacific had by the twentieth century shattered the Chinese idea of a world order based on the Middle Kingdom, and had smothered state practice of Southeast Asian ideas of a cosmic order focused on a Hindu-Buddhist god-king. In the tradition of Renaissance diplomacy, the Western imperial powers treated each other as legal equals; but in the tradition of social Darwinism, they treated Asian polities as legal and moral inferiors unless counterforce proved otherwise.

Only Japanese power kept native initiative in Asia. Japan removed herself from the traditional Chinese order, and strove for competitive equality within the rules of the Western traditional system. Then, after 1931, she moved toward a unilateral militarism as a way of ending a disequilibrium that was poised in her disfavor. In 1940, Japan defined herself "brazenly at the center of a new world order she was to create in the Pacific area."[1]

In promoting the Greater East Asia Co-Prosperity Sphere, Japan stressed frugal premodern agrarian values as a countermeasure to the decadence of modern industrial nature. In trying to construct a

[1] Miwa Kimitada, "Neither East nor West, but All Alone," in Harry Wray and Hilary Conroy, eds., *Japan Examined: Perspectives on Modern Japanese History* (Honolulu: University of Hawaii Press, 1983), 384–89; quotation, 388. The bibliography of this compendium of essays, 395–99, summarizes the state of discussion. Among influential earlier works are: Maruyama Masao, *Thought and Behavior in Modern Japanese Politics*, ed. Ivan Morris (London: Oxford University Press, 1963); Iriye Akira, *After Imperialism: The Search for a New Order in the Far East, 1921–1931* (Cambridge: Harvard University Press, 1965); and James B. Crowley, *Japan's Quest for Autonomy* (Princeton: Princeton University Press, 1966).

Gotō Ken'ichi, *Shōwaki Nippon to Indonesia* (Japan and Indonesia in the Shōwa Era) (Tokyo: Keisō Shobō, 1986) was published too late for systematic reflection in these notes, but contains a thorough examination of *nanshinron* ("southern advance theory"), with specifics on Indonesia and wider implications for Japanese naval, military, and civilian views of Asian expansion.

closed, self-sufficient regional autonomy that would guarantee prosperity, the Japanese actually fashioned an imperialistic autarky, justified by self-sacrificing idealism and flavored with nostalgic utopianism. "By 1941 Japan had become ethnocentric in ideas and egocentric in external affairs. . . . Posing as the big brother of all Asian nations whom she meant to liberate from the shackles of Western colonialism, she was imposing on them a more severe self-conceited order of particularistic nationalistic orientation."[2]

Frustrated by continuing resistance in China, seizing opportunistically on the apparent successes of the Axis in Europe, underestimating American power to mobilize and will to fight, Japanese leaders added fatally to their commitments with a decision to strike south.

DEFEATING THE BLUE-EYED ENEMY

In November 1941, General Imamura Hitoshi received a cable in Manchuria appointing him commander in chief of the Fifteenth Army. Imamura trembled with enthusiasm at the prospect of fighting the North Atlantic powers: "Oh! Holy War, in order to break a deadlock for our mother country, staking the existence of our country upon it! . . . At any cost we must win. . . . Giving thanks to God . . . and praying . . . for protection, I fell to my knees."[3]

The "deadlock" of which Imamura spoke involved oil. Peace without oil was excruciating; war without oil was impossible; oil without the Indies was unthinkable. The Dutch government had resisted Japanese attempts to negotiate for petroleum. They had tried to curb what they called "burrowing" in the Indies by Japanese

[2] Miwa Kititada, in Wray and Conroy, *Japan Examined*, 389. In another essay Miwa has examined idealistic-nativistic and geopolitical-economic strands of "new order" thinking: "The Japanese Policies and Concepts of a Regional Order in Asia, 1938–40," Sophia University Institute for International Relations, Research Paper No. 46 (1983). Examples of wartime Japanese expansionist literature focusing on "the Southern Area" include Izawa Shōji, *Nanpō Kyōeiken* (The Co-Prosperity Sphere in the South) (Takayama Shōin, 1940), Hayasaka Yoshio, *Nanpō kyōeiken to sono seikaku* (The Southern Co-Prosperity Sphere and its nature) (Kasumigaseki Shoin, 1940); Japan Nanpō Association, *Shigen Kaihatsu to sono keiei: Nanpō Jitsujo* (Natural resource development and management: the situation in the South) (Kyōiku kenkyūkai, 1942); and Takei Jūrō, *Nanpō kensetsu to minzoku mondai* (Construction of the South and the race question) (Japanese International Association, 1942).

[3] Imamura Hitoshi, "A Tapir in Prison," English translation of prison memoir, RVO-002460, 106–7. I have amended the English syntax without changing the sense of the passage.

businessmen, journalists, and military men, all in various ways agents for the Japanese national polity.[4] Now the burrowing and negotiation were over. Imamura's army was to invade Java.

The spirit of Japanese draftees early in the war was similar to Imamura's. Miyoshi Shunkichirō, a civilian who had served the Ministry of Foreign Affairs since 1920, chiefly in Indonesia and the Netherlands, was mild, dutiful, and unmilitant; but when he heard in Tokyo of the sinking of *Prince of Wales* and *Repulse,* he cried out in exultation. The evening of the same day he received an overseas assignment. The telegram moved him with the "beautiful" passage: "From today you will be cut off from your country and your kin."

Miyoshi left Tokyo secretly by special train in his first military uniform, wearing a heavy sword, with a "grand feeling of being a man." His outfit trained in Taiwan. Three days after the fall of Singapore, they sailed in sixty transport ships. From the deck, Miyoshi "faced the East in tears, deeply moved and in meditation."[5] He resolved to face death, and grew a goatee to remind himself of his resolution.[6]

The navy had begun capturing areas of Celebes on January 11; the army, Borneo on January 12; parachutists, Palembang on February 14 and the oil fields of southern Sumatra. The fleet approached a Java surrounded east, north, and west, its air under full control by units operating out of Singapore, and the seas swept nearly clear of enemy fleets after three engagements.[7] An impromptu night battle with two Allied cruisers resulted in slight losses, but the Japanese landed with minimal mishap the next afternoon.

That night Miyoshi slept deeply. When he woke, he found the river edge so crowded with early risers that it was hard to find space for his toilet. Fighter planes from Singapore flew overhead, and he composed a poem:

[4] Netherlands Information Bureau, *Ten Years of Japanese Burrowing in the Netherlands East Indies* (New York: 1942).

[5] Miyoshi Shunkichirō, "Jawa senryō gunsei kaikoroku" (Memoirs of the military administration in occupied Java), *Kokusai Mondai* (1965–67), pt. 1 (April 1965), 62–64; hereafter, Miyoshi, part number, page number. Anthony Reid and Oki Akira, eds., *The Japanese Experience in Indonesia: Selected Memoirs of 1942–1945,* Southeast Asia Series, no. 72 (Athens: Ohio University Center for International Studies, 1986), 113–25, contains well-edited selections from Miyoshi. My references, however, are to the published original, translated in full for me by Ōshima Kazuko, MS in my possession.

[6] Miyoshi, pt. 2, 80.

[7] Ibid., pt. 1, 65. David A. Thomas, *The Battle of the Java Sea* (New York: Stein and Day, 1968) gives detail.

> Bold eagles
> Circle above to protect us
> While we shit.

Miyoshi laughed.[8] Java was now Japanese.

When the Japanese reached the provincial capital of Bantam, the streets were filled with thousands of old and young waving Japanese paper flags, hailing the Japanese with "Banzai!" and shouting "Merdeka!" in anticipation of their own freedom. For Miyoshi, "who had experienced life in the Dutch Indies in the past, to witness such scenes was like a dream."[9] The grasp of Europe was released. Indonesians and Japanese shared a vision of triumph. The Indonesians' trust in the Japanese struck Miyoshi as "beyond imagination." A few years later, however, he would feel that the gap between the propaganda broadcasts and the reality of occupation was "beyond the comprehension" of the Indonesians.[10]

The Dutch retreated to Bandung, leaving Jakarta open. When the Japanese arrived in the capital, they were surprised to find "many Dutch, including women and children, talking gaily and drinking tea on the verandahs."[11] They apparently hoped for a kind of Vichyite modus vivendi with the conquerors, such as the French had contrived with Japanese troops in Indonesia. Dutch authorities, however, ordered stores to destroy their supplies of alcohol, lest the Japanese entering the capital get drunk "and start an orgy of rape and murder. Thousands of bottles of whisky, gin, champagne, and Bols were thrown in the Tjiliwang river, which streamed through the center of the city."

A small crowd gathered to watch the conquerors arrive. Standing near a Dutch woman and her small daughter, a young Indonesian writer overheard the child comment on the ugliness of the Japanese flag. Her mother immediately disagreed, praising the conquerors' flag and glancing about nervously, afraid someone might denounce the child to the Japanese. As her eyes met the young Indonesian's, they held an anxious, questioning look. "I smiled at her," he wrote later, "reassuring her that I would not denounce the pretty little girl." But her defensive reaction had awakened in him a realization of a new era.[12]

[8] Miyoshi, pt. 2, 81–82.

[9] Ibid., pt. 2, 82–83; pt. 4, 67.

[10] Ibid., pt. 2, 82–83; pt.4, 66–67; pt. 6, 74–75.

[11] Ibid., pt. 2, 83.

[12] Mochtar Lubis, untitled, undated MS fragment (written in jail during the Guided Democracy period, and lent to the author, February 1968), 15–16.

Not all Japanese arrivals were as joyous as in the Indonesian provinces, or as docile as in Jakarta. On Luzon the Japanese had to fight Filipinos and Americans in battles that lasted six months. The Americans declared Manila an open city and carried the fight to Bataan and Corregidor. A young Filipino watched the Japanese arriving in the capital and later recalled it:

> The Japanese! *Open city*, no? Open city; all they had to do was walk in. Then what? At the Odeon Theater, they picked this Chinese, they made him scrub the sidewalk with a coconut husk. . . . And after . . . they took a samurai sword and cut off his head, staging executions . . . four or five heads.
>
> When the Americans came back [in 1945] riding on tanks, they were throwing chocolate bars to us. Chewing gum, canned goods—that's the way to enter a city. They had to capture it, but that's the way they came in, canned goods.[13]

Such feelings would have been evidence to the Japanese of a spoiled culture, an Asian spirit devastated by American materialism. Not to be greeted as liberators was trying; to be shot at by those they liberated was infuriating.

SORELY STRETCHED by war in Europe as well as in the Pacific, the English, Dutch, and Americans were lax in preparation; they lagged in coordination, vulnerable to attack. The Imperial Japanese Forces, aroused, unified, and disciplined to a high degree, sped southward, achieving a series of blood-stirring triumphs that helped allay the frustrations of decades of competition with North Atlantic powers and humiliating discrimination at their hands. Only in the Philippines did conquest fall behind schedule, but that was merely a strategic backwater to the main objectives—Indonesia's oil and Singapore's defenses.

In Singapore over 100,000 British troops surrendered to 30,000 Japanese in what Churchill admitted to the House of Commons was a "debacle." The defenders of Java, almost 100,000 regular troops, about half of whom were Dutch, surrendered to 40,000 Japanese after only nine days of fighting. Even in the most prolonged defense, that of the Philippines, 31,000 American and 120,000 Filipino troops gave ground to an initial force of only 43,000 Japanese.[14] Throughout the area, the Japanese consistently won against numerical odds of at least 2 or 3 to 1.

[13] Paulino Capitulo, interview, November 21, 1967.
[14] Figures From A. Frank Reel, *The Case of General Yamashita* (Chicago: Univer-

The surrender scenes everywhere were strangely similar: faced with demands for complete and unconditional surrender, the Allied commanders declared that they had not sufficient authority to grant it. The Japanese commanders threatened further attacks and total extermination. Confronted with abrupt demands for a yes or no answer, the Allied commanders finally gave up, nodding or mumbling their replies.[15] Thus, with bloodshot eyes and muffled voices, North Atlantic armies surrendered their control of the Malay world.

As the fighting went on in outlying areas, the excitement of battle and prospect of completing "Southern operations" moved one Japanese general to exhort his troops: "I have not the slightest doubt that you will conquer hardships and privations and that with one blow you will annihilate the blue-eyed enemy and their black slaves."[16] Here in Japanese terms is an example of the pseudo-speciation[17] peculiar to the human creature, and fundamental to militarism and imperialism: the defining of other peoples as subhuman, that they might be killed without calling it murder, and subjected as a matter of duty. Victory for the Japanese meant amazement and exultation as defeating the corrupt enemy, at becoming the lords of lesser peoples, and at taking their rightfully dominant place in all of Asia.

Hakkō Ichiu and Absorption of the South

Japanese imperial power was equipped with a hierarchical theory of international affairs, summarized in the slogan *hakkō ichiu*. Freely

---

sity of Chicago Press, 1949), 44 (Singapore); Kanahele, "Japanese Occupation," 251, n. 4; Imamura, "A Tapir," pt. 3, 117–18 (Java); and Louis Morton, *The Fall of the Philippines* (Washington, D.C.: Department of the Army, 1953), 29–30, 350–52, and passim. See also John Toland, *The Rising Sun* (New York: Random House, 1970), 268–93.

[15] Reel, *General Yamashita*, 54–55; "Djen. Yamashita memaksa Singapura bertekuk lutut" ("Yamashita forced Singapore to surrender"), *Inti Sari*, February 1968, 33–41; Miyoshi, pt. 3, 49–52, 53; Imamura, Reid and Oki, eds., *Japanese Experience in Indonesia*, 42–49; Morton, *Fall of the Philippines*, 568–73.

[16] Major General Yamagata to his troops at Giruwa, November 25, 1942, in ATIS Research Report No. 76, pt. 3, "The Warrior Tradition as a Present Factor in Japanese Military Psychology," 5. The further citation to ATIS Bulletin No. 571, 18, is misleading because that Bulletin concludes with p. 15. Dr. Frank Joseph Shulman, curator of the East Asia Collection, McKeldin Library, University of Maryland, assisted me in tracking this reference. Another copy of the ATIS Research Report exists in the MacArthur Archives, Norfolk, Va.

[17] For complementary definitions of pseudo-speciation, see Konrad Lorenz, *On Aggression* (New York: Bantam, 1967), 76, 78–80; and Erik H. Erikson, *Gandhi's Truth* (New York: W. W. Norton, 1969), 431–33, 434.

translated, it meant "everyone under one roof." National textbooks in the 1930s conveyed the idea to Japanese school children in the popular form of "one big happy family" of nations. Japan was to be the father of the family and other peoples the children, a metaphor implying generalization of the Japanese imperial throne and expansion of its nation-state.[18]

In Southeast Asia, hakkō ichiu would take on different meanings for individual Japanese, depending in temperament and position. For General Imamura Hitoshi, it meant "all nations are brothers." As commander in chief on Java, he adopted four teenage Indonesian boys to live with him in the palace he had taken from the Dutch governor general. In a still more flexible interpretation, Nishimura Toha, who trained Indonesian officers late in the war, would cast his lot with the trainees during the Indonesian revolution against the Dutch and feel "reborn." To him, hakkō ichiu meant freedom and national identity for all peoples, the wisest of those peoples to be the leader of the rest.[19] Murata Shōzō, a shipping magnate who became chief civil adviser in the Philippines, and later ambassador to the Japanese-created wartime republic, was puzzled that the Filipinos did not make more demands on the Japanese. Hakkō ichiu meant that they had the right to do so, he told Jose Laurel, the wartime president, just as a younger brother in a Japanese family could make some demands on an older brother, to which the older brother was obliged to respond.[20]

Confusion and contradiction naturally arose in trying to accomplish imperial expansion and familial consolidation simultaneously. Some in the military simply concentrated on obtaining natural resources.[21] More complex motives led to statements like that

[18] Theodore Friend, "Hakkō-Ichiu and Dōgi: the Rhetoric of Japanese Expansion," app. B in Rōyama Masamichi and Takéuchi Tatsuji, *The Philippine Polity: A Japanese View*, ed. Friend, Yale University Southeast Asian Studies, Monograph Series, no. 12 (New Haven, 1967), 286–89.

[19] Imamura, "A Tapir," pt. 3, 119, 121–23; *Imamura Hitoshi Taishō Kaisōroku* (Memoirs of General Imamura), 7 vols. (Tokyo: Jiyū Ajiasha, 1960), Ōshima Kazuko, selected translations, MS in my possession. Reid and Oki, eds., *Japanese Experience in Indonesia*, include a selection from Imamura, 31–79, which once refers to hakkō ichiu, 53.

Moh. Toha Nishimura, interview, February 19, 1968. Here and throughout, Japanese names appear surname first; Nishimura changed the order of his upon becoming an Indonesian citizen.

[20] Fukushima Shintarō, ed., *Murata Shōzō: Ikō hitō-nikki* (Murata Shōzō: posthumous Philippine diaries) (Shinjuku: Hara-shobō, 1969), entry for July 21, 1944; hereafter, Murata diary, plus date.

[21] George S. Kanahele, "The Japanese Occupation of Indonesia: Prelude to Independence" (Ph.D. diss., Cornell University, 1967), 263n.

of General Matsui Iwane, head of the punitive expeditionary force against the Chinese in Nanking, 1937: "We do not do this because we hate them, but on the contrary because we love them too much. It is just the same as in a family when an older brother has taken all that he can stand from his ill-behaved younger brother and has to chastise him in order to make him behave properly."[22]

When the Japanese invaded insular Southeast Asia, they found little cultural commonality, which made hakkō ichiu propaganda still harder to get across. Here were none of the ideographic traditions shared in their northeast Asian empire, and little of Buddhist tradition in religion, philosophy, or art, except where faintly discernible in Hinduistic syncretism. Racial connection was distant and blurred. Lexical comparisons have shown no genetic relationship between Japanese language on the one hand and Tagalog, Malay, and Javanese on the other.[23]

Family systems were also distinctly different. Japan's was unilateral and patrilineal, descent being reckoned through the father's line only, with society, culture, and personality compacted in a manner that one observer has seen as a survival of the late Bronze Age.[24] Family systems in the Philippines and Indonesia were generally bilateral, the Filipino more "extended," and the Javanese more "nucleated." The Philippines had developed out of its extended bilateralism a *tayo-tayo* style of relationship, of shifting cliques rather than enduring clans, of constant renewal of ties, of bargaining and much impromptu diplomacy. This system involved frequently changing loyalties, which the Japanese found perfidious, and a fluent vocal democracy, which the Japanese found superficial. As bilateral extension led to the tayo-tayo phenomenon in the Philippines, bilateral nucleation in Java produced the *golongan*, also cliquish but more corpuscular and less fluid, with a stronger tendency to keep its members.[25]

In neither country did the Japanese find the steadfast-to-the-death

---

[22] Quoted in Maruyama, *Thought and Behavior*, 95, citing IMTFE, no. 310, November 7, 1947.

[23] Gerret K. DeHeer, "Japanese and Austronesian: Lexical Comparisons" (M.A. thesis, University of California, Berkeley, 1961).

[24] Robert Bellah, "Japan's Cultural Identity," *Journal of Asian Studies* 24 (1965): 573–94, and "Religious Evolution," *American Sociological Review* 29 (1964): 358–74.

[25] On *tayo-tayo*, see Theodore Friend, *Between Two Empires: The Ordeal of the Philippines, 1929–1946* (New Haven: Yale University Press, 1965), 27–29. On Javanese kinship see Hildred Geertz, "Indonesian Cultures and Communities," in Ruth T. McVey, ed., *Indonesia*, Human Relations Area Files, Survey of World Cultures, no. 12 (New Haven, 1963), 47–49.

sort of loyalty that was latent in their peacetime values and prominent in their wartime militarism. In neither culture was the patriarchal principle as strong as in Japan, and in both cultures, that of the Philippines particularly, women were of higher status than Japanese females relative to men. Even to one of the most sympathetic of all observers, interpreter Shimizu Hitoshi, the Indonesians seemed unpredictably "passionate." Their emotions were likely to strike the Japanese at an "acute angle."[26] As for Filipino emotions, they were often in head-on collision with those of the Japanese.

An archaic Japanese fusion of religion, state, and society, combined with military aggression, made hakkō ichiu difficult to practice even where the Japanese at least shared with others the Chinese ideographic tradition. Trying to add a southern wing to their imperial mansion would still more severely test the concept that "Asia is one." The cultural theorist, Okakura Tenshin, had early in the century given eloquent expression to Asian unity, even though he did not resolve a tension between Japan's inspiring and her liberating the rest of Asia.[27] Publicists of expansion from 1931 to 1945, such as Ōkawa Shūmei, shifted the tension to one between the liberation and the domination of Asia. A jurist and specialist in Oriental philosophies, deeply involved in ultranationalist movements and plots since 1919, Ōkawa late in the 1930s launched a private school that emphasized Asian languages, economic geography, and character building through "Japanese spirit." Ōkawa's graduates went into the "Southern Regions" to work for Japanese firms such as Mitsui and Mitsubishi. After war broke out they were in particular demand, despite dubious skills, because of their youth and knowledge of languages:[28] they constituted an avant-garde of trained political missionaries for Japan.

That Ōkawa should appear as the intellectual leader of expansion to the south suggests the theoretical and strategic weakness of the

[26] Shimizu, interview, June 5, 1968.

[27] Okakura Kakuzō, *The Awakening of Japan* (New York: Century, 1904); Fukukita Yasunosuke, ed., *Japan's Innate Virility: Selections from Okakura and Nitobe* (Tokyo, 1944); Maruyama Masao, "Fukuzawa, Uchimura, and Okakura—Meiji Intellectuals and Westernization," *The Developing Economies* 4 (1966): 594–611; Ikimatsu Keizō, "Okakura Tenshin," *The Developing Economies* 4 (1966): 638–51; Marlene Mayo, "Attitudes toward Asia and the Beginnings of Japanese Empire," in Grant Goodman, comp., *Imperial Japan and Asia: A Reassessment* (New York: Columbia University Press, 1967), 6–31, esp. 25–26.

[28] Interrogations of Ono Ichiru and Kuromachi Hiroshi, SEATIC Intelligence Bulletins 230, 232, RVO-014119, 014162.

movement.[29] A man drunk on ideology and conspiracy, a man whose love of other cultures masked a desire to dominate them, he found in proximity to military power a potency that seemed to promise realization of his view, as some of the military found in his writings an ennoblement of their aims.

MILITARY ADMINISTRATION: STRUCTURE AND LEADERS

Premier Tōjō Hideki set the official tone at home, as well as for military administration abroad, by attributing all inspiration to the radiance of His Majesty: "Were it not for this light, I should be no better than a pebble by the roadside."[30] Tōjō carried the imperial mystique southward on a grand tour in mid-1943, filled with marshaled crowds, militant rhetoric, fatiguing ceremony, and forced conviviality. After that year, however, no cabinet member went southward; exigent problems kept them at home. Tokyo remained the capital and symbolic center of the Greater East Asia Co-Prosperity Sphere. Increasingly, however, the headquarters of the Southern Area Forces made crucial decisions. Located initially in Singapore in June 1942, it moved later to Saigon, then to Manila a few months before the American invasion of the Philippines, and back to Saigon in November of 1944, where it remained until the war's end.[31]

Throughout the war the supreme commander of Expeditionary Forces to the Southern Area was Field Marshal Count Terauchi Hisaichi. As minister of war in 1936–37, Terauchi had called for "the renunciation of liberalism [and] the establishment of a totalitarian system." On the occasion of Tōjō's tour of the south, the emperor personally sent Terauchi a sword, which rested on a special pillow in the airplane and was carried above eye level, by white-gloved

[29] For a summary account of Ōkawa's character and his book, *Nihon Oyobi Nihonjin no michi* (The way of Japan and the Japanese), see Maruyama, *Thought and Behavior*, 35, 38, 91–92, 319; also, SEATIC Intelligence Bulletin 232, p. 38; and Takeuchi Yoshimi, "Ōkawa Shūmei," *The Developing Economies*, 6 (1968): 366–78 passim.

[30] Quoted in Maruyama, *Thought and Behaviour*, 17, citing Asahi Shimbun, February 6, 1943.

[31] The most authoritative source is Bōeichō Bōeikenkyūjo Senshibu (War History Division, Defense Research Institute, Japan Defense Agency), *Nanpō no Gunsei* (Military administration in the Southern Area) (Tokyo: Chōun Shimbunsha, 1985). Preceding its collection of documents and memoirs is a 22-page introduction that, in relation to changing war aims, narrates and displays in tabular form the changing objectives and organization of regional military administrations.

hands, from hotel to airport to hotel, until its presentation to the count.[32] Sea and air communication with Tokyo was still easy then, pomp and circumstance still possible. But by the latter half of 1944, sea and air lanes were highly endangered; toward the end of the war only radio communication remained sure. In the beginning of 1945 Terauchi delegated authority to area commanders beneath him, in Singapore and Jakarta, "who were allowed to act on their own judgment." Terauchi retained overall responsibility and ordered the area commanders to consult with him as much as possible, and when one did not agree, as Yamashita Tomoyuki did not on the defense of the Philippines, Terauchi was sticky and vindictive.[33]

Terauchi's relations with subordinates, and stresses in the sphere, are revealed in an incident that took place while Yamamoto Moichirō was chief of the General Affairs Department in Java. The Marshal, in Jakarta on an inspection tour, asked Yamamoto if he would like to play golf. The latter, puzzled but obliging, said he didn't know how but would carry the clubs. On the golf course, and out of earshot of the Kenpei man chauffeuring their limousine, Terauchi sharply questioned Yamamoto: "Which way is your head turned?" The supreme commander of the Southern Army answered his own question: "I think it is turned toward Tokyo. Is that the proper direction?" Yamamoto, who had been dealing directly with Tokyo in some matters rather than going through channels in Saigon, promised to be more observant of lines of command.[34]

Terauchi had direct experience of the Philippines when he transferred his headquarters there for several months in 1944, anticipating American landings and hoping to commit the Filipinos to engagement in battle. "The General said that the Japanese military . . . regarded the Philippines as indispensable for the war regardless of her participating or not. . . . He, as usual, denounced the Filipinos for being weak willed, but [sympathized with their want of food]. He thought that in any case the primary concern now was to prevent the Laurel Administration from getting alienated from the people."[35] Just before Terauchi returned his headquarters to Saigon in mid-November 1944, Ambassador Murata was inspired to describe

[32] Terauchi quotation from Maruyama; 66–67, sword anecdote, Hamamoto interview, June 14, 1968.

[33] Lt. Gen. Numata Takazō, interrogation, Singapore, June 4, 1946, RVO-008785-91; Robert Ross Smith, *Triumph in the Philippines* (Washington: Office of the Chief of Military History, 1963), 88–90.

[34] Yamamoto, interview, June 8, 1968.

[35] Murata diary, May 29, 1944.

him to his diary: "His emotion is serene like water, but once ignited, its passion will not stop until it burns everything in its way; an ideal general. His feelings on having left all the present Philippine battles in the hands of Commander Yamashita are unfathomable . . . ; his indifference could be called the spirit of the warrior, and is very admirable."[36]

As the war proceeded, Japanese officers, from Terauchi downward, felt called upon to summon and communicate a warrior spirit, even if they could not issue clear and feasible orders.

Terauchi burned on, then out. He suffered a stroke that partially paralyzed him on April 10, 1945. He was able to sign orders and remained in command, receiving the Indonesian leaders and transmitting the imperial decree of independence to Sukarno. The surrender in mid-August was "a complete surprise" to him. Two months later he lost his memory and thus never had to endure the trial as a war criminal he might otherwise have expected.[37]

Beneath Terauchi were a succession of commanders in chief: in Indonesia, Imamura Hitoshi, Harada Kumakishi, Nagano Yoshiuchi; in the Philippines, Homma Masaharu, Tanaka Suzuichi, Kuroda Shigenori, Yamashita Tomoyuki. As fighting men primarily, they did not bother much with indigenous politics and culture. The two who left the strongest impressions did so because of unusually powerful character combined with memorable circumstances: Imamura, preceded by the Dutch and followed by days of hunger, was remembered as the liberator of Java, kindly.[38] Yamashita, succeeding the womanizer and seashell collector Kuroda, tried to carry out a strategically and logistically impossible defense. His fate was to be remembered less as the Tiger of Malaya than as the ravager of the Philippines, because MacArthur wanted him hanged as a scapegoat.

Whatever the fame of the commanders in chief, the most important Japanese in the lives of the occupied peoples were the *gunseikan*, the chiefs of military administration. Of these Yamamoto Moichirō in Indoneisa and Wachi Takagi in the Philippines had the greatest impact. Yamamoto was *Sōmubuchō*, chief of the Office of General Affairs, from April 1943 to November 1944, then served as

---

[36] Ibid., November 15, 1944.

[37] Numata interrogations, RVO-008895-91, 006788-89.

[38] Nakamura Mitsuo has written "General Imamura and the Early Period of Japanese Occupation," *Indonesia* 10 (1979): 1–26, an excellent article whose range exceeds its title. See also Reid and Oki, eds., *Japanese Experience in Indonesia*, 75–77.

Gunseikan until the end of the war. Afterward he went through imprisonment in three cities, Singapore, Jakarta, and Tokyo, before finally being cleared of all war crimes charges. Yamamoto judged himself an Indonesian benefactor, a promoter of independence under imperial instruction, and he so declared to British and Dutch officers in September 1945.[39] He was moved, however, less by goodwill than by the military rule books. He rose after the war to become head of a large veterans' organization and a member of the House of Peers. He had always had a taste for government, and he likened himself to the Dutch governors general who preceded him.

Wachi Takagi was chief of staff in the Philippines from February 1942 to March 1944, and chief of military administration from July 1942 until November 1944. He had become a hero to his men in China campaigns by pitching his tent right on the battlefield. Crude in expression, abrupt in manner, highly conservative in domestic politics, he seemed the archetypal hard-line administrator. Nonetheless, he had seen many Japanese mistakes in China that he did not wish to repeat in the Philippines.[40] If errors were to be made, he chose to err on the side of leniency. Yamashita, as a consequence, thought him a dupe of the Filipinos.[41] Whether or not that was the case, Wachi won enough Filipino friends and was sufficiently free of guilt feelings to invest in iron mines in Surigao after the war.

Yamamoto and Wachi each had within his staff a dispute on policy orientation toward the subject people—open arms or closed fist? A classical argument occurred between Utsunomiya Naotaka and Nishimura, Toshio, Wachi's two vice–chiefs of staff. Utsunomiya helped formulate the policy of orderly government and development of Philippine interests as a way of furthering Japan's interests, using amenable leaders within the existing system. By the time Nishimura came in 1944, however, the war had worsened for Japan. He favored a tougher and more "military" policy. With Yamashita's chief of staff, Mutō Akira, he gave ear to Benigno Ramos's plan to overthrow the Laurel government.[42] Arguing against the use of all-out Japanophiles and opportunists such as Ramos, Utsunomiya's

[39] Sworn statement by Charles van der Plas, re meeting aboard HMS *Cumberland*, September 21, 1945, RVO 059375; Yamamoto interviews, June 3, 11, 1968.

[40] Wachi, interviews, September 25, 1958, June 8, 1968.

[41] Murata diary, November 12, 1944.

[42] Yamamoto, interview, October 1, 1958; Fukushima Shintarō, interview, September 17, 1958. I have been unable to identify Nishimura's first name. For further identification of Mutō, see Reid and Oki, eds., *Japense Experience in Indonesia*, 53n, and Maruyama, *Thought and Behavior*, 315.

side prevailed—probably because there were too few of Ramos's kind, and too many other Filipinos.

Flanking the military administration were civilian officials, usually supporting the flexible Utsunomiya type of advice, and Kenpeitai officials endorsing the stiff Mutō-Nishimura line. In Java there were three civilian advisers, of whom Count Hayashi Kiyūjirō was the most influential. Hayashi admitted to nationalist leader Hatta that Japan's behavior in China was imperialism of the same order as that of the Europeans.[43] He interceded several times with Tokyo on behalf of the Indonesian independence movement[44] before flying home, aged and ill, late in the war.

Hayashi's counterpart in the Philippines was Murata Shōzō, a prominent shipping executive who found being a civilian adviser to the military early in the war largely a powerless function. To justify himself he brought a team of first-rate scholars from Japan to make a sweeping research report on the Philippines, and recommendations for the prospective republic.[45] The military did not heed the report, and since it was in Japanese the Filipinos could not read it. By the time of publication, however, the military had supported Murata for nomination as ambassador to the new republic, a job he performed with grace and judgment. A hard-driving, self-made man, he intoned to himself lessons on the Greater East Asia Co-Prosperity Sphere and proper Japanese behavior, and committed them to his diary, along with records of some of the key conversations of the period.

Like the civilian advisers in viewpoint, and indispensable to the administration, were the top interpreters. For Java the leading pair were Shimizu Hitoshi of the Propaganda Division, and Miyoshi Shunkichirō. The former gravitated toward Sukarno and the latter toward Hatta. Yamamoto called Shimizu his "telephone system," for he had only to make an apparently casual statement and Shimizu, an irrepressible gossip, would immediately repeat it to Sukarno and report back the reaction.[46] Miyoshi was a more guarded

[43] Hatta, interview, February 17, 1968.

[44] Kanahele, "Japanese Occupation," 160.

[45] Of the four volumes published by the Japanese military administration in 1943, volume 2, *Hitō Chosa Hōkoku, dai ni hen: Tōchi* (Report of the Research Commission on the Philippines, politics and administration: history and analysis), had been translated by Takéuchi Tatsuji and published as *The Philippine Polity: A Japanese View*, ed., Theodore Friend, Yale University Southeast Asia Studies, Monograph Series, no. 12 (New Haven, 1967).

[46] Yamamoto, interview, June 11, 1968.

character, with sequestered emotions and a diplomatic sense of protocol, but like Shimizu he ventured beyond the role of interpreter to try to advance, discourage, or criticize given policies. The outstanding interpreter in the Philippines, Hamamoto Masakatsu, played a rare intermediary role between the liberal military and President Laurel; equally trusted by both, and nearly as adept at English as Laurel, he became a social and political buffer in tense circumstances.

Against the largely understanding posture of men like Count Hayashi and Ambassador Murata, and the intercessive pleadings of the interpreters, stood the complaints of the Kenpeitai. Basically a military police force, it tended to develop independent power and a distinct outlook, composed of fascist spirituality, nationalist fanaticism, free-floating sadism, and power-grabbing separatism. After the war some Japanese general officers made a case for Kenpeitai having shielded native populations from the ravages of internal disorder and lawlessness. Such achievements seem hardly to balance, in the end, the cruelty and callousness of the externally imposed order.[47]

Two very different types of military administrator, the rigorous Hayashi Yoshihide (first chief of the Japanese military administration in Manila) and the flexible Utsunomiya Naotaka, both agreed on one matter: in their wide army experience of Greater East Asia, the Filipinos were the most difficult people to handle. Hayashi had worked with Chinese, Mongolians, Siberians, Koreans, Burmese, Thai, and Filipinos. He liked them all except the Koreans, whom he said were suspicious, and the Filipinos, whom he recalled as lazy, deceitful, and lacking in national pride.[48]

Hayashi, however, spent only the first seven months of the war in the Philippines. Utsunomiya, who spent nearly three full years there and had also traveled to Indonesia, Indochina, and Malaya, tried to get at the cause of the Japanese difficulty with the Filipinos. Differences in religion, customs, and manners separated the Filipinos and the Japanese, but this was equally true of the Indonesians and the Japanese. The chief problem was previous colonial policy, and particularly language: the Filipinos were Americanized; a great many spoke English and they despised people who could not. "It didn't help, trying to make them learn Japanese," Utsunomiya recalled years later with a dry laugh.

[47] For more on the Kenpeitai, see chap. 9.
[48] Hayashi, interview, October 2, 1957.

After the war, in the fashion of a good samurai loser, Utsunomiya himself studied English more systematically. As a prisoner of war, he read *A Bell for Adano*, John Hersey's success story of American military administration in Italy. Utsunomiya had wanted to be a benefactor abroad, a deliverer to those in distress, a guide and up-lifter. But Japan had needed goods for her war effort, and instead of being able to give, "it was take, take, take."[49]

MILITARY ADMINISTRATION: POLICY AND STYLE

Almost three weeks before the attack on Pearl Harbor, an Imperial Liaison Conference had laid down policy objectives governing administration of occupied territory in the Southern Area: "to re-store public order, expedite acquisition of resources vital to national defense, and ensure the economic self-sufficiency of military per-sonnel."[50] The man who drafted the statement later told General Inamura that his Java policy was in accord with the emperor's in-tention, and that other armies had forgotten the governing princi-ples and had grown too high-handed.[51] Even in the rare cases when "winning hearts and minds" was uppermost in a commander's mind, however, there were countless subordinates for whom mili-tary-economic needs justified any means. The paragraphs of imple-mentation of policy adopted before Pearl Harbor would hardly deter the tough-minded administrator. Tersely summarized, they meant that Japanese occupation forces were to put down insurrection and to put up with existing governmental structures while living off the native economy and obtaining its defense resources for use in gen-eral plans devised by Tokyo.[52]

The Japanese divided up Indonesia administratively to minimize

[49] Utsunomiya Naotaka, interview, September 29, 1958.

[50] Harry J. Benda, James K. Irikura, and Kōichı Kıshi, eds, *Japanese Military Admınistratıon ın Indonesia: Selected Documents*, Yale University Southeast Asia Studies (New Haven, 1965), document 1, p. 1. Miyoshi, pt. 1, 62–63, gives different emphases to the main principle.

[51] Imamura, "A Tapir," 132, states that Col. Ishii Akiho, chief of mılıtary admin-istration in Southern Army HQ, had drafted the basic policy statement while a mem-ber of the Mılıtary Affairs Department of the Rikugunshō.

[52] "Principles Governing the Administration of Occupied Southern Areas," adopted at the Liaison Conference between Imperial Headquarters and the govern-ment, November 20, 1941, in Benda et al., *Japanese Mılıtary Admınistratıon,* 2–3. For illustration of prıncıples attempted, deflected, and forgotten in practice, see Ut-sunomiya Naotaka's memoir of the Philippines, *Minami Jūjusei O Nozomıtsutsu* (Looking at the Southern Cross) and Yamamoto Moıchirō, *Watakushi no Indonesıa* (My life in Indonesia), both ın section 8 of *Nanpō no Gunseı* (see note 31 above).

friction between army and navy, and thus added to divisive factors in native geography, culture, and language. In minimizing rivalry, they also minimized coordination, for "the Army and Navy governed their areas as if they were two foreign and sovereign states."[53] The navy allowed political participation only late and reluctantly, being generally more hesitant than the army to use nationalists.[54] The army in Sumatra grew annoyed with the army in Java, which despite itself became the pacesetter in Indonesian development.

The Japanese sent a surprisingly large number of civilians overseas in a short time, and stationed surprisingly few soldiers in Java to keep order after their initial occupation (See Table 3.1). Whereas Indonesia had represented almost the entire Dutch empire, now Japan's empire touched all of East and Southeast Asia. Only three hundred military men were spared for use in administration in Java, which left them spread thinly over the island. Nonetheless, the Japanese gave few administrative positions to Indonesians; even after they granted "political participation" in 1943, only two of seventeen residents were Indonesian. As bureaucrats, the Japanese were slow to acknowledge the merits of Indonesian officials, quick to interfere with their business, and apt to give unreasonable orders. Some took the best offices of residents and regents, or even their bedrooms, and "acted as if they were their instructors." Inexperienced Japanese personnel lacking native language advanced their own interests and promoted overall disunity, leading one Japanese analyst to fault them for arrogance, "regionalist utilitarianism," and "merit-deedism,"[55] doing whatever might look good on the record to get themselves promoted.

The rice situation best illustrates Japanese administrators' currying favor with superiors by excessive zeal in performance of duties. Because of the live-off-the-native-economy rule, the Japanese had to send rice to troops in islands other than Java, the greatest producer. Each residency had a delivery quota; each resident competed in fulfilling and exceeding his quota in order to gain merit, prohibiting transport of rice except as supervised by himself. People in non-rice-producing areas of Java therefore suffered, unable to obtain a supply from the accustomed nearby source because it was going to Japa-

---

[53] Kanahele, "Japanese Occupation," 39; quotation, 264 n. 6, citing interview with an officer, name not given, Twenty-fifth Army, Sumatra.

[54] Ibid., 111–15, 295–97 nn. 74–92.

[55] Miyoshi, pt. 11, 82; pt. 6, 69–70, 82.

TABLE 3.1
Dutch and Japanese in Java

Population Categories	Dutch	Japanese
Estimated prewar civilian population	300,000[a]	7,000–8,000[b]
Wartime civilian population	evacuated or interned	40,000[b]
Civil service	15,531 (1940)[b]	5,000–6,000[c]
Military strength	avg. 30,000–40,000 (1900–36);[d] max. of ca. 100,000 in 1941	max. of 40,000–50,000 in spring 1942 and in late 1944, after evacuation from New Guinea;[b] as low as 15,000 after June 1942[c]

[a] Miyoshi, pt. 4, 64–65, gives the prewar population with Dutch citizenship as 600,000, which is far too high; Kanahele, *Japanese Occupation*, gives 200,000, which may be somewhat low.

[b] Figures from Kanahele, 58–59, 65, 248 n. 43, 251 n. 4, 282 nn. 38–39. The Japanese wartime population is the total for the war years, including turnover.

[c] Includes both military and civilians in primarily administrative service (Yamamoto Moichirō, interview, May 31, 1986).

[d] *Indisch Verslag*, 1931–37, table 334. The Dutch buildup in 1941, however, included about one-half Indonesians, so that a "Dutch only" figure would be 50,000 or less.

[e] Imamura, "A Tapir," 132.

nese troops in the outer islands.[56] Thus the Japanese squandered much of the goodwill they had created by trouncing the Dutch. Only by generating a new spirit of expectation of independence did they persuade Indonesians to suffer bitter continuum in hope of tasting sweet millennium.

While the Japanese military administration continued to command in Indonesia, by October 1943 it had adopted a more discreet

[56] Ibid., pt. 6, 70–71; pt. 12, 80–81. For other comments by Miyoshi on Japanese military administration, see pt. 4, 64–67; pt. 5, 65–66; pt. 6, 66–68; pt. 7, 61–63; pt. 8, 71. For details on rice, see chap. 8.

advisory position in the Philippines. At the time of independence José Laurel announced that "the record of the Japanese Military Administration in the Philippines is unique in the annals of mankind and will never be forgotten by a grateful people. Triumphing over the passions of war and the tragic prejudices which at first separated our peoples, it consistently and untiringly sought the true welfare of the Filipinos and guided our swift progress toward the attainment of our national ideal of independence."[57]

Since Laurel has also said that American colonial administration was unique in the annals of mankind,[58] one may be tempted to feel that he was either right in each case or wrong in each, or that, as one Filipino put it, "we always play games with our conquerors." Laurel's judgments, however, were not eternal but existential ones. After the war, the senator, the constitutionalist, the pragmatic jurist would look back and bless Elihu Root and others for their contribution to the still-rising arc of Philippine development. In wartime, the nationalist, the Asianist, the ambitious Batangan was grasping independence, however tentative and compromised, as the culmination of his father's struggle against Spaniards and Americans, and as something to bequeath to his sons.

Laurel, moreover, was well enough versed in Japanese culture as well as Spanish histrionics to make the most of an opportunity for over-statement. The administration was now his to run. There were still Japanese inspectors, advisers, monitors, and spies; there was still the Kenpeitai; there were Japanese firms milking Philippine resources and Japanese soldiers eating Philippine crops. But the administrative structure the United States had erected stood in design even if shaken in spirit. The civil service had been overwhelmingly Filipinized for a quarter of a century, and the Japanese had no intention or capacity to revamp it. Visiting experts from Tokyo noted that it suffered from "American mechanistic rationalism,"[59] but there was neither the opportunity nor sufficient new imperial personnel to imbue it with the spirit of family affection and loyalty that, at its best, the Japanese believed that their bureaucracy could demonstrate.

Examine yourselves—and emulate the Japanese. Even the Harvard-educated Hamamoto thought such injunctions proper and believed they accounted for the propitious development of Taiwan un-

---

[57] Undated, probably October 1943, Malacanang Records Bodega: Japanese Military Administration, 1943–44, vol. 144, doc. 600, p. 5.

[58] Laurel, interview, August 4, 1958.

[59] Friend, ed., *Philippine Polity*, 114–15; see also editorial comments, pp. xiv–xv.

der Japanese rule.[60] The Japanese tutorial spirit also included an element of the didactically sentimental. In countless speeches the theme of "loving concern" arose, most ironically perhaps from the lips of Colonel Nagahama, chief of the Manila Kenpeitai.[61] Some leaders of the Southern Area picked up the theme. When Tōjō came south, Sukarno spoke of his "love for the Indonesian people," and Jorge Vargas, then the chief Filipino administrator, spoke of Japan's "radiant spirit of brotherly love."[62] This tepid spring of false sentiment wells up from two sources: the propaganda themes of Japan as elder brother and protector, and Japan as Asian liberator from alien dominance. The Japanese were not fighting only to protect their own country, Murata told one of Laurel's sons late in the war. "They were standing up to face attack with their own selves to attain a sublime aim, the liberation of East Asia."[63]

In fact, very few Japanese considered that they were dying for the Philippines, and extremely few Filipinos were willing to fight for Japan. At the same time, all the peoples of the Malay world, widely construed, could feel relief at the lifting of the Western social system and racial image from their minds. The Japanese imperial system was also onerous, and Japanese ethnicity strange, but a redefinition of identity could now take place, a relaxation into nativism, justified as "Asian." Many Southeast Asians were glad to get the white man off their backs, a burden they had carried too long. Then they grunted anew under the weight of the Japanese.

The results of Japanese propaganda—tutorial, sentimental, or militant—varied with different leaders. In the Philippines, Camilo Osias got into the cultural stream of things Japanese, Vargas affected the bowing gestures, and Benigno Aquino took on an uncompromising banzai spirit. He alone among major Filipino leaders surpassed Laurel in wartime militancy. Many Indonesian leaders, however, took real nurture from mass demonstrations and organization, once entirely prohibited under the Dutch. While keeping long-term native goals in mind, Sukarno filled his speeches with mobilizing rhetoric—phrases like "forging unity of spirit" (*memadu*

[60] Hamamoto, interview, October 1, 1958.

[61] *Offical Gazette*, 1942–43, 163–64.

[62] Sukarno speech of July 7, 1943, in *Sinar Matahari*, July 8, 1943, *Tjahaja*, July 8, 1943 (from copies of newspaper clippings made available to the author by George S. Kanahele [hereafter, GSK]); Vargas speech of May 6, 1943, in Armando J. Malay, *Occupied Philippines: The Role of Jorge B. Vargas during the Japanese Occupation* (Manila: Filipiniana Book Guild, 1967), 206.

[63] Murata diary, November 15, 1944.

roch), "with joyfulness of soul" (*dengan kegembiraan roch*), and "burning enthusiasm" (*semangat yang menyala-nyala*).

Sukrano's bombast and Aquino's banzais sound superficial in retrospect, just as Japanese exhortations sound either futile or hypocritical. If we accept all culture, however, as a condition of estrangement in which growth occurs by coping with an opposite, then these odd moments take on value. They are part of a process of identity building, of connecting and challenging and resisting, in which "all moments execute justice on one another all round."[64]

The fact remains, however, that the Japanese had not sufficient expertise or administrative numbers to manage well their Nanpō conquests. In the Southern Area their lack of planning, lack of direction, and lack of coordination would become clear long before their eventual surrender.

[64] Hegel, *The Phenomenology of Mind*, 542.

4

EXPECTATION AND MOBILIZATION

IN JAVA AND LUZON

When the Japanese sought to mobilize insular Southeast Asia in their holy war, they struck sharp limits. Javanese Muslims had their own idea of a holy war, and few were likely to fight jihad sincerely with those who made them bow toward Tokyo instead of Mecca.[1] Filipino Christians had some concept of a just war, and it was more likely to dispose them to fight against the Japanese for obstructing independence than with them to advance it.[2]

The Joyoboyo prophecy in Java and the "high Messianic potential"[3] of the Philippines both contained elements upon which skilled political manipulators might play. The Japanese, however, were unable to reach, let alone control, these two sources of feeling. They eventually lost one to Sukarno and the other to MacArthur.

---

[1] This understates the intensity of feeling still expressed forty years later by Mohammad Natsir, former prime minister, in an interview, December 2, 1983.

[2] The Japanese were able to get some contributions to *Tagapagturo*, an official diocesan publication under the imprimatur of Bishop Cesar Ma. Guerrero, who was later indicted for treason (David Joel Steinberg, *Philippine Collaboration in World War II* [Ann Arbor: University of Michigan Press, 1967], 52, 140).

[3] The phrase is from David Sturtevant, *Popular Uprisings in the Philippines, 1840–1940* (Ithaca: Cornell University Press, 1976), who in turn attributes it to his teacher, Felix Keesing.

Joseph Needham's discussion in *Science in Traditional China: A Comparative Perspective* (Cambridge: Harvard University Press, 1981) offers a supple vocabulary (107–131) for attitudes toward time and change. From the apocalyptic, one may descend through the messianic, the evolutionary, the progressive, and the cumulative. All are variants of a linear time sense, in contradistinction to a cyclical sense of time. Full discussion is not possible here except to demur from Needham's statement that "Cyclical time cannot contain apocalyptic time" (127). In Java the two could exist in contradictory adjacency, and they might even fuse, because apocalyptic events were expected to reveal and generate a new cycle.

CHAPTER FOUR

JAVANESE MESSIANISM AND FILIPINO MELIORISM

Times of great deprivation and great expectations tend to sharpen
the time focus of the Javanese, and to substitute for their ordinarily
cyclical expectations a sense of the imminent and impending. The
years 1942 to 1945 were one such period, in which Javanese invested expectation in a person, looked for redemptive promise, and
made ready to revolt. They anticipated the arrival of a Ratu Adil, or
righteous king, to save Java in a time of trouble.[4] The Joyoboyo
prophecy, with its latent power, provided mythic fuel for change.
The Japanese conquest of the Dutch colony engaged the clutch of
historical expectation; and the emergence of Sukarno, followed by
Japanese defeat, would move events in Java into overdrive.

In the Dutch period, being too explicit about Joyoboyo had led to
the downfall of the nationalist leader, Thamrin. He dared to bring
up the prophecy in the Volksraad, quoting a passage he interpreted
as meaning, "When the Netherlands government is gone, there will
come a time of prosperity and happiness for the Indonesian people."
In popular acronymic, cryptographic style he declared the future
contained and enclosed in the name of a kind of parsley used as
medicine, called *djintan: Dj*(epang) *I*(tu) *N*(anti) *T*(aklukkan)
A(ntero) *N*(ederland), "Japan will overcome the Netherlands." The
Dutch in January 1941 arrested Thamrin for interrogation on the
grounds that he had been discussing with Japanese a possible Indonesian government under Japan's "New Order." He died a few days
later in prison.[5]

Thamrin perhaps was too explicit for his own good about his Joyoboyo faith. Others kept it in their hearts. One, Soedjono, educated
in Dutch schools and in law at Leiden, believed and trusted in it
from childhood.[6] He accepted a language fellowship in Tokyo,

---

[4] Although differing in thrust and emphasis, my thoughts owe some inspiration to
Sartono Kartodirdjo, *Tjatjatan tentang segi-segi Messianistis dalam sedjarah Indonesia* (Notes concerning facets of messianism in Indonesian history) (Jogjakarta,
1959).

[5] On Thamrin's use of prophecy: Tjantrik Mataram, *Ichtiarkanlah terlaksananja:
Peranan ramalan Djojoboyo dalam revolusi kita* (Thus it was brought about: the role
of the Joyoboyo prophecy in our revolution), 2d ed. (Bandung: Masa Baru, 1950), 93.
Dutch documentation on Thamrin's activities: R. C. Kwantes, ed., *De Ontwikkeling
van de Nationalistiche Beweging in Nederlandsch-Indie* (Development of the nationalist movement in the Netherlands Indies), (Groningen: Tjeenk Willenk Wolters-
Nordhoff, 1975–1982): 714–17, 753–62. On Thamrin's fate: Bernard Dahm, *History
of Indonesia in the Twentieth Century* (London and New York: Praeger, 1971), 79.

[6] Mr. Soedjono, interview, April 2, 1968.

helped train Japanese expeditionary forces, and arrived back in Java in March 1942 wearing the Japanese insignia of a colonel. Referring to Soedjono afterward, Indonesians made an unconscious gesture toward their shoulders, referring to the insignia that placed him two ranks higher than the Dutch had ever allowed an Indonesian to rise.

When the Japanese arrived, joyous Indonesians were prone to tell them, "You are Joyoboyo,'" a compliment that some Indies-based Japanese had cultivated by intimating before the war that they would become deliverers. Even the knowledgeable interpreter, Miyoshi Shunkichirō, however, confusedly thought that Joyoboyo was a kind of god of luck and happiness.[7] When the Kenpeitai realized that it was a potent prophecy, they became just as anxious about it as the Dutch had been before them. A key passage in the prophecy anticipated not only their arrival in Java, but also their swift departure: "There will come from Nusa Tembini [the Northeast] yellow-skinned men, short of stature. They will occupy Java and rule it as long as the life of corn [saumure jagung]. Afterward they will go home to their country, Nusa Tembini. Java will return to its original state, governed by its own native sons."[8] "Saumure jagung" was the phrase that worried the Japanese. It takes four and a half months for corn to ripen. Whether interpreted literally or figuratively the prophecy might soon lead to rebellion.

The Kenpeitai began a series of interrogations. Three weeks after their conquest they asked the psychiatrist Slamet Imam Santoso if he believed the prophecy. Slamet answered, "I am a scientist. The only way a scientific prediction can be verified is after the fact, not before. Likewise with prophecy." This answer got Slamet off the hook, but even as he spoke with a scientist's tongue, he thought with a Javanese mind. Slamet mentally substituted the Javanese praja agung ("great kingdom") for jagung and transformed the prophecy into "as long as the kingdom is great." The hidden meaning in the Javanese seemed irrefutably true to him: the only question was how long the great kingdom, the Japanese Empire, would last. When it crumbled the Indonesians could not be held back. The Japanese did not note the gleam in his eye.[9]

[7] Miyoshi Shunkichirō, interview, June 12, 1968.

[8] Tjantrik Mataram, *Ichtiarkanlah terlaksananja*, 3.

[9] Dr. Slamet Imam Santoso, interview, March 9, 1968. Such mental gymnastics were also critical to Ranggawarsita's reply to a Dutch test of loyalty in the nineteenth century: "Dutch power will only come to an end when bamboo can produce paddy." This archetypal, if apocryphal, story is related by George Quinn in "The

The Indonesians continued to fit prophecy to current history and events to predictions all through the war. Sukarno did not use Joyoboyo's name publicly lest he rile the Japanese, but he found ways of playing loosely upon the prophecy. When he came back from Saigon to Jakarta on August 14, 1945, he carried at last an imperial promise of imminent independence for Indonesia. Prior to his departure for Saigon he had said, "Before the corn is ripe, Indonesia will be free." Now he said, "Before the corn tassels."[10] Thus Sukarno conveyed the message metaphorically without trapping himself in specific schedules; saved the face of the Japanese; and refocused his own vague promises. He joined his political identity closer to that of Joyoboyo's prophetic tradition, and to the Javanese expectation of deliverance.

In Luzon, the anthropomorphic Christian tradition, brought to the Philippines by the Spanish in the sixteenth century, encountered no Hindu-Buddhist cyclicalism. The idea of the second coming of Christ helped foster numerous anti-imperial or counterclerical movements in the Philippines, led by rural figures who felt the call to bring time to a focus and history to redemption. Such movements continued to emerge during American sovereignty, and the Colorums in particular tended to believe that the millennium and independence were one and the same thing.[11] If the Philippines had a "high messianic potential," why did it not experience messianic explosion in war or after?

The answer lies in the secular rather than the religious realm. By bringing sovereignty within reach, the Americans removed one combustible notion of the millennium from the consciousness of most Filipinos. American impact not only further linearized the

---

Case of the Invisible Literature: Power, Scholarship, and Contemporary Javanese Writing," *Indonesia* 35 (1983): 21–22.

[10] *Suara Asia*, August 15, 1945, 1.

[11] Sturtevant, *Popular Uprisings*. Religious phenomena in the largely nonviolent rebellion against the regime of Ferdinand Marcos, 1983–86, richly deserve analysis. The essential interpretative concepts are available in the work of Reynaldo Ileto—*Pasyon and Revolution: Popular Movements in the Philippines, 1840–1910* (Quezon City: Ateneo de Manila, 1979), and "Rizal and the Underside of Philippine History," in David K. Wyatt and Alexander Woodside, eds., *Moral Order and the Question of Change: Essays on Southeast Asian Thought*, Yale University Southeast Asia Studies, Monograph Series, no. 24 (New Haven, 1982), 274–337. In the latter essay, Ileto uses vital and popularly accessible ideas, such as *loob* ("inside" or conscience), *liwanag* (radiance or charisma), and *damay* (participation in the plight of others) to illuminate the dynamics that make Jose Rizal and his martyrdom the emotional and symbolic center of Philippine history.

time sense of many Filipinos, but secularized it, and colored it with noncatastrophic and remedial expectations. A rise in standards of living and the spread of education further secularized this thinking into a linear-meliorative mode. Concepts of social mobility and political reward, instead of deferral both social and political, suggested the possibility of a rising line of production, consumption, and popular education. In the short run, such a form of the idea of progress played softly upon the eschatological scale in Filipino minds. It made religious intensity diffuse, and revolutionary expectation dilute.

In Indonesia, where the idea of progress obtained weakly in a colonial situation expected to endure for generations, an apprehension of eventual crisis arose like awareness of a time bomb. In the Philippines, however, the idea of progress took hold in a colonial situation with a declared terminus. One sensed small crises going off like a string of firecrackers, but no revolutionary cataclysm impending.

LEADERSHIP: CHARACTERS, STYLES, AND SITUATIONS

Java

Having defeated the Netherlands in Java, the Japanese found themselves with a Dutch-trained native administration comprising an etiolated aristocracy and a small native civil service, both permeated with an aestheticized world view that had its symbolic center in the royal courts. Against them contended a small group of nationalist leaders, religious and secular, who envisioned new symbolic centers. Even these latter, however, were affected by the Javanese tradition through which king, court, and capital formed "an image of divine order and a paradigm of social order."[12] Spirituality was inversely proportionate to sociopolitical distance from the king; and the state was required not so much to govern—villages did that for themselves—as to give liturgical display to the dominant themes of Javanese culture. The Japanese cosmos differed sharply from this Javanese world view in sources and details, but at

[12] Benedict R. O'G. Anderson, "Japan: 'The Light of Asia,'" in Josef Silverstein, ed., *Southeast Asia in World War II: Four Essays*, Yale University Southeast Asia Studies (New Haven, 1966), 13–50. Daniel Lev provides a commonsense introduction to Benedict Anderson and Audrey Kahin, eds., *Interpreting Indonesian Politics: Thirteen Contributions to the Debate*, Cornell Modern Indonesia Project, Publication No. 62 (Ithaca, 1982).

the apex was roughly correspondent. The function of their own imperial court as social paradigm and moral pinnacle helped enable
the Japanese to effect a stylistic cooperation with the Javanese.[13]

The Japanese found the civil service pliable; the nationalists
much less, or not. The latter tended to think of statism, socialism,
or representative pluralism as possible routes to modernity. What
would be an effective apparatus of power in a religiously centered
Islamic state; or a marxist-inspired collective one; or a constitutional democracy covering all the islands, peoples, and traditions of
the archipelago? Even as they cooperated with the secular forms of
the Japanese state, imperial, sacral, and corporate, Indonesian nationalists kept their own agendas in mind.

Early in the occupation the management of Indonesian leaders
was a fairly tidy matter for the Japanese. They devised the concept
of the *empat serangkai*, loosely translatable as the four-leaf clover:
all leaves were bound to a Japanese stem with regard to policy. The
four were Kiai Hadji Mas Mansoer as Islamic leader, Ki Hadjar Dewantoro as a leading figure in Javanese culture and national education, and Hatta and Sukarno as nationalist politicians.[14] The group
lacked any figure from the civil service, which had been loyal if not
servile to the Dutch, and which now served the Japanese. Of other
forces that figured later in the revolution against the Dutch and the
politics of independence—the army, communists, and the young—
the army did not yet exist, communists were illegitimate and ane-
thema to the Kenpeitai, and the young were not yet politically visible.

Dewantoro and Mansoer were the lesser leaves of the clover,
Hatta and Sukarno the greater. Hatta was later described apprecia-
tively by a Dutchman as "the perfect picture of what [we] wanted
the Indonesians to be": bourgeois in values, balanced in views, dig-
nified in demeanor, persevering in duty—a sober, reliable, and un-

[13] Beneath any structural analogy, of course, were great differences in feeling tone.
Paul Stange's "The Logic of *Rasa* in Java" illuminates dynamics not easily likened
to anything Japanese: *Indonesia* 38 (1984): 113–34, esp. 130–34.

[14] Hatta, interviews, February 17, March 6, 1968. Biographical information on
these and other Indonesian leaders of the time is available in *Orang Indonesia jang
terkemoeka di Djawa* (Prominent Indonesians of Java) (Jakarta: Gunseikanbu, 1944);
Alamsjah, *Sepuluh orang jang terbesar di Indonesia* (The ten most renowned people
in Indonesia) (n.p., n.d.); and from RVO-007875ff., "Lijst van Indonesische prominen-
ten." The last was apparently an intelligence "Who's Who," compiled near or after
the war's end by English and/or Australian officials, of which Dutch intelligence
obtained a copy.

original civil servant.[15] Hatta, however, believed his duty was not to serve the Dutch but to free his people from them. His loyalty to his nation, his religion and personal rectitude also won him the admiration of some Japanese. Miyoshi, who worked closely with Hatta, said he did no "maneuvering, and was pure [junshin] and sincere [seijitsu]. But once he decided something, he did it, and said what he thought, bravely."[16] Perhaps the best measure of Hatta's character was his vow to forget all personal desires, and not to marry until Indonesia was independent. When he did finally wed, after his nation was sovereign, he was fond of saying that he had taken the Islamic limit of four wives: the first three were Indonesia.

In later years the contrast between the entourage of Hatta and that of Sukarno would emphasize their differences of disposition: Sukarno with four real wives, and a nearly constant need of female company; Hatta, prim, fussy, and punctual, with a small proper family and two male secretaries. In the era of Sukarno's Guided Democracy, Hatta finally declared that he couldn't stand being "married" to Sukarno any longer, and Sukarno banned Hatta's writings and prevented him from speaking. But during and after the Japanese occupation they needed each other, and the nation needed them. One who was a student at the University of Indonesia still remembers the thrill in 1942 of seeing them together in public for the first time, their separate skills blended, pledging to work together for independent Indonesia.[17]

News of Sukarno's release in 1942 spread by word of mouth from Sumatra to Java. Crowds thronged his first appearances and reporters noted his words and gestures. The themes of Indonesian freedom, youthful energy, and militancy burst into the very first speeches, even while he was summoning energies to the cause of Dai Nippon.[18]

Other major wartime leaders had lived in Holland; Hatta and Sjahrir as students and Ki Hadjar as jack-of-all-trades in exile there; Mansoer had been at least to Mecca. But Sukarno had never left the

[15] Niels Douwes Dekker, interview, May 4, 1969.

[16] Miyoshi Shunkichirō, "Jawa senryō gunsei kaikoroku" (Memoirs of the military administration in occupied Java), 15 pts., Kokusai Mondai 61–82 (April 1965–January 1967), pt. 7, 60, pt. 10, 65, 66; Taniguchi Goro, interview, May 30, 1968.

[17] The foregoing comes from a variety of sources and personal observations. The student was Subadio Sastrosatomo, who later wearied of their cooperation with the Japanese and joined Sjahrir.

[18] Berita Umum, Pemandangan, Tjahara, Sinar Baru, Sinar Matahari, Hong Po, March–July 1942, passim, esp. speech reported in Hong Po, July 13, 1942 (newspaper clippings provided to the author by George Kanahele).

Indies. As a young man he had lived with the family Tjokroaminoto and had absorbed from the father, Hadji Omar Said, greatest leader of the Sarekat Islam movement, a vigorous brand of religio-nationalism, and an example of charismatic leadership, Javanese style. Compared with more traveled leaders, Sukarno was a homebody with a radical reading list. His cosmic-syncretic approach to philosophy, and conversance with Marxist-Leninist thinking, led him to express his secret as "dialectics in the mind and God in the heart." Whatever the formula, there was no doubt of his charm. Constantly in motion, conveying intimacy easily to the humble and the great, Sukarno drew people to him as if the identity of each and the future of all were in process of being revealed in his words.[19] Other men, believing they were riding a wave of history, have acted as if on a surfboard—balancing carefully lest they be wiped out. Sukarno behaved as if history were his pet dolphin and he had only to whisper in its ear to make it carry him where he wanted.

Of his contemporaries in the nationalist movement, Sukarno would ultimately feel the sharpest conflict with Soetan Sjahrir. A slight, charming, quick-witted man, Sjahrir had a sharp tongue and an easy smile. Some likened him to the *cabe*, or red pepper. His exuberance and intellect won him followers as devoted as Sukarno's but far fewer. Sumatran by birth, Western by later education, a theorist without the religious fundamentals of Hatta or the syncretic capaciousness of Sukarno, Sjahrir was more understandable to Europe than either of them, but less to Indonesia.

Both Sukarno and Hatta had predicted a war in the Pacific and foreseen danger from Japan.[20] But when the Japanese actually arrived only Sjahrir kept an ideological distance from them.[21] He had

[19] Interviews in Indonesia, 1967–68.

[20] For Hatta's predictions, see "Economische Wereldbouwen Machtstegen-stellingen" (January 17, 1926), reprinted in C.P.J. van der Peet, ed., *Moh. Hatta Verspreide Geschriften* (Jakarta, 1952), 66. For Sukarno's, see *Indonesië klaagt aan* (Amsterdam: N.V. de Arbeiderspers, 1931), quoted in RVO 007880; also Bernhard Dahm, *Sukarno and the Struggle for Indonesian Independence* (Ithaca: Cornell University Press, 1969), 115–19.

[21] The three men converged at Hatta's house in Jakarta on July 9, 1942. The first historian of that meeting states that they decided "Sukarno and Hatta were to work above ground through the Japanese, and Sjahrir, while maintaining contact with them, was to organize an underground resistance" (George McT. Kahin, *Nationalism and Revolution in Indonesia*, 2d ed. [Ithaca: Cornell University Press, 1970], 104). Sukarno and Sjahrir give identical accounts in their autobiographies—*Sukarno: An Autobiography*, as told to Cindy Adams (Indianapolis: Bobbs-Merrill, 1965), 173; Soetan Sjahrir, *Out of Exile* (New York: John Day, 1949), 245–46. The story is tidy, but it bears too clearly the birthmarks of the revolutionary period, when all three

decided before his release from eight years of Dutch detention not to cooperate,[22] for the fascistic despotism of the Japanese offended him even more than the paternal tyranny of the Dutch. He spent the Japanese occupation not "underground" in the European sense of espionage and sabotage, but out of public view, listening to clandestine radio, educating his disciples, and biding the time until he might emerge as a national leader untainted by cooperation with any imperial power.

Hatta, in exile with Sjahrir for the same eight years, agreed to cooperate but under conditions that preserved his own dignity and independence. As a "free person" who could write and say what he chose in a technical and analytical role, he agreed to advise the Japanese Military Administration. He would run an information bureau of sorts, but there were to be no Japanese in his office.[23]

Sukarno arrived in Jakarta last, from Sumatra. The morning after seeing Hatta and Sjahrir, he talked with General Imamura, commander in chief on Java. Imamura said that the fate of Indonesia was in the hands of His Imperial Majesty and would not be decided until the end of the war. In the meantime, however, the Japanese wished to foster native prosperity and welfare, and to assist Indonesian participation in civil administration and state affairs. Sukarno later said of Imamura, "In my hands he would be a boy." He likened his own dramatic role to that "of the Philippines' hero, General Aguinaldo. He fought the Spaniards for years and when the Americans conquered the ex-conquerors [the Spanish], Aguinaldo first said to the Americans, 'Thank you.' Later when the U.S. wanted to stay in the Philippines, he tried hard to kick them out."[24]

Sukarno tried to extract from the Japanese as much freedom of action as he could, realizing that in an ensuing deadlock he, like Aguinaldo, might have to lead his people against successor-imperialists. Imamura's own account, squared with Sukarno's, leaves the net impression that Sukarno agreed to cooperate in Java in return for "people's welfare and administrative positions," with the question of independence left open.[25]

---

men had an interest in trying to mitigate the burden of Sukarno's overzealous collaboration with Japan, and in persuading the Allies of the unity among themselves and all Indonesians.

[22] George S. Kanahele, "The Japanese Occupation of Indonesia: Prelude to Independence" (Ph.D. diss., Cornell University, 1967), 53–54, citing interview with Djohan Sjaroezah, January 19, 1965

[23] Hatta, interview, February 17, 1968; Miyoshi, pt. 6, 75.

[24] *Sukarno: An Autobiography,* 175–76.

[25] Imamura Hitoshi, "A Tapir in Prison," English translation of prison memoir,

Sukarno, in fact, had already agreed to cooperate with the local military commander in Bukitinggi, Sumatra,[26] Colonel Fujiyama. Sukarno's autobiography devotes four pages to the meeting, and he often mentioned it in speeches during the war: "The Lord be praised, God showed me the way; in that valley of the Ngarai I said: 'Yes, Independent Indonesia can only be achieved by cooperation with Dai Nippon.' " He added: "For the first time in all my life, I saw myself in the mirror of Asia."[27]

Like Hatta and Sjahrir, Sukarno came to Jakarta with his mind made up. In each case the personal decision expressed the style of the man: Sjahrir, exuberant in life but fastidious in tactic, preferring noncooperation; Hatta, steadfast, dogged, and careful, choosing limited cooperation; Sukarno, tempestuous and dramatic, opting for passionate involvement in the hope that he might eventually turn events the way he wanted them. Several Javanese leaders quickly approached Sukarno and offered to contribute a substantial income for him so that he need not rely too much on the Japanese.[28] Sukarno declined. Perhaps the embarrassment of accepting money from friends was too great; but Sukarno's example would eventually show how compromising it was to accept salary, house, and automobile from an invading army. His style—embracing in order to use, endorsing in order to manipulate—showed little consciousness of how much he himself might be used and compromised in the process.

Luzon

Having no strategic use for Japanese help, and lacking a shared view of sociopolitical order, Filipino leaders were far more difficult for the Japanese to manage. American colonial rule, while it democratized the Philippine polity overall, helped secure an already landed, comfortable, and educated class in power.[29] The persistence of Filipino leading families from the late nineteenth through the mid-

---

RVO-002460, pt. 3, 123–25. Imamura says Sukarno arrived by plane in May, when in fact it was by boat in July. If weak in logistical details, Imamura is still trustworthy in the spirit of his recollections.

[26] Sukarno: An Autobiography, 159–63, esp. 161.

[27] Speech of November 7, 1944, RVO 008192-96.

[28] Soedjono, interview, April 2, 1968, confirmed by Soebardjo, interview, April 3, 1968.

[29] Harry J. Benda, "Political Elites in Colonial Southeast Asia: An Historical Analysis," Comparative Studies in Society and History 1 (1964–65): 233–51, esp. 243, 245, 250–51.

twentieth century was irregular, but still probably had no equal in colonial Southeast Asia.

Filipino leadership in 1941 consisted characteristically of land-wealthy lawyer-politicians. They had usually not traveled abroad for higher education, because it was available in the Philippines. Few of them were intellectuals in the Dutch-Indonesian sense, although Claro Recto had written plays and become a member of the Spanish Academy, and Jose Laurel had a disposition toward moral philosophy, also inspired mainly by Spanish heritage. Almost none of them fed on Marxist theory, for instead of having to rationalize a repressed desire for independence they could practice law and politics in advancing toward a scheduled goal of national sovereignty.

As Japanese critics noted, the Filipino elite resulting from the American system was lacking in engineers, businessmen, and military men.[30] In Indonesia, the Dutch devoted special effort to training native engineers, but native military officers were not desired, nor native businessmen nurtured. Indonesian lawyers educated in Holland, who numbered in the 1930s perhaps no more than one hundred, either slipped quietly into the civil service, or tried desperately to compete against Dutchmen for clients in the private practice of law. Some young ones, like Ali Sastroamidjojo and Achmad Subardjo, went into the nationalist movement, resolving the choice between functionary and politician in favor of the less secure alternative.[31]

The Filipino lawyer-politicians of 1941 were in charge of a stable autonomous polity with a split-level culture. Many of them, like Sergio Osmena and Benigno Aquino, spoke Spanish better than English. Few besides Laurel had even a theoretical interest in a Malay culture; none could be seen as leading the Philippines in resolving its state of cultural transition. Nonetheless, they ran a country where nobody starved. Population pressure had not yet made the man-to-land ratio intolerable, technological lag insuperable, or recourse to communism inevitable. Life expectancy had increased from fourteen years in 1900 to forty years in 1940, literacy from one in five at the beginning of the American period to nearly one out of two in 1938, and the electorate from 3 percent to 14 percent be-

[30] Rōyama Masamichi and Takéuchi Tatsuji, *The Philippine Polity: A Japanese View*, ed. Theodore Friend, Yale University Southeast Asia Studies, Monograph Series, no. 12 (New Haven, 1967).

[31] Interviews, Ali Sastroamidjojo, Subardjo, Soedjono, and others, 1967, 1968; Robert van Niel, *The Emergence of the Modern Indonesian Elite*, (The Hague and Bandung: W. van Hoeve, 1960).

tween 1907 and 1941.[32] All of these increases were modest, and co-existed with underdeveloped industry, increasing farm tenancy, exploited labor, and regressive taxation. For most Filipinos of that era, however, the changes they saw both created and to a significant degree fulfilled their vision of progress.

Presiding over this system was Manuel Quezon, surrounded by a group of lawyer-politicians, cronies, compadres, and Hispanic elitists who lived an ethos of tayo-tayo, or "just among us." The banter and plotting of this in-group and its proximity to Quezon affected the shape of the whole Philippine polity, the rise of careers, the definition of issues. Quezon himself developed a personal affinity with some Filipino radical leaders of the 1930s, but he could not or would not force this part of his social vision into major legislation or administrative reality. Presiding with some democratic compassion and much autocratic flair, he was the personal symbol of a sociopolitical system whose sense of hope was rising faster than its indexes of social quality.[33]

When General MacArthur evacuated Corregidor in 1942, he persuaded Quezon to go with him. Quezon in turn chose Vice-President Sergio Osmena and Manuel Roxas, a senator who had recently become an aide to MacArthur, to accompany him. Roxas, a dozen years younger than Osmena and Quezon, and a dramatic speaker with presidential ambitions, chose instead to remain. Quezon had already deputed Jose Vargas, his executive secretary, and Jose Laurel, his secretary of justice, to stay behind and arrange an orderly transition. Laurel's longstanding legal and personal relationship

---

[32] Life expectancy figures from Salvador P. Lopez, "The Colonial Relationship," in Frank Golay, ed., *The United States and the Philippines* (Englewood Cliffs, N.J.: Prentice-Hall, 1966), 24. Literacy figures based on ability to read and write in any language, from W. Cameron Forbes, *The Philippine Islands*, (Boston: Houghton Mifflin, 1928), 2: 495; and Joseph Ralston Hayden, *The Philippines: A Study in National Development* (New York: Macmillan, 1942), 604. Forbes and Hayden use the censuses of 1903 and 1938, respectively. Voting figures from O. D. Corpuz, *The Philippines* (Englewood Cliffs, N.J.: Prentice-Hall, 1965), 15, 133.

[33] The basic sources on Quezon are *Messages of the President* (Manila: Bureau of Printing, 1936–41), and the manuscripts in the Quezon Collection, National Library, Manila. The manuscripts particularly illustrate Quezon's appreciation of some Filipino radicals, and his contempt for standpat landlords.

Lewis E. Gleek, Jr., *The American Governors-General and High Commissioners in the Philippines: Proconsuls, Nation-Builders, and Politicians* (Quezon City: New Day Publishers, 1986) is a collective portrait of men with and against whom Quezon worked; Michael P. Onorato, ed., *Claude A. Buss in Manila, 1941–1942*, California State University Oral History Program (Fullerton, 1986) dramatizes the months of transition when Japanese occupation replaced the Fil-American system.

with the Japanese, Quezon reasoned, could help Vargas to ease the impact of Japanese power. Laurel tearfully protested, but Quezon did not relent.[34]

Laurel later recalled asking how he should behave with the Japanese. Vargas allegedly relayed the question to MacArthur, and Quezon himself gave Laurel MacArthur's reply: they might do anything they thought necessary except taking an oath of allegiance to Japan; "If you do, when we come back, we'll shoot you."[35] In 1945, however, Roxas apparently began telling newspapermen that Quezon, not MacArthur, was the authority for instructions to cooperate, short of an oath of allegiance;[36] and as early as 1943 MacArthur himself denied giving any such instructions to Laurel on this or any other subject. "I never trusted him," said MacArthur, "and believe him to be thoroughly pro-Japanese."[37]

Recollections on the question vary in almost perfect relationship with the depth of one's involvement for or against the Japanese. Laurel's legal mind, however, would certainly have posed the question and sought an answer. Perhaps the Filipino leaders remaining in Manila exaggerated an offhand remark that MacArthur conveniently forgot. If some of them may be unreliable on this point out of self-vindication, MacArthur is often unreliable out of self-glori-

[34] [Jose Lansang, ed.], *War Memoirs of Dr. Jose P. Laurel* (Manila: Laurel Memorial Foundation, 1962), 3–6; Laurel interview, October 21, 1958; John Toland, *But Not in Shame* (New York: Random House, 1961), 137–38, Royal Arch Gunnison, "The Filipinos Fight On," *Colliers*, July 1, 1944, 46.

[35] Laurel interview, and *War Memoirs . . . Laurel*, 5. For complementary and composite accounts see Armando J. Malay, ed., *Occupied Philippines: The Role of Jorge B. Vargas During the Japanese Occupation* (Manila: Filipiniana Book Guild, 1967), 15–16; Manuel Roxas, "Brief Summary of the Activities of Manuel Roxas, Brigadier General, Philippine Army Reserve and Presently President of the Philippine Senate," MS, copy, courtesy of Mauro Garcia, in author's possession; Manuel Quezon, *The Good Fight* (New York. Appleton-Century, 1946), 208–9; Steinberg, *Philippine Collaboration in World War II*, 32–33. General Basilio Valdez (interview, August 29, 1964) recalls no consultation with MacArthur. Teodoro Agoncillo writes to vindicate the actions of the two leading Filipino wartime executives as patriots, and concludes that MacArthur's treatment of them was *walang hiya* (shameless) (*The Burden of Proof: The Vargas-Laurel Collaboration Case* [Quezon City: University of the Philippines Press, 1984]).

[36] Manila *Chronicle*, May 24, 1945, 1 (not attributed to Roxas by name, but clearly his remarks by context); Manila *Post*, June 24, 1945 (quoting Roxas directly concerning the colloquy between Quezon and Laurel).

[37] Penciled comment by MacArthur on draft letter from Charles Parsons to President Quezon, September 14, 1943, secret, apparently not sent; RG 16, Box 12, MacArthur Memorial Archives (hereafter, MacA).

fication.[38] Laurel, in any case, came to believe in the efficacy of the remark attributed to MacArthur and on occasion said to his wartime interpreter, Hamamoto Masakatsu, that he expected to be shot if the Americans returned.

Within a week of the departure of the Quezon group, the Japanese military initiated consultations with the Filipino leaders remaining. The Filipinos met ten times in the next eighteen days, discussing the Japanese proposal that they constitute themselves a provisional government. They submitted three alternative proposals: (1) continuation of the Commonwealth, (2) an emergency civil administration, or (3) establishment of the Philippine Republic.

General Maeda Masami made clear his objections to the Commonwealth: born of American sovereignty, hence gone with American sovereignty; led by Quezon, who was against the Japanese; a government responsible for the death of many young Japanese by Filipino hands. The Japanese could install a "government of iron backed by military force," or a "puppet government," but they seemed to hold out the possibility of an emergency civil administration for the purposes of public peace, order, and relief, and to be willing to make the question of a republic the subject of future conversations. When a group of thirty Filipinos did agree to organize themselves into a provisional council of state, Maeda replied that he was extremely satisfied they had decided to "pledge [their] fidelity to our country."[39] Few if any Filipinos felt that committed yet, but the process of cooperation, co-optation, and collaboration, once begun, went inexorably on.

In appointing a leader of the new government in 1942, a split arose between a hard-minded bloc of Japanese army leaders, including the chief of the Kenpeitai, who had brought Artemio Ricarte back for the purpose, and Benigno Aquino, who had immensely wide political contacts and was favored by pro-Japanese Filipinos. The matter was resolved by turning to Jorge Vargas, a malleable functionary, who conveyed the legitimacy of the departed Quezon. When the Japanese later needed someone of genuine stature to lead the puppet republic they established in 1943, they considered the three men who had dominated the constitutional convention of 1935. But Manuel Roxas feigned illness and Claro Recto was too

---

[38] Theodore Friend, "Listen as a Grandchild: MacArthur's Reminiscences," *Solidarity* 1, no. 1 (1966): 107–11.

[39] Penafrancia mss., January 23, 1942; Mauro Garcia, *Documents on the Japanese Occupation of the Philippines* (Manila: Philippine Historical Association, 1965), 33–36.

idiosyncratic for them. Roxas threw his support, ultimately, to his friend and compadre, Jose Laurel.[40]

In selecting Laurel the Japanese chose a man with a law degree from Yale and an honorary doctor of letters degree from Tokyo Imperial University, a living knowledge of Filipino government at the highest levels since he had become a cabinet member in 1923 at age thirty-two, a vicarious knowledge of things Japanese as part of a longstanding pan-Asianism, and many prewar Japanese clients and contacts. Too little and too much had occurred in Philippine history for Laurel to find himself, like Sukarno, "magically mirrored" in the face of Japan. As early as 1926, however, Laurel had written against "a craze for Western standards" and for an educational system fostering native traditions and national unity.[41] Ten years later he sent one son to study at the Imperial Military Academy in Tokyo. The young man soon wrote to complain about conditions at the school, finding fault with the style and content of instruction and with living conditions. Laurel wrote back warning against "effeminacy" and urging him to persevere: "Affairs in the Far East . . . indicate the eventual preponderance, if not dominance of Japan. Yours is the opportunity."[42] The boy stayed, and several years later became an assistant to his father as occupation president.

Laurel was willing to take inspiration and guidance from the Japanese, but not command. In Tokyo he refused to don the striped cravat required, with morning coat, for an imperial audience. He insisted on the black necktie he always wore as a reminder of promises made to his mother on her deathbed. Laurel's desire to rest the Filipino government on a philosophic and "Asian" basis, formed the core of a harmonious relationship with Murata Shōzō, now ambassador to the republic. Despite this bond, however, and the Christian heritage they shared, there were basic differences of temper between the two. Beneath his professed Christianity, Murata was a Shintoesque Confucian, just as Laurel, beneath his professed Greater Asianism, was a Catholic jurisprudent. Murata eventually

[40] Grant K. Goodman, "General Artemio Ricarte and Japan," *Journal of Southeast Asian History* 1 (1966): 48–60; Ricarte-Quezon correspondence, Quezon Collection, National Library, Manila; Garcia, *Documents*, 39; "The Reunion of Prominent Filipinos in the House of Jose Yulo in Penafrancia, Paco, Manila," memo by Jose P. Laurel, October 23, 1944, JPL; interviews, Ohta Kaneshiro, September 20, 1958, Utsunomiya Naotaka, September 29, 1958, Wachi Takagi September 25, 1958; Marcial P. Lichauco, *Roxas* (Manila, 1952), 175.

[41] Jose P. Laurel to Miguel R. Acosta, October 11, 1926, JPL, II-a-7.

[42] Jose S. Laurel III to J. P. Laurel, May 13, 1936; J. P. Laurel to Jose S. Laurel III, June 10, 1936, JPL.

read *Yankee from Olympus* in an American prison, looking up the words in his English dictionary. Laurel knew the story and could quote Oliver Wendell Holmes on legal principle.

The distinctly Western character of Laurel's legal attitudes and political thought also set him off from leaders in Java. Whereas Sukarno used the romance and pathos of the peasant Marhaen to create a visionary imperative of social justice, Laurel founded his thought ultimately on Roman law, and quoted the maxim, *salus populi est suprema lex*. To help assure that "the public welfare is the supreme law," Laurel was devoted to the tripartite separation of powers, legislative, executive, and judicial. Even when wartime conditions and temperamental inclination drove him to strengthen the executive at the expense of the legislative power, he fought to preserve the sanctity of the judicial process from Japanese intrusion.[43] Laurel enjoyed working at trying to resolve the tension of claims between majority and minority parties, local and national government, labor and capital, church and state, nationalism and internationalism. He saw the Japanese as a major power factor that had to be accommodated in order to preserve a Philippine state; and he strove, accordingly, to keep disagreements with the Japanese small so that they might be resolved through compromise rather than confrontation. Sukarno, by contrast, rejected such a style of pluralistic contention as "free-for-all liberalism." His dramatic imagination moved him to exaggerate Japanese virtue and Dutch vice in the moral-political clash he foresaw as inevitable in the birth of an Indonesian state.

MOBILIZATION AND ORDER IN JAVA

Both Dutch example and their own colonial tradition told the Japanese, in the aftermath of victory over the Allies, to "divide and rule." Later their strategic predicament and anticipation of Allied return urged them to "unite for resistance." Tight control over indigenous peoples and resources prevailed from the beginning; military crisis made some controls relax, but intensified exploitive use of those remaining. Inadvertently, the Japanese created the conditions for general upheaval. Their manipulation of the power struc-

---

[43] On Laurel's defense of due process in face of Japanese violations, see Department of Justice, *Administrative order no. 45*, October 13, 1942, Fortunato Jose to Laurel, October 1, 1946, JPL; Fukushima Shintarō, ed., *Murata Shōzō: Iko hito-nikki* (Posthumous Philippine diaries) (Shinjuku: Hara-shobo, 1969), entry for February 21, 1944; Jose S. Laurel III, interview, June 4, 1968; *War Memoirs . . . Laurel*, 9.

ture released new group and individual energies; and their spirit of holy emergency awoke in the Javanese the peculiar sense of simultaneous culmination and beginning that may be called "liberation."

The Dutch had cultivated the native aristocracy (priyayi) and used them as civil servants, while establishing an uneasy modus vivendi with Islamic leaders and keeping the secular nationalists under sharp surveillance. The new Japanese policies had the effect of reducing the authority of the priyayi and enhancing both the nationalist and Muslim elements, though the Japanese generally tried to keep the latter two separate. Later, finding the nationalists getting out of hand, they attempted a restoration of influence to priyayi and ulama (Islamic legal scholars), only to change again, late in 1944, when strategic jeopardy called for a promise of independence. Ensuing events favored the nationalists once more, relative to priyayi and ulama, and introduced on the scene for the first time native military officers and aroused young activists.[44] None of this, however, was visible as the Indonesian leaders made their earliest association with the Japanese in 1942.

Hatta counseled Sukarno not to get involved with the first Japanese propaganda campaign, the Tiga-A movement, but Sukarno went ahead anyway.[45] For a few months there followed a noisy fanfaronade of Pan-Asianism, anti-Europeanism, and Japanese messianism with marching bands, posters, and meetings under the slogan, "Nippon the Light of Asia, Nippon the Protector of Asia, Nippon the Leader of Asia." The Chinese, Arabs, and Eurasians, who had money to contribute to it, obtained what seemed to the Indonesian nationalists an undue influence. The military administration did not mind the prominence of those groups and indeed would later return to solidaristic policies inclusive of them. They were, however, distressed to find the Tiga-A changing by Indonesian initiative from a propaganda movement into a mass organization seeking to promote activities in social welfare, education, religion, and youth work. A well-placed Japanese observer later summarized the Tiga-A as "a childish ding-dong party . . . without aim . . . or organization," for a people that "loved music and dancing, which is

[44] Dahm, Sukarno and the Struggle for Indonesian Independence, is excellent on this period (221–75). Although I follow in part Harry J. Benda, The Crescent and the Rising Sun: Indonesian Islam under the Japanese Occupation, 1942–1945 (The Hague and Bandung: W. van Hoeve, 1958), 117–19, 130, 156–57, 185ff., I agree with Dahm's critique (26–66) of Benda for overstating the consciousness and constancy of "divide and rule" in Japanese policy.

[45] Hatta, interview, March 6, 1968, Sukarno: An Autobiography, 174.

true of any backward race."[46] By September 1942, official favor withdrawn, it had withered away.[47]

Some time after, finding the Indonesian leaders "slightly neurotic from fatigue and ennui," the Japanese established a Commission for the Study of Customs and Polity (Komisi Menyelediki Adatistiadat dan Tatanegara; Kyūkan Seido Chōsa Kai). The empat serangkai members and a number of others served, including Haji Agus Salim, Oto Iskandardinata, Husein Djajadiningrat, Soetardjo, and Supomo.[48] They were charged to inquire into Indonesian society, religion, administration, industry, and other fields, and submit a report applicable to occupation policy. The Japanese hoped that Javanese love of debate would preoccupy them.

Javanese leaders, however, tired of impotent eloquence and useless analysis. Their thirst for more consequential participation in government led on August 1, 1943, to the replacement of the empat serangkai with the Chūō Sangi-in (Central Advisory Council) and analogous councils in each residency and special municipality. The Japanese simultaneously appointed symbolic Indonesian advisers to the military administration, the reverse of the case of the Philippines, where powerful Japanese "advisers" hovered beside key officials in an already Filipinized civil administration.

The commander in chief appointed more than half the members of the Central Advisory Council; Indonesians elected or nominated the remainder. The nationalists' numerical position increased from the ten in sixty among fellow Indonesians who had formed the Fraksi Nasional Indonesia in 1941 to twenty-one in forty-three. The rest included eight Indonesian civil servants, six Islamic representatives, three Chinese, and various others.[49]

[46] Kanahele, "Japanese Occupation," 45–52, 269 n. 26, 275 n. 61; Drs. R. de Bruin, "Sense and Non-Sense in the Three-A Movement" (paper presented to the Twenty-seventh International Congress of Orientalists, Ann Arbor, Mich., August 1967); Miyoshi, pt. 6, 72–73; Sukarno: An Autobiography, 174; Hatta, interview, March 6, 1968; Taniguchi Goro, interview, May 30, 1968.

[47] Miyoshi, pt. 6, 72–73; Miyoshi, interview, May 30, 1968.

[48] Miyoshi, pt. 8, 1968. Events through this period are also discussed in Prof. Mr. A. G. Pringgodigdo, "Tatanegera di Djawa pada waktu pendudukan Djepang Dari bulan Maret sampai bulan Desember, 1942" (The Javanese State System during Japanese occupation, March–December, 1942) (Yogyakarta: Jajasan Fonds Universitit Negeri Gadjah Mada, 1952).

[49] S. Van der Wal, ed., De Volksraad en de Staatkundige ontwikkeling van Nederlands-Indië (The Volksraad and the political development of the Netherlands Indies) (Groningen: Wolters, 1964–65), vol. 2, "Overzicht van de Samenstelling van de Volksraad" (Survey of the composition of the Volksraad); Miyoshi, pt. 9, 70; Kanahele, "Japanese Occupation," 95–105, 292–94.

The powers of the Chūō Sangi-in, however, actually fell short of the Volksraad's semilegislative function. The agenda for each council session was prepared by the planning section of the military administration and approved by the commander in chief, in whose name were framed a number of inquiries to which the council had to reply. The shape of the answer desired was implicit in the questions: "only the formulation of the answer was free for discussion."[50] Sukarno orchestrated the opinions of members who, at almost every meeting, appealed unsuccessfully for permission to use their flag and national anthem. Heads of departments in the military administration set the procedures of committees, then attended committee meetings to illuminate special problems and to "guide them so that they would not stray away from the demands of the Military."[51]

The Indonesians had initially welcomed the Chūō Sangi-in, but with each meeting their attitude turned more sour. "They were given instructions . . . as if they were children," one close observer said. "They arranged secret contacts between themselves and [other] national leaders, and began holding secret meetings in local districts to discuss measures for independence."[52] Hatta gave perhaps the most succinct description of the Chūō Sangi-in: "a House of Representatives in which you had to say yes."[53] He was the victim of manipulation at its very first meeting, in elections for chairman and vice-chairman. Through technical confusion, Hatta's name got onto the ballot for first vice-chairman against his will, and he won overwhelmingly, with Ki Hadjar Dewantoro second. The top military, however, considering Hatta a "dangerous communist," falsified the results so that Kusumo Utoyo and Dr. Boentaran were declared winners and were appointed in apparent deference to the wishes of the majority. "The affair left a bad impression on the Indonesian side, mingled with suspicion and doubt."[54]

The Chūō Sangi-in may have done something, as intended, to "ventilate" Indonesian minds "which were stagnated with irrita-

[50] Miyoshi, pt. 9, 71; quotation from Hatta, interview, February 17, 1968.

[51] Miyoshi, pt. 9, 71; pt. 11, 81. The only proceedings of a session I have been able to locate bear out in detail the general observations of Miyoshi: "Tjatjatan dan toelisan tjepat dalam sidang Tyuo Sangin jang ketiga" [Stenographic notes of the third session of the Chūō Sangi-in], RVO 048340.

[52] Miyoshi, pt. 11, 81.

[53] Hatta, interview, February 17, 1968.

[54] Miyoshi, pt. 9, 70–71; Hatta, interview, March 6, 1968; the quotation is from Miyoshi.

tion." But most Japanese, whose motto was "to use even a tree or a weed for increasing war power,"[55] never saw political participation of this kind as other than an instrument to aid the war effort. In June or July 1945, as the war drew toward its climactic end, the Japanese abandoned the Chūō Sangi-in and tried to create a new empat serangkai composed of Sukarno, Hatta, the enthusiastically pro-Japanese Oto Iskandardinata, and Wiranatakusuma, who was among the best educated and most influential of the regents. But the proposal never got beyond discussion. By then the young were a political factor too significant to ignore, and they strongly opposed the arrangement.[56] "Divide and rule," if ever an aim, was no longer a real option. The Japanese had initiated waves of "organize and inspire," and in strategic jeopardy these could not be reversed.

A Dutch lawyer after the war, composing a prosecution document for the Tokyo war crimes trials, wrote that Japanese policy was to isolate Indonesia from the rest of the world; to expel Western influence by ridicule, prohibition, or destruction; to organize all political, economic, social, and cultural activities along lines suitable to Japanese aims and similar to Fascist "corporations" in Italy; and to ensure all those aims by manifest and multifold expansion of police activity, spying, and terror. "All expressions of society were supervised and controlled by Japanese authority. Life itself had been forced into rigid moulds for the support of the Japanese army."[57] Seinendan (youth corps) existed in every town for young men fourteen to twenty-five years old. Keibōdan (vigilance corps), a civilian body for assisting the police, had over a million members. The Japanese organized women's and cultural groups, and functional or professional groups of every imaginable kind.[58] The use of Japanese words was required for most offices, official titles, and services, and the Japanese system of dating years was introduced, so that 1942 became 2602. All clocks were switched to Tokyo time, so that the sun no longer rose at six o'clock, but at half past seven in the morning.

The point of all this activity was, in various minds, to Nipponize,

[55] Miyoshi, pt. 11, 81.

[56] Hatta, interview, July 5, 1968.

[57] K. A. deWeerd, "The Japanese Occupation of the Netherlands Indies," IMTFE, Prosecution Document 2750, pp. 45–54, RVO 059697.

[58] One list shows four women's associations, fourteen Muslim groups, ten different "suicide corps," twenty-seven paramilitary youth organizations, and seventy-two "voluntary" mobilization and defense groups; OSS XL 19038, NARS, citing Royal Netherlands Weekly Intelligence Summary no. 136, August 20, 1945.

to mobilize, or to nationalize. A few Japanese thought full-scale Nipponization possible.[59] The military put mobilization of people and resources emphatically first; nationalization was a permissible means to that end. For Indonesian leaders, however, the true goal was nationalization, the means mobilization, and the by-product—Nipponization—inescapable but not profound.

This tension of ends and means spawned the first full-scale national organization. Its name, in Japanese and Indonesian, illustrated the different aims of the two peoples: to the Japanese it was Minshū Sōryoku Kesshū Undō, literally "people's total power concentration movement"; but the Javanese name was Pusat Tenaga Rakjat, "center of the power of the people." The Indonesian name itself, to believers in word-magic like Sukarno, was a substantial victory, for they could abbreviate it in the acronym Putera, meaning "son."

The concept originated in two days of frank discussion between members of the Gunseikanbu (Military Affairs Department, or, simply, military administration) and Sukarno, Hatta, and others. The Indonesians wanted an organization with the word Indonesia in its title, no limit on membership, and freedom to use the national flag and national anthem. The Japanese decided not to have a membership system at all, since that would resemble too closely a political party, but instead to "marshal public participation." They decided against flag, anthem, and "Indonesia" for fear of losing control of Java, and of angering army colleagues in Sumatra and navy colleagues in Borneo, Celebes, and the Moluccas. Opposition from within the military administration, and from the Naimubu (Internal Affairs Department) and the Kenpeitai, and the need for permission from Tokyo prevented the organization of Putera until March 8, 1943, four months after Sukarno had first alluded to it in a public speech.[60] Even then, military opposition slowed its operation until General Yamamoto arrived late in March and got it moving.[61]

Putera caught on. Sukarno exulted in his chairmanship of this first Java-wide network. The other three of the empat serangkai were vice-chairmen, above a secretariat and staff of over one hundred. An early Japanese intelligence report found public reaction very good, despite "no spirit of mutual aid and self-sacrifice."

[59] On limits to Nipponization, see Kanahele, "Japanese Occupation," 83–84, 289 nn. 109–11.

[60] Miyoshi, pt. 8, 71; Hatta, interview, March 6, 1968; Kanahele, "Japanese Occupation," 72–80, 285–88 nn. 68–99; Benda, Crescent and the Rising Sun, 117.

[61] Yamamoto Moichiro, interview, June 8, 1968.

Intellectual and moneyed Indonesians particularly "clung to their individualism. . . . They do not like to be brought into contact with the poor."[62] In a report on Putera's first year, Hatta himself was explicitly critical of the native Javanese civil service, which at its higher levels was recruited largely from the aristocracy. His implicit criticism of the Japanese was contained in a defense of Putera which, with a staff now of over five hundred, was supposed to unite the people behind the government to win the East Asian war.[63]

As the Allies drew closer in 1944 the Japanese felt that Indonesian leadership was sluggish and that the "hardening of the war situation" made it necessary to "enlarge" Putera by including Chinese, Arabs, and Eurasians. The new proposed organization, Jawa Hōkōkai (People's Service Association of Java),[64] was criticized loudly by Indonesian nationalists. They felt they were losing the most powerful organ ever to express their national identity, and were distressed at being lumped in with the Chinese, whose economic cooperation the Japanese needed, but whose political opportunism the Indonesians mistrusted.[65] Sukarno and Hatta pleaded for continuing Putera at least as a subordinate organization in the Jawa Hōkōkai, but the Japanese refused. Sukarno wept "in front of the Chief of Military Administration and other people," and "cried many times, that to see Putera dissolved was more tragic than losing one's beloved child."[66]

The Jawa Hōkōkai made no distinction among officials, civilians, races, or professions, and absorbed all preexisting social and functional groups except religious ones under Japanese policy command. General Harada, the Japanese commander in chief, emphasized the spirit of universal brotherhood in Jawa Hōkōkai, but this was little

[62] Sixteenth Army Beppan, Bandung branch, "The Start of the National Movement and the Natives' Reactions," March 24, 1943, translation in RVO 005798.

[63] Hatta wrote a quarterly report and a postmortem for the Gunseikanbu, "Poetera dalam tiga boelan pertama" (August 1943), and "Poetera satoe tahun" (March 1944). William H. Frederick has translated them with full introduction and copious annotation as *The Putera Reports: Problems in Indonesian-Japanese Wartime Cooperation* Cornell Modern Indonesia Project, no. 51 (Ithaca, 1971).

[64] Miyoshi, pt. 8, 71; "Proclamation of the Java Service Association," in Harry S. Benda, James K. Irikura, and Koichi Kishi, eds., *Japanese Military Administration in Indonesia: Selected Documents*, Yale University Southeast Asia Studies (New Haven, 1965), 145; *Jawa nenkan, 1944* (Java Yearbook, 1944) (Jakarta: Jawa Shimbunsha, 1944).

[65] Yamamoto, interview, June 8, 1968; Kanahele, "Japanese Occupation," 137; Benda, *Crescent and the Rising Sun*, 118.

[66] Miyoshi, pt. 8, 71, pt. 11, 83, pt. 12, 79; Hatta, interview, March 6, 1968. Quotations on Sukarno's reactions are from Miyoshi.

more than a mask for the Japanese necessity to combine for defense. Through a whole range of organizations, from parapolice to hyper-military, the Japanese hoped to repel any Allied invasion of Java. The Seinendan was an amorphous, multipurpose work force with an alleged five or six hundred thousand members.[67] The Keibōdan, with twice that number, was technically an anti-air raid corps, but often assisted local police and Kenpeitai.

The most militant Japanese spirit found expression in the fifty-thousand-member Jibakutai, whose name literally meant "self-explosion corps" (in Indonesian, Barisan Berani-Mati, or "the league that dares to die"). Armed with bamboo spears, they were a loose and landlocked analogue of the kamikaze pilots, pledged to die for the emperor and Greater East Asia, or, in this case, for "New Java." Also important was Hizbullah, a "self-sacrifice corps" formed in February 1945 of young Indonesians in Muslim schools and institutions. The Japanese continued to hope that their idea of a holy war for East Asian liberation would resonate with an Islamic idea of a holy war for national freedom.

The Indonesian nationalists, however, cherished organizations over which they had more influence, such as the Barisan Pelopor.[68] Taking advantage of the increasing urgency of the military situation and a phase of new latitude toward nationalism late in 1944, the Indonesians were allowed to create this youth corps under their own control. As an "institution of public duty" attached to the Jawa Hōkōkai, it resembled the Seinendan and Keibōdan but differed in being armed with bamboo spears. By the end of the war it was the most nationalistic paramilitary organization, and after the Japanese surrender it became the Barisan Banteng, or Wild Buffalo Corps.[69]

[67] R. deBruin, "Enkele Kanttekeningen: De Seinendan in Indonesia, 1942–1945." DeBruin modestly titles his work "a few marginal notes," but it contains ninety-eight pages of research and observations. See also Miyamoto in Anthony Reid and Oki Akira, eds., *The Japanese Experience in Indonesia: Selected Memoirs of 1942–1945*, Southeast Asia Series, no. 72 (Athens: Ohio University Center for International Studies, 1986), 235–36.

[68] Sudiro, interview, March 7, 1968. As its director, Sudiro reported directly to Sukarno and Hatta. His maximum estimate of membership, fifty thousand, is far below the eighty thousand that Japanese sources ascribed to it. *Pelopor* means "vanguard" or "pioneer," so a free translation conveying the feeling of this group in American terms might be "Minutemen."

[69] Statistics and basic information on the foregoing groups are from Japanese reports made available to English and Dutch forces after surrender: RVO 005111-16, "Organization of the Keibodan," with remarks by an Allied officer, and RVO 005117-23, "Explanations regarding All Kinds of Armed Bodies."

The critical organization for a future Indonesia, however, was Peta (Pembela Tanah Air; Defenders of the Fatherland), a regular military training corps. Begun experimentally in December 1943, by the end of the war it had 37,500 members armed with eighteen thousand rifles, one hundred trench mortars, and over seven million rounds of ammunition. Peta, nevertheless, was clearly a limited auxiliary force. Although some of its officers received sophisticated training in intelligence, most were taught just enough to be platoon leaders. They realized that the Japanese intended to use them only for defense of certain points, to relieve the strain on the Japanese army. The corps had no command or communication system of its own. The Japanese feared a disposition to combine and revolt against themselves.[70]

In 1945 the ultimate Japanese defense intended in the home islands and in the field was based on *takeyari shugi*, the bamboo spear principle. Local echelons were instructed to put up a last-ditch stand with the resources at hand, rather than surrender to the Allies.[71] The Japanese made a movie in Java on the manufacture and use of the bamboo spear, with classical Javanese war dance music in the background. The film concludes with Japanese and young Indonesians shouting wildly as they attack demonstration dummies.[72]

In such ways as these Japanese gave back to the Javanese the rudiments of what the Dutch had taken away: militant self-assertion and military capacity. Some could not wait to test their new power on the Japanese. They let off steam by dressing in civilian clothes and going out looking for a fight; they would jostle a Japanese in the marketplace, intimidating him in an Indonesian crowd. The more aroused died in a Peta revolt at Blitar.[73]

[70] Rvo 005117-23; Gen. Kemal Idris, interview, March 19, 1968 (Gen. Daan Jahja was also present at part of this interview). Miyamoto Shizuo in Reid and Oki, eds., *Japanese Experience in Indonesia*, agrees on Japanese mistrust and on size of the force (twice that of the Sixteenth Army), while giving larger numbers for Peta weapons. The Japanese had also formed Heiho, a body of about 42,000 Indonesians who served in Java and on various fronts for the Japanese as "assistants" to Japanese soldiers. Although equipped with rifle and helmet, their duties were largely menial.

[71] Maruyama Masao, *Thought and Behavior in Modern Japanese Politics* (London: Oxford University Press, 1963), 293.

[72] Movies described in Rvo 014009-10. The extensive collection of Japanese wartime films in the Library of Congress contains a number of items on Indonesia and the Philippines.

[73] Miyamoto (Reid and Oki, eds., *Japanese Experience in Indonesia*, 226–234) stresses the unreliability of the Peta as a military force, and Japanese forgiveness of many involved in the uprising.

Those with sense and system waited for the Dutch return. Even when they found the Japanese overbearing, they knew they were learning something invaluable. "The Dutch considered us good only for servants." But the Japanese, by putting weapons in their hands and new thoughts in their minds, even by lecturing, "taught us that we were men, neither more nor less than the Westerners."[74] The older order was shaken, the power structure transformed, countless individuals awakened, and fierce anticipations aroused. Javanese focused their expectations on the great change that was millennium, or utopia, or restoration of national dignity, or renewal of personal pride. All of these may be collected under the heading of revolution. Or they may just as well be suggested by Chairil Anwar's poem, "Aku":[75] "I," the first-person singular pronoun, symbol of the lord within, fed by a sense of nationality.

MOBILIZATION AND PLURALISM IN LUZON

The established church and ubiquitous police system of the Spanish Philippines were structurally more analogous to Japanese imperial institutions than were those the Japanese actually found in 1942. Such church and police, however, had provoked a revolution in 1896. The constitutional convention of nationalists at Malolos disestablished the one, and the United States, after the harshness of its conquest, softened the other. American imperialists actually implemented Filipino revolutionary will by separating church from state and subjecting police to representative government.[76]

Even after the impact of American pluralism and freedom of expression, church, school, and home in the Philippines all showed strong authoritarian influences. They were not, however, easily susceptible to totalitarian organization by the Japanese. Had a cunning Japanese statesman explored the mood of Philippine Falangists and tried to exploit the organizations that had supported Franco's Spain, he would have found only a superficial consonance with Japanese aims. The leading prewar Falangist, Andres Soriano, served in Quezon's cabinet-in-exile, and finally on MacArthur's staff. The Elizalde family had also supported Franco, but the Japanese threatened their economic, social, and political influence. And despite the pres-

[74] Gen. Kemal Idris, interview, March 19, 1968.

[75] See chap. 7.

[76] For a different perspective on these events, see Bernhard Dahm, *Emanzipationsversuche von Kolonialer Herrschaft in Südostasien: Die Philippinen und Indonesien, ein Vergleich* (Attempted emancipation from colonial rule in Southeast Asia: the Philippines and Indonesia, a comparison) (Wiesbaden: Otto Harrassowitz, 1974).

ence of a Japanese bishop and Japanese priests and nuns, the conservative Dominicans did not translate their prewar sympathies for Franco into wartime affinities for Tōjō; the cultural gap was too great to cross.[77] The state that the Japanese were trying to spiritualize and police may have shared some corporatist features with the Spanish, but it was a culture apart.

In the absence of any prominent pro-Japanese groups or readily adaptable currents of thought, the invading forces nonetheless tried to subject the Philippines to totalitarian mobilization. The military government installed Japanese advisers at the shoulders of the native administrators they found in charge, in order to see that key decisions emerged as desired. The prewar consul in Manila, Kihara Jitaro, hovered around Jorge Vargas and made annotations on the drafts of his speeches, and Shiohara Tamotsu was imported to scan the budgetary detail in Jose Laurel's Department of the Interior.[78]

The records of the presidential palace are the best index of early Japanese control.[79] They show that the commander in chief of the army or the director general of military administration had to agree to routine appointments, declarations of holidays (Japanese oriented), changing of street and place names (from Western to Asian orientation), and even the moving of garbage barges. Furthermore, the Japanese transacted a great quantity of business not by approving Filipino action, but by fiat: "You are hereby informed" . . . of the price of castor beans, of the location of pasturelands for Japanese army horses, of the takeover of Filipino companies, of special subsidies to Japanese firms out of appropriations granted to the Philippine Executive Commission.[80] Little room was left for Filipino error, and less for their initiative.

The laissez-faire economics of the American period came to an end with Japanese monopolies, economic controls, and forced production. Because Japanese firms were making Taiwan the sugar producer for Greater East Asia, Japanese policy cut back this most developed of Philippine industries to meet the demands of local

[77] Theodore Friend, *Between Two Empires: The Ordeal of the Philippines* (New Haven: Yale University Press, 1965), 171–72; A.V.H. Hartendorp, *The Japanese Occupation of the Philippines* (Manila: Bookmark, 1967), 1: 441, 632, 2. 94, 590, 593, 595.

[78] Kihara Jitaro, interview, September 1958; Shiohara Tamotsu, interviews, January, May, 1968.

[79] I am grateful to Mr. Rafael Salas, then executive secretary to President Marcos, for permission to consult these files.

[80] Malacanang Records Bodega: Japanese Military Administration, 1942–43, vols. 81–83, passim; hereafter Malacanang, period, volume, document number, and date if any.

consumption only. A significant percentage of capacity went into developing liquid fuel and alcohol. The balance of sugar lands were planted in cotton, again to meet the needs of the sphere.[81]

Social totalization went forward simultaneously. The Japanese organized households into groups of five to ten families; five to ten of these neighborhood associations composed a district association, headed by a president appointed with the consent of the Japanese military administration. These neighborhood associations might have tapped the Filipino spirit of *bayanihan*, or mutual help, just as in Japan the *tonari gumi* did at their best. But because installed in the Philippines as a spying and exploitative device, they tended to bring out lesser individuals and lesser motives.[82] The system worked better in Indonesia, where the *rukun tetangga* still bear traces of Japanese influence.

The lack of enthusiasm among Filipinos for the neighborhood associations was part of a larger pattern. Excepting the assorted followers of Benigno Ramos, who had tried to manage the Sakdal revolt of 1935 from Japan and now led the Ganaps, and the personal followings of Generals Aguinaldo and Ricarte, and of Pio Duran, the Japanese found little spontaneous answering among Filipinos to Japanese "sacrifices'" on their behalf. Determined to build such a spirit, the military administration abolished all political parties, then established the Kalibapi, an all-embracing "service association"[83] modeled after similar ones in China and Manchuria. Though the Kalibapi resembled the Jawa Hōkōkai in name, it resembled the Putera more in fact: a national political movement with nationalist officers, rather than a multiracial, multifunctional organization whose top officers were Japanese. But whereas Putera was a giant step forward for the Indonesians, the Kalibapi was a step backward for Filipinos. Multiparty discussion and open criticism of the colonial regime were now impossible.

Benigno Aquino, Sr., however, saw opportunity and progress in the Kalibapi. His vast gregarious knowledge of Filipino politicians and provincial personalities made him an excellent choice for its director general. The Japanese could not trust him to be always favorable to them, and in fact he several times contradicted them, but they could rely on his ambition to make the most of the job. Aquino

[81] On monopolies, Hartendorp, *Japanese Occupation* 1: 207–10; for a concise and useful account of sugar in particular, see Steinberg, *Philippine Collaboration*, 86–88.

[82] Teodoro A. Agoncillo, *The Fateful Years: Japan's Adventure in the Philippines, 1941–1945* (Quezon City: R. P. Garcia, 1965), 1: 353–57.

[83] On the Kapisanan sa Paglilingkod sa Bagong Pilipinas (Association for Service to the New Philippines), see Agoncillo, *Fateful Years*, 1: 357–58, 364–68, 374.

CHAPTER FOUR

enthusiastically developed his own gospel of the meaning of Japanese history in a series of provincial speeches:

> Japan has been master of her destiny for 2,603 years and she does not know what we vulgarly term "inferiority complex." ... The Filipino cannot be blamed for suffering from this complex because for four hundred years he had been under the domination of occidental countries [and] the white man had impressed upon our people [his] superiority over the brown; ... [but] ... the combined armies of the U.S., England and Holland were doomed to be defeated because while Japan fights for the glory of her spirit and the grandeur of her soul, the white man fights to preserve the flesh.[84]

The great Kalibapi purpose, he said, is "to develop a culture that is autochthonous and truly our own, not a culture like that which we had in Spanish times: half-Spanish; nor like that which we had under America; half-American."[85] Thus Aquino labored for a unified, and even a regimented, Philippines, in order to realize its cultural integrity in a reemergent Asia. What use would sovereignty be without spiritual independence? In asking the question, he was a generation ahead of his time.

The Kalibapi nonetheless aroused little support. A sympathetic Kalibapi official in Manila wrote to Laurel early in 1944 that, "while there are very few ... absolutely identified with and loyal to the republic, there is a greater number of people who are sworn enemies of the present administration and actively working against it."[86] The contradictions between Japanese imperialism and Philippine pluralism grew more intense. Kalibapi correspondents to the president asked him to restrain the Japanese, on the one hand, and warned him, on the other, that nothing he did could win the loyalty of some Filipinos. In Sulu, the Japanese navy took over the direction of the Kalibapi and required members to follow orders from naval personnel. "We enjoyed more freedom under the Military Administration," a local school official wrote the president. Laurel pro-

---

[84] Aquino to Vargas, April 2, 1943, reporting his speech at a public meeting in Vigan, Iloces Norte, March 24, 1943, before "10,000 people," Malacanang, 1942–43, 228, 980.11. In *The Aquinos of Tarlac: An Essay on History As Three Generations* (Manila: Cacho Hermanos, 1983), Nick Joaquin champions Benigno Aquino more for being anti-Saxon than for being pro-Nipponese. He sees the "Second Republic" (1943–45) as a bridge to present-day nationalism (pp. 164–69).

[85] Aquino to Vargas, February 1, 1943, "Official Report on the trip of the Kalibapi to Dagupan, Pangasinan, in January 30–31, 1943," Malacanang, 1942–43, 228, 980.11.

[86] Jose I. Baluyot to Laurel, February 19, 1944, Malacanang 1943–44, 48, 066.

tested vigorously to the Japanese naval commander and to Ambassador Murata,[87] but he could do little to relieve overall Filipino disaffection with his government.

Generalizing about relations with the Japanese, a keen Filipino observer said that "the only common understanding [of] which the two groups were aware is the unspeakable suspicion for each other and the unbridgeable chasm separating them."[88] Laurel had no illusions that he could bridge this chasm himself, harmonious as his relations were with some Japanese. But the Japanese presence gave him an opportunity to say from the presidential pulpit things that had long been on his mind. On the occasion of establishing a Bureau of Oriental Culture, he recalled how he had been advised in Tokyo to "wipe out all vestiges of Occidental culture." Rejecting such advice, Laurel argued that knowledge should be accepted and used no matter what the source: "Japan herself would not have reached her present position had it not been for her absorption of Occidental civilization."[89] As he struggled for a shift of emphasis, he put the matter in his own blunt terms: "We do not hate the peoples of the West, but we believe that the peoples of this part of the world can be happy only being permitted . . . to live a life that is peculiarly Oriental, even though it may be a stupid way of life and against the theories of the West."[90]

Laurel advocated and advanced Tagalog as the national language and promoted the nationalization and Filipinization of education. He quoted a character from one of Rizal's novels: "While the people keep their language they preserve the gift of their liberty, just as a man preserves his independence of thought while he retains his manner of thinking."[91] As in language, so in history: "We shall no longer teach history making Andres Bonifacio a bandit and George Washington the greatest patriot in the world."[92] To ensure that

[87] Yusop M. Tan to Dr. Celedonia Salvador, Director of Public Instruction, January 5, 1944, and subsequent correspondence culminating in Laurel to Highest Cmdr. Japanese Navy, Philippine Waters, February 7, 1944, and Laurel to Japanese Ambassador, July 7, 1944; Malacanang, 1943–44, 27, 043.1.

[88] Fermin Abella, "Reminiscences . . . Davao . . . March 1944," October 31, 1946, Jose P. Laurel Collection, Laurel Library, Manila (hereafter JPL).

[89] "Remarks . . . before Educational Leaders . . . ," January 22, 1944, records of the People's Court of Justice, Manila (hereafter PC/DJ).

[90] "Remarks . . . in Honor of Col. Saito and Col. Akiyama," September 8, 1944, collected articles, speeches, messages, statements, 239–41, JPL.

[91] "Statement on the Propagation of the Filipino National Language," December 23, 1943, 55–56, JPL; also Official Gazette, December 1943, 100.

[92] "Speech before Convention of Division Superintendents of Schools," June 26, 1943, 159–63, JPL; also Official Gazette, June 1944, 1003–7.

these changes were made, a National Education Board was created to study and recommend reforms in the whole system.[93] Thus Laurel strove to Filipinize his society half a century after its national revolution, while Sukarno zealously promoted use of the national language and a national perspective on history, in the service of the revolution yet to come.

The effectiveness of Japanese mobilization was markedly different in the Philippines and Indonesia. The Japanese found that the Javanese sense of *tata*, or cosmic-political order, was less explicit but not unrelated to their own sense of *kokutai*. They found much in Javanese cultural history with which to resonate, and little in Dutch colonial administration to counter their authoritarian and hierarchical style. In the Philippines, however, there was no magico-mythical tradition of the polity. Against the established church of Spain and its ecclesiastical police state the Filipinos had revolted two generations before.

Given their motives and their capabilities, it may be argued that the Japanese achieved a relatively high degree of success in an undertaking of low probability for gain.[94] But the Japanese military administration could find neither the cultural inclination nor the political interest among many Filipinos for them to change themselves and their country in the spiritual and structural ways that the Japanese desired. In Indonesia the Japanese left at least a heritage of nineteen words in the vocabulary of the growing national language. Two of the four most common of those words denoted violent self-sacrifice, and two of the next four were names of weapons. The others of the most common eight had to do with organization, and self-forgetfulness through alcohol.[95] One might admit that these very facts indicate the limited and specialized impact of the Japanese. But one cannot argue that they did not succeed in arousing and mobilizing Java.

[93] Executive order no. 5, October 23, 1943, no. 10, November 30, 1943—explained by Laurel speeches, April 17, 1944, 119–24, JPL; *Official Gazette*, 799–804.

[94] Grant N. Goodman advances this case in his paper, "The Japanese Occupation of the Philippines was a Success" (unpublished, 1963).

[95] In order of frequency, the most common eight words are (Indonesian spellings): harakiri, osake, romus(y)a, jibaku (self-destructive attack), kumico (chief of neighborhood association), taiso (gymnastics), takeyari (bamboo spear), tekidanto (grenade launcher) (Gōtō Ken'ichi, "Nihon Gunsei to Indonesia" (Japanese Military Administration, Indonesia), in Rinjirō Sodei, ed., *Sekaishi ni Okeru Nihon Senryō* [The Allied occupation of Japan in world history] [Tokyo: Nihon Hyōronsha, 1985], 31).

5

TOWARD A REPUBLIC:

INDONESIA

The Japanese took for granted their own political independence, coexistent with cultural identity. The intensity of both concerns for Southeast Asians, and the connection between the two, the Japanese did not readily understand. Their misunderstanding led to mismanagement. Even when they did understand, they moved only on their own strategic necessities, until events outran their control.

RELUCTANT PROMISES

When Premier Tōjō announced in January 1943 that Burma and the Philippines would be granted independence, he inadvertently revealed "How important and how passionate a matter national independence was" to the Indonesians.[1] In almost daily meetings with Miyoshi, the normally calm Hatta was furious: "If we have to suffer without gaining independence, we would rather be struck by a tidal wave and drowned." Sukarno, with "tears in his eyes," said they had expected "priority" in approval of independence, but "Even the name Indonesia is completely left out. . . . It's beyond our comprehension what evil we've done to be made to face such an insult." Why, Sukarno demanded, did the Japanese rip up railroads and round up laborers from Indonesia and send them to Burma, and then promise Burma independence? Why did the Japanese ignore Indonesians, the most cooperative people in the whole sphere, while

[1] Miyoshi Shunkichirō, "Jawa senryō gunsei kaikoroku" (Memoirs of the military administration of Java), 15 pts., *Kokusai Mondai* (April 1965–January 1967), pt. 9, 64. He expresses similar thoughts frequently in his narrative, including pt. 13, 67, pt. 14, 64, 65.

they promised independence to the Filipinos who were rebelling against them?[2]

Sukarno and Hatta might consider Indonesia preeminent in Southeast Asian civilization, but were discovering it was last in Japanese political accommodation. They did not yet appreciate the logic of Japanese policy: independence was not a reward for good behavior but an expedient against danger. Burma was engaged in a deadly struggle with the enemy, and the Philippines was riddled with anti-Japanese guerrillas. Java was as yet unthreatened, internally or externally. The army wanted to keep at least Sumatra after victory,[3] and the navy all its outer island territory.

Aoki Kazuo, the minister for Greater East Asia, came through Jakarta in May 1943. Three of the empat serangkai visited with him until midnight, their demeanor "like grandchildren asking a favor of the grandfather." Hatta referred to the Tōjō pronouncement as "an unmistakably cold and bitter insult," making them feel "as if we had been thrown into the bottomless pit." He asked for use of the national flag and anthem to raise their spirits; for transportation to and communication with Sumatra, Borneo, Celebes, and the Moluccas; and for union of the several different areas of military administration into one. "Should we not be able to obtain this long cherished wish of our people [for independence], we, as a race, would rather choose to perish."[4]

When a subsequent Imperial Liaison Conference considered the Indonesian demands, Premier Tōjō went so far as to propose granting independence, with Aoki and Shigemitsu Mamoru of the Foreign Ministry backing him up. But army and navy representatives strongly opposed the idea.[5] Tōjō, in order not to delay Burmese and Philippine independence, and to avoid confrontation with the military, compromised on a solution that would grant "political participation" to the islands (mentioned separately by name, not as "Indonesia") while the military would continue to govern.[6] With this pale concession—the Chūō Sangi-in—with a personal visit from Tōjō in July 1943, and with vague promises and exhortations, the Japanese temporized for another year and a half.

[2] Ibid., pt. 9, 64–65.

[3] Ibid., 66.

[4] Ibid., 66–67.

[5] George S. Kanahele, "The Japanese Occupation of Indonesia: Prelude to Independence" (Ph.D. diss., Cornell University, 1967), 92–93.

[6] Ibid.; Saito Shizuo discussed political development of this period, under interrogation, Singapore, June 1946, RVO 006911-15.

But they could not wholly evade the issue. In late 1943 Tōjō convoked a Greater East Asia Conference in Tokyo, which included Ba Maw of Burma and Jose Laurel of the Philippines, along with the leaders of other "independent" countries in the Japanese sphere. The Indonesians were not invited to participate, but Sukarno and Hatta were summoned to Tokyo four days after the conference ended to receive awards and assuage their disappointment. When they reached Manila on their way, Sukarno saw the bunting and national flags left over from celebration of the recently proclaimed Philippine independence. Enraged, he "cried out in a loud voice, tears streaming down his face like a crazy man." When they visited the statue of Rizal, he "gave out yells like an indescribable prayer," and he startled diners at the Manila Hotel by pointing to the ceiling and shouting "Flags! Flags!"[7] Stopping later in Taiwan, Sukarno was astonished and aggrieved to see locomotives from Java.[8] Still he continued to cooperate eagerly with the Japanese in the hope of hastening independence.

In the middle of 1944, Tōjō's cabinet gave way to one formed by Koiso Kuniaki. In what came to be called the Koiso Declaration, the new premier gave in to Indonesian requests, promising that "independence will be sanctioned in the future."[9] Hatta's response was "How long is sometime in the future?"[10] He was right not to rejoice. The Sixteenth Army had advance notice of the Koiso Declaration. Lest they lose Javanese cooperation, they began a "fight through to the end campaign" a week before releasing the statement on September 7.[11] On that day General Yamamoto Moichirō declared that there was an unavoidable climax ahead in which Indonesians must help "behead" the Americans and British. His "holy order as a God-fearing servant" was to command Indonesians

---

[7] Miyoshi, pt. 10, 68. The Indonesian "Bendera! Bendera!" may have been understood by other diners; the Tagalog for flag is *bandila*.

[8] Hatta, interview, February 17, 1968.

[9] Statement by Premier Koiso before the 85th Imperial Diet, "Independence of the East Indies," from Harry J. Benda, James K. Irikura, and Kōichi Kishi, eds., *Japanese Military Administration in Indonesia: Selected Documents*, Yale University Southeast Asia Studies (New Haven, 1965), 257–59. Kanahele, "Japanese Occupation," 163, 310, n. 5, gives a variant translation taken from Imperial Diet Lower House Proceedings, 85th Session.

[10] Hatta, interview, March 6, 1968.

[11] A close chronology of the whole process of independence, compiled by Sixteenth Army HQ, appears in RVO 005870. Miyoshi, pt. 13, 64–65, and Kanahele, "Japanese Occupation," 160ff., gives additional information on formulation and handling of the declaration.

to honor their national birthright and give peace to the heart of the emperor.[12]

Behind the scenes the chief of staff was circulating a top secret document to key army officers in which he interpreted the Koiso Declaration. Use of the flag, the anthem, and the term "Indonesia" was now permitted. Communists, of course, were prohibited. Further specifications expressed clearly the spirit of military administrators in late 1944:

> Especially the idea of colonial subjugation has to be banned and we must approach the natives with affectionate feelings although we must instruct and guide them sternly like parents or older brothers or sisters. . . .
>
> Although the insatiability which springs from the Indonesian character may sometimes provoke our resentment we must not regard them with hostility, but guide them, sternly showing the established policy. . . .
>
> Thorough measures shall be taken for the spreading of Japanese language, the adoption of Japanese institutions, and the infusion of Japanese culture.[13]

The correct propaganda line was reiterated:

> They must be made to [reflect] upon the glorious spreading of the creed of hakkō ichiu and [through references to independence] induced to increase their confidence in the sincerity of their deep feelings of gratitude for the August Virtue of His Majesty and their devotion to the Emperor. . . .
>
> In order to check absolutely the enemies' counter-propaganda, they must be reminded of the past when they groaned for ages in misery under Jewish oppression, under an external appearance of dazzling splendour, by tracing back the history of the atrocities of the USA, Britain, and Holland.[14]

Meanwhile the Japanese had been increasing Javanese quotas for military auxiliaries, laborers, foodstuffs, and construction materials. An "unofficial order" went out "concerning the construction

[12] Declaration by Chief of Military Administration, September 7, 1944, RVO 005922-23.

[13] Chief of Staff, Osamu Army Corps, "Notification regarding the Measures Ensuing from the Proclamation of Admission of the Independence of the East Indies," September 7, 1944, Top Secret, RVO 005913-14.

[14] Gunseikanbu, "Basic Main Points of Propaganda and Enlightenment Ensuing from the [Koiso] Proclamation," September 7, 1944, Secret, RVO 005915-16.

in each regency of barricades in ravines which were deathstand positions for the military."[15] Uncertain where to expect the next attack, the Japanese dug in as if it might be directly on Java-Sumatra. They promised independence, gave out flags, and made semantic concessions, but withheld authority and arms. For the time being, singing "Indonesia Raya," the anthem learned in secrecy under the Dutch, was a thrill. But songs do not satisfy for long; one yearns for greater forbidden games.

By mid-February 1945, American forces had defeated the Japanese at Leyte and were battling for control of Manila. Indonesian Peta officers, aggravated by Japanese demeanor, rose up in revolt at Blitar. Military administration officials on Java now took a step without prior consultation of Saigon or Tokyo. They authorized, on March 1, the creation of an Investigatory Committee for Indonesian Independence.[16] Higher military authority did not approve convening the committee until almost another three months had passed. By this time the war situation had deteriorated enough that the mandate was widened and strengthened.[17] The nationalist leaders learned what the Burmese and Filipinos had learned before them, that only pressure from without and uprising from within accelerated independence in the Co-Prosperity Sphere.

A Constitution and Its Ideology

Cameron Forbes, an early twentieth-century governor general of the Philippines, had been fond of making a distinction between "freedom," early given in various concrete forms—press, speech, assembly—and "independence," intended for the future. When independence was scheduled in 1934 for a dozen years later, what remained of the distinction became unimportant.

In Indonesia, however, the combination of millennial and messianic streaks in the culture and repressive strains upon the polity gave to the word "merdeka" both of these meanings—sovereign independence and freedoms of association and expression. Other

[15] Miyoshi, pt. 13, 64–65.

[16] Ibid., 66–67; Kanahele, "Japanese Occupation," 184–92, 315 nn. 1–8, 316 nn. 13–15.

[17] Kanahele, "Japanese Occupation," 195–97, 317 nn. 26–28; Bernhard Dahm, *Sukarno and the Struggle for Indonesian Independence* (Ithaca: Cornell University Press, 1969), 287, attributes the delay after the Koiso Declaration in September 1944 to an intentional effort by the military government on Java to slow down momentum and check enthusiasm for independence.

meanings accrued as well, including personal psychological liberation, and imaginative fulfillment of the longing for a golden age. After March 1943, the Japanese heard merdeka uttered constantly in Indonesian conversations, and among the enormous crowds gathered around news announcement boards and public radios strung on poles.[18]

These energies boiled up in the Investigatory Committee for Indonesian Independence (Badan Penyeledikan Kemerdekaan Indonesia, or BPKI), when it first met in May 1945. Japanese advisers said the purpose of the BPKI was not to vote but to advise, to act "not [as] a prospective mother, but as a midwife." Sukarno, however, advanced his own metaphor: "Independence seems like a marriage. Who shall wait until the salary rises, say to 500 guilders and setting up house is complete? Marry first!"[19]

Thus began what became a constitutional convention. In nine days of meetings, the Indonesians completed an exercise the Filipinos had gone through with revolutionary fervor in 1898, with moderate deliberation in 1935, and still again with pressured haste in 1943. The unleashing of repressed ideals, the lack of precedent and experience, a Javanese tendency to thought-spinning, and the Dutch-enhanced tendency to compartmentalize society would all tend to make the Indonesian meetings far more ideological than their Filipino equivalents.

Before and during the meetings of the BPKI, youth groups were formulating their own visions of the future Indonesia in an extraordinary series of articles in *Asia Raya*: a complete fusion of all classes of Indonesian society; a new mass awareness based on the sovereignty of the people, the establishment of a United Republic of Indonesia, and the defense of Indonesia hand to hand with Japan, but, if need be, unilateral seizure of independence.[20] Such groups opposed government by the traditional Javanese *perintah-halus* (gentle command from above), the influence of the civil service, and those Indonesians deeply affected by Dutch style even while critical of it. The youth groups wanted open meetings. The Japanese, however, kept the meetings closed for fear the situation would become uncontrollable. In the end, the course of the meetings satisfied nei-

[18] Miyoshi, pt. 14, 64.

[19] Quotations from Y. Ichibangse, "A Report of the Preparative Investigation Committee for Indonesian Independence," November 13, 1946, RVO 005850-59.

[20] Kanahele, "Japanese Occupation," 200–8, 318 nn. 35–50; quotation from 205. For a Japanese view of pemuda activity, see Nishimura Otoshi, interrogation, RVO 059330ff.

ther the youth groups nor the Japanese, nor did they go exactly as the Muslims or secular nationalists desired; but they did produce some fundamental compromises upon which to found a state.

The most divisive issue was the most general: What form should the state take? Hatta's attempts to avoid the question were foiled by the chairman, Dr. Radjiman Wedioningrat,[21] and basic clashes of outlook broke out at once. The nationalists wanted a republican form of government, the Muslims wanted an Islamic state, and a significant minority—including representatives from Yogyakarta and Surakarta, plus about half of the civil service element[22]— wanted a monarchy. The Japanese advisers were not averse to the last idea; earlier in the occupation some Japanese military administrators had discussed making the sultan of Yogya a monarch.[23] But even the sultan, eminent and respected as he was, represented only one of 270 feudal lineages. The monarchists could not overcome localized traditions, competitive genealogies, and the nationalization of court politics sufficiently to advance their view. The committee voted 55 to 6 in favor of a republic.[24]

The Muslim leaders wanted to make Islam the state ideology, give Islamic law superior legal status, and require that the president be Muslim. To Miyoshi, they seemed "conservative and almost fanatic, obstinately insisting on . . . the unity of religion and politics." Hatta, himself a devout Muslim, observed that the greatest modern Islamic country had become a democratic nation—Turkey under Kemal Atatürk. Indonesia should encourage faith and devotion, he felt, but to make Islam the national religion would be anachronistic.[25] The meetings ended on June 1 with the question still unresolved. Before they resumed in mid-July, several nationalist and Muslim leaders drafted a preamble to the constitution declaring that the state was founded on belief in God and that citizenship obliged Muslims to follow the precepts of Islam. When the plenary session resumed on July 15, however, division flared anew between Muslim leaders who wanted a clear statement of Islam as the state religion, and nationalists who wanted assured freedom of belief and services for all. In renewed discussions late that night, with the success of the meetings at stake, the Muslims conceded freedom of re-

[21] Hatta, interview, March 6, 1968.

[22] Ichibangse, "Report," RVO 005859.

[23] Officials of the Sultanate, interview, March 26, 1968.

[24] Kanahele, "Japanese Occupation," 209–10, Bernhard Dahm, *History of Indonesia in the Twentieth Century* (London and New York: Praeger, 1971), 104.

[25] Miyoshi, pt. 14, 63.

ligion with the stipulation that the president be a Muslim—not a particularly exclusive clause, for over 90 percent of the population was nominally Muslim. Sukarno next morning, with tears in his eyes, begged the delegates to accept this agreement. It carried easily, for a republic with religious liberty and a Muslim president.

The next question concerned the territorial boundaries of the new state. A group of nineteen, mostly civil servants, voted for the Netherlands Indies as it stood; six men, including Hatta, voted to include Malaya, if it were willing, and leave out Western New Guinea; thirty-nine men, led by Mohammad Yamin, voted to include New Guinea, Timor, British Borneo, and Malaya up to the border of Thailand. Sukarno, one of this last group, had thought of including the Philippines too, but it was already "independent."[26] More than two-thirds of the body thus voted in an expansionistic way, and 60 percent of them conceived of going far beyond any provable extent of historical Indonesian kingdoms. The spark of revolution had already ignited the fumes of empire.

The Japanese had expected a variety of opinions to be decorously expressed, carefully framed, and then respectfully submitted to the military. But on the second day of the July session Sukarno had introduced a "bombshell motion": since all opinions were now known, the assembly should proceed article by article "without sleep or rest" until they produced a draft constitution. The committee enthusiastically approved, and the Japanese, caught by surprise, could not object.[27] Hatta would always recall the pressure, the fatigue, the euphoria, of dashing off formulations on the spur of the moment.[28]

Afterward the republic would be plagued with problems stemming from the vagueness and inconsistencies of its organic law. Unlike the Netherlands and Japan, however, both of which enjoyed ethnic homogeneity, historical national institutions, and a compact sense of polity, Indonesia had been an idea for only a generation. Turning the idea into a state required not only constructing a constitution but also fabricating a common ideology. The former was the job of many, the latter the job of Sukarno. On the last day of the

[26] The fullest source for these proceedings is Muhammad Yamin, *Naskah Persiapan Undang-Undang Dasar 1945*, 3 vols. (Jakarta: Jajasan Prapantja, 1959–60). The details stressed are drawn from Kanahele, "Japanese Occupation," 210–12; Dahm, *Sukarno's Struggle*, 300–1; Dahm, *History of Indonesia in the Twentieth Century*, 104–7; Miyoshi, pt. 14, 62; and Ichibangse, "Report," RVO 005850-59.

[27] Miyoshi, pt. 14, 63–64.

[28] Hatta, interview, February 17, 1968.

first series of meetings, in the Volksraad building, on the spot where the Dutch governors had stood, and in the hearing of Japanese advisers, Sukarno spoke for an hour. He wove a cloth of abstraction in the tradition of Javanese universalism, drew a pattern of principle with a hand steadied by struggle, and dyed the whole with cosmopolitan influence. The resulting political garment might be worn by any Indonesian, of whatever ethnic group or religion. Its design consisted of five elements:

1. Indonesian nationalism. Appreciating the potential threat to Muslim religio-nationalists and Chinese, Sukarno tried to reassure these factions. To the former he explained that nationalism meant the unity, ordained by God, of the early Indonesian states of Srivijaya and Majapahit, and of the Japanese nation. To the Chinese Sukarno explained that Sun Yat-sen's Three principles, which included Chinese nationalism, had rescued him from the more cosmopolitan ideas of his youth.

2. Humanitarianism (kemanusiaan). The missionary urge to create a better world, and an alternative to Western materialism, could be consonant with either Gandhi's religion of humanity, or the Japanese idea of hakkō ichiu, world brotherhood, without the necessity of Japanese leadership.

3. Democracy (mufakat). This Sukarno used in a peculiarly Indonesian sense, meaning representation of all sides and deliberative discussion to an extent sufficiently satisfying to all groups, to yield collective agreement.

4. Social justice (keadilan sosial). Sukarno emphasized economic democracy in contradistinction to the West, and a modern manifestation of the spirit of the Ratu Adil, the mythological Indonesian "righteous king."

5. Belief in almighty God (Ketuhanan yang Maha Esa). This was not the God of Islam who demanded absolute submission to his commandments, but the God who stood behind all being and all religions, and whose inspirations each individual might receive and interpret.[29]

[29] Some major summaries of the Pancasila are: Sukarno: An Autobiography, as told to Cindy Adams (Indianapolis: Bobbs-Merrill, 1965), 197–99; George McT. Kahin, Nationalism and Revolution in Indonesia (Ithaca: Cornell University Press, 1952), 122–27; Kanahele, "Japanese Occupation," 197–200; and Dahm, Sukarno's Struggle, 336–43. Mohammad Natsir, as a critic of latter-day uses of Pancasila, considered it a concoction based on Sun Yat-sen and those influential on Sukarno as a teenager—H.O.S. Tjokroaminoto and the Dutch socialist high school teacher, Baars (interview, December 2, 1983).

Years later, Sukarno would speak of these five principles—his Pancasila—as having superseded the Declaration of Independence and the Communist Manifesto. The Western documents had served their purposes for national freedom and proletarian liberation, but, with mankind now divided between the two, only the Pancasila offered the necessary universal basis for peace, welfare, and brotherhood.[30] In this conceit, Sukarno combined the intellectual syncretism of an Arnold Toynbee with the political ambition of hakkō ichiu. If he did not succeed in roofing over the world with his thoughts, he did nonetheless lay an ideological flooring for Indonesian independence. Long after he had passed from power, his successors would tread the boards of Pancasila.

INDEPENDENCE: IMPERIAL DECREE

By July 16, 1945, the BPKI had drafted a constitution, but it rested on no imperial authority other than that of the military administration in Java. Javanese were continuing to lose faith in the Japanese, and the young to lose faith in their elders. Now, however, the Supreme War Council in Tokyo caught up with and passed the Java Gunseikanbu by adopting a policy of early independence for the Indies. Tōgō Shigenori, the foreign minister, was the chief articulator. Instructions from the minister of war to Saigon brought Field Marshal Terauchi into agreement. In return, General Itagaki in Singapore reluctantly summoned a conference—the last, as it happened—of military administrators from Java, Sumatra, Malaya, and the naval Territories, to respond to Tokyo's target date of September 7, the first anniversary of the Koiso Declaration.[31] The military administration on Java later decided to appoint a delegation of four;

[30] Sukarno, Independence Day Address, August 17, 1960, in government publication of his major speeches, *Dibahwa Bendera Revolusi* (Under the banner of revolution), 2: 433–34.

[31] Kanahele, "Japanese Occupation," 214–16, 319–20, nn. 69–76; de Weerd statement, IMTFE Prosecution Document 2750, RVO 059679, esp. pp. 110–29. For proposal to and decision of the Supreme War Guidance Council, see Benda et al., *Japanese Military Administration*, documents 78, 79. For a rationale of the proposal by the Foreign Ministry, see "Materials used for the Foreign Minister's Explanation," July 17, 1945, in Library of Congress, Captured Document Japanese Ministry of Foreign Affairs, reel 586, pp. 37–44 (translated for me by Prof. Mikiso Hane). For details of response from Saigon, Singapore, and Jakarta: interrogations of Numata Takazo, RVO 006788-89, Saito Shizuo, RVO 006911-15 and 005838-42, Nishimura Otoshi, RVO 59330-33.

they would not go to Tokyo, suffering daily air raids, but would travel to Saigon to receive the imperial decree of independence.[32]

Thus far everything was secret. Yamamoto told the interpreter Shimizu to bring Sukarno immediately without telling him why. Unable to keep silent, Shimizu told Sukarno at once, and the latter wept with joy as he rushed to Yamamoto's office. When Sukarno appeared at his door, Yamamoto ran from behind the desk and embraced him, speaking in "queer English," crying all the while. Sukarno again broke into tears, and Shimizu did too[33]—tears of solidarity and relief. An Indonesian wept with Japanese as he could not with Dutch, and Japanese wept with an Indonesian as they could not with North Atlantic men. Together they took a mighty step in undoing Western lordship.

The party for Saigon, which included Sukarno and Hatta, gathered secretly on the night of August 8 and began the dangerous trip the next morning.[34] On the way the Japanese heard of the Russian declaration of war and invasion of Manchuria. Miyoshi felt "as if my blood were curdling." What would become of Indonesian independence, and Indonesian feeling for the Japanese, if Japan were defeated? In the morning the Japanese heard further startling news: Hiroshima was destroyed, Nagasaki "carbonized."[35] All this they kept secret from the Indonesian party.

The ceremony was held in Dalat at noon the next day. Terauchi, recovering from a stroke, presided. The Japanese were afraid the Indonesians would not accept points 3 and 4 of the decree, which declared that independence should come after preparation on Java first, followed by Sumatra and the outer islands, and that all other necessary authority belonged meanwhile to the imperial government for the prosecution of the war. They thought of softening it, but were even more afraid of tampering with the emperor's words. To the great relief of the General Staff, however, Sukarno and Hatta, during a recess, demanded no explanations and requested no time for consultation. Sukarno simply asked Miyoshi's advice on how to compose an oath of acceptance.[36]

[32] Miyoshi, pt. 14, 65–66; Yamamoto, interrogation, RVO 168902.

[33] Interviews, Yamamoto, June 11, 1968; Shimizu Hitoshi, June 4, 1968.

[34] Kanahele, "Japanese Occupation," 218–19, 320 nn. 83–88, gives a fine circumstantial account of the trip.

[35] Miyoshi, pt. 14, 66–67.

[36] Ibid., pt. 15, 60. For other perspectives on the decree: Ichibangse, "A Report of the Preparative Investigation Committee for Indonesian Independence," November 8, 1946, RVO 005850-59; and Abdul Kadir Widjojoatmodjo, "Comite voor het onder-

The ceremony reopened with the oath. Sukarno requested Terauchi to convey to the emperor that seventy million Indonesians were "grateful beyond expression to His Majesty."[37] Bowing, Sukarno repeated his thanks, tears streaming. The General Staff stood in deep emotion. "Then Marshal Terauchi burst into happy tears, his face glowing, and not even bothering to wipe away the flowing tears, thanked them again and again." Sukarno raised banzais for the emperor, Great Imperial Japan, the Japanese army, and the good health of Marshal Terauchi. The latter, now "merry as a child," told Hatta he had heard of his vow not to marry until Indonesia was independent, and asked if he had his eye on a bride, "at which Mr. Hatta blushed."[38]

That night the Japanese woke Sukarno to tell him about Russian intervention. He was "furious" and said the Soviets "had done a very stupid thing." Hatta showed no emotion—another officer had leaked the news to them earlier—but asked about the consequences for Japanese policy.[39] The Japanese held back the news of the atomic bomb, perhaps not fully appreciating its impact themselves. The General Staff of the Southern Army had been in almost continuous meetings between ceremonies, evaluating the Potsdam Declaration and the Soviet action. They now dispatched a colonel to Tokyo with their conclusion: opposition to surrender; a decision to "fight to the end."[40]

Sukarno later dismissed the whole trip: "Although . . . they knew they were finished and we knew they were finished, not by hint or twitch of the eyebrow did any one of them let drop one solitary word about it. From my . . . young Java training I was still a good actor so I never let on either. . . . The whole thing was a farce."[41] But those banzais? The fury against the Soviets? The lack of questioning of the terms of the imperial decree? If this contained an element of "acting," it also represented the engaged action of a man committed to the Japanese as far as they would go, for as much as he could get for Indonesia. That tension had brought him to tears in

---

zoek naar maatregelen van voorbereiding van de Onafhankelijkheid," November 3, 1945, RVO 005843-48.

[37] Miyoshi, pt. 15, 60–61.

[38] Miyoshi, interview, June 6, 1968, for Sukarno's tears (characteristic); Miyoshi, pt. 15, 60–61, for Terauchi's tears (most uncharacteristic). *Sukarno: An Autobiography*, 204, mentions of Terauchi only that he was "tall, slim, European in appearance," but not that he was using a cane, mumbling, and overcome with emotion.

[39] Miyoshi, pt. 15, 60–62; Miyoshi, interviews, June 6, 12, 1968; Hatta, interviews, March 6, July 5, 1968.

[40] Miyoshi, pt. 15, 62.

[41] *Sukarno: An Autobiography*, 205.

the presence of the Japanese on at least six occasions in eighteen months.

INDEPENDENCE: NATIONAL PROCLAMATION

When his plane landed in Jakarta on August 14, Sukarno made another play upon the Joyoboyo prophecy: Indonesia would have merdeka not when the maize was ripe, as he had promised just a week before, but as soon as it tasseled. "Cries and applause exploded from the crowd."[42] Sukarno did not know when that would be, but twice he had asked Terauchi, who replied that it was up to them.[43]

Sukarno had no idea that Japanese surrender was only hours away.[44] On the fifteenth, Sjahrir came to see Hatta with radio-earphone news of Japanese capitulation. They went to Yamamoto's office to check and found only one person there.[45] Hot with hope, anxiety, and wild speculation, they collected Subardjo, went to the Office of Naval Liaison, and asked Admiral Maeda Tadashi if the news were true. Maeda hung his head, "a full minute," as Hatta recalls it, and finally answered that Allied broadcasts said so; however, pending official word from Japan, the military attitude was that Japan was still at war. To Subardjo, however, the presence of many drunken Japanese at naval headquarters confirmed what they wanted to know.[46]

Sjahrir and Hatta went to Sukarno and pressed him to pronounce Indonesia independent. He was reluctant to do anything until the

[42] *Suara Asia*, August 15, 1945, GSK; Miyoshi, pt. 15, 62; *Sukarno: An Autobiography*, 206.

[43] Miyoshi, pt. 15, 73; Hatta, interview, March 6, 1968; *Sukarno: An Autobiography*, 204.

[44] The history of the proclamation crisis is extensively recorded and intensively discussed. Benedict R. O'G. Anderson's *Java in a Time of Revolution*, chap. 4, gives a balanced account, and his *Some Aspects of Indonesian Politics under the Japanese Occupation: 1944–1945* Cornell Modern Indonesia Project, no. 29 (Ithaca, 1961), chap. 6, contains additional detail. Dahm, *Sukarno's Struggle*, 310–15, also gives a useful version. My condensation omits some well-known facts while bringing out some new ones relevant to themes of this work. Among my key sources are: Miyoshi's diary, RVO documents, and Drs. Soeroto, "Sedjarah proklamasi 17 Agustus 1945" (History of the proclamation of 17 August 1945) (MS, 1961), which is based on a review of then-published materials, plus ten personal interviews with participants. I have also relied on the following interviews of my own: Boentaran Martoatmodjo, March 11, 1968; B. M. Diah, November 28, 1983; Mohammad Hatta, March 6, July 5, 1968; Kasman Singodimedjo, March 11, 1968; Maeda Tadashi, July 28, 1967; Adam Malik, November 28, 1983; Nishijima Shigetada, March 21, 1968; Jusuf Ronodipuro, February 17, March 27, 1968; Achmad Subardjo, March 12, 1968.

[45] Hatta, interviews, March 6, July 5, 1968.

[46] Interviews: Hatta, July 5, 1968; Subardjo March 12, 1968.

surrender was verified. Subadio, one of Sjahrir's foremost followers in the youth movement, came to Hatta later in the day, and when Hatta replied in the same vein as Sukarno, Subadio said he was not "revolutionary" enough; the pemuda were ready to revolt against the Japanese. But, Hatta countered, they could not beat four Japanese battalions in Jakarta. They should organize and prepare to fight the Dutch, their real and ultimate enemy.[47]

A large group debated the same issue for hours that night at Sukarno's house. The young nationalists, with Wikana as spokesman, wanted an immediate declaration of independence signed by Sukarno and Hatta. Hatta said they could not yet do this but would follow anyone else who dared. Reasonably, Sukarno reminded them that Indonesian freedom was more than a matter of a coup in Jakarta—it involved millions of people over thousands of miles. One youth taunted him: "Perhaps our great Bung is scared. . . . Perhaps he still awaits orders from the Emperor." Then Wikana stepped forward and commanded Sukarno to begin the revolution that night, or else. Sukarno, furious, met his bluff. He stood up, pulled his own head forward and shouted, "If you want blood, here's my head, you can take me outside right now." Wikana backed down.[48]

The youths, daunted at night, sprang back in the morning. They abducted Sukarno and Hatta, as well as Sukarno's wife, Fatmawati, and baby son, Guntur. Outside the city, Sukarni, a youth leader, guarded them, while promising an uprising of fifteen thousand people that day. Subardjo initiated a search the next morning when Sukarno and Hatta failed to show up for a meeting of the BPKI. At first he feared the Japanese had imprisoned them, but Maeda was equally alarmed and the Japanese joined the search. Finally learning where Sukarno and Hatta were, Subardjo went to bring them back.[49]

First he had to argue with Sukarni, who was armed with a pistol and a long-handled knife. Subardjo explained that the surrendering power is obliged to enforce the status quo; thus it was not an opportune time to anger the Japanese. Sukarni replied that the youths wanted a declaration of independence by the next morning. All right, Subardjo finally said, but let Sukarno and Hatta go. If it doesn't work out, "you can shoot me dead." This appeal to Peta-pemuda bravado helped persuade Sukarni. Though it was already

[47] Interviews: Hatta, March 6, 1968; Subadio, February 27, 1968.

[48] *Sukarno: An Autobiography*, 208; interviews: Hatta, March 6, 1968; Subardjo, March 12, 1968; Diah, November 28, 1983.

[49] *Sukarno: An Autobiography*, 210–14; interviews: Hatta, July 5, 1968; Subardjo, March 12, 1968; Maeda, July 28, 1967.

dark, they drove back to Jakarta, hoping to convene a meeting of the BPKI at midnight.[50]

Since Maeda was now in on the event and some form of Japanese support was felt necessary, the admiral's house was chosen as the meeting site. Sukarni, with Maeda's aide, set off around the city to tell various detachments of youths that the uprising was not yet to come off. While others were trying to forestall any pemuda outbreak, Sukarno and Hatta were seeking Gunseikanbu authority for a declaration of independence. Major General Nishimura Otoshi, Yamamoto's next-in-command, declined. Sukarno and Hatta argued that independence was a samurai promise, good until the death; the Japanese were duty bound to fulfill the imperial decree. But the Japanese had pledged their word to the Allies to maintain the status quo, Nishimura replied, and the surrender of Japan had made its armies "slaves" of the Allies.

Sukarno, having responded to the Japanese and played noble-warriors-together with them for three years, now found the samurai code working against him. In wonder and anger, he blurted at Nishimura, "Why don't you just go and commit *harakiri?*" Sukarno's challenge prompted neither action nor concession. The talk ended in inconclusive argument,[51] and the two Indonesians left for Maeda's house, which armed pemuda had surrounded. After talking briefly with Maeda, Sukarno and Hatta joined the meeting of sixty-odd committee members and youths. The major questions remaining were, Who should proclaim independence? and What should be the content of the proclamation? The pemuda, who distrusted all bodies created by the Japanese, including the BPKI, wanted Sukarno and Hatta to sign and announce the proclamation, so the moment of national birth would be pure and free of Japanese influence. Sukarno, who had no mass party, felt he needed the ground of Japanese support; he was willing to sign a proclamation as chairman of the BPKI, but to the young activists that had a Japanese smell. Hatta thought everybody present should sign it, like the American declaration, and Subardjo wanted to fashion a list of grievances against the Dutch queen, in the style of 1776. But Sukarni and the young activists opposed them, and the consensus was that Sukarno and Hatta "should bear the responsibility."

[50] *Sukarno: An Autobiography*, 214–15; Hatta and Subardjo interviews.

[51] Nishimura Otoshi, interrogation, January 16, 1947, Singapore, RVO 059330-33; "Taken from the Documents of Capt. Nakamura Hiroshi. . . . Notes . . . of Talks between Soekarno and Hatta and the Japanese in mid-August 1945," RVO 011155-57; Miyoshi, pt. 16, 65; *Sukarno: An Autobiography*, 216; Hatta, interview, July 5, 1968. The last is the source for the quotation of Sukarno on harakiri.

So they did. A draft by Sukarni and Chaerul Saleh was turned down. Hatta, fretting over phraseology for some time, finally dictated a simple message which Sukarno scrawled on a lined pad:

> We the people of Indonesia hereby declare Indonesia's independence. Matters concerning the transfer of power and other questions will be executed in an orderly manner and in the shortest possible time.
>
> In the name of the Indonesian people,
> Soekarno   Hatta

Maeda came into the room and congratulated Sukarno, addressing him as "Excellency." His was the first unofficial recognition of the Indonesian Republic. It was about four o'clock in the morning.[52]

Sukarno, trembling with malaria and dosed full of quinine, rose late the next day. People were gathered in his yard awaiting the proclamation. When Hatta arrived, the two, a little frightened, went outside. Sukarno, blinking away tears of joy, read the proclamation. A Peta leader strung the red and white banner, sewed together by Fatmawati, on a short staff, and Sukarno led the crowd in an oath of loyalty to the flag.[53]

Afterward furious Kenpeitai officers took him inside and questioned him harshly: by whose permission did he do such a thing? "We have declared independence in the name of the people of Indonesia," Sukarno replied. "Look around you." Hundreds of youths with hatchets, sickles, and bamboo spears stood ready. "If you wish to take us away, you are welcome to." The Kenpeitai left quietly.[54]

In accord with surrender agreements made with the Allies, the Japanese would again prohibit the Indonesian flag, ban the national anthem, and withdraw recognition from the BPKI.[55] But there was no holding back events now. Young Javanese newsmen telegraphed the proclamation over the Domei wire, and it was broadcast over Japanese radio. The Kenpeitai took the broadcaster to jail and beat him up. Next morning the director of the station, an elderly Japanese, came down and set him free. "What's the use?" he said to the Kenpeitai. "We've lost the war, haven't we?"[56]

[52] Soeroto, "Sedjarah proklamasi," 33–34; Boentaran, Hatta, Maeda, and Subardjo interviews.
[53] Soeroto, "Sedjarah proklamasi," 35; *Sukarno: An Autobiography*, 218–30; Miyoshi, pt. 16, 65–66.
[54] *Sukarno: An Autobiography*, 221–22; Miyoshi, pt. 16, 65–66.
[55] Nishimura interrogation.
[56] Jusuf Ronodipuro, interviews, February 17, March 27, 1968.

6

TRANSITION REPUBLIC:

THE PHILIPPINES

The Japanese faced in the Philippines a nation that already had a political and geographic identity, a flag, an anthem, and a constitution. They behaved as if these had not existed—behavior that grew increasingly grotesque and counterproductive as the war moved on. Early in the occupation, Japan's only clear-cut policy was extraction of resources,[1] but Allied advances and native resistance brought about the establishment of a Preparatory Commission for Philippine Independence in June 1943.[2]

The Third Philippine Constitution

The Philippines had developed its first constitution during the revolt against Spain, and its second one, under American tutelage, in 1935. Now, just eight years after a full-scale constitutional convention, Jose Laurel deployed a corps of experienced lawyers to revise it under Japanese advice and surveillance. "Much as we honor that flag," he told the Kalibapi, point to the Rising Sun at his back, "my people, you and I would like to see in this place our own Filipino flag . . . the Sun and the Stars."[3] A new organic document was one of the prices of independence.

[1] Takéuchi Tatsuji, "Manila diary," December 16, 23, 1942, in Theodore Friend, ed., *The Philippine Polity: A Japanese View*, Yale University Southeast Asia Studies, Monograph Series, no. 12 (New Haven, 1967), 212–13.

[2] *Official Gazette* 2, no. 6 (1943): 547; Takéuchi, "Manila Diary," 244–74.

[3] "One Nation, One Heart, One Republic," extemporaneous address at Special General Session, Kalibapi, September 7, 1943, JPL, 1c-11; regarding this speech: Nakamura Koji, twenty-page condensation of testimony before People's Court, October 2, 1947–January 20, 1948, JPL 1c-11; and Jose Lansang, interview, October 19, 1967.

CHAPTER SIX

Laurel had already tried to dispel suspicion of puppetry by stressing that the new constitution, "expressly made transitory in character" for the duration of the war, "contains everything that is essential to the protection of individual rights." He placated the Japanese and expressed a personal conviction by saying that its stress on "the duties and obligations of the citizens" corrected a deficiency in Western thinking since the French Revolution. He asserted a number of ways in which the new constitution escaped from report to or review by Americans (implicitly, any foreigners including the Japanese) and stood (theoretically) free from foreign interference.[4] The constitution created a unicameral Assembly, of which representatives of the Kalibapi became members. It provided for election of the president by the Assembly, allowed the Supreme Court to find laws unconstitutional only by unanimous vote, and gave the president broad emergency powers. Heel-dragging and draftsmen's cavils had irritated many Japanese, but the Philippines had moved toward the strong executive government that their invaders wanted. Laurel defended it to the ratifying session as a necessary center of political gravity in time of crisis.

The president-designate made plain that the new constitution contained a "transitory" provision enabling the Philippines to enter into agreements concerning natural resources during the war:

> To merit fair treatment from Japan ... we should lay our cards on the table; we cannot be insincere in our purpose [or] deceptive in our method. . . . It may be that some of [the people] believe that this war is being waged ultimately ... for the territorial aggrandizement ... of Japan. But we cannot ... tell her ... in beautiful speeches that we believe in co-prosperity, that we believe in the fundamental purpose of this war to liberate

---

For incidents involving the Philippine flag, see Malacanang (see chap. 4; note 80), 1943–45, 5.

[4] Manila *Tribune*, September 5, 1943, 2. Japanese testimony on the constitution includes Nakayama Kazuma, July 27, 1947, People's Court case 315, and Nakamura Koji, extracts of testimony in the case of Camilo Osias, pp. 15, 16, JPL. Official texts in Tagalog and English, *Official Gazette* 2 (1943), 9A. For Filipino cabinet recollections on the constitution, see "Reunion del Gabinete del Presidente Jose P. Laurel Celebrada el Dia Jueves, 27 de Diciembre de 1945, a las 4:30 PM," in Mauro Garcia, ed., *Documents on the Japanese Occupation of the Philippines* (Manila: Philippine Historical Association, 1965), 223–29. Takéuchi, who followed the drafting closely, concluded that Filipino leaders other than Laurel tried in the final draft "to raise a defense in their own behalf ... [and] try to show ... that they have done their level best to keep the extent of their collaboration to a minimum" ("Manila Diary," August 28, 1943, 271–73).

Asiatic peoples, and then . . . when Japan says: "Give us copper, give us iron, give us manganese," we shall not be able to give her any of these things because by our Constitution we have closed the door to them.

Turning to the question of peace and order, Laurel explained that this constitution made it possible for Filipinos "to administer our own affairs without the Japanese military police, without foreign garrisons, without the intervention of any foreign government (Applause) . . . [but] we cannot just tell the garrison, with bravado, 'Please, get out of here,' and then run the risk of our being overthrown." Because of guerrillas, saboteurs, and crop burners, Japanese garrisons must stay, "and if that is unreal independence, the Filipinos themselves have made it so." In a concluding statement far more extraordinary in its frankness than in its error, Laurel warned that it would be six more years before the Allies, finished the war with Japan and that Filipinos must determine what attitude to adopt for the duration of that war.[5]

The war would actually last only two more years, during which Sukarno continued to exhort his people to a life and death struggle in holy cooperation with Japan. Laurel, however, spoke so bluntly about ultimate Allied victory, that interpreter Hamamoto went to the office of an experienced lawyer-politician, Quintin Paredes, to express consternation. Paredes himself thought of the speech as almost a "declaration of war against Japan."[6]

INDEPENDENCE IN ALLIANCE WITH JAPAN

The constitution struck many Japanese as an extraordinary concession to the Filipinos. Indeed it turned out to be a Filipino position paper for bargaining with Tokyo over a pact of alliance, and therein trying to minimize the extent of Filipino participation in the war against the Allies.

Tōjō had already pressed the Filipinos in July 1943 for a declaration of war against the Allies, appealing to their honor with a pithy Japanese poem: "To see what is right and not to do it is a want of courage."[7] The point was lost in translation. Now in late September

---

[5] "One Nation, One Heart, One Republic," September 7, 1943, JPL.

[6] "Reunion del Gabinete . . . ," December 27, 1945, in Garcia, Documents, 228.

[7] This was Tōjō's second trip to Manila in two months. Teodoro A. Agoncillo, The Fateful Years: Japan's Adventure in the Philippines, 1941–1945 (Quezon City: R. P. Garcia, 1965), 1: 384–85, based on Wachi Takeji [sic], Nihon no himitsusen (The

he called Laurel, Aquino, and Vargas to Tokyo. There his remarks took the declaratory form appropriate to conveying decisions of an Imperial Liaison Conference: the "hopes of the Empire" were for a quick declaration of war, active involvement in it, and submission of the Philippine army and police to imperial Japanese commanders.[8]

The Filipinos were shocked at this price for independence. Laurel "silently prayed" before rising to say politely that he could not comply with the request. His people would not approve of it, and he was not sufficiently popular to carry them in such a policy against their will. Furthermore, "it would not be 'decent' for the Filipinos to declare war against the United States that was their benefactor and ally."[9]

Tōjō, taken aback, tried to convey sensitivity to ingratitude with another saying: "I have a mixed feeling of joy and sorrow as I walk in the morning frost for your sake." Again his point was lost in translation. Thereupon Tōjō called General Wachi and Ambassador Murata to another room and produced modest sums "necessary for the achievement": 500,000 pesos for Laurel, 300,000 for Vargas, 200,000 for Aquino. Laurel, as spokesman, declined the offer. Later, however, Laurel would give in to one of Wachi's repeated offers of financial assistance. He accepted for distribution among the members of the Preparatory Commission for Philippine Independence a sum of 10,000,000 pesos. Two of the twenty members declined. Roxas was one; Laurel himself was not one.[10]

---

secret war efforts of Japan) (Tokyo: Yomiuri Shimbunsha, 1956). Professor Agoncillo's copy of the document was eaten by white ants; General Wachi did not respond to my request for a copy; and a research assistant, checking newspapers of its alleged time of publication, was unable to locate it in print. Despite being unable to verify the text, I include Agoncillo's account here because of its likely congruities to the events and personalities involved.

[8] *Tōjō Naikakusoridaijin yori, Hito-Dokuritsu Junbi Iincho ikko ni taisuru shitatsu* (Premier Tōjō's instructions to the chairman of the Preparatory Commission for Philippine Independence and his party), September 29, 1943, Gaimushō 0:124–28.

[9] (Jose Lansang, ed.), *War Memoirs of Dr. Jose P. Laurel* (Manila: Laurel Memorial Foundation, 1962, 17.

[10] Agoncillo, *Fateful Years*, 1: 390–92, based on Wachi document, reports initial refusal of offer; author's interview with Wachi, September 25, 1958, establishes later acceptance of funds. The question of Laurel family benefits from Japanese financing arose during the 1949 election campaign. Emmanuel Pelaez charged that Laurel's family deposited in Japanese banks over one and a quarter million yen in mid-1945 ("300,000 prewar pesos," or prewar U.S.$150,000). Pelaez said that this represented spending public funds for personal benefit after dissolving the government-in-exile,

Using arguments similar to Laurel's among his Army Ministry and Foreign Ministry colleagues, Wachi meanwhile rejected an army draft treaty that mentioned "every possible cooperation in all matters"[11] because of its anticipated effect on Filipinos: "They will become raging guerrillas near the cities, making it impossible to win the hearts of the people. What we should do now is to have Laurel gain the sympathy of the people and make his government stable. Then when an occasion comes . . . we can have them enter the war."[12]

Waschi's effort to keep the phrase "successful prosecution of the Greater East Asia War" out of the preamble foundered when a council of the relevant ministries the next day, a group led by the army, insisted on including the phrase.[13] Murata did manage, however, to get attached to the treaty a "Terms of Understanding," which declared that the "principal modality" of close military cooperation would be that the Philippines would "afford all kinds of *facilities* for military action to be undertaken by Japan."[14] Tōjō later revealed, in defending the terms before the Privy Council, that Laurel had sought such limitation in the treaty proper. That being unacceptable to Japan, separate terms of understanding had been added "to

---

a wrong compounded by Laurel's later presenting a claim for 47,440 pesos in back pay as associate justice of the Philippine Supreme Court. ("The Truth About Laurel," *Daily Commoner* [Manila], November 2, 1949). The essential facts on the yen accounts are confirmed by "Deposit account balance of the members of the former Republic of Philippine [sic] on 5th November 1945" (Yokohama Specie Bank document, PC/DJ). Felino Neri (interview, June 28, 1968) said that he believed Laurel's peso funds (obtained from the Philippine National Bank in Baguio late at night) were spent on Philippine exile community needs and were fully accounted for, and that Pelaez's charges were politically motivated. But he could not explain why large sums remained in the Yokohama Specie Bank in November 1945. Agoncillo (*Burden of Proof*, 89) on the basis of a letter to him from Vargas in 1979, says that Laurel and his phantom cabinet tried to return three million pesos to the Japanese government after its surrender, but Japanese officials did not accept it.

[11] *Denpo utsushi Jikan ate Hito Gunseikan* (Copy of a telegram, chief of military administration, Philippines, to vice-minister [of war]), September 28, 1943, Gaimushō 0:186–91.

[12] *Nippi Domei Joyaku ni kansuru uchiawase no ken: Joyakuan kettei ni itaru keii* (Conference on the Japanese-Philippine Pact of Alliance: particulars concerning determination of the draft pact), October 1, 1943, Gaimushō 0:168–75.

[13] Ibid., penciled note following typed text.

[14] Ibid., Murata comments; *Nihon-koku Filipin-koku kan Domei Joyaku ni kansuru Nihon-koku oyobi Filipin-koku no zenkennin kan ryokaijiko* (Terms of understanding on the Japanese-Philippine Pact of Alliance agreed to by the plenipotentiaries of the two powers), n. d., Gaimushō 0:185 (see also earlier versions, 0:116–22, and final version, 0:741). Emphasis supplied.

make it easy for Laurel's administration" to persuade the public that there would be no draft of Filipinos to fight Americans.[15]

Minami Hiroshi, a councilor who had earlier inquired sharply into Tōjō's pact with Burma,[16] now expressed concern that the Philippine constitution would impede proper access to resources. Why not require detailed stipulations in favor of Japan, as in the Japanese-Burmese pact and the pact with Thailand over its (wartime) Malay and Shan regions? Tōjō professed to be disheartened at the question and explained defensively: "It is common sense in politics to put emphasis on winning the hearts of people, and acting in consideration of each nation's historical and economic characteristics. We have taken different attitudes for Thailand, Burma, and the Philippines, from the perspective of grasping each nation, when these [attitudes] could have been the same from the viewpoint of Japanese necessities."[17]

The accomplishments of Laurel's trip to Japan were clear: a treaty that did not take the form of an offensive alliance, as Burma's did, and no immediate declaration of war.[18] The costs were also clear: the ready availability of all major Philippine war resources, mineral and agricultural, to the Japanese—and in the course of time, Laurel felt, a declaration of war, perhaps after the first American air raid on Manila.[19]

A series of questions and answers prepared in the Foreign Ministry to help sell the treaty suggests the sensitivity of the Japanese government to the charge that too much had been conceded:

> Q. What is the *kokutai* . . . the form and organization of the Philippine government?
> A. Our country had left it to the Filipinos to decide their *kokutai* . . . and [they] decided upon a republican form of government. Although this might seem rather "Western" and

[15] *Nihon-koku Filipin-koku kan Domei Joyaku Sumitsuin Shinsa Iinkai Gijiroku* (Minutes of the Investigation Committee of the Privy Council on the Japanese-Philippine Pact of Alliance), October 20, 1943, Gaimushō, 0:567–88.

[16] Frank N. Trager, ed., *Burma: Japanese Military Administration, Selected Documents, 1941–1945* (Philadelphia: University of Pennsylvania Press, 1971), 151.

[17] Investigation Committee, Privy Council, October 20, 1943, Gaimushō, 0:567–88.

[18] Filipino cabinet recollections are consistent here with *War Memoirs . . . Laurel* and with Gaimushō documents: "Reunion del Gabinete . . . ," December 27, 1945, in Garcia, ed., *Documents*, 218–23.

[19] *War Memoirs . . . Laurel*, 17; Wachi, in Gaimushō 0:168–75; Hamamoto Masakatsu, interview, June 14, 1968.

disagreeable . . . it is not advisable for Japan to say . . . that a monarchy is better than a republican form of government. Especially for the Philippines, where they do not have a king or a leader [shidosha]. . . .

Q. What are the reasons for the Philippines not declaring war against the United States and Great Britain immediately after her independence?

A. . . . The animosity of the general populace in the Philippines against America is not yet quite heightened like that of the Burmese. . . . We are expecting the Philippines to enter the war at some appropriate time.[20]

At the inauguration of the Philippine Republic on October 14, 1943, there were bamboo arcades, woven palm fronds, Shintō lanterns, and, for the first time since the Japanese occupation, Philippine flags.[21] In contrast with the Commonwealth ceremony in 1935, key figures present included men like Ricarte and Ramos, symbols of military resistance to America, and General Emilio Aguinaldo, who raised the national flag. Laurel rose to the occasion with a strangely mixed message of heroism and austerity, forgiveness of opposition, and eugenic improvement of the race, implicitly through intermarriage with more advanced Asian peoples. He concluded with a reference to the rallying symbols of the nation—flag, constitution, anthem, and president, "the chosen leader of our people . . . the visible personification of the State."[22]

As president, Laurel moved promptly to effect "as a matter of logic, propriety, and justice" the release from Japanese army control of Philippine government properties. He granted "as a spontaneous act" the republic's permission to the Japanese army to assume operational control of those corporations and activities necessary for the prosecution of the war.[23]

[20] *Nihon-koku Filipin-koku kan Domei Joyaku teiketsu ni kansuru ken ni tomonau gimon gito* (Hypothetical questions and answers concerning the conclusion of the Japanese-Philippine Pact of Alliance), Gaimushō 0:672–712.

[21] Agoncillo, *Fateful Years*, 1:392–95; del Castillo and del Castillo, *The Saga of Jose P. Laurel*, 217–20.

[22] Jose P. Laurel, 'Proclamation of the Independence of the Philippines," October 14, 1943, JPL; *Official Gazette* 1 (1943): 66ff. Also: "Radio Broadcast by His Excellency, Jose P. Laurel . . . [to the United States], October 14, 1943," and "Greetings to the Filipino People by His Excellency General Hideki Tozyo [sic] . . . October 15, 1943," JPL; *Official Gazette* 1 (1943): 74–76.

[23] Quotation from Laurel to Utsunomiya, December 10, 1943; further correspondence, Laurel to Highest Commander, Imperial Japanese Forces, February 16, 1944, and Wachi to Laurel, February 24, 1944; Malacanang, 1943–45, 34, 053.3.

CHAPTER SIX

DECLARATION OF WAR AGAINST THE ALLIES

The day drew closer when Laurel would have to give in on a declaration of war. Murata told Aquino in April 1944 that Laurel was "already decided" on the matter. Marshal Terauchi in May, "while as usual abusing weak-spirited Filipinos," said the "military will do whatever war makes necessary, whether [the Filipinos] enter it or not." For the sake of general stability, however, he agreed that the Laurel government should not be prematurely pushed and hence isolated from the public.[24] In August, Murata began bringing high army and navy officers into the periodic meetings between Laurel and the officials of the Japanese embassy. On August 11, Laurel told Murata that "it is a natural course for me . . . to proclaim martial law and, in case of an American invasion, to stand as the Commander-in-Chief of the whole defensive organization." A more difficult alternative, discussed at a meeting on September 4, would be to convene an extraordinary session of the Assembly and try to get the two-thirds vote constitutionally necessary for a declaration of war. Murata discounted the assurance of Aquino, the Assembly Speaker, that this could be done. Laurel was against such a course. He preferred to impose martial law and then, in the suspension of other authority, issue the declaration of war.[25]

American planes bombed Manila on September 21. Wachi sent Hamamoto running, under bombardment, from the Manila Hotel to military headquarters for an agreement with Laurel that was locked in his safe.[26] Murata hurried to Malacanang. He agreed with Laurel that it was no longer possible to convene the Assembly; a "difference of opinion . . . would prevent us from getting the desired number of votes even under Speaker's orders, and this would result in the use of military force, which is the last thing desired by the Philippine government."

Therefore Laurel must follow his own plan to declare a "state of war." Murata confided to his diary that, while another man might have done the job of president up until now, henceforth only Laurel

[24] Fukushima Shintarō, ed., *Murata Shōzō: Iko hito-nikki* (Post-humous Philippine diaries) (Shinjuku: Hara-shobo, 1969), entries for April 24, May 18, 1944.

[25] Murata diary (see chap. 3, note 20), August 11, 25, September 4, 1944.

[26] Hamamoto, interview, June 14, 1968. Felino Neri, secretary of the cabinet in 1944, did not recall such an agreement but acknowledged that Hamamoto was in a position to know of one where he, Neri, was not (interview, June 28, 1968). The existence of such a document would be consistent with Wachi's view expressed in Gaimushō 0:168–75, and with the cards-played-close-to-the-vest atmosphere of Laurel's relations with Murata and Wachi.

was equal to it and "we owe our future to . . . our true President Laurel!"[27]

To broaden the legitimacy of the action as much as possible, Laurel now put the problem before his cabinet. They consented but stipulated, with Roxas particularly insistent, that the Philippine government should not raise an army. The cabinet sought further legitimacy by submitting the question to a joint meeting with the Council of State, only three members of which showed up. Long argument followed: Refuse the Japanese, flee to the mountains, or find a compromise? Armed resistance, given the array of Japanese forces, hardly merited real consideration.[28] Nor did suicide, which as Laurel observed was "against our religion."[29] Refusal and flight appeared to be essentially the same thing, except that flight would leave others to take Japanese reprisals.[30] No one seriously counseled either, and everyone—with varying degrees of willingness—eventually spoke for compromise.[31]

The compromise was not an impromptu response to Japanese pressure; Laurel had been pondering the problem for over a year, had some form of understanding agreeable to Wachi locked in Wachi's safe, and had sketched to Murata a solution upon which he had

[27] Murata diary, September 21, 1945. After the compliment to Laurel, the editor of the diary has made a deletion for diplomatic purposes. One may infer that other persons are criticized.

[28] Laurel, in his defense, prepared a memo that showed Japanese troops in the neighborhood of Malacanang to number 7,000; spies, Makapilis, and other Japanese auxiliaries brought the total to 10,000. Aggregate Japanese forces in Manila and its immediate vicinity numbered 100,000. Against this: "Defensive strength of the President: 300 Presidential Guards armed with ordinary rifles which are usually defective and with no more than 20 rounds of ammunition apiece" ("Partial Disposition of Japanese Forces in Manila at the Time of Declaration of War, September 1944, with Particular Emphasis on those Garrisons Surrounding Malacanan," n.d., JPL).

[29] War Memoirs . . . Laurel, 24.

[30] Those who later had to defend themselves against charges of treason stress in recollection the strength, frustration, and fury of the Japanese. Recto recalled everyone feeling that refusal would make the Japanese produce una sarracina (a Saracen slaughter). Yulo asked Yamashita's opinion of a declaration of war without conscription, and Laurel, according to Recto, described his face as that of a "drunken tiger." Roxas had told Laurel it would be folly not to compromise, for the Japanese "would work up something messy" ("Reunion del Gabinete . . . , December 24, 1945, in Garcia, ed., Documents, 215–16). Whatever Yamashita may have looked like, he had not arrived in the Philippines at the time under discussion; General Kuroda did not resign his command until September 26, 1944.

[31] Don Miguel Unson, memo in Spanish on meeting of cabinet and Council of State, 22 September 1944, translation in Philippine Press, July 15, 1945 (HC); "Reunion del Gabinete . . . ," December 24, 1945, 202–17; War Memoirs . . . Laurel, 23–25.

been determined at least six weeks before. Moreover, he had managed to bring into critical deliberations as many establishment figures as he could to share responsibility. Neither Wachi nor Murata had demanded conscription,[32] and General Yamashita, who might have, did not take command until October 6.[33] Yamashita had to content himself with volunteers like the Makapili, a small armed group organized under Benigno Ramos on Japanese initiative, and with the declaration of a "state of war," a legalistic formula to which Murata had agreed. Although some Japanese, particularly Mutō Akira after his arrival as Yamashita's chief of staff, supported Benigno Ramos's plan for a coup d'état, this was not a live alternative in the September crisis. Wachi and his vice–chief of staff, Utsunomiya Naotaka, talked him out of it.[34] The Japanese army was developing its own defense plans. The watered-down declaration did no critical injury to any realistic Japanese intention. Only the most aggressive of newly arrived officers perceived an insult.

For Wachi and Murata, Laurel's declaration of a "state of war" on September 26, 1944 was the acme of Filipino-Japanese political compromise, in which they already had two and a half years' experience. Laurel received congratulatory messages from Tokyo, including one from his old friend, Aoki Kazuo. The minister for Greater East Asia commended Laurel for his defiance of the "poisonous fangs" of "insolent America."[35]

EVACUATION AND DISSOLUTION OF THE REPUBLIC

In mid-December as the military situation deteriorated, Yamashita informed Murata that he wished government and army to evacuate

---

[32] Laurel called on the republic "to render every aid and assistance to the Imperial Japanese Government, short of conscription of Filipino manhood for active military service." In so doing he denied nothing asked by the Japanese, and stated limits the conquerors were themselves observing (radio address from Malacanang over PIAM, September 26, 1944, JPL).

[33] Information supplied by Historical Office, Defense Agency, Tokyo, July 11, 1967.

[34] On the Makapili (Kalipunang Makabayan ng mga Pilipino, or Patriotic League of Filipinos), see Agoncillo, *The Fateful Years*, 2: 831–34. General Wachi is the source for knowledge of discussions between a restless military faction and Ramos on the desirability of overthrowing Laurel's government and installing Ramos (author's interview, September 25, 1958).

[35] Proclamation no. 30, two drafts with revisions by Laurel and final copy, "Proclaiming the Existence of a State of War in the Philippines," PC/DJ; radio address by Laurel from Malacanang, 8:00 P.M., September 26, 1944; Aoki to Laurel, October 19, 1944, JPL; Vargas to Laurel, conveying messages from Koiso Kuniaki, Shigemitsu Mamoru et al., September 26, 1944, PC/DJ.

to the moutains of Luzon: "I have received the order of His Majesty to defend the Philippines and to protect President Laurel." If Laurel agreed, Manila would escape becoming an enemy target and Laurel might avoid the defection of some of his cabinet to the guerrillas.

After "deep thought," Murata approached Laurel. He said yes, "but what I am afraid of is to be criticized for leaving . . . Manilans under starvation and air bombardment while I move to a safer zone with the cabinet members." Murata suggested it would lighten their criticism to say the move would keep the city from being burned to the ground. This was quite true, Laurel thought, and furthermore, there would be no "dropouts" from his cabinet: "Even Yulo, who has a special relation with Quezon, has clearly stated he will follow my move." Murata commented that he was proud for Japan and the sphere to have his agreement.

Laurel still felt uneasy: "I regret that some of the people of my country criticize me by saying that my efforts are not enough, or that I play golf, judging me thus when I am struggling in adminstration." Murata comforted him by saying that great men are unappreciated while alive: "Praise and fame are decided after the lid of the coffin is closed." Apparently reassured, Laurel proceeded to ask if Murata would live in the president's residence in Baguio with him, where there was a golf course and they could play together. Murata afterward "rejoiced" with embassy colleagues at "how quite smoothly it went."[36]

The day before leaving for Baguio, Laurel wrote a defensive and revealing "letter to Yamashita"—a letter he thereafter carried with him against the day the Japanese might ask him to leave the country altogether or, possibly, an American or a Philippine tribunal might ask him to account for his actions. "The gospel I have preached, to which I adhere," Laurel wrote, . . . is that 'we die together or survive together.' . . . I do not want to be the first to violate that injunction by saving my own self and leaving my people in the lurch. . . . It would be cowardice, pure and simple, if I should quit the Philippines now that it has once again become a battleground." It would show lack of Oriental courage and set back "the renascence of the Oriental spirit."

Laurel then shifted from patriotic arguments to ones aimed more at Japanese logic. The Japanese had criticized Quezon for leaving the Philippines when the fall of Corregidor was imminent. "I do not want to be subjected to the same criticism." Nor did he, now that Osmena had returned to Leyte with American troops, wish to bow

[36] Murata diary, December 17, 1944.

to the Commonwealth government by fleeing, or to attempt the "empty gesture" of opposition in exile. He also rang in a legal note: complete American occupation of the Philippines would render the republic hors de combat and the pact of alliance with Japan inoperative. The letter closed with an emotional allusion: "I have done no wrong . . . and I feel no fear. There is a saying in the Bible that 'the wicked fleeth though no man pursueth, but the innocent are as brave as the lion.' . . . If I should die because of this, perhaps it would be better in atonement for the suffering of my people whom I have not been able to serve any better and whom I would be powerless to help any longer."[37]

Early in the morning of December 22, on three days' notice, the cabinet and the embassy began their evacuation to Baguio with their families. The silent Filipino farewells "with the eyes and the hands raised" touched Murata, and the unanimity of the cabinet relieved his anxiety that they would break ranks: "Had these VIP's been [left] in Manila . . . the result would have cracked apart the Laurel administration."

On the way, near Angeles, enemy planes forced them to leave their cars. Murata, taking shelter with the president and his family in a clump of bamboo, was reminded of an incident during the flight of the fourteenth-century Japanese emperor Godaigo, as recalled by his retainer Fujifusa.[38] Murata's thoughts while hiding there with Laurel borrowed some of their pathetic complexity from Fujifusa's poem:

> Emperor Godaigo:
> When I left Mount Kasagi
> I found no place to hide,
> No place under heaven:
> I stand in the rain
> And power is in the balance.
>
> Fujifusa:
> I though I found a hiding place

[37] Laurel to Supreme Commander, Imperial Japanese Forces in the Philippines, December 21, 1944, Confidential, JPL. In an interrogation at the Yokohama Interrogation Center, October 25, 1945, JPL, Laurel asserted that Yamashita in a meeting about November 1, 1944 made it obvious he would defend Manila if the Philippine government remained there; hence he agreed to move to Baguio. Testimony at Yamashita's trial, however, made clear that he never intended to defend Manila. Murata's diary indicates that the decision to move the government was not put finally to Laurel until December 17.

[38] Murata diary, December 22, 1944.

By coming under the pine tree,
But even here rain reaches me
Dripping from the pine;
My sleeves are getting wet.[39]

American planes striking Baguio killed "more Filipinos than Japanese, more civilians than military." Laurel's son Salvador wrote, "I do not understand why they did not confine their target to military objectives. . . . Those P-51 and P-52 pilots were like schoolboys out on a binge."[40] The Filipino cabinet and their families were surrounded by Kenpeitai, on the pretext of guarding them from harm but "primarily," the Filipinos thought, "to prevent any contact with the guerrillas." The Filipinos often talked in guarded whispers or inverted Tagalog syllables in a kind of pig-Latin understandable only to native speakers. Then the Kenpeitai, always suspicious, grew angry.[41]

In the gloom of daily American bombings, Murata and Laurel reviewed the war together and pondered the failure of the Japanese to win Filipino loyalty. Noting Yamashita's dismay at having to fight Filipinos in battle, Murata commented: "No one remembers that our forces are combating the U.S. not by using the Filipinos, but only by shedding the blood of our officers and men."[42] Laurel said he too lamented the situation,

but to speak frankly, Japan has failed to understand the psychology of the Filipinos. [They] have begun to hold the view,

[39] I am grateful to Ōshima Kazuko for locating Fujifusa's poem, and for translating it. The final phrasing, and hence any faults in English tone, are mine. Whatever comes across of the original Japanese flavor is owed to Miss Ōshima.

> Emperor Godaigo: sashite yuku
> kasagi no yama o ideshi yori
> amega shita ni wa
> kakurega mo nashi
> Fujifusa: ikani sen
> tanomu kage to te
> tachi yoreba
> nao sode nurasu
> matsu no shita tsuyu.

For General Imamura Hitoshi's reflections on the same fourteenth-century crisis, see chap. 9, note 62.

[40] Salvador Laurel's diary, "Odyssey to Nara—A Boy's Footnote to History" (MS copy in my possession, courtesy of the author), 3–7, quotation from p. 4.

[41] S. Laurel diary, 6.

[42] Murata diary, March 1, 1945.

having come into contact with many Japanese for the first time
. . . that they are a cruel race. They sympathize in [the Japanese]
ideal, but [there is] . . . antagonism especially over the stern tyranny of the Military Police. . . . The retaliation of U.S. forces
began to look to the public like the second coming of the Savior.

Those like myself, who know and understand Japan, regard
[the cruelty] as a war-time phenomenon, but why does Japan
not face the Filipinos with affection instead of power, as in Taiwan, administered by Governor-General Kodama? . . . The U.S.
is well aware of Filipino psychology from its past forty some
years of experience; it paid much attention to conciliating
them, and is trying more than in the past to give the Filipinos
what they want.

Thus, Laurel explained, the minds of his people had turned more
and more away from Japan, though he himself did not share their
disappointment: "The ideal of establishing the Greater East Asia
Sphere, once planted, will see the time of sprouting, and even if I be
the last one, as long as I am living I shall cooperate for its realization."

Murata conceded that some Japanese policies for Greater East
Asia had been imprudent, a regrettable consequence of military exigencies before the American onslaught. With no time to face other
than immediate problems, his own administration had been unable
to do as Kodama had done on Taiwan, and he felt especially defi-
cient in consideration of the public welfare.[43] Having criticized
himself to Laurel, Murata later recorded in his diary a more solacing
self-appraisal: "The failure in the Philippines involved mostly Kenpeitai in outlying stations, especially minor officials. As to the major policy, I have been unwavering."[44]

The question of further evacuation, to Japan, came up as early as
mid-February. Murata had been in touch with Tokyo about it, and
suggested to Laurel that there might be room for four or five men.
Laurel asked who. Murata named Roxas, Yulo, Paredes, and de las
Alas. Laurel nodded approvingly, then asked, "And what about
Aquino? He thinks that he is the most watched by the U.S. forces."
Murata did not demur,[45] but six weeks later he was still hoping to

[43] Ibid.; S. Laurel makes similar remarks on Greater East Asia in his diary, December 17, 1944.
[44] Murata diary, March 1, 1945.
[45] Ibid., February 15, 1945.

get the other four,[46] perhaps because men less overtly pro-Japanese would be able to give more credibility to a government in exile.

By March 1 Laurel let surface another question: "What is unbearable for me [in case of going to Japan] is the problem of families. Those who handle the nation, theoretically speaking, should not be involved in their personal emotions, but I cannot help sympathizing with the weak and the young. I feel very envious of such a man as Chandra Bose on this point."[47]

A few days later a policy statement arrived from Tokyo authorizing Murata to bring Laurel and others to Japan in case of extreme crisis, but ruling out the use of force or intimidation, should Laurel not wish to go.[48] Laurel was still distressed over the necessity of choosing who could and could not go, and worried about the fate of families left behind. Murata met these hesitations by assuring Laurel that the Japanese would try to protect those remaining, and by reminding him of the many Japanese who had left their families to give their lives for the Filipinos and for Greater East Asia. To a third concern of Laurel's, Murata replied sympathetically:

Laurel: When Quezon in the past abandoned the people and moved to the United States, I attacked him as "most ruthless and unfair and irresponsible to the people," both verbally and in writing. But a practical joke of fate is making me take the same step. How can I face the people?

Murata: We who mocked at MacArthur's withdrawal [to Australia] at that time, thinking that it would not happen to General Yamashita, now feel ashamed. Therefore it must be more hard on Your Excellency.[49]

Laurel gave no sign that he was reassured by Murata's replies, but on the night of March 18 he gathered his family and told them of a Supreme War Council "order" that he thought he "could not evade." "They might kill all of us—all Filipinos here in Baguio, if I refuse to go." The matter was put to family decision: they all wanted to go, rather than separate or be left behind, so the family

[46] S. Laurel diary, April 2, 1945.

[47] Murata diary, March 1, 1945; Laurel may not have been aware of Bose's Austrian common-law wife and their daughter. In any event, Bose had vowed never to marry until India was free, just as Hatta had vowed for Indonesia.

[48] Murata diary, March 14, 1945, quoting the fourth in a series of cables from Tokyo, dated March 6, replying to his fifth in the series.

[49] Murata diary, March 14, 1945.

party was Laurel, his wife, four sons, three daughters, a daughter-in-law, and two grandchildren.[50]

For other key leaders it was a matter of individual choice.[51] Aquino chose to go out of competitive political pride as the "next president" and perhaps also out of fear of American forces. Osias defended his decision to go against his strong-minded wife in two nights of wrangling heard by the bachelors upstairs. Roxas and Yulo, the ones Murata most wanted, had no desire to go, and were not coerced.

Hamamoto was included in the orders to go. He decided, however, to stay and help the rest of the Philippine cabinet obtain passes through the Japanese lines, to rejoin their families or seek security elsewhere. When he told Laurel, falsely, that his orders had been changed, Laurel exploded that he would need him more than ever, with Tōjō in Japan, and strode off to Murata's house to get Hamamoto "reincluded." But Hamamoto took a shortcut down the hill and forewarned Murata, who advised Laurel to leave Hamamoto behind to look after the VIPs. Aware now of the reason for his staying, Laurel gave Hamamoto "queer looks" and at a farewell meal quietly placed half his meager ration of fish on Hamamoto's plate, a gesture the latter found "very touching."[52] Hamamoto was not actually able to be of much help, but he and Fukushima Shintarō of the embassy tried to make sure, through Murata, that the army would not be a hindrance.[53] No Japanese deterred any of the cabinet from heading down the mountains and back to the capital.

The day before his departure Laurel saw Yamashita for the last time. They exchanged toasts and diplomatic courtesies.[54] Still carrying the "letter to Yamashita" written in December, and wanting someone to see it, Laurel next day handed a copy to Murata, who felt deeply Laurel's "kindness in enduring the unendurable . . . in

[50] S. Laurel diary, 9–10, referring to the evening of March 18; original document quotes Jose P. Laurel in Tagalog. See also Agoncillo, *Burden of Proof*, chap. 4, esp. 78, 86.

[51] The summary that follows is based on interviews with Utsunomiya, September 29, 1958; Hamamoto, October 1, 1958, June 14, 1968; Fukushima Shintarō, October 4, 1957; Felino Neri, June 28, 1968; Emilio Abello, June 1968; and Jose P. Laurel III, June 4, 1968; and also on the diaries of Ambassador Murata and Salvador Laurel. See also Agoncillo, *Fateful Years*, 2: 875ff., which relies principally on *War Memoirs of Dr. Jose P. Laurel*.

[52] Hamamoto, interview, June 14, 1968.

[53] Emilio Abello, interview, June 1968; Fukushima Shintarō, interview, September 19, 1958; Hamamato, interviews.

[54] Murata diary, March 20, 1945.

his [forthcoming] trip to Japan. It only shows my impropriety in having criticized him, though not too severely, concerning his family ties, and I am overcome with shame."[55]

On the night of March 21, the moon was behind a cloud; there were no banzais. To Murata the Filipinos seemed to use their eyes to say goodbye, except for "the President's wife [who] had her hands over her eyes all the time, crying."[56]

En route to the airfield at Taguegarao, a week's journey, the twelve cars of the Laurel and Murata parties stalled one by one, necessitating transfer to trucks. The villages along the way offered only primitive accommodations and no privacy; Murata noted in his diary the "problem of shit." He found himself unable to go one morning because village children kept following him everywhere. Food ran low—a greater specter for the Japanese, aliens to the native diet, than for the Filipinos, who improvised dishes of unripe fruit. All at last arrived at Taguegarao and, after a day punctuated by heavy American strafing, met in darkness to board navy and army bombers for Formosa.[57] Despite the moonlight it was hard to distinguish faces. Low voices repeated "sayonara" . . . "goodbye." Murata had only one regret as the plane took off: a staff officer's report that in baggage arrangements "it seemed as if we were treating the President and his group like deported prisoners. Most regrettable, indeed. No matter how weak and lean his power . . . we treat him like a sovereign of a nation, and it is against our will to give him the same strict luggage limitations as the others."[58]

After almost two and a half months on Formosa, the party reached Japan in mid-June. The foreign minister honored Laurel with a dinner and the emperor gave him an audience, which, Laurel's later prosecutors said, left him "highly overawed."[59] Aside from such ritual the Filipinos were left much to themselves at a hotel in Nara, safe from major air raids, while they awaited the end of war and their inevitable arrest afterward.

One day the Japanese national anthem was played three times on the radio followed by announcement of the emperor's surrender address. Ambassador Vargas came up from Tokyo to suggest that Lau-

[55] Ibid., March 21–22, 1945.
[56] Ibid., March 22, 1945.
[57] Ibid., March 21, 22–29, 1945; S. Laurel diary, March 21–29, 11–23.
[58] Murata diary, March 29, 406–7.
[59] People's Court trial, Prosecution Exhibit 92, JPL; Armando J. Malay, *Occupied Philippines: The Role of Jorge B. Vargas during the Japanese Occupation* (Manila: Filipiniana Book Guild, 1967), 134.

rel proclaim dissolution of the Philippine Republic. Laurel temporized, reluctant perhaps to let go the symbol of a vanished valor, hoping perhaps that even now the "republic" had some barter value for his country, his family, or himself. Vargas got back on the train to Tokyo but changed his mind in midjourney and returned to Nara to talk with Laurel again. This time Laurel gave in.[60] He issued a statement that in view of the "reoccupation" of the Philippines, the "reestablishment" of the Commonwealth government, and Japan's acceptance of the Potsdam Declaration, "the Republic of the Philippines has ceased to exist."[61]

The date was August 17, 1945. That same day Sukarno declared the birth of the Republic of Indonesia.

[60] Malay, *Occupied Philippines*, 134–35. Vargas's wartime role is defended by Malay and by Agoncillo (n. 61 below). But most Japanese had little respect for him. Criticisms of Vargas for personal scandals, suspicion of appropriating government property, and incompetence as ambassador were excised from Murata's published diary (an authoritative private source to the author, June 23, 1969). Even Vargas's loyal Japanese assistant revealed that he "played tennis half the day," and got entangled with a Miss Ono, "sort of a high-class mistress," planted by the Kenpeitai (statement of Nakayama Kazuma, March 28, 1947, PC/DJ).

[61] Laurel statement, August 17, 1945, "Biographical Data," 388, JPL. Subsequent charges of treason against Vargas, Laurel, and others are treated in social and historical context by David Joel Steinberg, *Philippine Collaboration in World War II* (Ann Arbor: University of Michigan Press, 1967): "Did the elite show sufficient respect for the intelligence and integrity of its own people?" (176). Teodoro A. Agoncillo in his latest book, *The Burden of Proof* (Mandaluyong: University of the Philippines Press, 1984), implicitly repudiates the Fil-American perspective of his earlier volumes, *The Fateful Years* (1965), and adopts a tone of bristling nationalism. He treats Vargas and Laurel as heroes, while attacking MacArthur for "cynical betrayal" and illegal detention of them (216), and castigating Manuel Roxas for "canine loyalty" to the United States (214). Such rhetoric aside, Agoncillo's argument that Laurel was absolved by his people through near-election as president in 1949 is a compelling one.

7

ENCOUNTERS IN
THE ASIAN FAMILY

Few Japanese actually attempted to live according to their own propaganda, as older brothers among younger. Those who did often met bafflement at their best intentions, or resentment because of the rude behavior of many Japanese soldiers and overseas civilians. Japan's Co-Prosperity Sphere found it hard to absorb the insular world of Southeast Asia into the Greater East Asia family. Japanese saw obedient faces, but heard conflicting voices, and felt resistant spirits.[1]

OLDER BROTHER, YOUNGER BROTHER

Before the war, Sjahrir noted, the whole Islamic population in Indonesia was "pro-Jap": whites and Chinese were considered *kasar* (crude and uncultivated), whereas the Japanese were *halus* (refined and elevated).[2] Such attitudes did not long survive the arrival of Japanese troops. As with any army, there were drunks and petty thieves. Soldiers who innocently wandered around off duty in undershirts, an ordinary act at home, looked boorish in Java. Time did not make the social behavior of the Japanese more ingratiating.[3]

[1] Early exploratory essays on this subject are Benedict R. O'G. Anderson, "Japan: 'The Light of Asia,' " in Josef Silverstein, ed., *Southeast Asia in World War II: Four Essays*, Yale University Southeast Asia Studies (New Haven, 1966), 13–50; and Victor Gosiengfiao, "The Japanese Occupation: 'The Cultural Campaign,' " *Philippine Studies* 14 (1966): 228–42.
[2] Soetan Sjahrir, *Out of Exile* (New York: John Day, 1949), 186–87.
[3] Taniguchi Goro in *Hiroku Daitoa Senshi: Ranin-hen* (A confidential history of the Greater East Asian War: Netherlands East Indies) ed., Tamura Yoshio (Tokyo: Fujishoen, 1953); Diary of Minarsih, March 10, 1942 (original, in diarist's possession, made available to the author in Jakarta).

Those with special hopes of the Japanese were destined to disillusionment. Subardjo, the nationalist lawyer, had worked as a journalist in Tokyo in the 1930s. There Japanese naval officers made much of the theory of partial racial descent of Japanese from proto-Indonesian peoples, and called him "elder brother." But in Java the Japanese began calling Subardjo "younger brother."[4] Diplomatic persiflage had given way to *libido dominandi*. Such behavior awoke a painful analogy to the Dutch, who had elevated certain Javanese to the rank of regent, and then officially styled Dutch assistant residents as their "Elder Brothers."[5]

The Japanese tendency toward familial and cultural subordination took peculiar forms regarding Eurasians, who were considered "half-breeds." One Dutch citizen with a Dutch father and a Japanese mother served as an interpreter for the Kenpeitai, only to find himself being paid at a chauffeur's rate and being addressed by his mother's maiden name, Yamaguchi. Adding to these slights the Japanese called his mother Yamaguchi too, which deeply disturbed the devout Christian woman, legally married to a Dutchman. They commandeered her house on half an hour's notice. She began to hear voices, and eventually starved herself to death.[6]

Filipinos, who had no general yearning for an Asian redeemer, tended to be suspicious of the Japanese from the start. Those genuinely immersed in things Japanese were very few. A wartime survey of seventy-nine leading Filipino officials showed that 75 percent had been to Japan; but most had simply passed through on their way to or from the United States as students twenty or thirty years before. Almost none could claim more than a superficial knowledge of the country,[7] although a group of business and cultural leaders did form a Philippine-Japan Society.

President Quezon conducted a complex prewar diplomacy that kept up assurances to the Japanese of a certain economic stake in the Philippines, while he strove to make the islands defensible against Japan by building up a native army.[8] Carlos Romulo's pre-

[4] Subardjo, interview, March 12, 1968.

[5] *Continuity and Change: Collected Journal Articles of Harry J. Benda*, Yale University Southeast Asia Studies (New Haven, 1972), 243.

[6] Interviews, G. K. de Heer (son), July 6, 1968, G. H. de Heer (father), May 1969. For analysis of use of *konketsu* and similar disparaging terms, see Barbara Gifford Shimer and Guy Hobbs, trans., *The Kenpeitai in Java and Sumatra*, Cornell Modern Indonesia Project, Translation Series, no. 65 (Ithaca, 1986), 23–24n.

[7] "In Re Trips to Japan of Government Officials," Malacanang (see chap. 4, note 80), 1942–43, 227, 980.11.

[8] Grant K. Goodman has made detailed studies of Philippine-Japanese relations in this period, e.g., "Japanese Pan-Asianism in the Philippines: The Hirippin Sai Ajia

war relations with the Japanese illustrate his own genius for maximizing the training and opportunities offered by America, while quietly exploiting any nationalistic, pan-Malay, or pan-Asian opportunity as well. His dispatches to the *Philippines Herald* from a journey through Southeast Asia in late 1941 won a Pulitzer Prize. In them Romulo reported feeling "like the man in the legend who traveled the wide earth in search of the golden egg only to find it in his garden." The Philippines would be "the great Brown Democracy of the future," and even the Indonesians would look to the Filipinos as "the logical leaders in the movement to liberate all the colored races in Asia."[9] Romulo commented on the vulnerability of the British in Singapore and the Dutch in the Indies to surprise attack, and observed that the Japanese in Indochina were already forcing the occupied to buy protection in a manner that tied them economically to Japan.[10]

The Fil-American liberal in dread of Japan, however, had another side. The Japanese consulate in Rangoon secretly reported to Tokyo a tea party of influential Burmese, from which Romulo had asked that Europeans be excluded.

Accordingly, the former Minister of Trade and Industry . . . gave a tea party . . . with Romulo as guest of honor. Speaking cheerfully and frankly he emphasized the creation of an Asia for Asians and his opposition to white men, and he insisted there must be something like an Asian federation. . . . "The fact of Japan's presence in the Far East is of the greatest significance to all the people of the Far East. If it were not for Japan, we would have been destroyed by the white men. Even to me, the present Japanese assault on China is unpleasant, but to envision omitting Japan from a federation of Far Eastern countries is not only impossible, but Japan properly should be its leader."[11]

Kyokai," *Studies on Asia* (1966); "The Philippine Society of Japan," *Monumenta Nipponica* 22, nos. 1, 2 (1967); "Philippine-Japanese Professional Exchanges in the 1930's," *Journal of Southeast Asian History* (September 1968); "Pio Duran and Philippine Japanophilism," *The Historian* 32, no. 2 (1970). For Quezon's strategy, see Theodore Friend, *Between Two Empires: The Ordeal of the Philippines* (New Haven: Yale University Press, 1965), 169–83.

[9] *Philippines Herald*, November 11, 1941.

[10] Ibid., October 1, 7, 8, 10, 11, 17, 20, 29, 30 and November 11, 1941.

[11] Cons. Gen. Isono to For. Min. Tōjō, November 4, 1941, Gaimushō File A.3,5; 0.2–30. I am grateful to Grant Goodman, who discovered this document, translated it, and made it available to me. The interpretation of its contents is my own.

Romulo's public warnings about Japan became realities in a matter of weeks. He left in exile with Quezon, and during the war years in the United States he wrote *Mother America* and *My Brother Americans*. His secret wishes for an Asian federation led by Japan also came true, with stern impact on the Philippines.

"The true aim of our forces," General Homma broadcast to the Filipinos on December 30, 1941, "is to drive out the evil influences and power of the United States of America, which has persisted in availing itself of each and every opportunity to obstruct the natural development and healthy growth of nations in East Asia." Homma promised Japanese assistance to all who shared the ideals of Asia for the Asians, and the Philippines for Filipinos. He gave assurances that "we shall also fully respect culture and traditions."[12] After the surrender of Fil-American forces, however, Murata Shōzō averred in June that the Filipinos "have no culture of their own. How could a people, culturally bankrupt, be independent spiritually?"[13] And General Wachi, at a dinner in Malacanang for provincial governors and mayors in August 1942, lectured his audience: "You are orientals and you should have the soul and spirit of orientals. . . . You may pattern your education according to the standards of the West; you may dress yourselves and live as Westerners do, and learn and practice their habits; still all these things cannot change you Filipinos from being orientals. . . . We are here to collaborate with you in building up a real new Philippines."[14] Experience in the Philippines later modified Wachi's conviction that the Filipinos shared with the Japanese a fundamental Oriental nature. Few Japanese of the occupation, however, grasped that the supposedly Oriental soul and spirit of Filipinos were actually, like their education, dress, and habits, a distinctive Malayo-Western blend. Among urban Filipinos especially, Hispanic restraints worked in tension with American liberties, in feeling tones affected by a bilaterally extended family system.

An even more fundamental misconception misled many Japanese. "Asia is one," Okakura Tenshin had declared at the time of the Russo-Japanese war. In some geopolitical sense he may have

---

[12] CincC Imperial Japanese Army and Naval Expeditionary Forces to Quezon, December 30, 1941, Malacanang, 144, 600.

[13] *Japan Times and Advertiser*, June 5, 1942, quoted in *Foreign Relations of the United States* 1 (1942): 788 (Washington, D.C.: Government Printing Office).

[14] Notes on speech, August 15, 1942, reconstructed from memory by Dr. de Jesus and Mr. Reyes, Malacanang, 227, 970–72. For a similar statement by Tōjō, see Malacanang, 1, 004 to 007:01.

been right, and certainly he was effective in articulating in cultural terms a Japanese sense of destiny that implied a mission to save Asia from the West.[15] But in Greater East Asia, as in Europe, there were ample differences of language, religion, and history to have contributed to centuries of regional warfare. The Japanese political logic of "Orientalism," was perhaps not as pernicious and vicious as Hitler's "Aryanism." But even while proclaiming Oriental solidarity, they were behaving as if separate and superior. The gains the Japanese might have made among those who were fed up with Western pomposity, they tended to vitiate by their own arrogance.[16]

The essential symbolic expression of Japanese superiority to Malays was the required *saikeirei*, or deep bow in the direction of the imperial palace. Instructions for a public meeting in Manila were similar for gatherings throughout the conquered territories. Every participant had to carry a Japanese flag and each group of participants had its own placard in Japanese characters. When assembled, all stood at attention, heads bare, through the playing of the Japanese national anthem and a minute of silent prayer for the war dead. There followed precise commands for the *keirei*, a bow twenty to thirty degrees from the waist in salute to the commander in chief of the Imperial Japanese Forces, and for the saikeirei ninety degrees from the waist toward the northeast in homage to the emperor.[17]

However irritating to the political and religious sensitivities of the Filipinos, the saikeirei was more offensive still to the Muslims of Java and Sumatra. They saw a resemblance to the prayer bow performed by Muslims, and thus an implied transcendency of state Shintō over Islam.[18] One of Hatta's first acts as general adviser to the military administration was to urge the Japanese to drop this requirement as an affront to Islam. To his distress Muslim officials of the MIAI (Great Islamic Council of Indonesia) subsequently

---

[15] Okakura Kakuzo, *The Awakening of Japan* (New York: Century, 1904).

[16] On these matters, Christopher Thorne's essay is rich in citation and well-rounded in perspective: "Racial Aspects of the Far Eastern War of 1941–1945," Raleigh Lecture on History, 1980; Proceedings of the British Academy, 66 (London: Oxford University Press, 1982). See also John W. Dower, *War Without Mercy: Race and Power in the Pacific War* (New York: Pantheon Books, 1986), chap. 10.

[17] Program of Celebration . . . [February 8, 1943, in honor of Tōjō statement reaffirming the intention of granting independence to the Philippines], Malacanang, 1, 004 to 007:01.

[18] Author's interview, Mohammad Natsir, December 2, 1983; Harry J. Benda, *The Crescent and the Rising Sun* (The Hague: W. van Hoeve, 1958), 126. For excellent background, see Deliar Noer, *The Modernist Muslim Movement in Indonesia* (Kuala Lumpur: Oxford University Press, 1973).

agreed that the keirei could and should be rendered as an act of politeness.[19] Hatta did not press the issue thereafter, though some Islamic leaders continued to object. Finally, in late 1943, when Dr. Hoesein Djajadiningrat was appointed by the Japanese as head of the Religious Affairs Office, he announced that, in recognition of the possible slight to Islam, the keirei and saikeirei would no longer be required in meetings of Muslim believers.[20]

While Indonesian sensitivities were not always respected, a slight to the Japanese was dealt with swiftly. The Jakarta daily *Pemandangan* marked the fall of the Dutch by filling its front page with a picture of the emperor and a large red circle—the picture in the lower right-hand column, the circle in the center. This was lese majesty: nothing should be above or overshadow the emperor. The editor, Sumanang, not only did not know about this regulation but had been away at the time the issue appeared. He was slapped in the face by the Kenpeitai and jailed until a good-hearted Japanese official arranged his release two weeks later.[21]

Indonesians and Filipinos might have tolerated simple regimentation, even endured some insult and abuse. But face slapping as punishment deeply wounded Javanese pride (the head is noble) and Filipino dignity (man was created by God in his own image). Few Filipinos, even if willing to use their authority with courage, could convince the Japanese of their error. Paulino Gullas, commissioner for the Visayas, who had taught Japanese political history and represented Japanese as an attorney, wrote a long paper entitled "The Delicate Japanese-Filipino Problem."[22] After detailing what the Filipinos should do to cooperate with Japan, Gullas, "as an admirer," offered the Japanese some advice beginning: "For heaven's sake stop this slapping business, once [and] for all. You just cannot understand, cannot fathom the depth of the resentment it causes, the amount of pain it gives to the victim." But his voice had little effect.

In Ambassador Murata's view the key problem was not lack of understanding or kindness, but failure to communicate clearly. Complaining to Laurel that the Filipinos always failed to provide Japanese-speaking interpreters, Murata implied that they would get

[19] Hatta, interviews, February–March 1968; George S. Kanahele, "The Japanese Occupation of Indonesia: Prelude to Independence" (Ph.D. diss., Cornell University, 1967), 766–67, n. 16, based on interview with Hatta, August 26, 1964.

[20] Benda, *Crescent and the Rising Sun*, 126.

[21] Sumanang, interview, March 4, 1968.

[22] Malacanang, 1943–45, 158, 980.1 (probably July 1944); another copy is located in the National Library, Roxas Collection, Bundle 17.

more of what they wanted if they would work more in the medium of Japanese. The ambassador also expressed surprise that "the Filipinos were not more outspoken in making demands as a younger brother does of an older brother."[23] Who would tell Murata that most Filipinos felt neither love, nor brotherhood, nor more than the faintest ethnic fraternity with the Japanese; and that extremely few felt a parallelism, let alone a solidarity, of interests?

In Java, a short-term congruence of political interests helped to encourage cultural adaptation between occupier and occupied, but not without silent contests and head-on disagreements. At a council of Indonesian leaders Lieutenant General Matsuura, the chief medical officer on Java, tried to lay blame for the food shortage on the Muslim taboo on eating pork. He called the custom unrealistic, and insisted that pork was very nourishing and production could easily be increased. The ensuing uproar from every member of the council was, a Japanese observer admitted, "no laughing matter."[24]

Many of the silent victories went to those Javanese who learned to put Japanese prejudices to work in their favor. A prominent physician working beside a Japanese doctor in producing 100 percent alcohol noticed that the latter was getting only 70 percent because of an improper procedure. Also noticing that the Japanese had a better instrument made in the United States, the Javanese suggested that the discrepancy in their results might be due to the "obviously defective" apparatus, which he thereupon accepted as sufficient for his own lesser work.[25]

Such cultural judo could, in larger matters, assume heroic proportions—as in a rebuff of the chief of military administration of the Fourteenth Army.[26] Planning a tour of all Java, the general sent out an advance party that in Yogyakarta asked the sultan for an appropriate welcome: a feast for five hundred and the famous court dances of which they had heard (and that they may have been imagining in Japanese geisha terms). The sultan replied that he would be happy to provide a banquet but the dances could not be performed. During *puasa*, the month of fasting in which the general's visit

[23] Fukushima Shintarō, ed., *Murata Shōzō: Iko hito-nikki* (Post-humous Philippine diaries) (Shinjuku: Hara-shobo, 1969), July 21, 1944.

[24] Miyoshi Shunkichirō, "Jawa senryō gunsei kaikoroku" (Memoirs of the military administration of Java), *Kokusai Mondai* (April 1965–January 1967), pt. 8, 68–69.

[25] Slamet Imam Santoso, interview, March 9, 1968.

[26] The account that follows is based on B.P.H. Poeroebojo, interview, March 25, 1968; interviews with keraton officials, March 26, 1968; and Pangéran Poeroebojo to the author, April 18, 1968.

would fall, the tradition of the Yogya *keraton* (palace) forbade it. The deputation turned away, perhaps doubting the sultan's rationale or thinking it a pretext. Days later, five angry members of the Kenpeitai came banging on the door to ask why the sultan had refused to present the dances, when the *mangkunegoro* of Solo was willing to do so. Referring again to the traditional prohibition, the sultan explained apologetically, "If this were tradition simply and solely, and not a religious injunction, I would be ready to put aside the tradition; but because it is included in the religious prohibitions of Islam, I can only receive the Gunseikan with a banquet." Perhaps, the sultan suggested, the Japanese government would like to submit the matter to the Islamic scholars and leaders who lived in Jakarta—but the keraton heard no more of the matter.

An incident of similar character occurred in Yogya when the commander in chief, on an inspection tour, asked to be received at the keraton just as the Dutch governors general used to be.[27] The style of dress for such occasions in Dutch times had been formal-military, and so in adaptation to Japanese conventions the keraton officials dressed all in black as a sign of respect. Sincerely impressed, the commander in chief sent his officers to pay a visit to the mausoleum of the sultanate, southward of Imogiri, the royal burial place for more than three centuries. At the mausoleum the officers took off their boots respectfully—as was the custom both there and in their own ancestral shrines—but when the senior officer present wanted to proceed to the hall where Sri Sultan Agung, founder of the line, was buried, his keraton guide told him that foreigners were forbidden. The Japanese protested that they were not foreigners but elder brothers. The discussion went on for some time. The keraton official finally persuaded the delegation that the rules were absolute, that the sultan did not even permit other high-ranking rajas to enter there. High tradition involved lines that the invader could not cross; and "elder brother" was made to feel where brotherhood ended and brashness began.

The Yogyans in wartime, perhaps beyond other Indonesians, stood fast on their traditions. They intensified their wearing of traditional Javanese dress, including daggers. Some Japanese may have interpreted this as anti-Westernism or Asian solidarity, but to Yogyans it proclaimed their own identity—resolute and resourceful, meeting power with countervailing dignity. They had no answer to

[27] The account that follows is based on K.R.T. Notojudo, interview, March 26, 1968; and Notojudo to the author, April 18, 1968.

Japanese guns, but they were conscious of their place and its meaning, of what was dear and must be defended.

INTERPRETING: HAMAMOTO AND SHIMIZU

Of the Japanese cultural mediators in the Philippines, the most extraordinary was Hamamoto Masakatsu. A Harvard graduate (1928), Hamamoto spoke in a popular American idiom, having learned to move easily in that society by impressing his friendliness, rather than his intelligence, on strangers. Those who heard him interpreting for Yamashita at the war crimes trial in 1945 thought he was white American until they looked, and then nisei, until they were corrected. Beneath this protective linguistic and cultural coloration, Hamamoto was proudly and emphatically Japanese.[28]

War brought his abrupt transition from General Motors executive in Japan to private in the Philippines, a draftee with a distinctly civilian mentality and a reluctance to conform to military patterns. Sent early in 1942 to work in a camp for Filipino prisoners of war, Hamamoto soon acquired—by virtue of his experience and the lack of other Japanese fluent in English—the powers of a commandant. When Tōjō first visited Manila in May 1943, the military administration obtained Hamamoto as interpreter. Expecting a formal introduction, Tōjō asked, "Don't you have a card?" Hamamoto answered, "I used to, of course, but how do you expect me to in circumstances like this?" Perhaps Tōjō enjoyed having someone talk back to him, for Hamamoto found himself thereafter attached to the premier's office and, on a later trip through Southeast Asia, the bearer of the imperial sword to Field Marshal Terauchi.

With the inauguration of the Philippine Republic, Laurel obtained the appointment of Hamamoto as his interpreter.[29] As Laurel's adviser and sounding board, Hamamoto attended high-level meetings and was generally trusted, though sometimes Filipino leaders would switch to Spanish on subjects not intended for Japanese ears. Often, one official recalls, Laurel would "blow his top" in Hamamoto's presence, and Malacanang would worry about it getting back to the Japanese General Staff or Kenpeitai. But Hamamoto apparently kept these explosions to himself, or passed them on

[28] The information on Hamamoto that ensues is from interviews with him October 1, 1958 and June 4, 1968, and from impressions obtained from a variety of people who knew him in the Philippines.

[29] For correspondence on Hamamoto's appointment, see Malacanang, 1943–45, 64, 101, General Adviser.

where they might bring thoughtful responses rather than repressive reaction. In the spring of 1945, when several Filipino leaders including Claro Recto were planning to steal away from Baguio through Japanese lines into the lowlands, Hamamoto chanced by that very morning. Noticing their anguish, he promised not to reveal their plans. They made away safely.[30]

Hamamoto communicated with Laurel through the American culture and language they shared as businessman from Harvard, lawyer from Yale. At a deeper level, their communication was of compatible personalities—highly educated but direct in speech, pragmatic in action. If both employed egalitarian tactics suitable to the popular medium of politics, both were also animated by hierarchical values and pride of heritage. Although their traditions were separate and conflicting, Laurel was capable of subordination to Japan to preserve the substance of his nation, and Hamamoto was capable of subordination to Laurel in accord with his function and in the interests of both countries.

The chief interpreter of Japanese culture to Indonesia—not by qualification or appointment, but by exuberance and ubiquitousness—was Shimizu Hitoshi, son of a farmer. As with Hamamoto and Laurel, there was between Shimizu and Sukarno an emotional fit and congruence of egos, intensified by the presence of war. They each also had an appetite for sloganeering and speechifying. Despite their relative powerlessness during the war, Sukarno and Shimizu shared a political language in the making and the excitement of a nation emerging.

Shimizu was a division chief in the Propaganda Department during most of the occupation, then chief of propaganda for the Jawa Hōkōkai from May to June 1945; after that, he was theoretically attached to the news and press agency of the Sixteenth Army.[31] In fact, Shimizu was dismissed from his post in June 1945 and, after wandering around Java for a while, was shipped off to Singapore by the Japanese authorities. A friend flew him back to Java without permission. The Kenpeitai considered him dangerous because of "idling and living with Javanese," and locked him in jail just before the surrender. He escaped, was caught, underwent internment in a Japanese camp to await arrival of the British, escaped again, and was eventually recaptured. Throughout this period, Shimizu aroused exaggerated apprehensions among the British and the Dutch about the

[30] Emilio Abello, interview, July 1, 1968.
[31] RVO 059308.

— 148 —

"Black Fans," apparently a last-ditch Indo-Japanese organization dedicated to Asian solidarity and modeled after Japanese secret societies.[32] Major General Nishimura Otoshi thought Shimizu "a most insolent official, who disobeyed orders, gave himself enormous airs, and was not to be trusted with any secrets. He was most unpopular with his fellow officials, who regarded him as mentally unsound, though at the time a clever man. He would talk about being on a special assignment from General Itagaki, and scorn his fellows."[33]

Another influential Japanese officer described Shimizu as "half-genius, half-crazy."[34] British officials investigating his role in the occupation found contempt and dislike for him among Japanese, and emotional exaggeration of his own importance in Indonesian affairs.[35] At war's end Shimizu was declared insane by both British and Japanese psychiatrists. The diagnosis reflects their own limitations of culture at least as much as Shimizu's eccentricity.

Propagandists in other countries of the Southern Area generally confined themselves to iterating the lines sent out from Tokyo and passing out exaggerated statistics on Japanese "victories." Shimizu was as capable of embellishment as any, but Indonesians were usually willing to concede a grotesque sincerity in him. He had come up through the public schools, with strong "Japanese" characteristics of reverence for ancestors and nearly religious faith in the emperor. His idealism and expansionism had already expressed themselves in three years of military service in China.[36] Five days after landing in Indonesia in March 1942, Shimizu made a speech in which he exhorted Indonesians and Japanese to *samasama tidur, samasama makan*—"sleep together, eat together"—translating literally a common Japanese expression that conveys the idea of intimate fraternal community. Indonesians laughingly replied, eat together, yes—sleep together, no. The idea struck them as ludicrous, but he had won goodwill for trying the language as well as for his willingness to adopt native dress.

Shimizu quickly became voluble in Indonesian, though often inaccurate. Of his speeches, Indonesians remember the intensity of

---

[32] Various files, RVO.

[33] Maj. Gen. Nishimura Otoshi, interrogation, RVO 059337.

[34] Saito Shizuo interrogation, RVO 005842.

[35] Opinion attached to interrogation of Maeda Tadashi, RVO 006894.

[36] Facts on Shimizu's career and beliefs, and direct quotations from him, come from interviews of June 4, 5, 1968. Other material comes from a variety of sources, or represents my own interpretive comment.

emotion and the gesticulation of his stubby arms. Though Sukarno jokingly complained that he could not understand the man's Indonesian, Shimizu became Sukarno's interpreter. He served as go-between to General Imamura when Sukarno wished to endear himself to the commander in chief by having an Indonesian artist paint his portrait. None would trust him for policy advice, but when other Japanese were blocked from usefulness by cultural blindness or linguistic impotence, Shimizu was there ready to hurl himself into the breach. To Japanese he lacked decorum, and to Indonesians he lacked finesse. Yet he would with gusto reduce a situation to its lowest common denominator, and get the talk begun.

Convinced by his experience in China that the Japanese had made only superficial efforts to understand Chinese cultural imperatives and had not behaved as if they felt the *giri* (obligation) that filled their own propaganda, Shimizu resolved in Indonesia to exemplify oneness of understanding and behavior.

> I thought by escaping my Japanese "color" and becoming one with Indonesia, I could understand them. I wore the *pici* and *sarong* from the very first day. I spoke poor Indonesian but delivered speeches in it, feeling almost completely Indonesian. At that time I thought only blindly of giving independence. . . . You must love and become *part* of their people. I would have done the same in England or America. This is not anarchism, but a cosmopolitan idea. There is no deception in it. No "obligation" will make it work. I decided to throw myself into it, not just ideology but practice, not just in logic but in reality.

Even so Shimizu retained certain stereotypical ideas of Indonesians. All southern peoples were "wild, brutal, passionate." That made it easy for them to understand the Japanese idea of *jibaku* (self-sacrifice for a cause) and to develop kamikaze corps carrying bamboo spears to repel the Allies. Yet this Indonesian emotionalism could also destroy a negotiation: they would talk reasonably with the Japanese to a certain point and then confront them unreasonably and furiously, "at an acute angle."

Working through Pusat Kebudayaan, the major institution focusing on cultural cooperation, Shimizu was frustrated by the Indonesians' tendency to see everything—even flower arranging—in political terms. Here was the crux of the matter. For Japanese, there would be no culture without victory, because "culture" was Japanese, to be given to Indonesians who lacked one. For Indonesians, there could be no culture without independence, because "culture" meant their own, blooming at last without foreign interference, whether European or Asian. Years after the war, Shimizu, a frequent visitor to the new Indonesia, would come close to seeing the problem. "Guiding culture," he concluded at last, "was the grave mistake made by Japan."[37]

REINTERPRETING:
CHAIRIL ANWAR AND S. P. LOPEZ

To be conquered involves a question of voice. To be reconquered raises the question anew. To be young raises the question constantly. Chairil Anwar was born to a culture whose voice had long been stifled by the Dutch. When he was nineteen years old, the Japanese invaded and imposed their own vision of authority. Within a year the young poet had begun an explosion of creativity that signified the emergence of a new Indonesian culture.[38]

First Anwar rejected the alien Dutch language, tongue of the educated classes, of access to prewar power and status, and of assimilation into international culture. He also abjured the writers of the prewar Pudjangga Baru group. They had made the effort, brave for those days, of writing in Indonesian, but with such timidity of form and such affectations of style that their value was in "pointing the path not to be taken."[39] Anwar, after early trials of their path, now dismissed such writing as "warm chicken shit."[40] The real writer, he declared to Ida Nasution, a poet herself, hears "an immense roaring voice [that] whistles and shouts in his ear 'Stop! Stop! Hey, Destroyer, Peace-Breaker!' But I've got guts enough to barge right into the house of holiness, right into the parlor itself! I'm not stopping outside in the yard."[41]

---

[37] Quotations from Shimizu, interviews, June 4, 5, 1968.

[38] Burton Raffel, *The Development of Modern Indonesian Poetry* (Albany: State University of New York Press, 1967), 83. See also H. B. Jassin, *Kesusasteraan Indonesia Dimasa Djepang* (Indonesian literature during the Japanese period), 2d ed. (Jakarta, 1954), Anthony H. Johns, "Genesis of a Modern Literature," in Ruth McVey et al., *Indonesia*, Yale University Southeast Asia Studies (New Haven, 1963), 410–37; Boen S. Oemarjati, *Chairil Anwar: The Poet and His Language* (The Hague: Martinus Nijhoff, 1972); Liaw Yock Fang, ed. and trans., *The Complete Poems of Chairil Anwar* (Singapore: University Education Press, 1974); and Dra. Sri Sutjiatiningsih, *Tokoh Nasional: Chairil Anwar* (Chairil Anwar as national figure) (Jakarta: Departemen Pendidikan dan Kebudayaan, 1979).

[39] James S. Holmes, introduction to Chairil Anwar, *Selected Poems*, trans. Burton Raffel and Nurdin Salam (New York: New Directions, 1962).

[40] Quoted in Raffel, *Modern Indonesian Poetry*, 90.

[41] Ibid., 22; also in Burton Raffel, ed. and trans., *The Complete Poetry and Prose of Chairil Anwar* (Albany: State University of New York Press, 1970), 167.

For Anwar the cultural problem was both imperial masters from abroad, and traditionalists within. He would not necessarily admire those who had denied the Japanese entrance to the tomb of Sri Sultan Agung, for his style was cultural attack, not defense of inherited harmonies. Anwar wanted to see beyond decorative authority and naked power into the very organism of culture, into the heart of truth. "We don't want to take just ordinary pictures," he wrote Ida Nasution, "but x-rays right down to the white of the bones. . . . No one's going to make us play at being life's musical instruments, not any more they're not. We play life's own songs, so we have to be honest, blunt. Because we've got courage and awareness and confidence and the skill too."[42]

Anwar's courage was not physical. Arrested and tortured by the Kenpeitai for some names and addresses, he soon gave in—"it hurt too much."[43] The information apparently was not critical, and the incident did not disgrace him. But Anwar did not shrink from such acts of courage as repudiating the Japanese Cultural Center and ridiculing it for "the development of a strictly Greater Asian 'art'— Castor Oil—cotton—increasing farm yields—Indonesians driven to Japan as coolies—put your pennies in the piggy bank—shipbuilding and all the rest."[44]

Though militant poetry that spoke of common Asian causes was encouraged by the Japanese, few of Anwar's poems were published during the war. The bulk became known through typed copies circulated among friends.[45] His "Siap-Sedia" ("To Arms"), however, did slip through into print. His nationalism and his call to his contemporaries are clear, but a sleepy Japanese censor could have taken the reference in the fifth stanza to the "shining sun" as positive, and let it pass.[46]

---

[42] Raffel, *Modern Indonesian Poetry*, 223–24; also in Raffel, *Poetry of Chairil Anwar*, 169–70.

[43] Raffel, *Poetry of Chairil Anwar*, xv.

[44] Raffel, *Modern Indonesian Poetry*, 228; also in Raffel, *Poetry of Chairil Anwar*, 175.

[45] Raffel, *Modern Indonesian Poetry*, 85. Holmes, on p. 13 of his introduction to the New Directions edition of Anwar, errs in saying that none of his poems were published during the occupation.

[46] Having come upon the shorter version appearing in *Keboedajaan Timoer* (see note 49 below), I originally based my translation on that. I am grateful to Burton Raffel who first provided me a copy of the longer Indonesian version. My translation takes liberties with the syntax and vocabulary of the original in order to try to render tone, mood, and rhythm.

ENCOUNTERS IN THE ASIAN FAMILY

To Arms

To My Generation

Later your hand will stiffen
Later your heart stop beating
Later your bones turn to stone
But now we are gathering others
Carving a pillar to victory.

Later your eyes will be glass
Later your mouth done speaking
Later your blood stopped flowing
But now we are gathering others
Bearing victory toward the people.

Later your voice will be stifled
Later your name blown to ash
Later your steps will falter
But now we are gathering others
Surging forward to triumph.

Our blood is on the boil
Our bodies daggers of steel
Our spirit forbids us to kneel
We will color the sky
We are painters of destiny.

Friends, friends,
Feel the skimming fresh wind
Sweeping away the clouds,
The shining sun stabs through
Spraying all points of the compass
Spilling bright on paddy and jungle.

Everything's flaming!
Everything's flaming!

Friends, friends
We rise up in awareness
Stinging, cleansing to toughness
Friends, friends
We swing a sword at the bright world.

Publication of the poem early in 1944 "brought the Japanese down on the editors of the magazine," for some of them interpreted "bright world" (*dunia terang*) in the last line as an equivalent of the

Rising Sun.[47] They wanted no more Indonesian swords against them, metaphorical or real; the first had already been swung in revolt at Tasikmalaya in January. When *Keboedajaan Timoer (Eastern Culture)* reprinted the poem in April, the last thirteen lines were cut.[48]

Chairil Anwar lived to see the Japanese surrender and the revolution in being. He died young—syphilitic and tubercular, suffering from cirrhosis and stricken with typhus—self-depleted, but also self-discovered. He had stared in the mirror and asked of "this face . . . covered with wounds / whose is it?" He knew, and answered, not in the genteel language of Balai Pustaka Malay, but in plain Bahasa Indonesia: "Aku." "Me." His pact was not with the Dutch or the Japanese, or the past, but with his own emerging self. And that inner lord he projected and pictured poetically, for the generation that was making a nation, in his "Pact with Bung Karno." He spoke to Sukarno, in a voice that was terse, vigorous, concrete, and new, in a line expressing the revolutionary psychology of millions: "Bung Karno! Kau dan aku satu zat satu urat." Freely translated: "Bung Karno! You and me, same blood, same guts."[49]

In the Philippines there was no Chairil Anwar, no voice of youth for national revolution. Reassessment, rather than radical purification, was the theme of most wartime writing. Salvador P. Lopez epitomized such analyses in an essay that asked: "What are we Filipinos going to do with our soul? And by our soul I mean the essence of what we are as a people: our moral, spiritual, and intellectual faculties, our capacity for adjustment and survival, the assimilative power and creative genius of our race."[50]

Lopez described Filipino culture as mestizo, a thorough hybrid. He then enumerated some of the cultural losses as a result of Western conquest: the animistic faiths of pagan forefathers, the aggressive religion of Islam (except among the Moros), the slave system of social organization, and the tribal system of government under petty chiefs and kings; and, more lamented, the instinct for fine

[47] Raffel, *Modern Indonesian Poetry*, 85.

[48] *Keboedajaan Timoer* 3, no. 166 (1944).

[49] For Indonesian text and differing translations of "Aku" ("Me"), "Selamat Tinggal" ("Goodbye"), and "Persetudjuan Dengan Bung Karno" ("Pact with Bung Karno") see Raffel, *Poetry of Chairil Anwar*, 20–21, 54–55, 130–31, and Fang, *Poems of Chairil Anwar*, 48–49, 54–55, 106–7.

[50] This and following quotations are from Salvador P. Lopez, "The Problem of Our Culture," *Philippine Review* 2, no. 6 (1944): 3–10. Asrul Sane is more analogous to Lopez in genre, as a leading Indonesian essayist of the time, but he captures less wholly than Chairil Anwar the spirit of the age.

handicraft, the native art of writing and whatever wisdom was in it, and almost the entire body of native folklore. Yet, in Lopez's view, the Filipinos had gained much more than they lost. The Christian religion implied for every nation the right to be free, and for every man "an irrevocable condition of personal dignity." From imperial rulers, Filipinos had gained a zeal for learning and education from which "sprang a new confidence in [their] own powers," and the scientific spirit, a "counterpoise to the fatalistic and superstitious tendencies of the race." He even counted as a gain "an appetite for material well-being, for the benefits of the abundant life, for the comforts and conveniences that have become synonymous with modern civilised living."

Having gone that far in acknowledgment to the West, however, Lopez observed that "an enslaved people tend to copy the vices more avidly than the virtues of their masters." From Spain, Filipinos had absorbed "religious fanaticism and hypocrisy," "hair-trigger sensitiveness based on an extravagant sense of honour," and "apathetic indolence" as a result of oppression. From the United States, Filipinos had acquired "exaggerated and self-indulgent individualism," a "predilection for materialistic pursuits and pleasures," and an "artificial standard of living that encourages pretense, sham, and dissipation." Nonetheless, Lopez declared, "I still affirm that there remains a residue of good influences that far outweighs the bad."

Now the Filipinos, awakened by the Japanese to the need for cultural rehabilitation, had to face the question of future direction. Discarding all borrowings from the West, as suggested by some Japanese, would amount to a "spirit of stampede." Instead, Lopez turned ingeniously to the Japanese example of adapting "the more vital elements of Western civilization to their own requirements," which enabled them to resist and compete with the West. Despite the richness of their indigenous culture, he observed, it would be unreasonable to ask the Japanese to rid themselves of the entire body of their cultural borrowings from the West. "How much less reasonable is it to demand that the Filipino people, considering the undeniable poverty of their own native culture, undergo a process of general purgation!"

This essay, in a journal sponsored and censored by the Japanese, is itself a masterpiece of cultural balance, conservative craftsmanship, and self-definition under pressure. Its humility could only charm the conqueror; and its criticism of Indian and Chinese "inbreeding" flattered the versatile and tasteful borrowing of the Japanese. Lopez thus provided a defense for Philippine hybridization, under which cover any native soul might make his own cultural choices. Seldom has so much of Philippine experience and character been summed up in such brief compass.

The cases of Chairil Anwar and Salvador P. Lopez are not wholly analogous, but they are mutually revealing. Lopez's insights were cumulative, retrospective, and conservative where those of Anwar were discontinuous, prospective, and radical. The Philippine dilemma brought out realizations in balanced prose, with its axes shifted to a new angle. The Indonesian predicament brought out discoveries in jagged poetry, the shrapnel of an explosive beginning.

One further distinction: Lopez was speaking out of the psychological uncertainties of a loosely hybridized culture; Anwar from the relative security of a culture deeply syncretized. Filipinos were still dependent on the energies of America in fusing their language, culture, and ambition, whereas Indonesians, vastly more confident of their heritage, were in deep perplexity as to their constitution. Filipinos sought a restoration of known political and economic conditions so that they could continue to rely on known public order while looking for private cultural identity. Indonesians sought an overthrow of established order and, with confidence in private cultural identities, searched for new public selves. Thus were eclectics conservative, and syncretists revolutionary.

8

ASSISTANCE AND

RESISTANCE

Assist the Japanese or resist them? Filipino and Indonesian answers varied by year and area, by predicament and opportunity, by power and person. The questions arose most urgently and with the most controversy regarding food, labor, and military force.

RICE COLLECTION

The Philippines and Indonesia were both peacetime importers of rice from French Indochina and Burma. When war disturbed agriculture and disrupted transportation, the resultant shortage of food by late 1944 caused general hunger and widespread starvation. As military demands grew more insistent, the production of rice fell even further behind civilian need. Profiteering, black-marketing, inflation, and theft increased.

As president of the Philippines, Jose Laurel succeeded in substituting a new agency, Bigasang Bayan (BIBA), for the Japanese-run National Rice and Corn Corporation (NARIC), which he called a "rotten apple," bruised by Japanese and Filipinos alike. In April 1944, Laurel installed his compadre, Manuel Roxas, as head of the new agency and its parent body, the Economic Planning Board.[1]

By mid-May, however, *Tribune* editorials, noting a crop decline of

[1] Utsunomiya to Laurel, 20 November 1943, and Laurel to Utsunomiya, November 27, 1943, Malacanang (see chap. 4, note 80) 51, 066.14; quotation from English text of Laurel speech in Tagalog to presidents of District and Neighborhood associations, Manila, January 5, 1944, JPL; also *Official Gazette* 1, no. 4 (1944): 396–404. A.V.H. Hartendorp, *The Japanese Occupation of the Philippines* (Manila: Bookmark, 1967), 2: 268; Minutes of the Economic Planning Board, April 11–September 5, 1944, and BIBA board meetings, April 18–June 12, 1944, Bundle 17, R.

25 to 30 percent over the previous year and stocks on hand of only forty-nine days' supply of rice, urged immediate action on more imports, reduced rations, and rice substitutes. Prices began to soar.[2] An executive order failed to halt either hoarding or profiteering. Black market rice sold for as high as two and a half times the official price.[3]

Field Marshal Terauchi's staff, newly arrived from Siagon, wanted to resort to military authority alone.[4] Murata and other Japanese with Philippine experience, however, succeeded in softening the military stance while toughening that of the Laurel government. They asked for production quotas, reinforcement of control organizations, enforced adherence to fixed prices, and punishment of all black marketeers. Eight Japanese were appointed to help BIBA with purchase and distribution. Colonel Utsunomiya assured Roxas that the army not only would strive to keep peace in the rice-growing districts but would help in production and procurement.[5]

Profiteering and pilferage, however, continued to rise. Utsunomiya, suggested that the major black market operators who "enjoy political influence and are connected with big financial groups . . . should be executed publicly and their names published in the papers."[6] Utsunomiya accused governors, Constabulary officers, and junior officials in Central Luzon of "connivance with the landlords who have bribed the former in an attempt to make black market dealings." What, he asked Roxas, are you going to do about malefactors and about the government's own "tacit approval" of the black market?[7] Roxas finally prevailed in his view that BIBA was being frustrated not by political subversion but by purely economic factors; Japanese modification of the BIBA plan had made it impossible to compete with the black market.[8]

Pressures for intensified Japanese control continued to mount as American forces drew near. Murata warned a newly arrived political adviser on rice policy, "that we should take great care . . . as an ad-

[2] Manila *Tribune*, editorials, mid-May 1944, collected in Malacanang, 50, 062.14.

[3] Hartendorp, *Japanese Occupation*, 2: 269.

[4] Fukushima Shintarō, ed., *Murata Shōzō: Ikō hitō-nikki* (Post-humous Philippine diaries) (Shinjuku: Hara-shobō, 1969), entry for June 7, 1944.

[5] "Orally stated by the Japanese Ambassador at his conference with H.E. the President on June 12, 1944," Bundle 17, R; also Murata diary, June 12, 1944.

[6] "Conference between Col. Utsunomiya and Secretary Sabido and Mr. Sanvictores," Malacanang, June 5, 1944, Bundle 16, R.

[7] Utsunomiya to Roxas, July 18, 1944, Malacanang, 50, 062.14.

[8] Roxas to Utsunomiya, July 20, 1944, Malacanang, 50, 062.14; Utsunomiya to Roxas, July 31, 1944, and Roxas to Utsunomiya, August 4, Bundle 16, R.

viser, since we tend to be narrow-minded toward foreign peoples."
Meanwhile he remonstrated with Laurel: "Your people, especially
those in Manila, think the cause of rising prices in rice and other
foodstuffs is supplying numerous [Japanese] soldiers and officers,"
whereas actually their needs were covered by imports.[9]

Collusion became obvious among some drivers of BIBA trucks,
the Constabulary, and thieves, as the latter punctured bags and
caught spilling rice while guards looked the other way. A Japanese
officer reported in September that middle class families had begun
selling possessions to raise money for rice while the lower classes
were reduced to a diet of vegetable leaves. Community kitchens by
this time were feeding an average of 120,000 people daily.[10] The average daily caloric intake of Americans in the Santo Tomas internment camp fell from 2,112 in June to 1,402 in October. As the situation worsened, mortality increased sharply among weaker people,
and some began salvaging condemned vegetables from the camp
garbage.[11]

Shortly before the American landing at Leyte, as rice import by
sea from French Indochina became increasingly perilous, the Japanese military took over from Laurel's government to ensure that
their troops were fed. The Japanese general responsible cautioned
that "publicity would run counter to the objectives . . . in mind."[12]
When allowed in November to make the new organization public
as the Rice and Corn Administration (RICOA), Laurel summarized a
wretched history: "The NARIC, which rendered a great deal of service to the military authorities and to the military administration,
[did not succeed from our point of view]. . . . Unfortunately for us,
the BIBA also failed. And we are manly enough to say that that organization of the Republic *bitterly* failed to achieve the purpose for
which it was organized. . . . [Therefore] I have gone to the extent of
appealing to the Imperial Japanese Army to help . . . [in] the primor-
dial purpose of procuring food for our people."[13]

[9] Murata diary, August 25, 28, 1944.

[10] Memo, HQ of CinC Kuroda to Ministry of Economic Affairs, rec'd. September
20, 1944, Bundle 16, R.

[11] Hartendorp, *Japanese Occupation*, 2: 431, 437, 441.

[12] "Transcript of the Stenographic Notes . . . First Meeting of the Rice and Corn
Investigating Committee . . . Manila Hotel . . . October 11, 1944," Bundle 17, R. The
Filipino contingent was led by Pedro Sabido, the Japanese by General Takahashi. See
also Hartendorp, 2: 271n.

[13] Remarks on the Oath-taking of Members of the Rice and Corn Administration,
November 28, 1944, JPL. Laurel had admitted to Murata in July that "he knew the
BIBA corrupt and untrustworthy" (Murata diary, July 14, 1944).

In Manila, only imminent American invasion made the Japanese discard cooperation and override Filipino rice management. In Jakarta, however, they could either deign or decline to take advice from Indonesians. Questions on production, collection, and price of rice, after first being raised in the Chūō Sangi-in by the gunseikan, were referred to the Sanyo Kaigi, an advisory group comprising some of the most eminent Indonesian leaders, under the chairmanship of Sukarno.[14]

Late in 1944, distribution of rice in capitals of residencies, in regencies, and in municipalities like Jakarta was regularly between 100 and 230 grams per person per day, far below the 400 considered sufficient.[15] Outside major cities only civil servants received a regular distribution at all. As in Luzon, the Japanese rice shortage was compounded by black market activity. Malnutrition, even starvation, clearly contributed to the sharp upward turn in the death rate in and after the second quarter of 1944.

The Javanese harvest of *padi* (unmilled rice) was far below normal because of extremes of hot and dry spells followed by late rains in 1944, and the people remained confused about what the government expected. The collection system was insufficiently supervised, especially between middle-man and government, and the complement of village leaders was too small to cope with the complex padi delivery system. "All kinds of dishonesty and muddle" led to manipulation and spoilage en route or to delays, which stimulated the impulse to hoard. The black market was "an immense obstacle." The "sense of social solidarity [was] still quite superficial at all levels," particularly among wealthy peasants, as among the rich and influential in general.[16]

Oto Iskandardinata deplored the mass starvation and the "Punishment of Tantalus" inflicted on the poor who saw padi piled in storage while they went hungry. At the same time he complained

[14] Ben Anderson, ed., "The Problem of Rice: Stenographic Notes of the Fourth Session of the Sanyo Kaigi, January 8, 2605," *Indonesia* 2 (1966): 77–123, translated by Anderson from RVO 036627. Professor Anderson has generously provided me his forty page unpublished continuation of the same translation, which I will cite as "Anderson MS" below.

[15] Anderson, "Rice," 90–91, 93. Hartendorp states that at this same time Americans interned in Santo Tomas were receiving 225 grams per person. Miyamoto Shizuo, in Anthony Reid and Oki Akira, eds., *The Japanese Experience in Indonesia: Selected Memoirs of 1942–1945*, Southeast Asia Series, no. 72 (Athens: Ohio University Center for International Studies, 1986), 244–46, gives gross production and consumption statistics along with considerations of military logistics.

[16] Anderson, "Rice," 84–88.

that the war spirit had weakened, war labor had declined, and the work of "enemy spies" had been made easier. Attuned to Japan, he appealed to the ideals of hakkō ichiu.[17]

A wholly different perspective came from Abikusno. He also saw "an unparalleled situation. . . . The man who plants doesn't eat." Rather than hakkō ichiu, however, he called for "Islamic justice." Abikusno suggested creation of a food supply agency within the military government with "widest possible powers," plus a grass roots anti-black market organization.[18]

The group, however, voted down Abikusno's proposal and focused on one by Oto and his committee: to ban private marketing and storage of rice and create a state monopoly to buy the entire padi crop.[19] Hatta, arguing that padi and *beras* (husked rice) should remain market commodities, pressed for rationing instead and finally won over Oto. A per capita ration was calculated and on this basis the amount of padi to be left in each village was established, the rest to be turned over to the government for distribution as beras at a set price in the cities. Opposition rose from various considerations of economics, peasant psychology, and military efficiency. The first vote on the matter split 7 to 7.

After a break, Hatta presented a concluding argument: lack of rationing, an absurdly low official price, and government issue of paper money, had caused padi prices to rise twenty-eight-fold. "Our strategy can only be to apply brakes to the process." Reset the price of padi and introduce rationing for the whole population. A "majority" at last agreed to the basic points of the proposal.

The debate not only illustrated basic economic conditions in Java, but the unique quality of political considerations entertained there. The discussants absorbed themselves in the argument that if plowing, planting, storage, and delivery were done by decree, the peasants would become "robots" instead of independent men. Furthermore, "if everything is put under government orders, there will be no more music in the villages." A discussion of music, rice, and authority ensued, revealing Javanese aristocratic benignity; a regard for the souls of the peasants, which overlooked their stomachs and purses; dubious premises about peasant psychology; underawareness of the needs of urban dwellers, whether poor or not; and an aesthetic test of the commonweal which, if appropriate to Javanese

[17] Ibid., 92–93, 103; Anderson MS, 6.
[18] Anderson, "Rice," 105–10.
[19] Ibid., 111–19; Anderson MS.

culture in ordinary times, was a poor measure of the urgency of the crisis. Others concluded more sensibly: "the padi required to feed the village will remain in the village and be distributed to its inhabitants. Those who have no padi of their own for personal consumption can buy from the rice barns."[20]

The discussion of rice problems was certainly more elevated on Java than in Luzon—more deliberate in exploration of basic principles, more thoughtful in assay of information. But the difference was between a seminar and a negotiation. The Javanese, lacking control over government and economy, could afford to express the beauty of their sentiments. The Filipino leaders, grappling to retain partial control, were more nakedly political, responsible, and subject to humiliation. In both situations the increase of hoarding and hunger, of profiteering and deprivation, pointed toward societies in breakdown, requiring restoration or transformation.

As for the Japanese, whose war aims stressed from the beginning the acquisition of resources for the war effort, reversals in the field made them more desperate and nakedly extractive. On May 19, 1944, a meeting of the commanders of the Seventh Field Army, which included armies in Malaya, Sumatra, Northern Borneo, and Java, determined that for the sake of aiding other military operations they should "maintain the natives' [genjūmin] standard of living at *the lowest possible level*." Reiterating the need "to win the hearts of the people,"[21] they did not say how this should be done while emptying their bellies.

LABOR CONSCRIPTION

In the use and treatment of labor, the Japanese dealt far more sternly with Indonesians than with Filipinos. The latter benefited from a stronger buffer in native administrative authority, and from a history of incipient unionization.

The Indonesian laborer, while being encouraged to think of himself as a volunteer (sukarélawan) in building a new Java, was called by the Japanese term rōmusha, meaning "laborer in the war effort." Later Indonesian usage transformed the meaning of the term closer to reality: "involuntary worker, or even convict," and concocted a

[20] Anderson MS, 1, 3, 7, 9, 10, 16–17, 27–28.
[21] Bōeichō Bōeikenkyūjo Senshibu (see chap. 3, note 31), Nanpō no Gunsei, 30–31. Emphasis added.

passive verb, "being forced to work hard."[22] The Japanese military machine consumed both male labor for construction projects and female for "comfort." "In the cities of Java, many Indonesian women were forced to become prostitutes for the Japanese military." The greater number of rōmusha, however, were Indonesian youths sent "like oxen and horses" to work overseas, much like Dutch prisoners.[23]

Estimates of the actual number of rōmusha range widely. Miyoshi gives a figure of 5 to 8 million, higher even than the 4.1 million the Indonesians put forward in reparations talks. Regular and rotation workers for whom the Japanese had to supply rice numbered 2.6 million. But the crux of dispute was over relocated labor, a high percentage of whom died. General Yamamoto, as former Gunseikan, dismissed Miyoshi's figure as logistically impossible but, pressed for his own, evasively replied, "Perhaps 50,000?"[24] A more realistic figure, deduced from postwar Dutch and English reports, is 300,000 transported rōmusha,[25] as distinct from regular forced labor on local projects. Although the great majority were

[22] S. Wojowasito and W.J.S. Poerwadarminta, *Kamus Indonesia-Inggeris* (Indonesian-English dictionary) (Jakarta: Penerbit Tiara, 1961); John M. Echols and Hassan Shadily, *An Indonesian-English Dictionary*, 2d ed. (Ithaca: Cornell University Press, 1963), 303; W.J.S. Poerwadarminta, *Kamus Umum Bahasa Indonesia* (Jakarta: Balai Pustaka, 1982), 831.

Gotō Ken'ichi, "Nihon Gunseiki No Indonesia Ni Okeru Rōmusha Mondai" (The rōmusha problem in Indonesia during Japanese military administration), Shakai Kagaku Tōkyū 28, no. 3 (1984): 607–640 is a sensitive review of the problem, including the anti-Japanese cultural nationalism that arose over the banning in Indonesia, upon Japanese protest, of "Romusya," an Indonesian-made movie, in 1973.

[23] Taniguchi Goro, in Tamura Yoshio, ed., *Hiroku Daitōa Senshi: Ranin-hen* (A confidential history of the Greater East Asian War: Netherlands East Indies) (Tokyo: Fujishoen, 1953), 128.

[24] Miyoshi Shunkichirō, "Jawa senryō gunsei kaikoroku" (Memoirs of the military administration of Java), 15 pts., *Kokusai Mondai* (April 1965–January 1967), pt. 6, 71, pt. 13, 64; Miyamoto Shizuo in Reid and Oki, eds., *Japanese Experience in Indonesia*, table 11, p. 247, on rōmusha fed rice in Java; interviews, Yamamoto, June 11, 1968, and Miyoshi, June 12, 1968.

[25] My calculations are based on data in several postwar documents: N(E)I Red Cross, "Het Antaal Romushas," June 26, 1946, RVO 048080; "Coolies Situation on Sumatra Medio January 1946," RVO 048072; "Het Coelie Probleem op Sumatra," undated, RVO 048081; RVO 005422; holograph translation of introduction to "Survey of Measures [re Siam-Burma railway] . . . ," RVO 005537-38; Lt. Col. P. W. Kent, "Report on Medical Care . . . N.W. Siam," RVO 005405. Kanahele independently refers to a postsurrender Japanese estimate of 270,000 transported rōmusha, and an Allied Red Cross estimate of 294,000. Miyamoto, in Reid and Oki, eds., *Japanese Experience in Indonesia*, 249–50, puts the number of rōmusha actually transported at 150,000 maximum, as distinct from 228,000 "assigned."

transported within the Indies, a significant fraction, probably over 50,000, were shipped overseas. Perhaps one-quarter obtained official assistance to return after the war. Probably half had died.

Figures do not convey the tragedy as well as a Japanese description of how rōmusha were recruited:

> The Japanese and Indonesian government officials undertook compulsory collection [of laborers] by unbelievable and even immoral deceptions in order to meet the orders of their superiors and to earn merit. . . . Since it was obvious there would be no applicants if the dates were announced previously, they commanded the subdistrict and village chiefs to assemble young males at a designated place on an appointed day and time. The townsmen gathered, thinking there would be special distribution [of food or clothing]. With clever words, the military men loaded them on prepared trucks and took them away to ports where ships awaited them. The men were then shipped to the battlefields of New Guinea, to the Andamans and Nicobars, to Burma, etc., as laborers. They had no idea once they left when they could return home, and they received no opportunity to bid farewell. When their families, worrying over the whereabouts of their long missing fathers, children or brothers, inquired of the government, the latter, not knowing, could only tell lies. . . . The public had no voice nor right . . . in the matter for it was wartime and orders were almighty.[26]

Labor collection differed little from rice collection in using compulsory delivery quotas and arousing competition among foreign military and native civil bureaucrats to comply. From Gunseikanbu to residency to regency to district to village, Miyoshi wrote, there existed a massive systematic official complicity which, in delivery of food, left masses of the poor starving and, in delivery of laborers, left many bereaved. Most Japanese would concur in his judgment that dragooning of rōmusha was "a great blot on the record of the Military Administration."[27]

Under interrogation, General Yamamoto later claimed that all orders for the export of laborers came from General Itagaki in Singapore; and that the implementer of policy in Java, one Takahashi, had given the orders in Yamamoto's name through the civil authorities to collect manpower for factories, railways, and textile works.

[26] Miyoshi, pt.12, 81.
[27] Ibid., pt. 6, 71.

"This labor was voluntary and was paid," Yamamoto insisted, but the numbers were always insufficient, in the last months especially, and the system broke down. Yamamoto denied knowledge of any forced labor, admitting only that some of his subordinates might have exceeded their orders.[28]

Years later Yamamoto would admit to more knowledge. His office compiled lists of those who had volunteered for transmigration to Sumatra and Borneo. Village officials used these lists when Singapore demanded men for those areas. Often, however, Singapore set quotas for extra-Indies locations that had to be met suddenly, when ships were ready, lest publicity leak to the Allies. Such rapid roundups, Yamamoto conceded, might have had a tendency to become ruthless.[29]

Charismatic enticement and deceptive impressment were common. The regent of Bandung was reputed to have the ability to transform water by his touch into a liniment that induced "exhilaration" in believers. When he lent his voice to the *sukaréla* enlistment, many trustingly joined.[30] In the absence of such collaborators, the Japanese used their own wiles. In Central Java, those responding to an offer of transportation to movies in a nearby village might find themselves going to the ships instead.[31]

One elder statesman later recalled the erosion of popular trust in the civil service and the ensuing acts of sometimes bloody retaliation. He observed that "Bung Karno shares moral responsibility for this, because of his publicizing *rōmusha* . . . because of saying if you sacrifice for the Holy War you earn merit and a reward from Allah. Bung Hatta, by contrast, said this was not *sukarela* but *terpaksa* [forced] labor. Hatta was brave in this respect and Sukarno was not."[32]

Sukarno, pestered by Cindy Adams,[33] eventually confessed having known about rōmusha packed into boxcars, shackled to prisoners of war, dying on the Siam-Burma railway. "In fact, it was I, Sukarno, who sent them to work. Yes it was I. I shipped them to their deaths. Yes, yes, yes, I am the one. . . . It was horrible, hope-

---

[28] Interrogation of Yamamoto, RVO 16903.

[29] Yamamoto, interview, June 11, 1968.

[30] Interview, name of source withheld.

[31] Slamet Imam Santoso, interview, March 31, 1968.

[32] Arudji Kartawinata, interview, March 16, 1968.

[33] Cindy Adams, *My Friend the Dictator* (Indianapolis: Bobbs-Merrill, 1967), 184–86.

less. And it was I who gave them to the Japanese. Sounds terrible, doesn't it? . . . Nobody likes the ugly truth."[34]

Sukarno's style of recruitment of rōmusha was as enthusiastic as this later confession was candid. One of many dates Sukarno declared "never to be forgotten" was September 3, 1944, because "for the first time in history, Indonesia leaders together with intellectuals [kaum terpeladjar] gave clear evidence of their devotion to the government. An event of this kind never took place in the period of Dutch government."[35] The "event" was one in which about five hundred educated Indonesians (some of Arab, Chinese, Japanese, or mixed-blood background) marched to the railroad station amid cheers of "Long live the Rōmusha Volunteer Corps," and were conveyed for a limited period of labor on defense installations outside the city. There Sukarno spoke. Even though many of these rōmusha were around sixty years old, all worked as if young, he proclaimed; and he asked them not to shave for two weeks as evidence to the world that their only desire was that the Javanese live and die along with the Japanese army in achieving final victory.

To the restless pemuda of Jakarta, Sukarno was already defending himself before the war was over: "If I must sacrifice thousands to save millions, I will. We are in a struggle for survival. As leader of the country I cannot afford the luxury of sensitivity."[36]

Some said that every able-bodied Indonesian male between fifteen and fifty was a rōmusha, because at some point every man or boy had to contribute to one Japanese project or another. In that sense, perhaps, many Filipinos were rōmusha too. But the Japanese went more lightly on their proclamation of "holy war" in the Philippines, and did not systematically conscript military auxiliaries. They also lacked sufficient common cause to permit propagandizing about "heroes of labor."

In February 1944, General Wachi, seeking more then seven thousand laborers distributed in various provinces, expressed the hope to President Laurel that "Your Excellency [will] be pleased to exercise the influence of your good office to afford positive assistance, and to induce the general public to respond to our needs." He enclosed a long list of working conditions to be publicized concerning wages, quarters, promotions, raises, accident compensation, mail

[34] Sukarno: An Autobiography, as told to Cindy Adams (Indianapolis: Bobbs-Merrill, 1965), 192.

[35] Tjahaja (Bandung), September 5, 1944, GSK.

[36] Sukarno: An Autobiography, 193.

service, and even, should need be, burial expenses.[37] The irony of the last item should not obscure the variety of the preceding ones. Wages were promised in Indonesia too, but assurances in the Philippines had to cover the whole range of sensibility created by American unionism and employment practices.[38]

The pro-Japanese mayor of Manila, Leon Guinto, publicly denied in July 1944 a charge of having empowered village chiefs to recruit labor under threat of punishment by military law. Such a denial, he explained to Laurel, was necessary because "under the present circumstances, any insinuation, however insignificant or inoffensive, may be interpreted in an erroneous way not only by the Japanese authorities, but also by Filipinos, specially those *elements who, while their bodies and stomachs are in the Philippines, have their minds and souls on the other side of the ocean."[39]* In other words, there lurked for Filipino officials the possibility of assassination by guerrillas, who did not wait for explanations.

A report of the Labor Recruitment Agency established by Laurel is full of unlikely numbers suggesting success, and words acknowledging failure. It complained of an already depleted pool of manpower because of employment by the Japanese in mines, factories, and defense projects or in food production; a lack of order in the provinces; and insufficient inducements in wages and rations (for example, ten hours of unskilled work brought only 2.60 pesos plus six hundred grams of rice). Other deterrents included maltreatment of laborers by Japanese to the point of death, violations of contract including nonpayment of wages or rations, and transport to places not designated. Twenty-five men from Tarlac, for instance, were contracted to work in Pasay and then taken to Davao. One in five were able to return to their families. The story spread quickly and stirred a general fear of being shipped outside the Philippines or being forced to fight the Great East Asia War.[40] That such a minor

[37] Wati [Wachi] to Laurel, February 1944, "Asking the Cooperation of the Government concerning the Enlistment of Personnel in the Philippines," Malacanang, 42, 054-03.

[38] Undated, but apparently written sometime after establishment of the Labor Recruitment Agency, April 11, 1944, Malacanang, 43, 054.5.

[39] Guinto to Laurel, July 8, 1944 (emphasis in original), Malacanang, 42, 053.5. Guinto's enthusiastic collaboration is traceable in Guinto to Hasimoto, July 7; and Guinto to Laurel, July 8, Malacanang, 42, 054.3.

[40] Executive Order no. 47, "Creating a Labor Recruitment Agency," signed by Laurel April 11, 1944, Malacanang, 36, 053.3. The first draft reads "upon request of the Imperial Japanese Army and Navy"; the final draft reads only: "attending to the needs of the Imperial Japanese Forces." Pablo Manlapit, "General Report of the Ac-

instance of unwilling interisland transport created rumors far and wide illuminates the sensitivity of Filipinos to maltreatment and their aversion to serving the "greater cause."

Even in the Philippines, however, the day of direct pressure finally came. In later September 1944, after the first American bombing of Manila, the Japanese chief of staff asked Laurel to give strict orders to every military governor to supply laborers to the army for military projects under the "state of war" just proclaimed. Laurel complied, sending martial law telegrams to the provinces in early October, followed by an executive order in early November, authorizing military governors to require the participation of all males aged eighteen to fifty.[41] Laurel's postwar defense against treason justified this labor recruitment "so as to avoid conscription which was threatened, and which he feared." The facts are congruent with his claim. Colonel Utsunomiya and Captain Hiraide jointly complained that Filipino efforts were insufficient and "that the Republic should show by deeds and not by words its adherence to the Pact of Alliance by conscripting laborers for the Japanese army and navy projects."[42]

The pressure from the Japanese did not go much further, but criticism from Filipinos continued manifest and sharp. Laurel had inherited a context affected by American living standards and labor practices and his countrymen did not forget it. Sukarno, emerging from exile and the shadow of Dutch police, worked in a context of shorter life expectancy, a history of corvée labor, and less developed modern unionism. In Java the invaders could also exploit more sluggish communication of apprehension, lower levels of wage and ration, and much higher cooperativeness. Sukarno's nearly unlimited concessions of rōmusha to the Japanese were the result.

MILITARY AUXILIARIES

As their holy war against the West became defensive, the Japanese were clearly going to have to arm some of the Southeast Asians they

tivities of the Labor Recruitment Agency from April 1, 1944 to September 30, 1944," Malacanang, 36, 053.3; Manlapit to Minister of Health, Labor, and Public Welfare, December 14, 1944, Malacanang, 42, 054.3; interview, Felino Neri, June 28, 1968.

[41] Gen. Imamura Yuzura, CofS, Imperial Japanese Forces, to Laurel, September 26, 1944, Malacanang, 43, 054.5; Exec. Sec. Abello to Military Governors, October 3, 1944, Malacanang, 43, 054.5; Executive Order no. 100, November 2, 1944, draft, with insertions by Laurel and others, Malacanang, 42, 053.03.

[42] "Conscription of Labor, Abello's Statement," n.d., JPL, Ic-11. Abello says the documents proving this were left in Baguio, possibly recovered by the American Counter-Intelligence Corps or possibly lost.

professed were brothers. But whom? Gurkhas in India and Karen in Burma had been used by the British, and Ambonese and Minahassans in Indonesia by the Dutch, because they saw in colonial military service a means of upward social mobility and protection from the majority oppression that nationalist movements portended. Even in the Philippines, the Americans found that a relatively high percentage of volunteers for the Philippines Scouts turned out to be mountain tribesmen and Moros, fearful of the lowland Christian majority. The Japanese, however, could not rely on minorities loyal to white imperialists. Reversal of the tides of war and the cumulative message of their own appeal to nationalism-within-Asianism required them to look for native auxiliary military forces among ethnic majorities. They announced plans for the formation of Peta in Indonesia later in 1943 and Makapili in the Philippines a year later.

Peta in Indonesia (*Pembela Tanah Air*, Defenders of the Fatherland) later became the leadership core of the army that fought the Dutch. Its birth is therefore understandably clouded with exaggerated claims of fatherhood. Sukarno alleges that he handpicked the head of Peta, chose "young men whom [he] could control," and "singlehandedly proposed" men who "could eventually become the heroes of [the] Revolution."[43] Juxtaposed with this gross untruth is an engaging half-truth from Gatot Mangkupradja, a nationalist who had stood trial with Sukarno under the Dutch in 1929. Gatot claims that his proposal of a volunteer army, countering one for a conscript army by a prominent Javanese in September 1943, led the Kenpeitai to pick him up for questioning and take him to the Japanese chief of staff, Major General Satō, who came around to the idea.[44]

In fact, the idea of Peta is traceable to Japanese contingency planning. Early in 1943, withdrawal of troops to fight in the Solomons–New Guinea area had reduced their defense force in Java to ten thousand. General Inada, then commander of the Seventh Army in Singapore, conceived the idea of arming Indonesians during an inspection tour of Java and obtained Tōjō's approval (but no funds) during the latter's visit to Singapore in July 1943. The army in Java, ready with arms surrendered by the Dutch KNIL (Royal Netherlands Indies Army), began organizing and training unarmed military

[43] *Sukarno: An Autobiography*, 186–87.
[44] Gatot Mankupradja, "The Peta and My Relations with the Japanese," *Indonesia* 5 (1968): 115–17.

auxiliaries called Heiho. For the next step, native sponsorship was needed. Gatot spoke out at the right time.[45]

Still the Japanese were jittery. Are you willing, Satō asked Gatot, to take the proper punishment if few or none volunteer? While Lieutenant Yanagawa Motoshige and Captain Maruzaki Yoshio watched, Gatot pricked his left arm with a pen until it bled and then in his own blood wrote a letter of request to the government in Tokyo. *Asia Raya* published it in ordinary newsprint—and so launched the idea to the public. Fortunately for Gatot, the rate of volunteering was high.[46]

Sukarno and Hatta did not learn of the plan until spring.[47] A year later at a large meeting, Sukarno proposed a conscript militia in a fiery speech that ended with the entreaty that all in favor stand. Gatot sat. His counterproposal was for another volunteer organ, which eventually materialized, again with Japanese support. This was the Hizbullah, a paramilitary unit of Islamic youths designed as a reserve to the Peta, some of whose Muslim officers were assigned to train it.[48] The Japanese were willing to let Sukarno employ his tongue and image in their behalf but would not let him, whatever he later said, screen or indoctrinate candidates for the military. That job went to Beppan, a "special forces" unit with some experience in training Indonesians for intelligence work, now responsible for giving basic military training to Peta volunteers.[49] Candidates applied from all over Java, and Beppan chose them on military grounds, without significant political participation or interference.[50] Total enlistment rose to 38,000, "four times the actual combat strength" of the Japanese Sixteenth Army.[51]

---

[45] Kanahele, "Japanese Occupation," 116–20.

[46] Gatot, "The Peta," 117, 121.

[47] Kanahele, "Japanese Occupation," 120–21.

[48] Gatot, "The Peta," 126–27; Harry J. Benda, *The Crescent and the Rising Sun* (The Hague and Bandung: W. van Hoeve, 1958), 178–79.

[49] Nugroho Notosusanto, "Instansi jang melaksanakan pembentukan tentara Peta," *Madjalah Ilmu Ilmu Sastra Indonesia* 2 (1964): 285–90, outlines the history of "The Outfit that Undertook the Formation of the Peta Army." *Beppan* was Japanese military jargon for the duties that evolved for the Isamu Butai Tokumu Kikan, Bunjitsu (special section, special division, Isamu unit [detached from the Second Division of the Sixteenth Army]).

[50] Gatot, "The Peta," 121; Yanagawa Motoshige, interview, February 21, 1968.

[51] Miyamoto Shizuo, in Reid and Oki, eds., *Japanese Experience in Indonesia*, 223, gives this figure in a valuable section on the Peta, 220–34; Kanahele, "Japanese Occupation," 131–32, says "over 30,000." Nugroho Notosusanto, "The PETA Army in Indonesia," in William H. Newell, ed., *Japan in Asia* (Singapore: Singapore University Press, 1981), 32–45, is one of a series of his articles, and perhaps the last before

1. Princess Kartini (standing, right) as a teacher in a school established for children of Indonesian officials, 1903

2. Arithmetic, English, and geography: classroom in the Philippines, early twentieth century. Note central photo of George Washington, and review questions on the Russo-Japanese War.

3. Toothbrush drill, La Carlota, Negros Occidental, Philippines, 1928.

4 Drill with wooden guns, Javanese children under Japanese occupation.

5 Governor General Tjarda's address at the opening of the Volksraad, Jakarta (Batavia), June 15, 1938.

6. Ceremonial farewell ride in carabao cart for Secretary of War George H. Dern, Zamboanga, November 19, 1935

7. Surrender of British General Percival to General Yamashita, Singapore, 1942, painting by Muy-amoto Saburo, 1944 (Yamashita is second from left, gesturing with wristwatch.)

8 Surrender of General Yamashita to American troops, Baguio, Luzon, September 3, 1945. (Yamashita is second from right, and General Mutō Akira is at far right)

9 Premier Tōjō visits Manila, July 10, 1943, and dines with Laurel (dark suit) and other Philippine leaders Painting by Kawashima Riichiro, 1943, entitled *Birth of New Philippines*

10. Laurel enjoys merienda in his honor with Filipino cadets in Tokyo at the time of the Greater East Asia Conference, November 4, 1943

11. Sukarno leading the Seinendan (youth corps) in banzais for the emperor, responding to the promise of independence.

12. Chinese-Filipino youth association arrives at airstrip, Tacloban, Leyte, to help American engineers rebuild it, October 21, 1944.

13 Raising the Indonesian flag at Sukarno's home following the Proclamation of Independence, August 17, 1945, Sukarno and Hatta at attention, Latief Hendraningrat, as senior Peta officer present, at halyard; women watching.

14. Conference aboard flagship H.M S. *Cumberland*, Jakarta, mid-September 1945, Japanese commanders come to terms with advance military party of the Allies. Seated (right to left), Rear Admiral Maeda, Major General Yamamoto, Major General Nishimura.

15 Indonesian nationalist slogans painted on monument to Governor General van Heutsz of the Netherlands Jakarta, October 1945

16. Surabaya, November 1945· two British soldiers take aim from behind a barricade in battle against Indonesian revolutionaries.

17. General of the Army Douglas MacArthur greeted by Manuel Roxas, president of the Philippines, on arrival from Japan, July 2, 1946, for Philippine independence ceremonies.

18. Sjahrir, Sukarno, and Hatta in custody of a Dutch officer, after Dutch capture of presidential palace, Yogyakarta, December 1948.

19 Revolutionary poster photographed by the Dutch and translated as "Capitalism has caused her downfall." But the Indonesian is more explicit: "Capitalism made me become a whore."

Tahoe kamoe, bahwa kapitalismelah yang membœat akœ mendjadi djalang.

20. Training of the women's auxiliary of the Republican Army (Tentara Wanita Indonesia), Solo.

21. Indonesian revolutionaries
interrogating a fellow countryman.

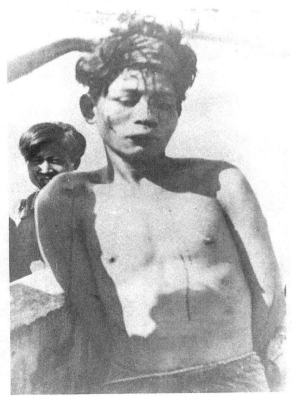

22. Before execution: humiliation of
a prisoner sentenced to death by
revolutionaries

23. Bung Tomo and Radio
Berontak, Surabaya, 1945.

24 Dead revolutionary with his bamboo spear, Gombong, August 1, 1947.

Lieutenant Yanagawa was ideal to convey the Japanese idea of militancy and agreed with Lieutenant General Harada Kumakichi's advice not to trust Indonesian politicians.[52] Yanagawa put Peta trainees through three months of basic military tactics, formations, and techniques including use of the rifle, hand-to-hand fighting, and jujitsu. He emphasized physical stamina, and "spirit," which the Japanese stressed at all their youth training centers, schools, and auxiliaries. Here it meant "an almost reckless kind of physical courage, defiant of bodily injury and even death." Other indoctrination themes included defense of homeland, holy war against white infidels, and final victory for Dai Nippon. Military theory and organization were not offered.[53]

Japanese strategy called for using Indonesians as a first line of defense at the beaches, Japanese as a second line for frontal encounters, and Indonesians together with Japanese for guerrilla war in the mountains.[54] The strategy was of course masked from Indonesians. Hatta observed positively, nonetheless, that the KNIL had been mercenaries trained to fight an enemy from within, but the Peta were volunteers trained to fight an enemy from without.[55] Their new rationale, defense of the fatherland, was, whether the Japanese intended it or not, a foundation in nationalism. Maruzaki, who had seen the KNIL collapse, swore that if the Peta succeeded he would cut off a finger. Yanagawa vowed to do the same if it failed. In the end it was Maruzaki who lost the wager, and a finger.[56]

FILIPINO military support of the Japanese is a story of tension among Jose Laurel, Artemio Ricarte, and Benigno Ramos. Nationalism and a sense of practical politics made Laurel refuse to conscript soldiers for the Japanese; he was averse even to a volunteer pro-Japanese army. Ricarte, however, saw the Japanese as an agency for realization of the revolutionary Malolos Republic of 1896. His lack of rapport with the new Philippines so embarrassed the Imperial Japanese Forces that they removed him to Tokyo, in quasi de-

---

his death. Ulf Sundhaussen, *The Road to Power, Indonesian Military Politics, 1945–1967* (Kuala Lumpur: Oxford University Press, 1982), 2–18, puts the Peta in perspective in the development of the Indonesian National Army.

[52] Yanagawa, interview.

[53] Kanahele, "Japanese Occupation," 125, Gen. Kemal Idris, interview, March 1968.

[54] Nugroho, "Instansi," 289.

[55] Kanahele, "Japanese Occupation," 132.

[56] Gatot, "The Peta," 120.

tention at the Imperial Hotel, from December 1943 to April 1944. When released to return, Ricarte offered to organize a "national volunteer security force," partly because he felt that Laurel had begun to "turn his back" on the Japanese.

Given Ricarte's historic reputation, Laurel had difficulty saying no, especially because the Philippine Constabulary alone was obviously insufficient to maintain order in the country.[57] The wartime Constabulary was made up of some prewar members, some former members of the Philippine army, and civilian volunteers. It admitted to "incompetence ... excessive display of authority ... misbehavior and unhealthy conduct."[58] Often patrolling in wooden sandals or barefoot, wearing civilian clothes, the Constabulary in Central Luzon could easily be mistaken for guerrillas.[59] The chief in Mindanao depicted his force as extremely low in morale, with some men unpaid for six months, many malaria stricken, and all wanting in clothes and medicine.[60] Under such circumstances, Laurel acknowledged Ricarte's offer of help but gave no tangible support.

Ricarte and his aide-de-camp, Ohta Kaneshiro, bought food with a large financial contribution from a Filipino, obtained clothing from bales of American wares kept at Old Bilibid Prison, and assembled a supply of weapons from a warehouse of American arms surrendered at Bataan. Next Ricarte made a recruiting trip through North Luzon, but the value of his initiative was minimized when American planes began bombing Manila and some key Japanese officers decided to find a collaborator of Benigno Ramos's kind.[61]

Ramos, in jail at the outbreak of war, had written a letter to Quezon offering cooperation, which events proved a sham.[62] Upon being freed by the Japanese in April 1942, Ramos thanked the commander, donated five hundred pesos to "the cause,"[63] and began to gather his followers to help the Japanese. Of the Ramos-inspired Sakdal rebels of 1935 against the Americans and the Commonwealth, many had joined his later creation, the Ganaps. The lineage

[57] Ohta Kaneshiro, interview, September 20, 1958.

[58] Gen. Mateo Capinpin to Pres. Laurel, December 4, 1943, Malacanang, 147, 605.2.

[59] Maj. Gen. Guillermo Francisco to Pres. Laurel, March 8, 1943, Malacanang, 146, 605.2.

[60] Maj. Gen. Paulino Santos to Pres. Laurel, May 15, 1944, Malacanang, 146, 605.2.

[61] Ohta interview, September 20, 1958. In a further interview, on June 10, 1968, Ohta observed that Ricarte's defense force, which he saw as "within the constitution," unlike the Makapilis, has been "wiped out of Philippine histories."

[62] Agoncillo, *Fateful Years*, 2: 74–75.

[63] Ohta interview, September 20, 1958.

would continue for some in the nonparty service organization, Kalibapi, and would emerge again in the Makapili, the hard core of the Ganaps transformed into a self-immolating military group.[64]

Ramos's impatience with the Filipinos in power grew to the point of violence. Just before the wartime republic was inaugurated in October 1943, Narciso Lapus, secretary to Ricarte, showed Ohta a list, concocted by Ramos, of people to be assassinated at the ceremony—all the leading officials except Laurel and possibly Aquino.[65] Although Ricarte and others clearly pro-Japanese would have succeeded to places in government, Ricarte scotched the plan. Ramos persisted. Several months later, he proposed a coup d'état. Radical officers of the Japanese army and navy, most belonging to the ultranationalist Black Dragon Society, endorsed assassinating Laurel and his cabinet, and putting the government in the hands of Ramos and his followers as the only way materially to help the Japanese. General Wachi and Colonel Utsunomiya prevented the plot from being carried out,[66] but others kept the idea simmering. Mutō Akira, who arrived in September 1944 as Yamashita's chief of staff, had to be dissuaded by Wachi and Murata from backing a coup; Ramos might be loyal to the Japanese, but how many Filipinos were loyal to him?[67]

If too few followed Ramos to credit him as leader of a government, there were still enough to constitute him leader of an auxiliary force. The Japanese army had asked the help of the Laurel government in building a defense line from Quezon City to Pasay City. No one showed up.[68] Yamashita's staff, in exasperation, debated the question of arming Filipinos. Some agreed with Utsunomiya that to do so would alienate the Laurel government and give Filipinos weapons for possible use against the Japanese; others agreed with Major General Nishimura Toshio, newly arrived from China, that Laurel was no help, and they ought to organize guerrillas fighting for the Japanese to offset those already fighting against them.[69]

At Japanese instigation, Ramos called a meeting to organize such

[64] Goodman, "The Case of Benigno Ramos," Four Aspects of Philippine-Japanese Relations, 181–82, summarizes this sequence.

[65] Ohta, interview, September 20, 1958. Lapus later tried to save himself from a collaboration charge by fabricating evidence against Yamashita (A. Frank Reel, The Case of General Yamashita [Chicago: University of Chicago Press, 1949], 126–30).

[66] Nakamura Kōji, the leading Japanese political journalist in the wartime Philippines, testified to this effect in the collaboration trial of Pio Duran; Claro Recto, Laurel's lawyer, so reported in a letter, September 23, 1947, to Laurel (JPL, I-C-11).

[67] Gen. Wachi Takagi, interview, September 25, 1958.

[68] Ohta, interview, September 20, 1958.

[69] Hamamoto Masakatsu, interview, June 14, 1968.

a force. On learning that Laurel had not been informed, Ricarte objected. The situation was resolved at a second meeting when a Japanese representative announced that the commander in chief would proceed to organize the Makapili despite objections, and that its inauguration would be held in Malacanang. Laurel, privately informed about these arrangements, declared his intention to boycott the inauguration because the organization would owe its allegiance neither to him nor to the republic; but Murata persuaded him to be present anyway, arguing that defiance, on top of his unwillingness to declare outright war, would provoke a military reaction.[70]

At the inauguration, on the anniversary of the Pearl Harbor attack, Ramos described the Makapili as a nonpolitical, nonpartisan, nonsectarian organization dedicated to the destruction of the nation's enemies "within and without." Ricarte unfurled its flag: the sun with eight rays, symbolizing the eight provinces that first took arms against Spain, and the spirit of hakkō ichiu. General Yamashita made his first public speech in Manila, pledging to prevent the Anglo-Americans from reconquering the Philippines. After the program, Yamashita's chauffeur drove to the platform first, but "in a demonstration of sincere esteem for President Laurel" Yamashita walked Laurel to his car and watched it drive away before entering his own.[71]

The Makapili possessed two thousand rifles in their organizing stage.[72] Apparently, however, they were never deployed as a unit against American forces. Ramos evacuated to Baguio about two weeks after the Makapili inaugural ceremony. Cut off from Manila, he spent his time in the mountains zealously organizing Igorot scout-spies until his death while retreating with the Japanese army. The Makapili thus served as little more than the last angry symbol of Benigno Ramos's opposition to the Filipino leaders and to American imperialists.

Ricarte died of dysentery in the mountains. Ohta fulfilled the general's last wish, to be buried both in his native land and his second country, by burning his body and carrying some of the ashes back to Japan.[73]

[70] Agoncillo, *Fateful Years*, 2: 831–34.

[71] Manila *Tribune*, December 9, 1944; also November 26, December 7, 1944, on organization and aims of Makapili.

[72] Agoncillo, *Fateful Years*, 2: 833.

[73] Goodman, "Benigno Ramos," 182, implied that Ramos died in a kamikaze effort with Makapili troops. My sources on Ricarte are Ohta interviews, September 20,

Undergrounds and Guerrillas

Resistance to the Japanese, like assistance to them, was a function of differing kinds of hope. Among Indonesians, few resisted. In collaboration lay prospects of arms, organization, and morale, with which to challenge Allied forces. Only political affinity for the Netherlands or an ideological antifascism could account for underground activities. The Kenpeitai proceeded ruthlessly against those with, or suspected of having, communications with the Dutch: mostly ethnic minorities and Eurasians, or "half-breeds" as the Japanese called them.[74] Of a different nature was the cell led early in the war by Amir Sjarifuddin. Politically volatile and unpredictable, Amir was probably moved by the idea of a "united front against Fascism." He accepted Dutch monies and instructions for the purpose, but the Kenpeitai caught and tortured him, executed a number of his communist associates, and intimidated any who had intended to work with his unit.[75] Open opposition never reached the systematic level; the Japanese were able to put down any hostile uprising with abundant force to spare.

Armed rebellion against the Japanese, as distinguished from covert resistance, symbolic opposition, or intellectual criticism, had three major and distinctly different focal points: the Cirebon, Tasikmalaya, and Blitar incidents. The first of these was a response to oppressive economic conditions. Rice delivery quotas for Cirebon residency, the traditional granary of West Java, had been set high to fill military needs throughout the southern theater, and ambitious Japanese officers strove to exceed even those high quotas. Their oppressive methods, later described by one Japanese official as "disgraceful," led to two outbreaks in Cirebon in 1944, during which rioters attacked not only Japanese officers but also Indonesian bureaucrats who, "as the the tools of the Japanese, forced sacrifices by direct orders." Strong military action quelled the disturbances, with many deaths and injuries.[76]

The revolt in Tasikmalaya regency at Sukmana, Singapurna, although similarly grounded in economic conditions, intensified into a religious phenomenon. Kiai Zainal Mustafa, a famous conserva-

---

1958, June 10, 1968, and segment from Kozuma Hitoshi, *Wartime in the Philippines*, MS translation by Kamiya Yoshiko, author's possession.

[74] *Nihon Kenpei Seishi* (Tokyo, 1976) and *Nihon Kenpei Gaishi* (Tokyo, 1983) (see chap. 9, note 2).

[75] On Amir's wartime network, Ali Sastroamidjojo, interview, March 1968.

[76] Miyoshi, pt. 12, 80–81; also Benda, *Crescent and the Rising Sun*, 268 n. 46.

tive religious educator allegedly blessed with divine powers, was expected to give a mystical sign in the month of Muhammad's birthday that would protect those who believed and leave those who doubted to be punished. The Kenpeitai, hearing rumors of unrest in late February 1943, went to inspect and found the town roads blockaded against intruders. The Japanese began skirmishing with students and villagers to gain entrance. When the chief of the detachment was killed with his own saber, reinforcements came, and in the ensuing battles 153 villagers as well as 86 Japanese died. The Kenpeitai rounded up 23 Indonesians, including Zainal, many of whom presumably were later executed.[77]

At Blitar, East Java, in February 1945, a detachment of Peta trainees rebelled against their training officers and the Kenpeitai. Discrimination in wages and conditions had moved them, as had humiliating punishment for violation of regulations, in particular the slap on the head or face. The Japanese were "prepared for the emergency," and crushed it in a few hours with rifles and machine guns. A court-martial in Jakarta tried sixty-eight men and condemned eight to death, two of whom later had their sentences commuted. Supriyadi, the leader, disappeared without a clue, either in battle or by execution. His name, thereafter, took on magical life.[78]

These three incidents pointed up three major aspects of conditions under the Japanese—economic mismanagement, religious misunderstandings, and military officiousness—but neither singly nor together did the incidents seriously alter Japanese practices. The uprisings in Cirebon and Tasikmalaya echoed events occurring throughout the Dutch period and after, for economic deprivation and messianic expectation had been and remained prime causes of Indonesian unrest, particularly when combined. But men short on rice and long on religion, armed with bamboo spears and swords, did not worry the Japanese as much as the Peta revolt at Blitar. These were men with nationalist ideology, modern expectations, and some military training. Sukarno, still "loyal unto death"

[77] Miyoshi, pt. 13, 79–80; also Benda, *Crescent and the Rising Sun*, 160–61, 163, 268–73; Benedict R. O'G. Anderson, *Java in a Time of Revolution: Occupation and Resistance, 1944–45* (Ithaca: Cornell University Press, 1972), 35–36; Bernhard Dahm, *The History of Indonesia in the Twentieth Century* (London and New York: Praeger, 1971), 92. The Kenpei histories, *Seishi* and *Gaishi*, are silent on the punishments. They stress Zainal's "3000 adherents," his vision of an Islamic kingdom, and the fanatic fighting abilities of those pursuing a holy death.

[78] Miyoshi, pt. 12, 80; Gatot, "The Peta," 124; Benda, *Crescent and the Rising Sun*, 182, 270, 283; Anderson, *Java in Revolution*, 36; Dahm, *History of Indonesia in the Twentieth Century*, 98, 116–17; Sundhaussen, *The Road to Power*, 2, 7, 19.

to the Japanese, openly condemned the Peta revolt at a Chūō Sangi-in meeting on June 18, 1945,[79] and also repudiated the revolt to some critical youth, telling them it brought bloodshed and death prematurely.[80] Most nationalists subscribed to his reasoning and avoided active resistance. Even the pemuda confined themselves to symbolic gestures and intellectual preparedness.

Against this background, one can better understand the several youth groups who applied to themselves the term "underground." With its implications of clandestine war, the term was more useful in suggesting to the Dutch an aura like that of their own actively anti-Nazi underground than in describing the actuality. The groups of young political activists were actually above ground, and none engaged in espionage or sabotage. As nascent centers of agitation, these groups gave vent to passionate discussions and, as the war came to a conclusion, assumed active involvement with the national destiny.

Delineation of these groups is difficult because of some measure of overlapping, but the following division into major nuclei may illuminate their character:[81]

1. Sjahrir's group, a mutation of the 1930 discussion group, Pendidikan Nasional Indonesia, over which the Dutch police had kept close watch, was the most sophisticated and the most elaborate in the sense of exchanging information by courier between major cities.
2. The Prapatan 10 group, drawn from the *asrama* (dormitory) of the Medical Faculty and led by Soedjatmoko and Sudarpo, was intellectually Western-oriented and close to Sjahrir.

---

[79] Gatot, "The Peta," 124.

[80] *Sukarno: An Autobiography*, 193. Anton Lucas, ed., *Local Opposition and Underground Resistance to the Japanese in Java 1942–1945*, Monash University, Centre of Southeast Asian Studies, Paper on Southeast Asia, no. 13 (1986) is a Blitar-centered collection of reminiscences by communists who were jailed, or were on the run from the Kenpeitai. It reveals little about the Peta uprising, but on that and other matters is fascinating for its dreams, dreads, and nostalgia for purity. For an example of active Marxist resistance against the Japanese and partial cooperation with the returning British that was significant in shaping postwar Burma, see Robert H. Taylor, ed., *Marxism and Resistance in Burma, 1942–1945: Thein Pe Myint's "Wartime Traveler,"* Southeast Asia Translation Series, vol. 4 (Athens: Ohio University Press, 1984).

[81] The listing I give is compounded of information in Bendict R. O'G. Anderson, "The Pemuda Revolution: Indonesian Politics, 1945–1946" (Ph.D. diss., Cornell University, 1967), 38–50, revised in *Java in Revolution*, 36–49; Kanahele, "Japanese Occupation," 156–60; and author's interviews.

3. The Menteng 31 group, comprising members of the Asrama Angkatan Baru Indonesia, was a "new generation" group set up by the Sendenbu (the Japanese Propaganda Office) and encouraged especially by Shimizu Hitoshi. Their training ended in April 1943, but most members, including Sukarni and Chaerul Saleh, remained close to the Sendenbu and were strongly anti-Dutch.

4. The Kebon Sirih 80 group, from the Asrama Indonesia Merdeka, was set up by the Bukanfu (Admiral Maeda's Naval Liaison Office) in 1944 after the Koiso Declaration, primarily to develop leadership cadres for an independent Indonesia. Wikana was a leader of this group.

5. Barisan Pelopor was a "vanguard group," led by Muwardi, whose younger elements were less military and more political than the Peta, less political and more military than the three asrama groups. After independence this group renamed itself Barisan Benting.

6. The Gerakan Indonesia Merdeka consisted chiefly of young communists—notably Aidit and Lukman—who would emerge after 1948 as party leaders.

Distinctly young, rarely wielding more dangerous implements than the radio and earphones that Sjahrir employed, these groups signified the emergence on the Indonesian scene of varieties of young nationalism. But their very youth and lack of arms, in addition to inadequate organization, poor liaison, and the alertness of the Kenpeitai and Beppan, made overt activity hardly profitable at the time. Their professed purpose was not to combat imperial Japan "but to make her fulfill her promises."[82]

The Philippine situation differed from the Indonesian in one very significant respect: the diffuse availability of arms. Filipino society bore the influences of both Latin American machismo and North American frontierism. A man's own gun meant protection and identity, and it might also lead to provocation and extinction. Private possession of firearms in the peacetime Philippines enormously exceeded that of Indonesia. In addition, MacArthur, trying to develop a defensive Philippine army for President Quezon and to bolster American forces (which numbered thirty-one thousand in December 1941), had trained and armed over one hundred thousand Filipinos. Surrender to Japan legally meant surrender of those arms, but by no means all usable items wound up in Japanese warehouses,

---

[82] Kanahele, "Japanese Occupation," 159–60; Anderson, "Pemuda Revolution," 49.

despite repeated instructions. A significant proportion of USAFFE (United States Armed Forces Far East) arms, American and Filipino, disappeared with those who faded out of the regular army to bloom later as guerrillas.

The Japanese tried to rebuild the Philippine Constabulary along their own lines, selecting officers from among prisoners of war who were "experienced, high-ranking . . . [and] of superior character." The basic force was constituted from "volunteers" among other prisoners, and nearly twenty thousand were trained for two months from May 1942 through March 1943. Many were used successfully on antiguerrilla expeditions, and four hundred to seven hundred guerrillas per month were induced voluntarily to surrender, and released on a pledge of good behavior. Nonetheless, the Japanese officer in charge of these activities found it heavy going with Philippine poverty and dependency, against American material culture, education, and propaganda.[83]

Filipino resistance groups were initially short on arms and ammunition, which required some to go on forays to capture Japanese arms. But in contrast to the isolated outbreaks in Indonesia and the subdued dissidence of intellectuals there, the Philippine scene, within a year of effective occupation, was one of a steady level of espionage, sabotage, and ambuscade, all seriously detrimental to Japanese interests. From early 1943 to late 1944 the collaboration government moved from special entreaty to general amnesty and finally to admitted incapacity in dealing with resistance. The Japanese mood meanwhile shifted from harassed tolerance to suspicious fury.

Quintin Paredes, who had been associated with the American colonial government since his youth and its first decade, found the habit of power too hard to break. Like most of his fellows, he collaborated with the Japanese. In a letter to Macario Peralta, an early and prominent guerrilla leader on Panay, Paredes named the men who were cooperating with the Japanese military administration and asked if all of them were wrong and Peralta alone right: "the leaders of our former political parties . . . men whose record of services have been recognized by the former Government, and men whose political slogans have merited popular approval, can they all have changed from patriotic Filipinos into traitors overnight? I hope

---

[83] Col. (later Maj. Gen.) Utsunomiya Naotaka, *Minami Jūjisei O Nozomitsutsu*, in *Nanpō no Gunsei*, 506–8.

you will not insult them or your intelligence by holding that they all have, without exception."

Paredes said that he had secured immunity for Peralta from the Japanese General Staff, and added that "your mother has already become thin out of worries." Peralta did not move. He persisted in touch with MacArthur's headquarters in Australia.[84]

Several months later, after taking office as president, Laurel declared a general amnesty to all citizens who had committed political crimes, if they would surrender and turn in their arms within sixty days. He conceded that the guerrillas "want to keep that freedom in the way they believe is honorable and patriotic. And so do we, but it is clear now beyond argument that this freedom is here within the pale of law and order, where it is real, tangible, and fruitful, and not where they think it is, for it is only the ghost of liberty and freedom that walks with them in their solitary exile."[85]

The number reported as surrendering over the next six months was 123,385—an incredible figure, including a round sum of 60,000 for Leyte.[86] If one-tenth of this total actually turned themselves in, obtained a bit of rice and peace of mind, and went back soon after to old units and pursuits, Laurel probably succeeded in his immediate objective of reducing the possibility of repressive measures by the Japanese.

One of Laurel's most loyal informants nonetheless expressed profound doubts about the effect of a conciliatory policy. He said that enemies of the administration interpreted it as a sign of weakness; they "make an active and insidious whispering campaign to convey that misimpression to the masses. And when the law-abiding citizens, the majority of whom are usually passive and timid, observe how the . . . lawless elements are practically running the government in their respective communities . . . is it any wonder that even the good elements . . . acquiesce to many subversive acts?"[87]

As the Americans drew nearer, there was nothing further Laurel could do to lessen hostilities between guerrillas and the Japanese

[84] Commissioner Quintin Paredes to Col. Macario Peralta, February 26, 1943, Malacanang, 227, and RG 4, MacA, passim. Alfred W. McCoy pictures Peralta's activity in a setting of regional political conflict in " 'Politics by Other Means': World War II in the Western Visayas, Philippines," McCoy, ed., *Southeast Asia Under Japanese Occupation*, Yale University Southeast Asia Studies (New Haven, 1980), 191–245.

[85] Message to accompany General Amnesty Proclamation, December 15, 1943, JPL; also *Official Gazette* 1 (1943): 292–94.

[86] "List of Persons . . . Surrendered . . . in Accordance with Proclamation N. 2, as per Reports Received" (as of May 3, 1944), Malacanang, 20, 037-3.

[87] Jose I. Baluyot to Laurel, February 19, 1944, Malacanang, 48, 066.

army. Late in August 1944, Murata told Laurel that the "worsening" of public security was giving the military an "uneasy feeling." After recalling the early occupation when Japanese tended to have "friendly feelings" toward the Filipinos, he warned that now, despite the "absolute faith of the Japanese Government in Your Excellency. . . . I can positively assert that we do not trust your people."[88]

Communications between MacArthur's headquarters in Australia and such guerrilla leaders as Peralta and Tomas Confesor on Panay, Ruperto Kangleon on Leyte, and Wendell Fertig on Mindanao were well established by 1943. Confidence in American return gave these forces, which faced a relatively smaller number of Japanese than those on Luzon, a certain boldness in operation. MacArthur's headquarters even referred to their districts as the "free areas." Confesor likened surrender overtures to the "tranquility . . . of a carabao," and declared that "personal privileges and civil liberties . . . were practically a gift from a generous and magnanimous people—the people of the United States of America. Now that Japan is attempting to destroy these liberties . . . should we not be willing to suffer for their defense?"[89]

In Luzon, communications to MacArthur's headquarters were much more dangerous where they existed, and relations between units were sometimes more hostile than relations with the Japanese. The clear disposition of most units—as many as forty-one have been listed[90]—was for Filipino-American cooperation to oust

[88] Murata diary, August 25, 1944.

[89] Gov. Tomas Confesor to Dr. Fermin Caram, February 20, 1943, copy in Quezon Collection, the National Library, Manila; also reprinted in Agoncillo, *Fateful Years*, 2: 986–76. For full analysis of Confesor's actions and motivations, see McCoy, " 'Politics by Other Means.' "

[90] Maj. Robert T. Yap-Diangco, *The Filipino Guerrilla Tradition* (Manila: MCS Enterprises, 1971), 153–57. One of these was Ang Mga Maharlika, organized by Ferdinand Marcos. Neither Yap-Diangco's book nor Willoughby's (note 92 below) give it narrative attention, as distinct from mere listing. My efforts through the Philippine Embassy and Malacanang Palace to interview President Marcos about it were given the runaround (October–November 1982). Records made available at the National Archives in November 1984 reveal that Marcos's postwar attempts to build a history of the unit, in order for it to receive backpay, were denied as "fraudulent." Professor Alfred McCoy disclosed that fact to influential American newspapers shortly before the Philippine presidential election of 1986 (*New York Times*, January 23, 1986, p. 1). Reading the full file makes it clear that Marcos was involved in light espionage and sabotage, as well as some heavy politicking. He followed that with extensive fabrication and exaggeration of the importance of what he had done (NARS RG 407, special segregated copy of Guerrilla Unit Recognition File, Maharlika). Charles C. McDougald, *The Marcos File* (San Francisco: San Francisco Publishers, 1987) sorts

the Japanese. But the closer that major units were to the power center, Manila, the more they reflected differing socioeconomic status and interests.

In the lordly center of MacArthur's headquarters, prewar and postwar economic interests gave a neo-imperial cast to the thinking of some key personnel.[91] Most closely related to that military-patriotic connection were the various units with unsurrendered American commanders from the United States Armed Forces Far East, such as the ECLGA (East Central Luzon Guerrilla Area), of which Major Ramsey's unit claimed seven thousand arms and forty-five thousand members.[92] The Hunters ROTC originated in Rizal and had the largest unit in Cavite. They were led by young Filipinos, mostly college and university students. Their leader recalled later: "We didn't hate anybody . . . unlike the Indonesians with the Dutch. Still, even then, we were careful not to look 'pro-American.' When we were in times of idleness indoctrinating our troops, we said we were fighting to help get our independence from the Americans. We were pro-Filipino and definitely anti-Japanese. We just wanted the Americans to come back [so we could] win the war, and go back to college. That was our thinking, pretty short range politically."[93]

The political thinking of the Markings, led by Marcos Villa Agustin and Yay Panlilio, was hardly any longer range than that of the Hunters, as their correspondence with MacArthur's headquarters shows.[94] But they were older, more numerous, and more plebeian than the Hunters, and were led by an ex–truck driver. The two groups expended much energy in rivalry with each other over spheres of influence, arms, supplies, and women.[95] Still lower on any scale of affluence or social status, while clearer in their motivations and their impact, were the Hukbalahaps. They were also further from contact with MacArthur, and almost wholly independent in initiative. The hungry and disaffected peasantry of Central

---

all the inconsistencies and discrepancies and concludes (p. 106) that "Marcos the soldier was an illusion."

[91] Col. Jesus A. Villamor, *They Never Surrendered* (Quezon City: Vera-Reyes, 1982), 235–36.

[92] Maj. Gen. Charles A. Willoughby, *The Guerrilla Resistance Movement in the Philippines* (New York: Vantage Press, 1972), 452.

[93] Proculo L. Mojica, *Terry's Hunters* (Manila: Benipayo Press, 1965); quotations from Eleuterio Adevoso, interview, October 15, 1967.

[94] Yay Panlilio, *The Crucible* (New York: MacMillan, 1950), 2d ed., *Marking* (Manila: Venceremos, 1979); RG 16, MacA.

[95] Mojica, 270–336, esp. 273–76; Agoncillo, *Fateful Years*, 2: 763–70.

Luzon were recruited in significant numbers by a brittle Stalinist political leadership, and an unorthodox socialist field commander, Luis Taruc.[96] All the guerrilla groups made life hard for the Japanese army and the puppet Constabulary. But the Hunters also fought the Markings and the Huks. And the Huks fought everybody. They and the USAFFE units struggled to the "last drop of blood."[97]

The ideological error of all the other guerrilla forces, as the Huks saw it, was to "lie low" following MacArthur's orders and wait for his return. When the Americans came back, most units fought with them, but "as orderlies." The Huks had pride of initiative as well as continuity of struggle. They tried to organize not only for battle, but for a government based on "nationalism, democracy, justice." They did raise the Philippine and American flags together in 1945. But when a major in the CIC offered Taruc one-star rank if he would have his Huks lay down their arms, Taruc replied, "OK, if you will disarm Stalin at the same time."[98]

The class tensions that produced bloodshed in Indonesia in 1948 and 1965 had their analogue in the Philippines. They would emerge

[96] Taruc wrote of these experiences from within the movement in *Born of the People* (New York: International Publishers, 1953), but mentions them only briefly in a subsequent memoir, written in prison from a Christian democrat viewpoint, *He Who Rides the Tiger* (New York: Praeger, 1967). For orientation to doctrinal and tactical splits, see Francisco Nemenzo, "Rectification Process in the Philippine Communist Movement," in Lim Joo-Jock, with Vani S., ed., *Armed Communist Movements in Southeast Asia* (New York: St. Martin's Press, 1984), 72–105.

A Soviet analyst of six peasant societies in South and Southeast Asia finds Java and Luzon at opposite ends of a spectrum of class consciousness—Java weak with archaic collectivism and conformism, Luzon the most fertile for the formation of an aggressive class atittude (Zhanna D. Smirenskaia, *Peasants in Asia: Social Consciousness and Social Struggle*, trans. Michael J. Buckley, Ohio University Monographs in International Studies, Southeast Asia Series, no. 73 [Athens, 1986]).

[97] Willoughby, *Guerrilla Resistance Movement*, 450–64; Villamor *They Never Surrendered*, 182–84; quotation from Agoncillo account, 2: 761–63; various guerrilla commanders to MacArthur, RG 16, Box 110, and Col. Eusebio Aquino, Field Cmdr., No. Luzon, Hukbalahap, to Cmd. Ofcr. [U.S. Army], Concepcion, Tarlac, January 26, 1945, Box 6, MacA.

[98] Interview with Luis Taruc, Commander Liwayway, Agaton Bulaong, and Rufino Regalado at Barrio San Marcos, Calumpit, Bulacan, November 23, 1982.

After the war, the U.S. Army provided back pay to cooperative guerrilla units contributing substantially to the defeat of the Japanese. Huk units under Eusebio Aquino made documented submissions, but were turned down. The Markings were recognized, despite a good deal of contentiousness, for their raw courage in significant engagements with the enemy. The Hunters were clearly the most cooperative, most sought cooperation with other units, and were most readily recognized (NARS RG 407, Huks [Boxes 369–70], Marking's Fil-Americans [Boxes 325–31], Hunters ROTC [Boxes 493–501]).

in the postwar struggle of a new body of Huks against the society, and later in the upsurge of the New People's Army. But the generational and national tensions that helped to feed the Indonesian revolution had no Philippine analogue. Where young men joined in nationalist discussion groups designated by Jakarta street addresses, their educated Filipino equivalents mainly joined the Hunters ROTC and like guerrilla units, which had restorative aims.[99]

In supplying food and labor and trainable military manpower to the Japanese, Indonesia was incomparably more accommodating than the Philippines. During wartime there were just three significant moments of uprising in Java against the Japanese. Only in the postwar power vacuum that helped foster national revolution, when the Japanese stood as embarrassed surrogate police for the British and Dutch, did Indonesians mortally challenge them.

In their dogged withholding of manpower from Japan, the Filipinos were unique in the Greater Asia Co-Prosperity Sphere; and in the audacity of their open and mortal resistance they were alone among Southeast Asian peoples. In public sentiment, apparently, the revolution of 1896 was being realized through American constitutional means and institutional manners. In fighting as proxies and auxiliaries to the return of American power, many Filipinos were striving to complete an old revolution. Some were simply working for restoration of the prewar system. Only a few, the Hukbalahaps, labored for an imagined new era.

[99] L.E.L. Sluimers looks at these matters from a different angle in *Samurai, Pemuda und Sakdalista: Die Japaner und der Radikalismus in Indonesien und der Philippinen, 1941–1945* (Amsterdam: Antropologisch Sociologisch Centrum, University of Amsterdam, 1972). Susan Sternglass has done a summary translation (MS in author's possession).

9

JAPANESE REPRESSION IN
VICTORY AND DEFEAT

Japanese imperialism, like other varieties of modern empire, aimed to do good. Its unique cultural form and its militant enthusiasm, however, contained a high propensity for misunderstanding and harsh action. One organization came supremely to represent the terror latent in Japanese presence overseas. Long after the goodwill and kindness of individual Japanese were forgotten, the shadow of the Kenpeitai remained in the minds of conquered peoples.[1]

REPRESSIVE STYLE AND AGENCY

The Kenpeitai was founded by the Meiji government in 1881 to police the army and control the populace.[2] Although a separate organ-

[1] For a balanced retrospective and prospective view of Japanese-Philippine relations, see Miwa Kimitada, "Not Another Greater East Asian Co-Prosperity Sphere," *Solidarity* 1 (1983): 14–20. The stimulus for the article is the concept of Pacific Basin Cooperation, which the author compares in its antisentimentality and economic pragmatics to Rōyama Masamichi's 1943 report on the Philippines.

[2] Barbara Gifford Shimer and Guy Hobbs, trans., *The Kenpeitai in Java and Sumatra*, Cornell Modern Indonesia Project, Translation Series, no. 65 (Ithaca, 1986). Mrs. Shimer precedes the work with an informative translator's introduction, toward which in turn I have written a general introductory essay. The corpus of fact and opinion from which we three proceeded is contained in a trilogy of works by the Editorial Committee of the National Federation of Kenpeitai Veterans' Associations, the first two chaired by Moriyasu Seiichi, and the other by Iizuka Jun: *Nihon Kenpei Seishi* (The authoritative history of the Japanese Kenpeitai) (1976) and *Nihon Kenpei Gaishi* (The general history of the Japanese Kenpeitai) (1983), both published in Tokyo by Zenkoku Kenyūkai Rengōkai Honbu; and *Junkoku Kenpei No Isho* (Last testaments of Kenpei who died for their country) (1982), published in Tokyo, by Tōkyō Kenyūkai, 1982. Subsequent references will be simply to *Kenpei Seishi*, *Kenpei Gaishi*, or *Kenpei Isho*.

ization, the Tokkōka, was established in 1911 as a thought police, the Kenpeitai developed its own thought control division in the 1920s. Stifling foreign ideas, pacifist sentiments, and irreverence for the emperor made the Kenpeitai focus particularly on students, socialists and communists, and workers and farmers, as targets. Intimidation, imprisonment, torture, and occasional murder were among its methods.

In 1939 the Japanese Diet enacted an extraordinarily strong anti-espionage law, expanding counterespionage services and application of the death sentence. Antispy campaigns worked normal Japanese insularity into unprecedented suspicion and hatred of foreigners. The chief beneficiary of the legislation and chief rouser of the mood was the Kenpeitai.[3]

Although the Kenpeitai was organized as a combat force of the army, its provost marshal general was responsible only to the minister of war. The organization took its name seriously (ken pei means "law soldier" or "judicial soldier"); and it assumed a charge of being exemplary of the discipline required for the expanding Meiji state.[4] Overseas in the Second World War it was active everywhere—Formosa, Korea, China, and all the occupied territories of Southeast Asia—in censorship, surveillance of public places, monitoring of suspected subversives, and eradication of networks of spies. Its numbers grew to thirty-six thousand in Japan and overseas.[5] Its influence was nearly uncheckable. At the end of the war many Kenpei leaders opposed surrender; nearly all files were burned; and some field leaders fled to the hills to continue resistance. One of MacArthur's early acts was to abolish the organization, on November 1, 1945.

Before defeat, however, the Kenpeitai had so effectively established its power in security, counterespionage, censorship, propaganda, and counterpropaganda, that it could potentially influence any thought, behavior, movement, or expression. The core of this power was its supreme responsibility for army discipline. A mem-

[3] Ronald Seth, Encyclopedia of Espionage (Garden City, N.Y.: Doubleday, 1972), 325–28; Richard H. Mitchell, Thought Control in Prewar Japan (Ithaca: Cornell University Press, 1976), 25; John W. Dower, Origins of the Modern Japanese State: Selected Writings of E. H. Norman (New York: Pantheon Books, 1975), 58, 355; Ōtani Keijirō, Shōwa Kenpei-shi (1979), 5, cited in Shimer and Hobbs, trans., Kenpeitai in Java and Sumatra.

[4] Kenpei Seishi, 125.

[5] Shimer, translator's introduction. American intelligence estimates, 1945, were 70,000 Kenpei of which 24,000 were officers, not including native recruits and auxiliaries in occupied territories (Seth, Encyclopedia of Espionage, 325–28).

ber of the Kenpeitai could arrest an army officer up to three ranks higher than himself and carry out punishment in the field. Noting instances of Kenpeitai corporals beating captains if the latter were found drunk, and of Kenpeitai field units holding courts-martial, an Allied research unit report concluded that "the authority of the Japanese military police is undoubtedly limited by regulation; in practice, however, their power appears to be limitless."[6] For a Kenpeitai captain to be able in theory to arrest an army general is not of course boundless power; but it does describe a potency of military police probably unsurpassed in modern industrial nations.

The Kenpeitai was not the only part of the Japanese imperial machine transgressing in Indonesia and the Philippines. Misunderstandings and misdeeds were commonplace. Japanese logic of doing the impossible, of spirit over machine, or pure motive over corrupt system, served as inspiration to Japanese troops and civilians alike, as well as to many cooperating with them. But such logic also filtered out contrary information, blinded the Japanese to their own errors and defeats, and served as a rationale for cruelties against occupied peoples.

One man's reason may be another's repression; and one's militant enthusiasm,[7] another's terror. From the very beginning cultural frictions arose over symbolic things. Two sensitive matters were hair length and face slapping. Nineteenth-century samurai had seen political significance to hair style: a shaven head expressed commitment to retention of the old ways and expulsion of the Western barbarians; a bushy head, commitment to replacement of the shogunate and adaptation to Western pressure and precept.[8] The bushy heads had won. But now, in the twentieth century, shaven heads defended the imperial system. Even Japanese university students cut their hair down to one-half inch or less, like soldiers, to show their wartime spirit.

As the tide of battle began to turn in late 1943, Japanese professors at the University of Indonesia became increasingly irritated by the long hair of Indonesian students. Were not Japanese boys dying

[6] Seth, *Encyclopedia of Espionage*, 327; quotation from Allied Translator and Interpreter Service (ATIS), Research Report 119, "The Japanese Military Police Service, p. 26 (MacA).

[7] I use this term as it is employed by Konrad Lorenz, *On Aggression* (New York: Bantam, 1967), 253–65, esp. 259ff.

[8] Kosaka Masaaki, ed., *Japanese Thought in the Meiji Era*, trans. David Abosch, Centenary Culture Council Series, no. 9 (Tokyo: Pan Pacific Press, 1958), 57–58.

for them? The professors ordered the students to shave their heads.[9] Feelings ran high. When a Japanese doctor slapped a recalcitrant longhair, the medical students went on strike. With the help of their own professors, particularly lawyers, the striking students defended the sacredness of hair and head in Javanese culture, and the Japanese backed down. But when the students renewed their strike after a Japanese soldier slapped another medical student, the Kenpeitai abruptly arrested eight ringleaders, including Sudarpo, Soedjatmoko, Daan Jajah, and Subandio. They interrogated the eight for a month, trying to implicate Hatta, still a bete noir to them, as was Roxas in the Philippines. Soedjatmoko had in fact consulted Hatta, who, aware of being under close surveillance, dared only to convey implicit approval.[10] But they kept that secret against Kenpeitai pressure, and the eight were eventually released.[11] Indonesian students shaved their heads, but that only accelerated the revolution growing inside their brains.

Face slapping (binta) was an acceptable form of social control in many Japanese relationships. The military had developed it to a particularly high degree. Officers and soldiers alike considered binta swift and memorable, less demeaning then demotion, a dock in pay, confinement, or even a tongue-lashing, which would be mentally grievous.[12] Although someone in the Japanese bureaucracy had sufficient insight to prepare a booklet warning soldiers arriving in Indonesia against slapping Muslims, most of them did not grasp the seriousness of the offense.[13] Few or none showed sensitivity to those for whom Javanese syncretic culture meant far more than pure Islam. "With a true prijaji, you wouldn't dare touch his head with all peaceful intent, let alone slap him."[14] Japanese soldiers and

[9] Yamamoto Moichirō, interview, June 11, 1968.

[10] Interviews: Soedjatmoko, March 21,1968; Hatta, July 3, 1968.

[11] Sukarno (Sukarnro: An Autobiography [Indianapolis: Bobbs-Merrill, 1965], 194), says that the strikers were sentenced to death and "Sukarno . . . freed them." Nothing in my interviews with Soedjatmoko (March 21, 1968), Yamamoto (June 11, 1968), or Hatta (July 3, 1968) suggested there was any such sentence or any such intervention.

[12] Interview, Yamamoto Moichirō, June 11, 1968, G. H. de Heer; May 27, 1968.

[13] Miyoshi Shunkichirō, "Jawa senryō gunsei kaikoroku" (Memoirs of the military administration of Java), 15 pts. Kokusai Mondai (April 1965–January 1967); Miyoshi and Yamamoto interviews.

[14] Quotation from Rosihan Anwar, interview, February 24, 1968. Clifford Geertz distinguishes nicely between santri, from whom Islamic tradition prevailed and priyayi, for whom Hindu-Buddhist mysticism was admixed with Western bureaucratic values (The Religion of Java [Glencoe, Ill.: Free Press, 1960], 5–6).

civilians nevertheless tended to slap indiscriminately, right hand or left (though warned particularly against the latter), not only insulting strangers but their own Indonesian co-workers and servants.

Among Filipinos the reaction to the face slap was at least as keen, although the psychology was different. Christian belief in the unique worth of every "child of Christ" was accompanied by acute sensitivity to anything that smacked of treatment as an inferior. The physical pain was less than the humiliation—being abused in one's soul by an armed man, and unable to respond or to find redress.[15] Benigno Aquino, Sr., on Kalibapi speaking tours, tried to reassure the populace that he had cautioned the Japanese against face slapping.[16] Paulino Gullas, another willing collaborator, understood it was a mild matter with the Japanese, "but with the Filipinos it is extremely humiliating, degrading, insulting. It may leave no scare in the face [sic], but surely it leaves a wound in the heart, most probably bleeding, never healing down to the grave."[17] He asked for courage in the highest Filipino officials to stop the practice. But it continued.

At their war crimes trials the Japanese joked, a bit desperately, about binta: one slap of a man, three years in prison; five slaps, death; slapping a woman, death sentence for sure.[18]

Repression, Japanese style, went far beyond insult to maltreatment of prisoners of war, forced labor for prisoners and rōmusha, forced prostitution, and mass political executions. Overall figures on Japanese prisoner-of-war camps show that 27 percent of the inmates died, compared with 4 percent of those captured by the Germans and Italians.[19] In the so-called Koo operation in various parts of Java from July 1943 to March 1944, the Japanese executed 239 persons without trial, ostensibly to eliminate individuals considered dangerous in case of Allied invasion. The "Ji operation" in Sumatra was similar.[20] In Pontianak, Borneo, at the end of 1943, the

---

[15] Theodore Friend, "Japanese Totalism, Philippine Pluralism," Solidarity 3, no. 3 (1968): 24–30, esp. 25; Juan Collas, Sr., interview, May 7, 1968; del Castillo and del Castillo, The Saga of Jose P. Laurel, 140–41; A.V.H. Hartendorp, The Japanese Occupation of the Philippines (Manila: Bookmark, 1967), 1: 224–25.

[16] Aquino to Jorge Vargas, February 15, 1943, "Official Report of the Kalibapi Tour of Baguio, Mountain Province, and San Fernando, La Union," Malacanang, 228, 980.11.

[17] Malacanang, 158, 980.1, probably July 1944.

[18] Yamamoto, interview, June 11, 1968.

[19] IMTFE, Judgments, pp. 1002–3.

[20] "Extracts of Extreme Cruelty by the Japanese," undated memo, RVO 008762-5; R. John Pritchard and Sonia Zaide, eds., International Military Tribunal for the Far

Japanese executed or tortured to death about 1,500 people on the basis of a rumored plot; few got a trial.[21] The war crimes prosecution of General Yamashita in the Philippines centered on the alleged killing "without trial or apparent cause" of 35,000 men, women, and children, exclusive of prisoners of war and civilian internees.[22]

The Japanese had little difficulty finding justification for their actions. Since Japanese troops who became prisoners of war were considered nonpersons, spiritually dead, why should enemy prisoners be considered any better? Since the "primitives" (dojin) of the Southern Area were blessed with Japanese intervention and sacrifice of blood on their behalf, why should they not work diligently, even to death? Since women were creatures subordinate to men, and men needed comfort, why should some Indonesian women not be pressed into service in Japanese military brothels? And since the success of the holy war depended on extermination of subversives, why should rebels not be liquidated?

The postwar explanations multiplied. To many Japanese among themselves, the maxim "motive purifies mode" seemed to justify most or all that they had done.[23] Even a non-Kenpei officer could argue that because beating was still practiced by the police in Japan, penal responsibility for such acts was incongruous.[24] A scholar could explain, without justifying base acts, that Japanese soldiers, "mere subjects" at home, could get inflated ideas of superiority

---

East: The Tokyo War Crimes Trials, 1946–48 (New York: Garland Publishing, 1981) 6: 13701–2, 13810 ("Narrative Summary of the Proceedings"). Another document, "Establishment of Military Court (Gunritsu Kaigi) and Outline of its Jurisdiction," RVO 005134-39, composed by the Japanese for Dutch investigators, gives an actual total of 438 death penalties imposed by the court in Java, March 1942–August 1945. In that light, the figure of 239 additional executions without trial during "Koo" is easily credible.

[21] "Extracts of Extreme Cruelty," RVO 008762-5. Dr. Bahder Djohan, a postwar minister of education, saw ten mass graves in Kalimantan and estimates the dead as high as 4,000 (memo to the author, March 27, 1968). In response to the Japanese Education Ministry's elimination of such matters from textbooks and to Indonesian journalistic exaggeration of them, Iseki Tsuneo, a wartime member of the navy's special police unit, quoted his squad leader's figure of 1,486 killed in the Pontianak incident (Philadelphia *Inquirer*, November 6, 1982, UPI (Tokyo) dispatch).

[22] Theater Judge Adv. to CinC Pac, December 26, 1945, SCAP, Box 164, Washington National Records Center.

[23] [Nakamura Hiroshi], RVO 048339. For a description of this document see chap. 10, note 18.

[24] Ichibanse Yoshio, interrogation, April 17, 18, 1947, RVO 006202-08.

abroad.[25] At more nakedly self-defensive levels, non-Kenpei Japanese tended to blame what went wrong on the Kenpeitai alone. Of cultural rationales and juridical problems there is no end.[26] Some of what actually happened, however, deserves to be clarified.

THE KENPEITAI IN JAVA

On December 8, 1942, celebrating a year of freedom from Dutch oppression, Mohammad Hatta told a wildly applauding audience of a hundred thousand that he would rather see Indonesia at the bottom of the ocean than under another colonial regime. Thereafter the Kenpeitai kept a close surveillance over him. In July 1943 Hatta's reports began to come back from the Japanese military administration heavily red-inked with criticism and deletions. Sometime in August 1943, Miyoshi heard of a plot from an officer in military government: Hatta was to be summoned to Bandung, driven and accompanied by Miyoshi; at a precipitous curve near Puntjak Pass a band of military police in a plain car would ram the car over the cliff. Announcement of accidental death would follow.[27]

Feeling "wretched and horrified," Miyoshi went to Yamamoto and in a private two-hour session got the full story. The Kenpeitai had inflamed their own objections to Hatta with material from the files of the Dutch secret police and attorney general that labeled him, like many other nationalists, a "communist." Major General Nishida of the Sixteenth Army staff had approved a report by the two top Kenpeitai officers, Lieutenant Colonel Murase Mitsuo and Major Cho, calling Hatta a dangerous man who, in consideration of public peace, could not be left alive.[28] Sanction from Tokyo had followed. It was too late, Yamamoto said "very sadly," to interfere with the plan. The commanding general's chief of staff gave Miyoshi the same excuse. The Sixteenth Army and the military administration in Java were unwilling or unable to ask the Kenpei-

[25] Maruyama Masao, *Thought and Behavior in Modern Japanese Politics* (London: Oxford University Press, 1963), 18–19. Ienaga Saburō sees the same phenomena unredeemed by an anthropological explanation, as a "disgraceful and bloody rampage," *The Pacific War, 1931–1945; a Critical Perspective on Japanese Role in World War II* (New York: Pantheon, 1978), 180 (1st Japanese ed., *Taiheiyō Sensō* [Tokyo: Iwanami Shoten, 1968]).

[26] Some are recently examined in Richard L. Lael, *The Yamashita Precedent: War Crimes and Command Responsibility* (Wilmington: Scholarly Resources Inc., 1982).

[27] Miyoshi, pt. 10, 65–67.

[28] Ibid., 65; Miyoshi interview, June 6, 1968.

tai to retract its report and reverse its decision—most likely unwilling. Great loss of face would follow for Nishida, Murase, and Cho.[29]

Fortunately for Hatta, Miyoshi was more daring than Yamamoto. He sought out Murase and discovered that the latter had acted on the reports of junior officers without ever having met Hatta. Miyoshi argued so effectively against this "simple blind decision without due investigation," that Murase finally agreed to meet Hatta face to face. The next night Miyoshi brought the unsuspecting Hatta to Murase's residence, on the pretext that Murase knew all the Indonesian leaders but him. "Murase had imagined Hatta as . . . cruel, unsmiling, making only sour faces, but when he met him in person, Hatta did not once fail to smile, and answered frankly and ardently all of his quite sarcastic inquiries."[30] Did he not write articles against Japan before the war? Miyoshi tried to suggest that the Dutch had forced him to do so, but Hatta said he wrote them out of his own conviction against what Japan was doing in China. You've been reading too many American books, Murase said, and don't understand the Japanese spirit. Hatta answered that he read many books—European, English, and American. He couldn't read Japanese, but he had read Nitobe in English.[31] Murase suggested Hatta needed further study of the "imperial way."

The interview, just as Miyoshi had hoped, convinced Murase that to assassinate Hatta would be to give "seventy million Javanese" a martyr around whom to rally. There remained the problem of saving face for the Kenpeitai. The problem was resolved by the decision to send Hatta to Tokyo for "transformation." After a year of study with Yasuoka Seitoku at the Kenkei Gakuin School, Hatta would be acceptable as a *ma ningen*—a good citizen, upright man, true person.[32] His friends feared for his life, but Hatta felt there was less chance of his being murdered in Tokyo than in Jakarta.

Thus a group comprising Sukarno, Ki Bagus Hadikusumo, Hatta, and Miyoshi arrived in Tokyo in November 1943, Hatta the only one expecting to stay.[33] But war pressures in the capital were high.

[29] Miyoshi interview, June 6, 1968. Yamamoto disclaimed knowing about the Kenpeitai plot (interview, June 8, 1968). But he had had two hours of argument with Miyoshi on the subject and there was certainly further discussion in the Gunseikanbu. Yamamoto in interview either lied, or had lost his acuity with advancing age, or had repressed the memory of his passivity in this affair.

[30] Miyoshi, pt. 10, 65–66; Hatta, interview, February 17, 1968.

[31] Hatta, interviews, February 17, July 3, 1968.

[32] Miyoshi, pt. 10, 67.

[33] Hatta, interview, February 17, 1968.

Tōjō stormed that he was so busy he could not spare even a lieutenant to look after the Indonesian. When Miyoshi objected that it was
impossible to escort an unwanted Hatta back to Java, Tōjō responded with a cable *ordering* that Hatta go back.[34]

Hatta did undergo a kind of transformation while in Tokyo,
though not a mental one. The emperor received the Indonesian delegation and gave each member a small medal. It thereafter served
Hatta as a protective amulet. No Kenpei would dare harm a man
who wore an imperial decoration.[35]

The Kenpeitai, however, did not abandon the assassination plot
at the orders of any superior authority, military or civilian, or because of its arbitrariness or supralegality. The death of Hatta, it was
decided, would serve to fan rather than extinguish the flames of nationalism in Indonesia. The decision not to assassinate, like the decision to assassinate, was made within the Kenpeitai, and only after
a means of saving face had been found.[36]

Considerations of face played an important role in another case
involving the Java Kenpeitai, the Muchtar affair. The incident arose
from the death in September 1944 of five to ten thousand rōmusha
who were assembled at a camp at Klender, outside Jakarta, in preparation for shipment to other parts of the Indies or the sphere. The
deaths were eventually traced to tetanus, and the tetanus bacteria,
in the official Japanese story, to Dr. Muchtar, a professor at the Jakarta Medical College, at whose bacteriology research institute the
culture of tetanus bacteria was found to be under way. Motivated
by misguided nationalism, Mochtar had, according to the Japanese,
"mixed tetanus bacteria with anti-epidemic injections" in order to
"induce shot-rejections by the romusha, to save Indonesian laborers
from being dispatched overseas." The tetanus bacteria content was
too high, however, and the doctor's error had resulted in countless
deaths. After an investigation implicated Muchtar, he was court-
martialed and convicted.[37]

So pictured, Muchtar, out of desperate nationalism, practiced

[34] Miyoshi, interview, June 6, 1968.

[35] Miyoshi interviews; George S. Kanahele, "The Japanese Occupation of Indonesia: Prelude to Independence" (Ph.D. diss., Cornell University, 1967), 107–8. George
McT. Kahin, *Nationalism and Revolution in Indonesia* (Ithaca: Cornell University
Press, 1952), 107, alludes to the same story without details. Bernhard Dahm, *Sukarno
and the Struggle for Indonesian Independence* (Ithaca: Cornell University Press,
1969), 259n, disbelieves Kahin, but without benefit of interview of principals.

[36] Nothing about the incident appears in the *Kenpei Seishi* or other Kenpei works.

[37] Quotation from Miyoshi, pt. 12, 81; ibid., pt. 6, 71; see also *Kenpei Seishi*, 1034.
Sukarno (*An Autobiography*, 194) says "tens of thousands died."

either criminally clumsy medicine (if he intended only to induce rejection of the vaccine) or mass euthanasia (if he intended to kill thousands of laborers on the grounds that death by lockjaw was preferable to life as a rōmusha). The account satisfied the Japanese need to find a culprit, and was consistent with their low estimate of the "native" level of medical science, relative to that of the Japanese military establishment. In fact, however, the *dojin* doctors in Indonesia were generally more competent than their counterparts in the Japanese military,[38] for, after initially sending some excellent physicians to Java, the Japanese sent many whom Indonesian experts believed to be "sixth rate."[39]

Dr. Bahder Djohan of the Jakarta Medical School was summoned to the Klender camp that September, and informed by a Japanese doctor that there had been an outbreak of meningitis among the rōmusha assembled there. Two laboratory assistants helped Bahder Djohan ready equipment for lumbar puncture, and, though the scores of men sprawled, writhing, or cramped in grotesque positions, did not seem to fit a meningitis diagnosis, several spinal taps were performed.

The results, confirmed by an Indonesian and a Japanese doctor in attendance, were all negative for meningitis. Bahder Djohan suspected tetanus instead. After ascertaining from several camp officials that eight days earlier the men had received a typhoid-cholera-dysentery inoculation, he proceeded to give antitetanus injections to those who had been taken to the hospital. By nightfall, nonetheless, about a hundred there were dead.

The Japanese immediately closed the camp to visitors. Bahder Djohan's request to see samples of the inoculant was refused by a Japanese, who said that civilians should not meddle in military matters. Two Japanese professors arriving the next morning took away the records with the explanation that so unusual a case warranted publication in Japanese medical journals. His last effort to pursue the matter was a suggestion to Muchtar, chief bacteriologist at the Eykman Institute, that incisions be made at the points of injection in the corpses to try to obtain tetanus cultures.[40] Muchtar's

[38] Maruyama, *Thought and Behaviour*, 14–15.

[39] Interviews: Dr. Slamet Iman Santoso, March 1968; Dr. Bahder Djohan, March 14, 23, 1968. On human vivisection and noneuthanasia killings, see ATIS Research Report 117, "Infringement of the Laws of War and Ethics by the Japanese Medical Corps," RG 3, Box 93 (MacA).

[40] Dr. Bahder Djohan, interviews, March 14, 23 1968, and memo to the author, March 27, 1968.

nephew, a physician, and other doctors at the General Hospital, examining rōmusha brought there, went further. They took spinal serum together with samples of antitetanus serum from the camp and sent it to the Eykman Institute, whose doctors found the latter faulty. Muchtar signed the report concluding that the working methods of the Pasteur Institute in Bandung should be examined carefully. He and his entire staff were soon arrested.

The vaccine had in fact been prepared, not in Muchtar's laboratory, but by Japanese at the Pasteur Institute in Bandung, where the Dutch before the war had been working on a multipurpose inoculation without complete success. The Japanese had continued the work and either were testing the inoculant prematurely on rōmusha or, far more likely, had unknowingly permitted defective antitoxins to be used. In either case, the Japanese at the institute under General Matsuura would appear to be, and in great probability were, at fault. Such fault being inadmissible, the Japanese were in need of someone to blame when Muchtar's report implicitly blamed them. Japanese officers searched his house and found a book in which before the war he had discredited a famous Japanese expert on tropical diseases.[41] Muchtar, having already produced loss of face in Japanese medicine, was now threatening it on a massive scale. He became the perfect scapegoat.

The Kenpeitai, imagining or concocting a nationalist conspiracy, also arrested Suleiman Siregar and Mohammad Arif, who had administered the inoculations. Both were highly respected physicians of whom colleagues believed mass euthanasia, let alone mass murder, impossible. Bahder Djohan saw Arif's body when it was returned to the family by the Kenpeitai—emaciated almost beyond recognition and covered with burn marks. As for Siregar, another medical school professor, Slamet Iman Santoso, when called to attend him in prison, did not recognize the putrefying body or hideously swollen face of his old colleague until the dying Sirergar managed to croak a greeting. The Kenpeitai had tattooed him from head to toe with cigarette burns and had slashed both legs open from buttock to heel, then stuffed the wounds with maggots.[42]

[41] Abu Hanifah, *Tales of a Revolution* (Sydney: Angus and Robertson, 1972), 125–27); Dr. Slamet Iman Santoso, interview, March 9, 1968; Dr. Badher Djohan, interviews.

[42] Interviews: Dr. Badher Djohan, March 14, 1968; Slamet, March 9, 1968. Badher Djohan gives the names of the two other doctors as Suleiman Batangilung and Mohammad Arif; Slamet gives them as Suleiman Siregar and Arifin. I use in each case the name given by the source who knew him better. Slamet himself was questioned

Japanese medical men and the Kenpeitai, having fabricated the case, focused upon Muchtar; the Gunseikanbu called Indonesian leaders in to read them the charges and the sentence of death. Sukarno believed Muchtar guilty, but the others had doubts about both the evidence and the verdict. Hatta gathered Mansoer, Dewantoro, and Oto Iskandardinata, and they went to Yamamoto to appeal for clemency. Yamamoto, by this time chief of staff, had power of intervention but was not willing to use it; he told the Hatta group that the Kenpeitai was not in his line of command.[43] Later, two nieces of Muchtar who sought his release were told sentence had been passed on July 3 and he had been decapitated on July 8. His nephew learned years after that the Japanese had then driven a steam roller over the body and trucked it to a mass grave in coastal swamps.[44]

In the nine months between the rōmusha deaths and Muchtar's execution, why did Sukarno not intercede on the doctor's behalf? This was the period of the Pancasila speech and preparations for independence, when Sukarno had more influence with the Japanese than at any previous point. One may infer that he dreaded the Kenpeitai and readily found reasons not to cross them.[45]

---

by the Kenpeitai after he asked Lt. Gen. Kurusawa, a psychiatrist and friend, to show him some of the tetanus cases, and implored that the deadly inoculation be discontinued. When asked by the Kenpeitai why he opposed the inoculations, Slamet replied that Indonesians could not receive injections during *puasa*, which was to begin in two days. The Kenpeitai officer checked this story with the Department of Religion and seemed relieved to find it true. After Slamet's release, Kurusawa and his associates held a feast in his honor, evidence that they sided with him, though they were unable to support him openly against the military and the Kenpeitai. Bahder Djohan, as a material witness, also feared for his life; he believes that a Japanese radiologist intervened to protect him.

[43] Hatta, interview, July 3, 1968.

[44] Bahder Djohan to the author, March 27, 1968; "List of persons executed by the Military Court," RAPWI to NEFIS, October 3, 1945, RVO 006296; Abu Hanifah, *Tales of a Revolution*, 127. The *Kenpei Seishi* account (p. 1034) says that the "world-famous Indonesian bacteriologist" injected workers with "dysentery bacillus" in a "plot to obstruct Japanese military construction." Because the professor was "influential . . . renowned . . . and popular," he "was treated with kid gloves" and "his punishment was relatively light." Only ignorance, carelessness, disingenuity, faulty memory, protective motives, or all combined could produce such a story. Of Japanese commentators, only Nishijima Shigetada articulates the possibility of a false confession extracted by Kenpeitai torture ("The Nationalists in Java: 1943–45," in Anthony Reid and Oki Akira, eds., *The Japanese Experience in Indonesia: Selected Memoirs of 1942–1945*, Southeast Asia Series, no 72 [Athens: Ohio University Center for International Studies, 1986], 266).

[45] Sukarno (*An Autobiography*) recalls a confrontation with medical students who

As for Yamamoto, there is no evidence of his being willing to alienate the Kenpeitai, no matter how elevated his rank, on any crucial matter. Agencies of repression have a way of intimidating everyone, not just the obvious targets. Men who have the power to disapprove prefer to be too busy to oppose, and became inert accomplices. Indonesians, Filipinos, and other Asians, however, found little solace in the fact that Japanese regular army personnel feared the Kenpeitai almost as much as they.

THE KENPEITAI IN LUZON

If the Kenpeitai thought Yamamoto a "leftist-Marxist" for his cautious sympathy with the cause of Indonesian independence,[46] what must they have thought of Wachi, his counterpart in the Philippines? As chief of military administration, Wachi pursued a policy of guarding Philippine autonomy in order to prevent revolt. Murata Shōzō abetted him, first as chief civilian adviser to the military, and later as ambassador to the republic. So did Hamamoto, the interpreter and intermediary. Together these three protected basic Philippine interests and leaders with an eye to long-run international relations. They represented a counterweight to the Kenpeitai, imperial zealots pursuing the short-run interests of an embattled expeditionary force.[47]

Colonel Nagahama Akira, the Kenpeitai commander, met with ambassador Murata on the same terms as General Wachi for the army and Admiral Oka for the navy. The military police thus appears to have been an autonomous party, equal in status to the army and navy, with the embassy a civilizing element, fainter in effect as the war neared its end. Through Murata, and sometimes directly from Nagahama, President Laurel found out about and discussed their major policies and deeds. He considered them "particularly presumptuous." When they did not ask his consent in important cases of detention, Laurel expressed his "displeasure" to Murata, who in turn remonstrated with the Kenpeitai.[48]

---

asked him why he did not save Muchtar. He replied with the "enormity" of the Japanese charge against the doctor (193–94). Miyoshi (interview, June 6, 1968), like Sukarno, continued to believe Muchtar guilty on the basis of the Japanese wartime sources—Yamamoto, the Kenpeitai, and the Jōhōbu (Dept. of Information).

[46] Yamamoto, interview, June 8, 1968. According to Yamamoto, the Ministry of War replied that he was if anything a "rightist."

[47] Felino Neri, interview, June 28, 1968.

[48] Fukushima Shintarō, ed, *Muratra Shōzō: Ikō hitō-nikki* (Posthumous Philippine

Leaders in Manila had made pleas early in 1942 for Jose Abad Santos and Manuel Roxas, both of whom had followed the Commonwealth regime southward and, when captured, declined to collaborate. Laurel found the matter was not under the eye of Homma, who was fighting a humiliatingly slow battle, but under Hayashi Yoshihide. That hardened military administrator had no desire to intercede for either Filipino and erroneously reported them both dead. The Japanese did execute Abad Santos; but a field officer, Colonel Jimbo, impressed by Roxas, delayed his execution until higher orders saved him.[49]

While serving as commissioner of justice, Laurel himself was interrogated in Fort Santiago by the Kenpeitai after he protested against Japanese disregard for due process of law. He seems to have drawn conservative conclusions about what ground the Kenpeitai could be made to yield.[50] When he became president, Laurel occasionally intervened for those nationally important, or near to him personally, but no others, lest he weaken the stands he took on larger policy matters.

Letters to the president on behalf of prisoners were handled by the assitant executive secretary in Malacanang, who wrote a liaison officer in the Ministry of Foreign Relations, who probably took the matter up with the assistant chief of staff, who might eventually contact the Kenpeitai if he felt the case significant and the time propitious, and if he could reach an appropriate person. The result depended on the will of each person contacted to pass on the communication, and concluded with the whim of the Kenpeitai.[51] A typical appeal was that of a woman whose husband had been detained for some months on suspicion of possessing hand grenades.

diaries] (Shinjuku: Hara-shobō, 1969), entries for February 7, 24, March 8, 14, 23, 1944.

[49] Laurel, memo, January 29, 1946, "Gen HQ SCAP, Legal Section," JPL; Teodoro A. Agoncillo, *The Fateful Years: Japan's Adventure in the Philippines, 1941–1945*, (Quezon City: R. P. Garcia, 1965), 1: 343–44. Roxas's mortal danger for a while was generic to all prisoners of war. Lieutenant Colonel Imai, commanding the 141st Infantry Brigade, disobeyed an order to "shoot to death immediately all captured enemy soldiers." Some, but not all, field commanders carried out the order, instigated by Lieutenant Colonel Tsuji Masanobu. Imai instead disarmed and freed his captives (Imai Takeo, *Shina-jihen no kaiso* [Recollections of the Chinese incident] [Tokyo: Misuzu-shobō, 1964], 178–81).

[50] [Jose Lansang, ed.], *War Memoirs of Dr. Jose P. Laurel* (Manila: Laurel Memorial Foundation, 1962), 9; interviews, J. P. Laurel III, June 4, 1968, and Emilio Abello, July 1, 1968.

[51] Malacanang, 1943–45: in all seventeen volumes, there is no surviving record of any inquiry resulting in release or clemency.

She pleaded in a letter to Laurel that he be allowed to return home to support his seven children, surviving only through the charity of friends and relatives. Eight months later, her letter came back to Malacanang with a form attached: "Respectfully returned . . . with the information that [blank for name filled in] Felipe D. Galang was found to have committed acts against Japanese Military Laws."[52] Sometimes forms came back marked "present whereabouts not known."

After the war Utsunomiya asserted that "in the name of the commanding general" he was able to do a lot toward getting relatives of the Philippine cabinet ministers out of Kenpeitai jails, but he gave no details.[53] A former executive secretary to Laurel, questioned closely on efforts made for political prisoners, finally answered, "If you're looking for success, there was no success."[54]

Energy was better spent keeping people out of the hands of the Kenpeitai in the first place. Major Jesus Vargas, an aide to Laurel, interrupted him at golf one day to say that he had been ordered by the Kenpeitai to appear for questioning at Fort Santiago about contacts with guerrillas. Such contacts Vargas indeed had. Laurel told him to explain by phone that he was on duty with the president, who could not dispense with his services. The Kenpeitai replied that theirs was not an invitation but an order. Laurel then positioned a hundred presidential guards near the gates of the palace grounds and ordered them to shoot any Japanese soldier who tried to enter.[55] They never came for Vargas.

For Roxas, however, Colonel Nagahama himself once came to Malacanang. Early in the occupation, Laurel had pledged to the Japanese commander in chief to guarantee the behavior of Roxas, his friend and compadre. After a while Roxas nonetheless made contact with a Manila intelligence group that reported Japanese troop, ship, and air movements to MacArthur's headquarters.[56] The Japanese,

[52] Mrs. Ursala Galang to Laurel, January 11, 1944; Liaison Officer, For. Rel., to Asst. Exec. Sec., September 11, Malacanang, 17.

[53] NARS, WWII Records, reel 3210, p. 579.

[54] Emilio Abello, interview, July 1, 1968.

[55] J. S. Laurel III, interview, June 4, 1968; Agoncillo, Fateful Years, 1: 400–402. Hamamoto tells a similar story about another suspect member of the Presidential Guard. Laurel stuck a .45 caliber revolver in his belt and said, "You watch, Hamamoto. If any Kenpei comes in, I'll shoot him myself." Hamamoto immediately telephoned General Wachi (interview, June 14, 1968).

[56] Roxas, "General Summary of My Activities," draft MS; Roxas affidavit, October 18, 1945, on his relations with Jose Ozamiz, R. Evidence in RG 16 (the personal papers of Gen. Courtney Whitney), in the MacArthur collection, establishes that the

long suspicious of him, discovered correspondence about the intelligence ring in February 1944 and arrested Senator Jose Ozamiz, Juan Elizalde, Enrico Pirovano, and others, whom they executed in August without trial.

Colonel Nagahama's further aim, apparently, was to extract enough information from the ring and other sources to seize Roxas, whom he had been watching for two years. One day in mid-1944 he arrived at Malacanang with two truckloads of Kenpeitai, stormed in, and insisted on seeing the president, who was in a meeting of the Council of State. Confronting Laurel in the president's office, Nagahama demanded that he turn over Roxas, and threw a sheaf of allegedly incriminating papers on the desk. Laurel belittled the evidence and met Nagahama with his own fury. "You can go and get Roxas," Laurel declared, "but you'll have to kill me first." With Roxas only two rooms away, Laurel completed Nagahama's frustration by telling him to go through channels. The Kenpeitai chief left, muttering that he would get Roxas yet. Laurel immediately phoned Murata and Hamamoto and asked them to intercede with General Kuroda.[57] They were all aware of Roxas's activities but did not dare harm him—the army for fear of an uprising, the embassy for the sake of postwar relations.[58]

Although he endangered his position for his compadre, Laurel did nothing for the arrested members of the Manila intelligence group. A sister of Senator Ozamiz tried three times to see Laurel in order to visit her brother, but she could not get access to the president.[59] The net record of national leaders in the Philippines and Indonesia in saving prominent political colleagues from Kenpeitai intentions is one apiece: Roxas and Amir Sjarifuddin. The difference between the cases is that Amir's espionage group barely accomplished anything before his arrest. Roxas avoided arrest, was in occasional indirect communication with Australia, and even received in his home a secret emissary from President Quezon in Washington.[60]

intelligence connection was substantial. The Roxas presidential campaign of 1946, however, exaggerated both the importance of the Manila group to SWPA intelligence and of Roxas to the Manila group.

[57] Interviews, Felino Neri, June 28, 1968, J. S. Laurel III, June 4, 1968; J. S. Laurel III, "A Consummate Leadership in Its Finest Hour," *Philippines Herald*, Laurel Special Issue, September 2, 1967; Agoncillo, *Fateful Years*, 1: 411–15; del Castillo and del Castillo, *Saga of Jose P. Laurel*, 170–72, 258–68.

[58] Fukushima Shintarō, interview, September 17, 1958.

[59] Nieves Ozamiz, interview, January 24, 1958.

[60] Hatta, interview, July 3, 1968; Benedict R. O'G. Anderson, *Java in a Time of Revolution: Occupation and Resistance, 1944–45* (Ithaca: Cornell University Press,

The commander of the Kenpeitai in Manila was two men. The more civilized Nagahama told an inquiring group of Japanese scholars that "To govern alien nationalities, it is absolutely essential to know something of their national traits and idiosyncrasies. . . . Slapping a Filipino on the face [is] an unbearable insult. . . . It is often more effective to appeal to his sense of duty rather than to try using a third degree method to get truth out of a Filipino." Nagahama had ordered the anthropologist H. Otley Beyer released three hours after capture that he might give the Kenpeitai regular lectures on the Filipino peoples; and fifteen Americans from Santo Tomas internment camp periodically gave them English lessons.[61] So Nagahama pictured his cultural sensitivity to inquiring Japanese scholars. He told the Filipinos that all discipline came out of love. He quoted to his subordinates an ancient Chinese maxim to inspire police to be educators: "Arrest seven times, reform them, release seven times."[62] On such evidence the chief of the Kenpeitai in the Philippines would appear to be a man of intelligence, education, and professional dedication.

Prosecution at the Manila War Crimes Tribunal, however, documented the other Nagahama. Personnel at Kenpeitai headquarters, Fort Santiago, forced prisoners to clean latrines with their hands; beat them with baseball bats, wet ropes, and muzzles of guns; burnt them with matches and cigarette butts; and even barbecued some whole. The defense did not contest points established by the prosecution: 200 military and civilian prisoners beaten, of whom many died; 10 Filipino prisoners of war executed without trials; 35 Filipino noncombatants beaten, tortured, and killed; 450 civilian and military prisoners permitted to suffocate in one insanely packed cell, in December 1944.[63] Nagahama exercised no restraint over

---

1972), 37–38; Maj. Gen. Charles A. Willoughby, *The Guerrilla Resistance Movement in the Philippines* (New York: Vantage Press, 1972), 394–95.

[61] Takéuchi Tatsuji, "Manila Diary," January 19, 1943, in Theodore Friend, ed., *The Philippine Polity: A Japanese View*, Yale University Southeast Asia Studies, Monograph Series, no. 12 (New Haven, 1967), 225–26.

[62] *Official Gazette, Republic of the Philippines*, 1: 163–64; testimony of Yanase Shōichi, USA *vs.* Akira Nagahama, p. 79, JAG, Box 1457, Washington National Records Center.

[63] USA *vs.* Akira Nagahama, vol. 1, review of the case, JAG, Box 1457, FE 43-29. Only one-tenth as many people died in the celebrated Black Hole of Calcutta (calculation based on Brijen K. Gupta, "The Black Hole Incident," *Journal of Asian Studies* 19 [1959]: 53–63). The *Kenpei Seishi* account (p. 941) of the "mass suffocation incident" uses the figure of 460 dead. Although the Kenpeitai saw mitigating circumstances—incessant air raids that hindered ventilation of the room—they were "ap-

brutalities of subordinates, permitted release of prisoners only when desired information was obtained, and never punished the officer responsible for the mass suffocation. Manuel Elizalde, arrested with his doomed brother Juan, spent fifteen weeks in Santiago, periodically beaten with baseball bat and billiard cue before release. He testified that "during the entire time" he heard moaning, screaming, and cries of pain. Nagahama's office was only "30 to 40 yards" from the "continuous noises of prisoners suffering."[64] General Yamashita testified in his own defense that he had removed Nagahama from office and ordered him back to Japan, in February 1945, because he was too cruel to Filipinos.[65]

Was this the same man who abjured face slapping and quoted the ancients? Nagahama recognized the disparity himself. Instead of taking the stand in his defense, he submitted a written statement accepting responsibility for the actions of his subordinates while pointing to events that made an ideal of admonition impossible—chiefly the rapid American military advance, which played into the hands of those preferring a policy of force and fear.[66]

REPRESSORS AS LOSERS

The Japanese were victims of their own style when it came to suppression of negative military intelligence. Part of Japanese militant enthusiasm was refusal to admit reverses publicly even when they were conceded privately. After a series of early military victories that gave Japan hegemony over Greater East Asia, the United

palled" by this "careless mistake," and ascribe foremost responsibility to the chief of secret police, Capt. Yanase Shōichi. He, however, turned states's evidence to save his own life during the war crimes trials. His colleagues find his "selling out" understandable, but not his "perjury, which ascribed crimes where none had been committed." They castigate him for "utter absence . . . of guilt for his betrayal." On return to Japan he was "lucky not to have been killed by the Kenpeitai."

[64] USA vs. Nagahama, p. 685–703, esp. 695. For vivid detail on Japanese torture in the countryside, and Filipino vengeance, see Col. Yay Panlilio, Marking (Manila: Venceremos, 1979).

[65] USA vs. Nagahama, 696; A. Frank Reel, The Case of General Yamashita (Chicago: University of Chicago Press, 1949), 156–57.

[66] USA vs. Nagahama, defendant's statement. Teodoro Agoncillo, in The Burden of Proof (1984), has criticized the behavior of the American Counter Intelligence Corps in 1945 toward alleged Filipino collaborators. "In the minds of thinking Filipinos, the CIC agents were no better than the Japanese Kempeitai, who as enemy, acted with unusual brutality and unreasonableness" (p. 122). The offenses ascribed to the CIC—being uncouth and arbitrary, violating Filipino privacy, and breaching "Jeffersonian principles"—are indefensible. But the comparison with the Kenpeitai neglects Kenpeitai torture and murder, and is therefore grossly unjust.

States mobilized, flew into super-production, and launched a return across the Pacific. By the time Admiral Tanaka Shiichi went south to Burma, only a year after the Pacific war began, he felt that the Japanese "were at the bottom of the hill . . . powerless at Saipan and the Marianas."[67]

At the time, no such admissions could be made. General Imamura, transferred from Java to Rabaul in November 1942, considered it a "Minatogawa," and thought that future Japanese historians would deplore operations beyond the limit of naval capacity. "However, my emotion, raised in me when I was ordered to this duty," he later recalled, "was very large, [and] repressed me from criticism. . . . The end comes once to everybody."[68] When Saipan fell in July 1944, Prince Konoye noted in his diary that the top Japanese military realized they were beaten, "but none of the army and navy leaders had the courage to state their conclusions publicly."[69]

Nobody admitted skepticism to soldiers in the field. Throughout the Southern Area, superior officers told them that do-or-die fighting would turn the tables on the Allies, and still give Japan victory in the holy war. Japanese soldiers made ready for the "decisive battle," which would happen on one's own front, in one's own sight, and be won with one's own blood.

In Java, the army and navy fixed a new plan of operations in April 1945, anticipating a "decisive battle" late in the year, or no later than the first half of 1946. The army, concentrated in fortified positions in the interior of East and West Java, was to launch suicide attacks on land, sea, and air, in concert with their air force. The navy was to concentrate in the areas of Malang and Bandung and create bases for suicide squads (tokkōtai, or special attack troops), at over one hundred locations along the coast. The various branches of the military began removal of factories, ammunition, and hospitals to the interior.[70]

[67] Adm. Tanaka Shiichi, interrogation, NARS, WWII, reel 3210, pp. 433–61, esp. p. 451.

[68] Imamura Hitoshi, "A Tapir in Prison," English translation of prison memoir, pt. 3, 139, RVO 002460. Minatogawa: in 1336, the forces of the emperor Godaigo there fought and lost a crucial battle to an opposing feudal army. Imamura implies analogy to the great warrior Kusunoki Masashige, who thought it the wrong place to make a stand, but fought loyally and valiantly for the emperor and died on the battlefield. For the thoughts of Murata Shōzō upon the emperor Godaigo, see chap. 6, note 39.

[69] Manila Times, December 9, 1967; UPI (Tokyo) dispatch, December 8, on publications of part of Konoye's diary in Tokyo newspapers.

[70] Adm. Maeda Tadashi, undated summary of events from roughly April 1945 onward, RVO 006825-29.

In the Philippines, Yamashita clashed with Terauchi on where to
make the decisive stand. He opposed dispatching forces to Leyte because transport was too hazardous; he wanted the enemy hit at sea
by naval and air power, and Japanese troops saved for battle on Luzon. Terauchi, as theater commander, won the argument.[71] Yamashita, as army commander, would lose both battles, Leyte and Luzon.

The logic of the impossible meant desperate readiness for the future, and inflated propaganda for the present. Japanese news sources
transmitted reports in early October 1944 of a massive air-naval battle east of Taiwan in which Japanese forces sank ten aircraft carriers, two battleships, and three cruisers.[72] In fact, the Japanese had
hit three American ships and sunk none, while they had suffered
the loss of over five hundred planes and serious damage to installations on Formosa. Imperial General Headquarters, believing its own
propaganda, actually proceeded to plan on the assumption that
America would give up its invasion of the Philippines.[73] Terauchi's
headquarters trusted the propagandistic news enough to disbelieve
first reports of American landings on Leyte, and to think that the
enemy "had not yet had enough time to renew their invading
strength." As the invasion of Leyte continued, so did further fabrication of news: eight more American carriers, three cruisers, six
other ships sunk, and five hundred planes shot down.[74]

Murata found out that Laurel and many Filipino leaders were listening to enemy radio broadcasts. He felt the embassy should do the
same to keep abreast of the news, because Japanese sources were
growing "outrageous" and "foolish" in their exaggerations. When
he heard from Australia that Americans had secured most of Leyte
and ten thousand Japanese were dead, he found the news "unbearable" and switched off the radio.[75] Most of his countrymen, however,
approached major defeat fed by gargantuan tales of triumph.

Eventually many individual Japanese faced an inescapable reckoning—surrender or death? Some found a way out through explosive
aggression against noncombatants, or as kamikaze pilots, or in
other self-immolation units. Members of the Manila Defense Unit

[71] Interrogation of Lt. Gen. Nukada Hiroshi, G-3, Gen. Staff HQ, NARS, WWII, reel
3210; Utsunomiya interrogation, same source, pp. 580, 584–86, 593.
[72] Manila *Tribune*, October 17, 18, 21, 1944.
[73] Samuel Eliot Morison, *The Two-Ocean War* (Boston: Little, Brown, 1963), 429–
32.
[74] Manila *Tribune*, October 24, 25, 26, 28, 1944, and well into November.
[75] Murata diary (see chap. 3, note 20), October 28, 1944.

were urged on by their commander, Admiral Iwabuchi, after three days of American bombardment: "If we run out of bullets we will use grenades; if we run out of grenades, we will cut down the enemy with swords; if we break our swords, we will kill them by sinking our teeth deep in their throats." Later he summoned those who had survived the onslaught of American bombs, tanks, napalm, and bazookas to his headquarters. He apologized for putting them in such a situation. "If anyone has the courage to escape, please do so," he counseled. "If not, please take your lives here." The admiral retired to his own room and disemboweled himself.[76]

When news of the emperor's surrender finally reached the Manila Kenpeitai, they felt "deep indignation and sorrow, gazed up to the heavens and wept." A first lieutenant "transcended his sense of defeat" by uttering a high-pitched wail and breaking into rapid, heavy machine-gun fire.[77]

In Indonesia, one who spoke Japanese, Indonesian, and Dutch and who lived the war years there was asked who suffered the greatest cultural shock: the Dutch, in the capitulation and loss of their colony in eight days; the Indonesians, with the changes of imperial regimes and wartime deprivations; or the Japanese, in final surrender? He answered firmly, having watched all three: the Japanese, surrender. For the first time in all history their nation was vanquished. Men prepared to win or die had to live with loss. "We never dreamed up to the last moment that the war should end so quickly and in such a form as this."[78]

Japanese commanders resolved on rapid concentration of their troops, cutting all possible connections with Indonesians, and paying out suitable allowances. "The shock of defeat being too great, some were entirely at a loss what to do, [and] others showed an attitude of utter despair."[79] Drunken and disorderly men kept officers constantly busy with problems of discipline and morale. A considerable number, trainers of the Peta and others, kept their passion alive by joining the struggle for Indonesian independence. For most,

---

[76] Battle diary of Lt. Miyazawa Hōichiro, quoted in Okochi Reiko, "Watashi no chichi no tsumi o otte shikei ni natta Yamashita Tomoyuki; bōryaku to iwareru Manila genchi saiban no shinsō o saguru" (General Yamashita, who was sentenced to death for my father's crime; investigation into the truth of the Manila [war crimes] trial, which is said to be a frame-up) *Gendai*, June 1968, 302–10 (quotation, 304).

[77] Ibid., 306; *Kenpei Seishi*, 944.

[78] G. H. DeHeer, interview, May 26, 1969.

[79] Maeda Statement, RVO, 006825-29.

however, defeat brought their involvement with Indonesia to a bewildering end.

General Imamura, who had recognized as early as 1942 that Japanese defeat was inevitable, transmitted the emperor's surrender message to his men between sobs, then struggled to express his reflections on the past and future: "The Holy War has not been [successfully] accomplished. But our great efforts are the greatest achievement since the dawn of our history. I am sure that future historians will appreciate this Holy War properly and praise its world-historical value."[80]

THE HOLY WAR IN KENPEI MEMORY

Some Japanese now see their holy war as indispensable to the destruction of the myth of Western superiority, vital to the growth of the Southeast Asian nationalism, and intrinsic to the political and military organization of the new nations. One expert believes that the Japanese occupation "was on the whole constructive and enlightened." He concedes that "Japanese military administration was undoubtedly destructive and brutal in physical terms," but "I make no apology for it."[81]

Java offers the best case for the Japanese—wholeheartedly undoing the work of the white man and halfheartedly promoting national unity and organization. But other phenomena must also be kept in mind. Historical writings by surviving members of the Kenpeitai bring out their values in sharp relief. The Japanese army in general and the Kenpeitai in particular tended to replicate Dutch fears about communism and Islam. They distrusted them both as blind faiths, fanatical and unpredictable.[82] They inherited Dutch police files and they exaggerated Dutch suspicions. At the same time they felt tricked and bedeviled by the ingenuity of Netherlands colonial policy. As they saw it, Holland had developed a large number of Dutch-Indonesian mixed bloods, or "half-breeds,"[83] who were loyal to them. They had enlisted as well a number of racial minority

---

[80] Imamura, "A Tapir," pt. 3, 156–57.

[81] Akashi Yōji, "Japan and Asia for the Asians," in Harry Wary and Hilary Conroy, eds., *Japan Examined* (Honolulu: University of Hawaii Press, 1983), 323–30 (quotations, 323, 329).

[82] *Kenpei Seishi*, 1038.

[83] Ibid., 1029ff. The Japanese word *konketsu* has derogatory implications. "Mixed-bloods" translates it adequately, but the disdain for racial impurity felt by many Japanese overseas in wartime is better conveyed by the term "half-breeds." See Shimer and Hobbs, *Kenpeitai in Java and Sumatra*, 23–24n.

groups to their side. In both groups festered a "full-scale anti-Japanese movement," which, together with the "infiltration of armed spies from abroad . . . drew the entire island of Java into a vortex of strategems."[84]

Suspiciousness rose toward paranoia as the war progressed and the Allies drew closer. After defeat at Guadalcanal, the Kenpeitai commander, Murase, felt that following normal procedures from investigations through courts-martial was "thwarting Kenpeitai goals and paralyzing the army, thereby impeding the work of the military government." He recommended a policy of investigation, reporting to Kenpeitai headquarters, and, with approval by the army commander, execution without trial. To this, the Kenpeitai gave the name *kikōsaku*, which translates roughly as "Operation Hades."[85] This new policy, approved by Lieutenant General Harada, at best meant indefinite imprisonment on cursory investigation, and, at worst, summary execution upon suspicion. Nearly three hundred people were killed this way.

The Dutch response in the war crimes trials was thought by Kenpeitai memoirists to be pursued with "a terrible vengeance." To the Dutch themselves, who engaged civilians in military strategies, should be ascribed "the principal fault." Such at least is the opinion of the National Federation of Kenpeitai Veteran's Associations. Of the 538 members of the Java Kenpeitai in 1945, 199 were convicted of war crimes. Of the other 20,000 regular army troops on Java, only 58 were so convicted. Forty Kenpei received the death penalty, or one out of every thirteen men in the force.[86]

In the Philippines there was no Kenpeitai nomenclature as evocative as "Operation Hades," but there was plenty of hellcraft of various sorts: tributes to limited but exaggerated heroism, fierce efforts to protect the dignity of the military police and to recover it when lost, and drastic action taken on misinformation. The Kenpeitai romance with its idea of itself is clear in a memoir identifying a sergeant major as "worthy of the highest honors for distinguished service" for allegedly having arranged "an agreement of mutual non-

---

[84] *Kenpei Seishi*, 1040.

[85] Ibid., 1031–33. For a colloquial English equivalent of this term, I am grateful to Professor Kataoka Tetsuya.

[86] Quotation, *Kenpei Seishi*, 1041. Statistics from *Kenpei Seishi*, 1323, 1381; *Kenpei Isho*, 580–84. Resentment at Allied "vengefulness" also permeates the pages of Lt. Gen. Fujiwara Iwaichi, *F. Kikan: Japanese Army Intelligence Operations in Southeast Asia During World War II*, trans., Akashi Yōji (Hong Kong: Heineman Asia, 1983).

aggression between the Japanese garrisons in Central Luzon and the Huks." The same source states Huk troop strength at 50,000, but the most careful historical analysis puts the number of armed Huk guerrillas in April 1942 at "less than 300," before growing to 5,000 by year-end. The Kenpei writer states that the Huks had taken a prewar stand against American forces, when in fact, through United Front tactics, they had pledged loyalty to the Commonwealth and American government. What could have been the impact of the supposed agreement of February 11, 1942 if, in the view of a close Filipino student of the Huks, they were actually "at their fighting-est in the first nine months, from March 1942 to about December?"[87] These instances of gross misinformation suggest of the Kenpeitai a badly overrated espionage network, clumsy intercultural skills in communication, susceptibility to being duped by wily Filipinos, and a syndrome of self-congratulation despite proven misconceptions and tactical errors.

The Kenpeitai's reputation was clearly at stake when an assailant critically wounded President Laurel while he was playing golf in August of 1943. Their account describes Laurel's Kenpeitai bodyguards as "ashen-faced from the shock." The military police went into action and captured a large set of suspects. The chief one escaped and hid under water, breathing through a reed. A sentry shot him dead when he came out from the cold. The Kenpeitai account implies regret that he did not survive for torture and execution, and expresses satisfaction that they had "preserved the dignity of the Kenpeitai." In fact they had missed the actual perpetrators altogether,[88] and they continue to congratulate themselves on erroneous killings.

[87] The account in *Kenpei Seishi*, 919, is refuted with regard to numbers of Huk troops by Benedict J. Kerkvleit, *The Huk Rebellion* (Berkeley: University of California Press, 1977), 87; and on intentions and actions of Huks by Eduardo Lachica, *Huk: Philippine Agrarian Society in Revolt* (Manila: Solidaridad, 1971), 103, 108; quotation p. 114. Luis Taruc to the author, February 1984, specifically denies that there was a mutual nonaggression agreement.

[88] *Kenpei Seishi*, 927–28, identifies the would-be assassin as one Jirano Marcelino. Agoncillo, *Fateful Years*, 1: 379, 506n, says that the assailant was disclosed in 1962 as being Capt. Palma Martin, acting on instructions of Col. Enrique Arce of the (Hunters) ROTC guerrilla unit; but in *The Burden of Proof* [Mandaluyong: University of the Philippines Press, 1984], 51, he attributes responsibility to the Markings guerrillas, on Col. Yay Panlilio's say-so in 1947. With more concrete authority, Dommini Torrevillas-Suarez, "The Day of the Jackal," *Philippine Panorama*, July 4, 1978, 14–18, establishes that Feliciano Lizardo was the triggerman. Laurel recognized him, but refused to identify him to the Kenpeitai, and several years later hired him as a bodyguard. In any event, the Kenpeitai clearly killed the wrong suspects.

The Kenpeitai could sympathize with heroic allies or heroic enemies—with General Artemio Ricarte, because he had steadfastly
opposed the Americans since 1898, and with an unnamed girl who
substituted herself for her younger brother when the Japanese were
breaking up a spy ring in Jakarta, to be executed in his place. The
first, however, was a case of failed sponsorship of a political exile;
Ricarte was too old and out of touch to take leadership of the Japa-
nese-occupied Philippines. The second was another case of mistaken identity, in which the redeeming feature is Kenpeitai admiration—when they learned the truth about the young woman they
had executed—of her "great composure . . . a heart rending memory."[89] Inward-turning tales of small-scale heroism and narcissistic
pathos—such is the literary residue of the Kenpeitai overseas.

Manila, by July 1944, was seen as filled with armed guerrillas,
who, "disguised as vegetable carriers would suddenly shoot at a sentry on duty in front of the military headquarters and then get away.
Even Kenpeitai drinking coffee on the streets would be shot at, and
in the evenings Kenpeitai on their way to the cabarets would be met
by assassins lying in waiting. Day or night, Manila was a city in-
fested with assassins." This phenomenon the Kenpeitai described as
a "bloodbath."[90] The blood, of course, was their own. No other
blood shed, of all that flowed in the wartime Philippines, rises in
their recollections to the rhetorical proportions of a "bath."

Being sniped at was bad enough. War crimes trials were worse.
The Kenpeitai memoirists repeatedly shunt away blame and disa-
vow guilt. They deride the Allies, the Dutch especially, for "victors'
justice."[91] At the time, however, Colonel Nagahama composed
himself to his fate. To a fellow inmate later freed, Ambassador Murata, he entrusted his will. He cheerfully umpired baseball games.
When his day of execution came, all of the Buddhist and Shinto
priests had been repatriated to Japan. Nagahama consented to be
attended by a Catholic priest.[92]

Colonel Murase went out more defiantly, with a written message
to those in his cellblock: "The mind of the enemy is transparent.
. . . An attack on my character is the real crux for the death penalty

[89] *Kenpei Seishi*, 929 (quotation, 1033).

[90] Ibid., 935.

[91] *Kenpei Seishi; Kenpei Gaishi.* Non-Kenpei felt the same way. See Yamamoto
Moichirō, *Watakushi no Indonesia*, 211–12, and *Kaisōroku* (Memoirs) (Tokyo: Yamamoto Akiko, 1978), 52, 54.

[92] Murata diary, February 20, 1946; USA *vs.* Nagahama, administrative memo.

judgment. . . . I was wondering whether to expect a frame-up, but it was written so viciously that I remain in mute amazement. . . . Having in mind sorrowful memories of my fellow soldiers who have already fallen and died, I intend to attack the enemy until the end."[93]

[93] *Kenpei Isho*, 444; translation by William Shimer.

10

REVOLUTION IN JAVA

Had Douglas MacArthur had his way, and had Allied armies invaded Java in June of 1945, Indonesia afterward would have confronted a complex and heavy array of forces, and endured a cumbrous transition to independence. In fact, however, in August of 1945, the sudden end of Japanese capacity to dominate, memories of Dutch repression, the eloquence of Sukarno, and the high pitch of the pemuda, rushed together in revolutionary combustion.

POWER VACUUM

A national power vacuum, itself the consequence of an international power vacuum, was indispensable to the uprisings in Java that eventually freed Indonesia. Early in the war, the Allies had divided their theaters of operations at the Sunda Straits. The British were responsible for Sumatra, Singapore, Malaya, and points west, and the Americans for Java, Borneo, Celebes, Makassar, and points east. The Dutch, forced to rely on the military power and logistical support of their allies, were split in their affinities. The Netherlands government-in-exile in London believed Churchill and the British would support them after the war, whereas Roosevelt was avowedly anticolonial. Hubertus van Mook, lieutenant–governor general of the Indies, and his exiled associates in Australia, trusted MacArthur, the Americans, and the Australians more. Later the Australians in fact helped the Dutch reoccupy East Indonesia in 1945 with great efficiency. Roosevelt's death had no immediate impact. But the fall of the Churchill government in the summer of 1945 badly upset the calculations of the Dutch in London.[1]

---

[1] Debates on strategic decisions revealed differences among and within the Allied governments on the "colonial question": Evelyn Colbert, *Southeast Asia in International Politics* (Ithaca: Cornell University Press, 1977), 27–53; Robert J. McMahon, *Colonialism and the Cold War: The United States and the Struggle for Indonesian Independence, 1945–1949* (Ithaca: Cornell University Press, 1981), 43–73.

The problem was where to fight the Japanese. At Honolulu, in August 1944, the British had proposed to skip Java and Sumatra in order to reach Singapore faster; the United States Navy wished to skip Luzon and the Visayas, in order that Admiral Chester Nimitz might have MacArthur's ground, naval, and air forces at his disposal in attacking Formosa and Japan. MacArthur vigorously opposed any bypass of Luzon or Java, which would victimize Filipinos, Indonesians, and Western internees.[2] He won his basic point and subsequently his battles against the Japanese at Leyte and on Luzon.

When MacArthur turned his gaze on Java, however, and proposed to attack there in June of 1945, he found both American and British chiefs of staff firmly against him. They forbade him to carry out any operations in Indonesia lest he dangerously overextend forces required to attack the Japanese home islands. In mid-July, MacArthur suggested to Lord Louis Mountbatten that the latter assume responsibility for all of the Southwest Pacific Area south of the Philippines. At the Potsdam Conference later that month the Combined Chiefs of Staff made such a change into policy, effective August 15.[3]

Van Mook regretted this change more than anyone. Anticipating American liberation of Java, he had negotiated an agreement with MacArthur in December 1944 giving the latter *"de facto authority to take all necessary measures"* in combat areas, while stressing the most rapid possible return of authority to Dutch civil administration, and elaborating principles of jurisdiction consonant with

---

[2] Robert Ross Smith, *Triumph in the Philippines* (Washington, D.C.: Office of the Chief of Military History, 1963), 3–18. See also Idrus Djajadiningrat, *The Beginnings of the Indonesian-Dutch Negotiations and the Hoge Veleuwe Talks*, Cornell Modern Indonesia Project, No. 14, (Ithaca, 1958), 7–11; Vice Admiral the Earl Mountbatten, *Report by the Supreme Allied Commander South-East Asia, 1943–1945* (New York: Philosophical Library, 1945); *Enquete Commissie Regeringsbeleid, 1940–1945* (The Hague: Staatsdrukkerij en Uitgeversbedrijf, 1956), the report of a parliamentary inquiry into policies of the Dutch government in exile.

[3] McMahon, *Colonialism and the Cold War*, pp. 73, 78–79; D. Clayton James, *The Years of MacArthur* (Boston: Houghton Mifflin, 1970–1985), 2: 738; William R. Manchester, *American Caesar: Douglas MacArthur, 1880–1964* (Boston: Little, Brown, 1978), 429; Djajadiningrat, *Beginnings*, 12–16; F.S.V. Donnison, *British Military Administration in the Far East, 1943–1946*, (London: HM Stationery Office, 1956), 417–18.

Samuel Eliot Morison, *The Two-Ocean War* (Boston: Little, Brown, 1963), 491, asserts, regarding the invasion of Java, that the Combined Chiefs "fiddled around with this plan until August, when it was too late." He is wrong. MacArthur knew he had been overruled, never conceded the wisdom of it, and later rolled out a humanitarian rationale for such an invasion, explicitly critical of his superiors (*Reminiscences* [New York: McGraw Hill, 1964]).

Dutch sovereignty.[4] The change in command undermined this agreement. The Japanese surrendered on the very day Mountbatten assumed wider responsibility. That precipitated a power vacuum.

Responsible for law and order, rescue of Western prisoners, and repatriation of Japanese everywhere in Southeast Asia except the Philippines, Mountbatten found himself seriously shorthanded. His one ethnically British division was already committed to India-Burma. Because of the fermenting political situation in India itself, he calculated he had only seven months to use his other troops, mostly Indians, in Indonesia. Military weakness, his recent success at permissive dealings with Aung San in Burma, and a basically liberal outlook on politics led Mountbatten to declare, "Our one idea is to get the Dutch and Indonesians to kiss and make friends . . . [so we can] pull out."[5] The Dutch, who had been alternately concerned about American anti-imperialism and British military weakness, now found their two concerns merged in one command and one man—Mountbatten—who had neither the strength nor the desire to restore Dutch power in Indonesia.

The Dutch were in no position to reassert their own authority. The leading personnel of NICA—the Netherlands Indies Civil Administration—had been supplicant to more powerful forces ever since escaping to Australia in 1942. When their government returned to power in Holland, its major concerns were with a war-torn homeland, barely freed of German occupiers.

The men at the head of NICA returned to Indonesia like seismologists without recording equipment, engineers without bulldozers, farmers without seeds. A political earthquake was underway and they did not realize it; the ground was riven beneath them and they

---

[4] "Principles of Governing Arrangements for Civil Administration and Jurisdiction in Netherlands Territory in the Southwest Pacific Area," and exchange of letters, MacArthur–van Mook, December 10, 1944, RG 4, Box 2 (MacA). Van Mook expressed his concern in a letter to MacArthur, July 14, 1945, personal and confidential, referring to MacArthur to van Mook, June 17, RG 3, Box 2 (MacA). Top-level Dutch planning documents, 13–15 August, stressed disarming Japanese and the highest priority of liberating Allied prisoners of war and civilian internees: S. L. van der Wal, *Officiële Bescheiden Betreffende de Nederlands-Indonesische Betrekkingen, 1945–1950*, (The Hague: Martinus Nijhoff, 1971), 1: 16–31, 60–62 (hereafter, *Betrekkingen*).

[5] Benedict R. O'Gorman Anderson, *Java in a Time of Revolution: Occupation and Resistance, 1944–1945* (Ithaca: Cornell University Press, 1972), 132–35 (quotation, 135); McMahon, *Colonialism and the Cold War*, 80, 83–84. Peter Dennis compares situations in Vietnam and Indonesia in "Other Peoples' Empires: Britain and the End of the Second World War in Southeast Asia" (paper presented to the Tenth Conference of the International Association of Historians of Asia, Singapore, October 1986).

had no machinery with which to close it; the people were hungry and they had little to feed them with. They brought to bear a legalistic and moralistic restorationism that made them view the Sukarno government as "Japanese formed and completely under Japanese control."[6]

Three key figures illustrate the flavor and the intentions of NICA: van Mook, Dr. Charles O. Van der Plas, and Lieutenant Colonel Raden Abdul Kadir Widjojoatmodjo. Born in Semarang, Java, the son of two schoolteachers, van Mook was fiercely loyal to the Indies. In the early 1930s he had been the chief legislative and journalistic voice of the reform-minded Stuw-group. He spoke for the administrative autonomy of the archipelago, but like many Eurasians he could not contemplate the severance of the Indies from the Netherlands itself. On the basis of a speech by the queen, van Mook foresaw a commonwealth of the Netherlands, Indonesia, Surinam, and Curacao, with "complete self-reliance and freedom of conduct for each part regarding its internal affairs, but with the readiness to render mutual assistance." At the same time he described nationalist leaders as "collaborators" and youth activists as "unsettled youngsters." He implied prosecution and punishment for the former and discipline of the latter through the restoration of stability and resumption of education.[7]

Van der Plas, former governor of East Java and a member of the Council of Indies, wore a distinctive beard and moustache, trimmed according to Muslim religious prescription. His friendships with indigenous leaders in East Java, and his visits to Rumah Indonesia in Melbourne to "eat with the natives," opened him to criticism from Dutch bureaucrats and businessmen. He was damaging his government and lowering the prestige of the white man. But he also was steady in pursuit of the queen's solution for the Indies. When he returned to Jakarta his first political report on the "fascistic? republic" was studded with anguished and astonished exclamation points.[8]

[6] Van Mook to Mountbatten, 3 September 1945, in van der Wal, *Betrekkingen*, 1:82–86 (quotation, 86).

[7] Dr. H. J. van Mook, "Past and Future in the Netherlands Indies" (Address to the Institute of Pacific Relations, San Francisco, 18 May 1945), quotations from 10, 13. Sources for my sketch of van Mook, as for that of Van der Plas following, are from a number of interviews of Indonesians and Dutch. Anderson makes a stimulating comparison of Van der Plas and Shimizu Hitoshi in "Japan: 'The Light of Asia,' " in Josef Silverstein, ed., *Southeast Asia in World War II: Four Essays*, Yale University Southeast Asia Studies (New Haven, 1966), 16.

[8] Van der Plas to van Mook, September 18, 1945, in van der Wal, *Betrekkingen*, 1: 121–28. For the evolution of Van der Plas's views of Sukarno in 1929, see B. Hering,

Abdul Kadir, a graduate of Batavia Law School who had worked his way to the top of the native civil service, was, like van der Plas, also adept in both cultures. Now, as the foremost Indonesian in NICA, he was even discussed for the governor generalship.[9] An obedient, congenial man, he hid any hard feelings behind the smiles and grace of a cultured Javanese, tendering his criticisms of the Dutch indirectly, in terms of praise for American public education and technology. He prepared an article that declared that Indonesia's civilizing influences had all come from the West—Hindu, Islamic, Chinese, and Dutch—but now, for the first time, there came from the "East" the liberating civilization of the Americans. The Dutch never allowed the article to be published. They instead encouraged Abdul Kadir in radio broadcasts that threatened punishment to Sukarno and other collaborators with the Japanese.[10]

When Abdul Kadir and Sukarno finally met, the favor of the Dutch queen mattered far less than the ferment of the Indonesian people. Abdul Kadir's plea for binationalism and negotiation was losing to Sukarno's confrontational nationalism. "Maybe you can make it rain," Abdul warned Sukarno, "but later let's see you stop the flood."[11] The warning was prophetic, but impotent. NICA could neither unleash a rain nor dam the flood.

The British had to use the Japanese to control the situation until Mountbatten's SEAC troops arrived in any quantity. Formal terms having been reached between SEAC and General Itagaki at Singapore on 12 September, General Yamamoto came on board HMS *Cumberland* at Jakarta to arrange local surrender terms. After the talk, the British cabled headquarters in Singapore: "Have just had Yamamoto on board to rub in his responsibilities which he assured us he fully realizes. Japanese control is undoubtedly deteriorating and new Indonesian nationalist flag is appearing in increasing numbers. Extremists continuing old Japanese-created organisations ... are effecting a measure of terrorism and underground movements especially communists are coming to the surface."[12]

---

ed., *Ch. O. Van der Plas and the P.N.I. Leadership*, James Cook University of North Queensland, Centre for Southeast Asian Studies, Monograph No. 20 (Townsville, 1985).

[9] RVO 007883-85 consists of sketches of Indonesians active "in the Allied cause," of which Abdul Kadir was the most prominent.

[10] Abdul Kadir, interview May 12, 1969; unpublished MS headed "De Opdracht," dated April 25, 1945, made available to the author by Abdul Kadir; for radio broadcasts see RVO, particularly RVO 048339, pp. 17–18.

[11] Abdul Kadir, interview, May 12, 1969.

[12] Rear Adm. Comdg. HMS *Cumberland*, Batavia, to SACSEA, September 15, 1945, RVO 005376-400; CS5 to SACSEA, secret, September 16, 1945, RVO 059376. An early

Next time on board Yamamoto suggested that Allied military administration continue his own policy. The Indonesians would cooperate "if we make full use of their desire to attain ultimate independence by peaceful means." Law and order, he said, depended on permission to use the national flag and anthem, on clothing and food, on ultimate independence, and on restored financial equilibrium. Van der Plas differed. Food was most important. The 4.5 million tons of rice that the Japanese considered a good year was only half of a normal prewar corp. He was particularly unreceptive to flag, anthem, and independence. Without commenting on Yamamoto's defense of Sukarno and Hatta—that they had cooperated not because they liked it, but as a means of gaining independence—Van der Plas said only that people had to be protected against a "very undesirable type of nationalist" using "organized terrorism."[13] Afterward Van der Plas drew up a sworn statement,[14] presumably for legal use against Yamamoto, recording Yamamoto's declaration that on imperial instruction, "he had planned and conducted the whole campaign for Indonesian independence from the beginning."

Van der Plas himself took to Radio Batavia on September 30, presuming "to put an end to violence, brutality and injustice. Our object is to work as hard as we can for the welfare of the people, remembering the old Javanese saying, 'When there is order and peace the country can prosper.' "[15] He made no mention of independence, or autonomy, or even of further representation; there was no suggestion of anything but the Dutch intention to resume where they had left off: *rust en orde* plus paternal welfarism. His use of an "old

British intelligence report concluded "once transport and security problems are solved, other tasks will become comparatively simple" (Major Alan Greenhalgh, "Java Situation Report, Batavia, 14 Sept 45, 1900 hours," RVO 5160-67). American intelligence reports, beginning a week later, were more realistic; e.g., "Indonesian Unrest Portends Most Critical Situation in Southeast Asian Command" (Office of Strategic Services files, R + A Summary Reports 3261, September 21, 1945, and 3265, September 28, RG 59, National Archives [hereafter, OSS, R + A]).

In addition to sources cited hereafter, useful contemporary pictures of the situation include David Wehl, *The Birth of Indonesia* (London: Allen and Unwin, 1948); Charles Wolf, Jr., *The Indonesian Story* (New York: John Day, 1948); and P. S. Gerbrandy, *Indonesia* (London: Hutchinson, 1950).

[13] "Meeting on Board HMS *Cumberland*," September 21, 1945, RVO 059376. Yamamoto Moichirō's account in *Kaisōroku* (Memoirs) (Tokyo: Yamamoto Akiko, 1978), 140–41, is consistent with Anglo-Dutch notes on the event.

[14] Rvo 059376.

[15] "Official Statement by Dr. Ch. O. Van der Plas as representative of the Netherlands Indies Government," Radio Batavia, September 30, 1945. See also untitled, undated translation of earlier propaganda leaflet, RVO 048084.

Javanese saying" nicely served Dutch intentions. The Filipinos meanwhile quoted Douglas MacArthur's "I have returned"—a promise in the first person, dramatically and victoriously realized in a return that meant fulfillment of the prewar American promise of independence.

Both the Gunseikanbu and the Indonesian nationalists expected the Allies to prosecute collaborators, as Abdul Kadir's broadcasts had warned. The Dutch had plenty of evidence against Sukarno for treason: an oath of "eternal fidelity" to Japan; criticism of Italy for lacking the will to fight; a tribute to the "gallant German nation" on V-E day for holding out against a numerically and materially stronger enemy; an "ecstasy of joy and gratitude" at the Philippine declaration of war against the Allies; several messages of support to Laurel; endorsement of a proposal of general military conscription against the Allies; presiding over the burning in effigy of Roosevelt, Churchill, and Van der Plas; and repeated denouncements of Dutch "lies" and of Van der Plas's petty promises of "welfare and blessings."[16] Sukarno phoned the Gunseikanbu almost daily to ask if there was any Allied order to arrest him.[17] Hatta prepared a trunk in case of arrest, and joked cheerlessly to Miyoshi, "I am well accustomed to . . . jail life."

A controversial speech by Lieutenant General Sir Philip Christison changed the picture. As the Seaforth Highlanders landed in Jakarta, he broadcast that Great Britain had but two main objectives: protection and evacuation of Allied prisoners, and disarming the Japanese. "The British have no intention of meddling in Indonesian internal affairs, but only to ensure law and order." Pending Dutch-Indonesian agreement, he asked nationalist leaders to treat him and his troops as guests and said they would not move outside occupied areas in certain major cities.

The report of the broadcast shook the morale of the Dutch. The

[16] Extracts from Sukarno's speeches, April 29, 1943, September 28, 29, 1944, October 1, 25, 27, 1944, May 14, 1945, RVO 08211-13; *Asia Raya* September 14, 1943 (re Italy); Manila *Tribune*, November 4, 1944 (re battle of Leyte); extract, August 16, 1944, RVO 08211-13; *Tjahaja*, September 2, November 9, 1944, GSK.

[17] "Beschouwingen over de algemeene en financiele voorbereiding v.d. Indon. Onafhankelijkheidsbeweging door de Japanners" (hereafter "Beschouwingen . . . financiele"), RVO 048339, pp. 17–18. The author, anonymous, was a first lieutenant, later a captain in the Kikakura (Planning Section) of Gunseikanbu HQ. Anderson (*Java in Revolution*, 66n), giving an RVO number 059397 for the same document, believes the author was Nakamura Hiroshi, who served a long prison sentence at the end of the war. I use this apparently knowledgeable source only with care, when other evidence is lacking, or when its narrative consists in tone and content with other sources.

"last to be liberated in Europe" now felt betrayed by their allies in Asia. Van Mook remarked that Great Britain had given virtual recognition to the Indonesian Republic.[18] They were treating Sukarno, the detestable collaborator, as a political equal, and erasing the possibility of war crimes and collaboration trials against major Indonesian leaders. The Dutch proceeded with some trials nonetheless and achieved a few convictions, including that of Gatot Mangkupradja. In May 1947, however, van Mook would declare an amnesty,[19] one of a series of concessions attempting to save Dutch imperial sovereignty.

Only a full Allied invasion of Java could have restored Dutch power. Then, postponement of Indonesian independence might have been a strong possibility. Land war on Java would have left thousands of Javanese, including many Peta officers, dead by the time of Japanese surrender; the revolutionary impulse would have been bled to weakness and much of the material means for rebellion consumed. A transfer of authority under the MacArthur–van Mook agreement might then have allowed the Dutch to restore order, try collaborators for treason, and put down any uprisings by ill-supplied, demoralized nationalists.

Instead events played into the hands of Indonesian nationalists. While full-scale warfare ravaged Luzon, in bypassed Java Indonesian paramilitary personnel were poised to take as much of Japanese materiel and installations as they could. The British, though willing to restore the prewar imperial order, lacked the personnel to do so. Dutch troops did not arrive until December, by which time the Indonesian nationalists were psychologically and physically prepared for struggle and attrition. Before the war they had not dared oppose 40,000 Dutch troops. By 1949 they were able to achieve their will against the presence of 145,000.

POSTURES OF THE JAPANESE

Hoping to curb disorder and despair among their forces and to restrain Indonesian rebels, the Japanese navy did not issue an order to

---

[18] Dutch-British confusion on questions of recognition and jurisdiction may be traced in van der Wal, *Betrekkingen*, 1: 110–11, 148–49, and the Dutch-British schism and confusion over the Christison broadcast, in *Betrekkingen*, 183–202, 233–35; "British Policy Toward Nationalists in Indonesia Strengthens Sukarno's Position," OSS, R + S 3270, October 5, 1945; Anderson, *Java in Revolution*, 133–39.

[19] Staatsblad van Nederlandsch-Indië, 1947, No. 79, Praerogaties, Amnestie, RVO 048380.

suspend hostilities until August 19, nor the army until August 22. They shared the news with Hatta and Sukarno, who were informed that the Japanese could no longer participate in the BPKI, which had been preparing for independence.[20] In this "stolen week," the Japanese tried to figure out what to do. According to one summary, about 90 percent of the Japanese were too stunned to have any definite opinion, or were effectively neutral. The remaining 10 percent favored policies ranging from armed suppression of the rebels to armed assistance to them. General Nishimura Otoshi felt that Japan, having surrendered, had lost jurisdiction over the Indonesian problem and should abide by international law, offering no help to the rebels.[21] Others of the Gunseikanbu, while willing to allow Indonesian theft or bloodless seizure of arms, took the same legal view. Admiral Maeda Tadashi challenged them with his own conviction that "Indonesian independence comes from the will of the Emperor based upon the sacred ideal of *Hakkō Ichiu*." Nishimura countered that the emperor's will could change; before, they had fought for him; now "the same Emperor has ordered us to stop fighting." Why cease hostilities at the emperor's command, and yet incite the nationalists against the Dutch? The Allies, with the future of Japan in their hands, had decided to permit the emperor to remain on the throne; both gratitude and common sense argued that the Japanese should do nothing to antagonize the victors.[22]

Nishimura's superior, Yamamoto, had at one point promised Hatta that his men would surrender their arms to "attacking" Indonesians if both sides would shoot in the air. But in places where Indonesians particularly hated the Japanese, they shot level and killed. Yamamoto furiously rescinded his order and "turned his back" on the Indonesian leaders.[23] This episode neutralized the

[20] Miyoshi says this occurred on the eighteenth, "Jawa senryō gunsei kaikoroku" (Memoirs of the military administration of Java), 15 pts. *Kokusai Mondai*, (April 1965–January 1967), pt. 15, 63, pt. 16, 68–69). Yamamoto says it was the morning of the nineteenth (RVO 168902).

[21] "Beschouwingen . . . financiele," RVO 048339, esp. pp. 12–15. Lt. Col. Miyamoto Shizuo, staff officer in charge of Supply, reporting to the commander in chief of the Sixteenth Army, subsequently detailed the army's critique of the hasty actions of the Naval Liaison Office and Admiral Maeda (Reid and Oki, eds., *The Japanese Experience in Indonesia*, 325–27).

[22] RVO 048339, pp. 21–22. Nakamura's source was Major General Nishimura himself, which may account for the general having the best lines.

[23] Hatta, interview, July 5, 1968, is the basic source of this story. Yamamoto, in interviews, June 1968, would not discuss his original order. His reluctance is understandable, because such an order contradicted surrender terms, was unsamurai, led

army to some degree, and made Yamamoto's ambiguous behavior bear to some Japanese "the stink of pretending."[24]

The navy went its own way, with less inhibition. Some of its commanders in Indonesia, such as Admirals Shibata and Maeda, had shifted "from a policy of fighting World War II to one of fighting World War III." They got behind the independence movement, making a long-term goodwill investment in areas where bases and resources would potentially more than compensate for possessions in the Pacific now lost.[25] The navy assisted the Indonesians with munitions, personnel, and funds. They were most effective outside of Java, but significant in Java too, particularly through the dump at Cililitan, interior "fortresses" at Bandung and Malang, air bases at Madiun and Yogyakarta, and, most of all, at Surabaya, Admiral Shibata's headquarters.[26]

Whatever the emperor's orders and victor's expectations, Japanese help to Indonesian nationalists widened as a result of the power vacuum, anti-Allies sympathy, and Indonesian pressure. Since mid-December 1944 the Japanese army had been collecting diamonds (to polish airplane propeller shafts), gold, and platinum. In the first month the Javanese yielded up more than thirty million guilders' worth of these precious goods, and by March 1945 the Japanese had collected more diamonds in Java than in Japan itself.[27] In Hindu mythological tradition, jewels for battle, bangles for justice, were part of the thread of heroic narrative. These actual donations were a sign of the fear and trust in which Javanese, encouraged by Sukarno, continued to hold their Asian conquerors—fear of reprisal for noncooperation, trust in aid against the Dutch.

Help from Japanese forces never took the expected form of armed struggle, although several hundred individual Japanese soldiers deserted to fight with Indonesia against the Dutch. The Japanese legacy to the Indonesians, in addition to funds and key buildings, consisted of fighting spirit, military training, and weapons.

The self-proclaimed republic was inexperienced and ill-prepared to get the most out of the resources available. Its people were tired of the war and many were weak with hunger. Nonetheless, enough

---

to deaths among his own troops, and did not fit the public image of a man who, at the time of interview, was a leader of a Japanese veterans' organization.

[24] Rvo 048339, pp. 12–15.

[25] Ibid., pp. 25–28.

[26] Ibid., pp. 20–21.

[27] Ibid., p. 26, citing *Shin Jawa*, March 1945, p. 47; see also Abu Hanifah, *Tales of Revolution* (Sidney: Angus and Robertson, 1972), 142.

of the fractured establishment, its offices and factories and finances, passed into Indonesian hands to make occupation difficult for the late-arriving British, and imperial control impossible for later-returning Dutch. The Japanese made available, or the Indonesians took over, significant assets, which in a probably exaggerated estimate, exceeded three hundred million guilders.[28] When ordered to concentrate in new camps, the Japanese completed construction of "fortresses" previously planned, and paid the construction monies into the hands of regional nationalist governments to the extent of probably one hundred million guilders. When ordered to continue their administration as before, the Japanese were able to "play two jokers": to pay three months' salary in advance to Indonesian employees, plus an advance bonus for Lebaran (New Year), or a minimum of ten million guilders more, and to release generous amounts of food, clothing, and medicine they had stored to sustain them for three years of fighting.[29]

The military and paramilitary units trained by the Japanese may have totaled sixty thousand men, plus another two hundred thousand in groups with at least some military indoctrination. Three thousand Javanese officers with noncommissioned officers began organizing these. By theft, hand-over, or other appropriation illegal under surrender terms, the Javanese apparently obtained, among other items: 53,000 rifles and 16,000 pistols, including automatics, with plenty of ammunition; 3,000 light and heavy machine guns, with 107 million rounds; 318,000 hand grenades; 50 tanks; and a variety of field guns, antiaircraft guns, cars, trucks, and explosives.[30]

[28] "Beschouwingen . . . financiele," RVO 048339:

Funds designated for general fortresses	f. 10,000,000
Funds for local fortresses	9,000,000
Ordinary managing funds for the Gunseikanbu and civilian business organs financed by the Gunseikanbu	200,000,000
Reserve funds at local specie banks	18,000,000
"Contributions" (voluntary, compulsory, or stolen) from Japanese soldiers; based on an estimate of f.1,000 each from 70,000 men	70,000,000
	f.307,000,000

The funds themselves were inflated to one-tenth of their original value. Bernhard Dahm, *The History of Indonesia in the Twentieth Century* (London and New York: Praeger, 1971), 115–16, cites smaller figures for Central and East Java only.

[29] Rvo 048339, pp. 8–10, 35–36.

[30] Miyamoto's memoir (Anthony Reid and Oki Akıra, eds., *The Japanese Experience in Indonesia: Selected Memoirs of 1942–1945*, Southeast Asia Series, no. 72

Many were willing to fight with simpler weapons, even bamboo spears.

Sukarno formed his first cabinet on August 31, 1945. The Christison broadcast a month later made it clear that the British would not abet the prosecution of major Indonesian leaders. The stage was fully set for the events that ensued.

NATIONAL REVOLUTION

Independence proclaimed, flags were on display. A British air force commandant in Central Java saw them everywhere, and nearly everybody wore armbands of red and white. "Normally quite peaceful people, whose memories of the Dutch regime could only have been pleasant, but whose feelings had been exacerbated by three and a half years of Japanese rule, stood forth now as opponents of any form of Dutch infiltration and as champions of their own 'MERDEKA.' "[31] He misunderstood prewar rule, but identified two critical factors correctly. The people had seen Dutch armed forces completely routed and Europeans subjected to "every form of humiliation and ill treatment." Then, "the Dutch on their return to Java did not return as conquerors of the Japanese in the same degree as [the British] did in Burma [where reinvasion preceded Japanese surrender] and Malaya."[32]

Dutch wartime internees, escaped or released, thought mainly of *status quo ante bellum*. They began demanding the immediate return of industries, dwellings, and automobiles taken over by Japanese or Indonesians. By mid-September, disputes arose suddenly and sharply. On September 19 a Dutchman raised the red, white, and blue flag of the Netherlands over the Hotel Oranje in Surabaya, and an Indonesian climbed up and ripped off the blue, leaving the *Merah Putih* (red and white) flying. The incident touched off a riot, which led to more mass demonstrations and riots. The Japanese evacuated contested buildings; they did not wish to risk large confrontations that would force them to choose between using heavy weapons against the Javanese or being overrun.[33] In Yogyakarta, a flag-hoisting incident involving ten thousand Indonesians at the

[Athens: Ohio University Center for International Studies, 1986]) contains an extensive table from which these figures are drawn and rounded.

[31] Report of Wing Cmdr. Tull, RAF, attached to RAPWI, on Operation "Salek Mastiff," September 10–December 15, 1945, RVO 059388.

[32] Ibid.

[33] Vice Adm. Shibata Yaichiro, interrogation, RVO 006948-67.

sultan's residence showed the same depth of ferment, and by September 25 the city was in Indonesian hands. On the twenty-eighth Bandung began to go over to the Indonesians, and by the thirtieth the main public buildings in Malang and Solo were out of Japanese control.[34] Sukarno wrote to Mountbatten: "We do not ask the Allied Military Forces to recognize the Republic of Indonesia. We only ask you to acknowledge facts, namely that to the feelings of the people there exists a Republic of Indonesia with a government."[35]

The period of "gentleman's agreements" between the Japanese army and the Indonesian rebels now came to an end. Sukarno and Hatta were accepted as leaders not only by aggressive nationalists, but by many who hoped to gain independence wholly by negotiation, by nationalistic radicals for whom Mohammad Yamin was a representative voice, and even, until their disastrous left-adventurist initiative at Madiun in 1948, by Indonesian communists, again on the rise. The "united religious, cultural, regional, and purely political forces of varying Indonesians" surprised and impressed American intelligence agents.[36] The prospects for the Dutch were clear and ominous.

The revolution in Indonesia had three major flare points in the late months of 1945: Bandung, Semarang, and Surabaya. Events in each city overlapped events in the others, and were partially connected, but with distinct local flavor. From West to Central to East Java the scale of death and destruction rose.

In Bandung, foreign arms were a significant but not determining factor in the situation.[37] A small group of nationalist politicians, establishing political committees and military units, displaced the civil servants and the Islamic leaders who had carried on administration or come to the fore under Japanese encouragement. Disorder erupted in late September. The committees gave way to struggle groups (badan perjuangan). Although elsewhere in Java, Japanese

[34] Sixteenth (Japanese) Army HQ, Public Peace Intelligence Bulletins, September 1945, RVO 005178 et seq.

[35] Sukarno to Mountbatten, September 30, 1945, in van der Wal, Betrekkingen, 1: 202–6 (quotation, 204).

[36] "The Political Issue and Occupation Problems in the N.E.I." and "The Communist Movement in Indonesia," both October 19, 1945, OSS, R + A 3278,79. Re British: Wehl, Birth of Indonesia, 66–67.

[37] The following account is based on John R. W. Smail, Bandung in the Early Revolution, 1945–1946: A Study in the Social History of the Indonesian Revolution, Cornell Modern Indonesia Project, no. 33 (Ithaca, 1964). See also M. Slamet, "West Java, 1945–1948," in Moenander et al., Indonesian Nationalism and Revolution: Six First-Hand Accounts (Monash University, 1969?), 19.

were colluding in Indonesians' obtaining arms and control of offices and establishments, in Bandung the Japanese regained control on October 10. Two British battalions arrived shortly afterward and helped maintain calm for another several weeks. Meanwhile Indonesians continued to form struggle groups and units of the Tentara Keamanan Republik (TKR, or Security Army of the Republic; later the Tentara Republik Indonesia, or TRI, Army of the Indonesian Republic).

On November 23, young activists in the army and the struggle groups attacked British units in Bandung. They failed to dislodge the occupiers, but they did produce a "state of almost complete anarchy" in December, which periodically recurred until March. During this time, activist elements kidnapped or murdered over fifteen hundred people, mostly Eurasians and Chinese. The British created a protective zone in the northern part of the city for Europeans, which drove many Indonesians to the southern part of the city, from whence fighting and bombardment drove them again. The struggle groups, in evacuating southern Bandung on March 24, 1946, turned it into a "sea of fire."[38]

These months of turmoil in Bandung made the civil authorities, especially the traditional native bureaucrats, impotent; diminished the influence of nationalist leaders and made political parties irrelevant; and robbed the Islamic elite in the city of much of the ground it had gained under the Japanese.

Meanwhile, in the nearby villages, religiously educated pemuda came forward leading a militant rural Islam of the kind always feared by the Dutch. Young activists, urban as well as rural, santri and secular, educated and illiterate, were drawn to the struggle groups. Here lay the opportunity for exuberant daredevilry, for romantic heroism, for defiance and violence—for the thrill of bringing down the Japanese, British, and Dutch, as well as their own complicit elders, all in the name of the people. Such action, such intoxication, could not last forever. By May 1946 the TKR Third Division began absorbing the larger and more effective struggle groups. Some pemuda, appreciating the power of larger-scale organization, developed an interest in the relation of force to diplomacy and even the possibility of postrevolutionary stability.

In Semarang the British arrived later and in small numbers. The

---

[38] Anderson, *Java in Revolution*, 139–43, gives a condensed account of the earlier weeks of activity in Bandung, relying on Smail, while elaborating some controverted points.

Japanese commander of the area possessed fewer men than the commander in West Java, and was much more sympathetic to Indonesian independence. The local resident, Wongsonagoro, cultivated contact with the pemuda, negotiated with both Japanese and British, and was appointed governor of Central Java. But a growing British presence aroused suspicions. To prevent the kind of nullification of Indonesian power that had temporarily taken place in Bandung, activists moved against the Japanese in Semarang in mid-October. There followed a bloody series of incidents reflecting fear and pent-up vengeance, reprisal and counterreprisal. In six days of fighting the Japanese lost over five hundred men, and an estimated two thousand Indonesians died.

On October 20, Brigadier General Bethell, commander of the Forty-ninth Brigade, took control of the city. He negotiated with Wongsonagoro a respect for Indonesian sovereignty in return for help with supplies, and freedom from interference with British rescue of internees, many of whom were women and children. Events in Surabaya reinflamed the situation. Sukarno and Amir Sjarifuddin flew to Semarang on November 1 and arranged a cease-fire, but news of the British assault on Surabaya on November 10 aroused hostilities again. With the aid of air strikes, heavy artillery, and shelling from the cruiser *Sussex*, the British forces, largely consisting of Gurkha troops, managed by the end of the month to complete the major assignment of evacuating internees. Their power prevailed in Semarang, but they had left the rest of Central Java in the hands of the Indonesian Republic.[39]

In Surabaya, the initial mood of revolution, one of ecstatic release, grew with early victories, leaving "the people even more intoxicated than before. Their faith in the new god continued to grow and they abandoned the old god entirely. They fell in love with carbines and revolvers as if they were beautiful girls: they caressed them, kissed them, and sold them at very high prices. Their faces were happy and proud."[40]

Surabaya's mood resembled that felt elsewhere in Java, but its social fabric and history promoted a special intensity of feeling. Jakarta was primarily a city of bureaucrats and intellectuals, and even Bandung and Semarang were strongly conditioned by the ethos of educated civil servants. Surabaya, however, had a more independent and loosely "democratic" character. The major naval base there

[39] Anderson, *Java in Revolution*, 147–51.
[40] Idrus, "Surabaja," trans. S. U. Nababan and Ben Anderson, *Indonesia* 5 (1968): 3.

helped foster independent labor, which made machine parts and
spare equipment for marine purposes as well as for sugar mills and
other enterprises. An Indonesian middle class had grown up in the
city, much more competitive with the Chinese than was the colonial norm, and Indonesian professionals there had an unusual autonomy of view. Militant rural Islam was closely connected to the
city, as a result of the years of Hadji Omar Said Tjokroaminoto's
leadership of Sarekat Islam. In addition to that once fiery movement, Surabaya was also the site of Muhammadiyah activities under K. H. Mansoer; the Nahdatul Ulama under K. H. Hashim Ashari
and K. H. Wahab Chasbullah; the Studiclub and PBI/Parindra under
Dr. Soetomo; the Nationalist party movement under Dr. Samsi, Ir.
Anwari, and Doel Arnowo; and it was the seat of communist party
activity led by Musso and Alimin.[41]

Surabaya, then, resembled a preindustrial Hanseatic city more
than the other focal towns of Java; and its diversity, independence,
and relative freedom from hierarchy and bureaucracy made it more
mature for revolution. Surabaya had also escaped one corollary of
Dutch educational style, which by selecting a small group to be
"educated to perfection," often reduced them to sycophancy. The
city's unique combination of disadvantage and leverage included
not only having no university, but having no senior high school for
Indonesians. There was only one for Dutch, which perhaps 30 to 35
Indonesians attended, of a total of 750 students. Three kinds of junior high schools existed for Indonesians aged approximately twelve
to seventeen: Perguruan Rakyat, which fostered militant nationalism; Taman Siswa, cultural nationalism; and Muhammadiyah, Islamic centeredness. From them came young leadership before and
during the revolution. A strong Surabaya chapter of Indonesia Muda
in 1933 forced the national organization to be opened to all, not just
to university students. This chapter took social action in Surabaya
against illiteracy, and was involved with labor strikes abetted by
adult education. The spirit of neighborhood organizations for mutual assistance, and the energy of sons and daughters of free profes-

[41] Roeslan Abdulgani, *Semangat dan Jiwa Kepahlawanan Dalam Peristiwa 10 November 1945 Untuk Kelanjutan Pembinaan Bangsa* (The courage and spirit of heroism in the affair of 10 November 1945 advancing creation of the nation), Prasaran
Untuk Rapat Penjarahan Proyek Biografi Pahlawan Nasional Cibogo-Bogor, June 14–
18, 1976, 3–4; idem, "The Values of the 1945 Struggle," *Prisma*, Indonesian Journal
of Social and Economic Affairs, no. 4 (November 1976) 33–39; interview, Roeslan
Abdulgani, December 2, 1983.

sionals and free labor, gave Surabaya a stubborn, independent style distinctive in Java.[42]

In this city, the Japanese commander, Admiral Shibata Yaichiro, favored Indonesian independence. By the time a Dutch representative arrived in early October 1945, the Indonesians had already seized a quantity of arms. Shibata knew he was obliged to surrender them to the Allies, but was not prepared to fight Indonesians to do so. He ordered his troops on no condition to use force; if no peaceful resolution could be found, they were to let Indonesians take the weapons.[43] The arms went not just to the KNI (Indonesian National Committee) and Special Police, but to a variety of irregular groups, new bodies, and strenuous claimants on behalf of their own visions of necessity. Authority leaked everywhere into anarchy. Bung Tomo, calling on the name of Allah for Radio Rebellion, was the local voice of arousal for those outside of the power structure of the Dutch and Japanese eras.

By the time the British arrived in the harbor on October 25, a confrontation was inevitable. They intended to disarm the population, take key buildings and communication centers, and free internees. They were well armed, but their small number of troops were divided between internee camps and the harbor at opposite ends of town. Indonesians, estimated at over 120,000 with every variety of arms, many of them primitive, attacked. Sukarno, at the urging of Major General Hawthorn, commander of a Gurkha brigade of Seaforth Highlanders, flew with Hatta and Amir Sjarifuddin to Surabaya on October 29. They achieved an agreement by which the British would withdraw to fixed positions, free passage would be allowed between them for evacuation of internees, and the Indonesians' right to bear arms would go uncontested.

The afternoon that Sukarno flew back to Jakarta, firing broke out amid the effort of joint patrols to establish the agreement. Brigadier General Mallaby was killed. His death was possibly by a mistake of his own men, as many Indonesians believe, but it certainly aroused the fury and punitive instincts of the British. The threat of massive bloodshed drove Sukarno to a radio broadcast on October 31, which concluded, "I order all fighting with the Allies to cease. Carry out my orders. Merdeka!"[44]

The calm that followed was destroyed by Major General Man-

[42] Roeslan Abdulgani, interview.

[43] Shibata Yaichiro, "Surabaya after the Surrender," in Reid and Oki, eds., *Japanese Experience in Indonesia*, 341–74; Yamamoto Moichirō, Kaisōroku, 143–46.

[44] Anderson, *Java in Revolution*, 152–64.

sergh, arriving with the Fifth Indian Infantry Division and tanks. With Dutch foreknowledge, he issued an ultimatum on November 9 that all arms in Surabaya be turned in the next morning, and that the "murderers" of Mallaby be surrendered.[45] Impossible demands. Rejected.

The British attacked on November 10 at 6:00 A.M., with heavy naval and aerial bombardment. Street-to-street battles lasted for more than three weeks. The Indonesians at first fought with "fanatical self-sacrifice, with men armed only with daggers charging Sherman tanks"; then later in a more organized mode, following Japanese military manuals.[46]

British forces now consisted of about six thousand Seaforth Highlanders strengthened by twenty-four thousand "battle-hardened" troops of the Fifth Division; twenty-one Sherman tanks, eight Thunderbolt and sixteen Mosquito planes, and divisional artillery. Indonesian forces were neither countable nor accountable. They took shape from within and against imperial history, Dutch, Japanese, and now, incidentally, British. They expressed the spirit of Surabaya and the ideal of merdeka. Their casualties were incompletely numbered. The British counted 1,618 corpses, and another 4,697 Indonesians who died of wounds. In the first five days of fighting one Indonesian source saw 300 fallen in mass burial, and another 3,000 treated for injury, before the wounded were evacuated to hospitals in a variety of other cities in East Java.[47]

The British won the city. Indonesia won respect for its cause. The shadow of Surabaya made both British and Dutch cautious thereafter. Direct conflict initiated by the Dutch in the two "police actions" of July 1947 and December 1948 involved incomparably less intensity and fewer losses to either side than occurred in Surabaya late in 1945. The Indonesian will to fight remained clear. It was to a great degree disorganized and spontaneous, and prone to attacks on Allied, Eurasian, and Chinese noncombatants; but its latent energies were formidable and fierce. Java was in full revolt. The Dutch had only to recognize that an era was ending. To do so systematically took them four years.

---

[45] For the ultimatum in full, see ver der Wal, *Betrekkingen*, 2: 15n; for Dutch foreknowledge of it, see van Mook to Logemann, November 8, 1945, *Betrekkingen*, 1:565ff.

[46] Anderson, *Java in Revolution*; 164–66; quotation from Wehl, *Birth of Indonesia*, 66.

[47] Roeslan Abdulgani, *Semangat dan Jiwa Kepahlawanan*, 1–2. *Abdul Haris Nasution: A Political Biography*, by C.L.M. Penders and Ulf Sundhaussen (St. Lucia: University of Queensland Press, 1985), gives Nasution's view of the battle of Surabaya, pp. 21–22.

Rebelling and Governing

Before violence broke out in Bandung, the nationalist leaders were conceiving how to govern Indonesia, as well as to free it. As violence was ending in Surabaya, they were vexed over how to liberate Indonesia into the family of nations, while trying to rally and lead it. Two events dramatize their dilemma, and help illustrate the nature of the Indonesian revolution.

On August 30, 1945, before having assembled the first cabinet, Sukarno and Soetardjo convened a Java-Madura conference of the *pangreh praja*. Young activists were dismayed and disillusioned at the high priority given to a civil service organized by the Netherlands and used by Japan. Sjahrir, whose three cabinets covered most of the vicissitudes of the first year of revolution, nonetheless followed the same path. Would not the bureaucratic lackeys of the Dutch and the Japanese retard the revolution? Hatta's reply is hard to fault: to try to circumvent the existing civil servants and build up two administrations would create inefficient conflict, and leave open to capture a working structure that could be handed from the Japanese to the British and back to the Dutch. To start a totally new structure with presumably pure personnel would not be rational. "And what is not rational in a revolution is not revolutionary."

Sukarno told the pangreh praja conference itself that the government of the Republic of Indonesia needed to get "as much real power and activity as possible" through the "gentleman's agreement" with the Japanese authorities. He and Hatta were concentrating on diplomacy, which in turn was based on "an aggregate collective will of the people," expressed through national committees down to the village level. In this regard the pangreh praja had an important role, not "simply as secretaries, clerks or petty foremen," not "degraded" or "lowered" as before, but as part of the uprising of the people.[48]

Partisans of struggle and partisans of diplomacy tend to present the Indonesian revolution with some disdain for each other. Leadership, however, required adeptness at both. Sukarno had shown himself capable of heating the struggle; now he had to show himself also capable of cooling it for the sake of international credibility, and support. When he did so, he evoked criticism for everything from bad timing to intrinsic cowardice.

One can, of course, imagine a revolution conducted with kami-

[48] Re Sjahrir: author's interview, Soedjatmoko, November 16, 1983; Anderson, *Java in Revolution*, quotes Hatta, 112, Sukarno 113; Miyoshi's memoirs discuss the early effort at assembling a governmental structure (*Kokusai Mondai* 16: 68–69).

kaze sincerity and pesantrèn purity. Conceivably it might have prevailed over the Dutch in two years, instead of four, and bequeathed to Indonesia a brighter revolutionary heritage, instead of what one pemuda leader, in mature perspective, called a "soft revolution."[49] But just as likely, it could have failed to win international support, could have taken longer to achieve its objectives, and could have been vastly more costly in blood, Surabaya-style.

Those leading the revolution were clear in their choice at the time. Late in 1945, Harold Isaacs, who was covering Vietnam for the *New York Times*, brought a letter from Ho Chi Minh to Sukarno. The Vietnamese leader invited coordination between their two revolutions, and proposed a joint statement of solidarity against returning colonialists. Hatta, as vice-president, referred it to Sjahrir. The prime minister discussed it with two of his adherents among young activists, Soedjatmoko and Sudarpo. Soedjatmoko argued strongly for it, only to find that he simply fueled Sjahrir's opposition along these lines:

1. Indonesia's adversaries were different from Indochina's. The French were tough and would last a long time, but the Dutch could be outlasted with patience, and defeated at less cost.
2. The international contexts and strategies of the two revolutions differed. Indonesia was courting international opinion and support, whereas Vietnam was not. To join hands with them would be to lose such support.
3. The internal leadership and their alliance patterns differed. The Viet Minh was clearly communist; but Indonesian leadership was nationalist, and to veer toward "coordination" with Ho would cost the movement rural and Muslim followers, and might even precipitate change in the leadership itself.

Sjahrir convinced himself, and his arguments persuaded Soedjatmoko over time. Nobody answered Ho Chi Minh.[50]

The Character of the Revolution

Understanding the Indonesian revolution as it focused in Java requires grappling with two further questions: (1) What was the role

---

[49] Quotation, B. M. Diah, interview, November 28, 1983.

[50] Soedjatmoko, interview, November 16, 1983. Harold Isaacs to the author, December 27, 1983, confirmed the existence of a letter of such nature in "November or so, 1945," the fact that he was the courier, and the fact that it went unanswered. On the particular importance of American example and opinion at this time, see McMahon, *Colonialism and Cold War*, 56–57.

of the pemuda? and (2) What was the level and nature of violence that took place?

Benedict Anderson, the eminent Javanist and sensitive analyst of politics, has provided a stimulating backdrop for the first question. He sees the revolution as guru-determined, particularly by Muslim *kiai*, and by those working in special pockets of folk culture and fighting traditions known as *jago*. His accent is right insofar as a power vacuum led to the plausibility of any kind of initiative, collection under any banner, the following of any who would or could lead, either as counters against further anarchy or counselors toward merdeka. But the emphasis is wrong when it goes this far:

> Traditional deviant aspects of *santri* culture—sexual abstinence, fraternal solidarity, selfless devotion, nomadic wandering, and dealing with the supernatural—were seen as in harmony with the times. The sense that everything was in suspension while disorder raged in the cosmos seemed to be reflected in the suspended quality of the pesantrèn's inner order. *The society itself became a larger pesantrèn, in which the pesantrèn life-style assumed the mode of normality and necessity.* For in periods of great crisis the whole society moved to free itself from the cycle of routine and regularity and accepted the suspended soaring of the spirit which underlay the pesantrèn's conception of itself.[51]

Evocative as this passage is, we may well ask what proves "the society itself" to be "a larger pesantrèn," as distinct from a ferment of revolutionary hopes and hatreds? What is meant by "the suspended quality of the pesantrèn's inner order," or by the "suspended soaring of the spirit which underlay the pesantrèn's conception of itself"?

In Java, late in 1945, there certainly existed plenty of suspense (in the sense of unresolved political and social conflict with high stakes); of soaring of the spirit (for brief periods of time; humans cannot live solely by soaring any more than by bread alone); and of religiosity (the historical connection of which to the sentiments of nationality Anderson has brilliantly analyzed in a subsequent book).[52] To compose all three elements into a society-embracing metaphor of a pesantrèn, however, is to commit a fallacy of romantic concreteness.

[51] Anderson, *Java in Revolution*, xiii, 2–10 (quotation, p. 10; emphasis added).
[52] Benedict Anderson, *Imagined Communities: Reflections on the Origins and Spread of Nationalism* (London: Verso Editions and NLB, 1983).

Memoirs of the time, even the memoirs of pemuda leaders, do not suggest such a tone, and interviews suggest contrary thoughts. Hatta, as Islamic as any major leader, and as pesantrèn-affected, took a highly skeptical view of youthful attempts "to seize power without any backbone and mature planning."[53] Young Adam Malik's view differed dramatically, but his memoirs do not support Anderson either: pesantrèns made Malik fed up with Islamic feudalism, and interested in retail business and national unity.[54] The perfervid pesantrènesque thinking conjured forth by Anderson may be a better testament to his own imaginative love of Java than a valid controlling metaphor for the times he scrutinizes.[55]

Anderson is surely right in saying about the pemuda movement that its "emergence . . . as a political force was certainly the most striking aspect of the early revolution."[56] To agree still allows questioning his use of "pemuda" as a ubiquitous adjective—as in "pemuda consciousness," "pemuda tradition," "pemuda nationalism," and "pemuda revolution."[57] Translation simplifies matters and raises new questions. What does the concept "youth consciousness" mean, when the consciousness of urban and rural youths may have significantly differed from each other; and "youth tradition," when the very point being advanced about the politically aroused young is a relative traditionlessness, a radical desire to begin the world anew? "Youth nationalism" and "youth revolution" sound like more concrete terms, but are actually abstractions without substantiation.

[53] Miyoshi Memoir, *Kokusai Mondai* 16: 66–68, documents Hatta's views at the time. Hatta elaborated them in "Legend and reality surrounding the 17th August," an article in *Mimbar Indonesia*, no. 32/33 (August 17, 1951) (reprinted in *Portrait of a Patriot* [The Hague: Mouton, 1972], 518–27). In interviews with the author (March, July 1968), Hatta spoke consistently with both earlier writings, and on later occasions, he likened pemuda activity at the time of the proclamation to Hitler's abortive putsch in Munich: C.L.M. Penders, ed., *Mohammad Hatta, Indonesia Patriot, Memoirs* (Singapore: Gunung Agung, 1981), 229, 231; quotation from *Bung Hatta's Answers: Interviews, Dr. Mohammad Hatta with Dr. Z. Yasni* (Singapore: Gunung Agung, 1981), 121.

[54] Adam Malik, *In the Service of the Republic* (Singapore: Gunung Agung, 1980), 6–7.

[55] In interviews, both B. M. Diah (November 28, 1983) and Roeslan Abdulgani (December 2, 1983) took exception to Anderson's emphasis on the pesantrèn, each on his own initiative. Diah's memoirs, *Angkatan Baru '45* (Jakarta: Masa Merdeka, 1983), develop thoughtful distinctions between the generation of 1928 and the generation of 1945, 66–95, but do not ascribe a tone of religious inflammation to the latter.

[56] Anderson, *Java in Revolution*, 407.

[57] Ibid., 151, 157–58, 187–88, 408.

When one comes to such usage as the "pemuda masses," and to "Indonesians, estimated at over 120,000 pemuda" attacking British encampments in Surabaya,[58] further queries arise. How can 120,000 people attacking at night be known to be all youths? How old are pemuda? From what classes do they come? How do they think?

Anderson's own research is an abundantly helpful place to start on definitional questions. His excellent biographical appendix gives sketches of 144 key actors, Indonesian and Japanese, in the story he is telling. Of these, 23 Indonesians appear to have been aged 30 years or less by the end of 1945.[59] Some of the most significant names on the list push that age limit: Adam Malik (28), Chaerul Saleh and Sukarni (29), Sudirman and Soedjono (30), among others. The latter two were of very different character and style than the former three, and remind us that people behave with regard to a great many factors besides age. Because Anderson, however, treats both B. M. Diah and Wikana in "pemuda" context,[60] let them be added with Rasjidi to the list. Then one can say that more than one-sixth of the key actors in Java in 1945 were 31 years of age or less.

Anderson occasionally identifies a specific pemuda by age, such as Mudjitaba bin Murkam, "a 27-year-old pemuda who was second in command of the Lasjkar Hitam and head of intelligence for Hadji Achmad Chairun's Direktorium in Tanggerang." He is more likely to speak broadly of "pemuda of all social classes—pedicab drivers, tradesmen's apprentices, and pickpockets, as well as students and school children."[61] The last phrase takes the age boundaries down to 12 at least, and conceivably lower. So Anderson appears potentially to have embraced in the concept of pemuda Javanese of all social classes aged 12 to 31.

Such a category either includes too many people to be significant, or does not clearly convey the phenomena it is meant to describe. Among Javanese aged 12 to 31, there were obviously a great variety of moods and interests, and states of activity and passivity. Some in that age group came forth for the idea of the nation and/or merdeka, as different cities went through crisis. Some did not. People older than that, or even much older, came forth too. But how often is marching and fighting chiefly an activity of the middle-aged and elderly? Demonstration, riot, and battle involve youthful energy. In that Java was not unique.

[58] Ibid., 109, 161.

[59] Ibid., 411–58. In cases of disputed birthdays, I take the latest, "most youthful," offered.

[60] Ibid., 55–57 concerning Diah; 70–77 concerning Wikana.

[61] Ibid., 186n; 126.

What happens if we take an abbreviated age census of leading Philippine revolutionaries of 1896 and their slightly older precursors, the propagandists? Comparing it with a list of Indonesians of the generation of 1945, and the preceding generation of 1928, "propagandists" from abroad before they became revolutionaries at home, yields little difference.[62]

Filipino Leaders	Age on Dec. 31, 1896
Emilio Aquinaldo	27
Andres Bonifacio	34
Antonio Luna	33
Apolinario Mabini	32
Gregorio del Pilar	21
Artemio Ricarte	30
Jose Rizal	34
Avg. age of 7 above	30 yrs., 3 mos.
Graciano Lopez-Jaena	40
Marcelo H. del Pilar	46
Avg. age of all 9	33 yrs., 1 mo.

Indonesian Leaders	Age on Dec. 31, 1945
D.N. Aidit	22
Chairul Saleh	29
B.M. Diah	28
Adam Malik	28
A.H. Nasution	27
Sudirman	30
Wikana	31
Avg. age of 7 above	27 yrs., 7 mos.
Mohammad Hatta	43
Sjahrir	36
Sukarno	44
Avg. age of all 10	31 yrs., 10 mos.

[62] Data compiled from Gregorio F. Zaide, *Great Filipinos in History: an Epic of Filipino Greatness in War and Peace* (Manila: Verde Book Store, 1970), as well as Anderson, *Java in Revolution*, 441–58. Anderson's preferred date of birth for Diah is 1914 (with 1916 as a parenthetical alternative), 417, whereas internal evidence in Diah's *Angkatan Baru* would place it in 1917 (ix, 80). I am dealing, however, not with the fact here, on which I would yield to Diah, but with Anderson's reasoning.

For provocative essays on the Filipinos listed, and Jose Burgos, who died a generation previously, see Nick Joaquin, *A Question of Heroes* (Manila: Filipinos Foundation, Inc., 1977; reprint ed., Manila: National Book Store, 1981).

The similarity in the Philippine and Indonesian averages suggests that the business of conceiving and planning a revolution in Southeast Asia was the work of young men, and the work of fighting it of younger ones still. Emilio Aguinaldo was 27 at the outset of the Philippine Revolution, but to call him a "pemuda" or a "youth general" would seem tangential and distracting. The leaders of major Philippine intelligence networks and pro-American guerrilla groups against the Japanese from 1942 to 1945, were also young, but it would be equally incongruous to refer to them as "youthful restorationists" working for reestablishment of the Philippine-American system. Youthful consciousness may or may not be revolutionary. Revolutionary consciousness may inhere in people of different ages.

What happened in Indonesia in 1945 is not conceivable without older leaders like Sukarno, Hatta, and Sjahrir, and twenty years of work on national consciousness toward independence. The opportunities of wartime furthered the possibility. Dutch intransigence made hostilities inevitable. In the power vacuum created by Japanese defeat and Anglo-Dutch delay the idea of violent revolution flourished; arms and equipment were gathered; some fundamentals of organization were applied; and force was expressed in the age group biologically most able to bear arms, wield daggers, hurl bottles, and outrun police.

To charge a Sherman tank without firearms takes courage. Respect for that courage, however, does not require one to characterize what happened as a "pemuda revolution." That would leave out the work of too many others. Sjahrir, indeed, in November of 1945, wrote of the dangers of youthful fascism and feudal militarism. He was concerned to change pemuda attitudes "so that they do not lower themselves to the level of wild beasts, but can develop into a revolutionary youth looking forward to a new world."[63] Anderson, who translates Sjahrir so well, nonetheless clings to his own tone of pathos about the revolution, over lack of a driver to put the pemuda engine in gear, over the pemuda movement being "condemned to be frustrated," and over "the search for 100 percent merdeka . . . to remain sentenced to disappointment."[64] How appropriate is such lamentation?

In fact the Indonesian Revolution had a prime leader in Sukarno, formidable secondary leaders in Hatta and Sjahrir, and a significant number of men who had fomented a nation in their twenties who

[63] Sutan Sjahrir, *Our Struggle*, trans. Benedict R. O'G. Anderson, Cornell Modern Indonesia Project, no. 44 (Ithaca, 1968), 36; see also p. 21 on youth's susceptibility to action as a "psychological opiate."

[64] Anderson, *Java in Revolution*, xiii, 409.

now struggled practically for it in their forties. That did not make it a *revolusi setengah tua*—a revolution of the middle-aged—any more than it was a pemuda revolution. Indonesian sovereignty was sought and won by leaders and visionaries who felt unfree under the Dutch, and resented being characterized by them as semi-intellectuals.[65] They had matured politically in the 1920s and 1930s, were aided in energy by those who came suddenly to political prominence in 1945, and were buoyed up by the many of various ages willing to fight for the idea of a nation, with or without Japanese training, even with or without arms.

A question still remains about the nature of the fighting that took place from 1945 to 1949. George Kahin's first-hand account of the revolution is still admirable for the personal courage, tenacity of inquiry, and careful documentation that it represents.[66] The Dutch, however, typically appear in it as powerful villains and Indonesian nationalists as persisting heroes. With hindsight we can appreciate more clearly that the Dutch were blind and weak. Van Mook warned about "Fascist terrorism" in October 1945, while protesting the Christison broadcast. But Mountbatten believed that "he could not recommend to H.M. Government that British/Indian troops should be used to crush the Indonesian Republic." As commander, he proceeded from his experience in Burma, "where he had decided to treat Aung San, who had fought on the side of the Japanese, not as a traitor but as a Patriot who had his own country and its independence most at heart."[67] The Dutch were unwilling to adopt such a view of Sukarno, and unable to express a contrary view with force. A month later, while Surabaya was still seething, and while discussions were about to take place with the Sjahrir government, van Mook wrote to Christison that the Dutch should be released from their "present humiliating position of being everybody's head-ache and nobody's help."[68]

[65] For comparable demeaning of educated Vietnamese leaders by the French, see David G. Marr, *Vietnamese Tradition on Trial* (Berkeley: University of California Press, 1981), Chaps. 4, 8, and particularly p. 330.

[66] George McTurnan Kahin, *Nationalism and Revolution in Indonesia* (Ithaca: Cornell University Press, 1952; reprinted, 1970).

[67] Minutes of the thirty-fourth mixed meeting of the Supreme Allied Commander in Southeast Asia, Singapore, October 10, 1945, in van der Wal, *Betrekkingen*, 1: 300–18 (quotations, 307–8). Citing Aung San strengthened Dutch intransigence and alarmed some leaders in London, where the First Sea Lord said, "More than fifty percent of people in England would like to have seen him shot" (Peter Dennis, *Troubled Days of Peace: Mountbatten and South East Asia Command, 1945–46* [Manchester: Manchester University Press, 1987], 96).

[68] van Mook to Christison, 16 Nov. 45, *Betrekkingen*, 2: 83–85 (quotation, 84).

That humiliating position continued even after the British departed and the Dutch returned. Heartache was added to headache; and so were shadowboxing, irresolute bloodletting, and negotiations in less than full faith. Not much fighting. Through the whole Indonesian revolution, the total number of Dutch combat fatalities was only approximately three hundred. Even with British and Indian deaths of the same order included, the total combat dead of Western powers across the entire revolution only ran between five hundred and seven hundred men.[69] Considering the number of Dutch troops eventually present—variously reported as 140,000 or 145,000—the Netherlands could have risked far more for colonial mastery. But that also would have cost far more. The will to dominate was clearly weakened by European war, and sensibly restrained in the Indonesian circumstances. Because Mountbatten's liberalism was followed by American and Soviet support for Indonesia, self-interested and vacillating as it was in both cases, there were good reasons for the Dutch not to try to rely on protracted force.

The Indonesian will against Western dominance was clearly powerful. At the same time the diffuseness of Indonesian combat deserves remarking. The British initially put a thousand men ashore to control Surabaya, a city of 330,000 people. They were surprised and divided when attacked by twenty thousand armed Indonesians and a large mob, but held on until reinforcements came.[70] In the first police action, from July 21 to August 4, 1947, total Dutch losses were 74 killed, 178 wounded, and 11 missing. The British lost as many to the Americans in their one-day, seventeen-mile march retreating from Lexington to Boston, April 19, 1775. The facts suggest at least that Indonesian sniper fire was not effective.[71] The second police action, from 19 to 31 December 1948, was centered upon the so-called Battle of Yogyakarta. The one or two thousand Dutch troops sent to occupy a city of 400,000 met little resistance. Indonesian forces failed to anticipate and act upon clear indications of impending attack. The principal political leaders revealed a glaring

[69] Karl D. Jackson, "Loyalty Behavior in Post-War Indonesia," unpublished paper, October 1967, 51, 56. The total number of Japanese killed after their surrender was 1,057, of which 544 died in action (*Kenpei Gaishi* [see chap. 9, note 2]; 1129). That the number of Japanese dead equalled or exceeded that of the British and Dutch combined may help explain Japanese resentment over the role forced on them in this period. The figures certainly illustrate Dutch unwillingness to risk lives to save their own empire.

[70] Ibid., 15–23.

[71] Ibid., 29.

absence of planning for their own safety and for the initiative of the revolution. They were captured.[72]

Colonial armies with slender forces could then still achieve major tactical objectives with light casualties, no matter how massively outnumbered they were. But they could not approach success in the major strategic objective, to retain Indonesia as a Dutch colony. The Indonesian army, in turn, could be thought of as a surprisingly effective phenomenon, given how recent was its birth and how limited its training. There was probably far more noncombatant blood shed during the revolution—including that of Chinese, Eurasians, and some Allied internees, as well as unarmed civilians on both sides of the Madiun Affair—than there was blood shed by soldiers. But in any case, the Dutch had lost Prospero's wand. The colonial magic that had appeared so potent as late as the 1930s in the hands of Colijn, de Jonge, and the queen, was now gone. A revolutionary mystique took its place, and eventually a successful revolution.

Some historians wish that more had been achieved in the years 1945–49 and after. They note in tones of regret that there was no "social revolution." But what full social revolution might have consisted of, and what its costs in lives would have been, they do not clearly analyze. Is their model the Vietnamese revolution? The great costs in blood for that among Vietnamese themselves have thus far yielded weak comparative productivity and development, much internal repression, and naked imperialism against their neighbors.

The Indonesian revolution in retrospect can be seen as successful in ending the Dutch plantation system, chiefly in sugar, followed less dramatically by rubber and tobacco; and ending Dutch transporation of labor, both Indonesian and Chinese, to serve that system. The other major sectors of the colonial economy, tin mining and petroleum, relied on protective intervention by the colonial state in similar ways, and suffered similar changes when the protection was gone. The Dutch retained property rights until the sequestration of their assets in 1957. But they could not recoup or transform their economic or social control after 1945, still less after 1949. Because Dutch-owned economic activity depended utterly on the colonial state, and that state was shattered, Dutch neocolonialism was impossible.[73]

---

[72] Ibid., 49.

[73] Alec Gordon, "The Indonesian Revolution 1945–1949 as a Social Revolution," paper presented to the Tenth Conference of the International Association of Historians of Asia, Singapore, October 1986, and "Colonial Mode of Production and the

The end of the Dutch economic system was a massive fact by itself, accompanied in turn by the end of the power of the sultans in Sumatra and of aristocratic royalties in Java, and a thorough turning over of the personnel among village headmen. To argue that the Indonesian revolution was "merely political" flies in the face of such realities. Transfer of sovereignty in Indonesia signified a total realignment of relationships of political and economic power. To ask for more "social revolution" in historical retrospect is equivalent to asking for much more bloodshed, with an uncertain outcome, or even a more totalitarian outcome.

Many more Indonesians died as a result of the Dar'ul Islam Rebellion (1948–62) than were killed as a consequence of the Indonesian revolution. And a vastly larger number died in the months following the failed coup of September 30, 1965.[74] But neither fact should be used to belittle or overshadow the Indonesian revolution. Both reveal it to have accomplished much more with relatively modest human cost: a major sovereignty transfer at a key period in world history, which changed the politico-economic order and sealed the society against neocolonialism.

Indonesian Revolution," *Economic and Political Weekly* no. 32, 21 (August 9, 1986): 1417–26. Contrary to the lament of "no social revolution," Gordon argues that these economic changes constituted one.

[74] Karl Jackson's estimate of deaths through the Dar'ul Islam Rebellion is 40,000 (*Traditional Authority, Islam, and Rebellion* [Berkeley: University of California Press, 1980], 1). The lowest estimate regarding the coup/countercoup of 1965 is Sukarno's 80,000, and the highest journalistic figure, 1.2 million.

11

BINATIONAL RESTORATION

IN LUZON

POWER PLENUM

Instead of a power vacuum, the Philippines in August 1945 experienced a power plenum.[1] In Indonesia at the time there were no Allied troops at all, and Japanese benumbed by surrender were giving arms to nationalist struggle groups. The Philippine situation, however, flowed from the American strategic decision to bypass Java for a showdown on Luzon. Faced with at least 450,000 Japanese in their former colony, the Americans went in to overpower them. Sixteen American ground combat divisions were deployed in the Philippines, forces several times larger than those that had ended the Philippine revolution in 1901, and even larger than the American forces that carried out operations in North Africa and Italy in 1943–45.[2] With American troops now fought Filipino guerrillas as allies and auxiliaries, coliberators of their own land.

After winning Manila, MacArthur, without informing the Joint Chiefs of his intentions, planned and executed a series of major amphibious landings over a four-month period in the central and southern Philippines and Borneo. He would have turned back to enhance his glory as liberator of Java as well, had not the Joint Chiefs finally drawn the line.[3]

Sundered governmental authority, as in the Philippines in 1945,

---

[1] Robert Ross Smith, *Triumph in the Philippines* (Washington, D.C.: Office of the Chief of Military History, 1963), 651–52, 658, 694; Col. Vincent J. Esposito, ed., *The West Point Atlas of American Wars*, (New York: Praeger, 1959), 2: 154, map.

[2] Smith, *Triumph*, 584–85.

[3] William R. Manchester, *American Caesar: Douglas MacArthur, 1880–1964* (Boston: Little, Brown, 1978), 428–30; D. Clayton James, *The Years of MacArthur* (Boston: Houghton Mifflin, 1970–1985), 2: 738.

is a classical opportunity for revolution. The actual Philippine circumstances, however, narrowed the possibilities. American troops had accompanied President Osmena at Leyte and helped him begin restoring native civil administration under the Philippine Commonwealth. Conditions for revolution were clearest in the unrest that fed the wartime Huk movement in Central Luzon. They, however, were a minority among Filipino guerrillas, even if their units were especially effective. Maximum Huk strength was 10,000 to 12,000 among a total of at least 118,000 guerrillas still in action with the Americans when the Japanese surrendered.[4]

Most guerrillas were, if politically minded, constitutional nationalists, or sympathizers with Fil-American establishmentarian values, or psychically dependent on the United States in some manner. Some were personal opportunists: a figure of 260,000[5] Filipinos eventually given back pay as guerrillas contains inevitably exaggerated and falsified cases. But the major point remains: in contrast with their Indonesian counterparts, who exploited the revolutionary potential of a power vacuum, the Filipinos themselves contributed to the power plenum that fashioned a binational restoration.[6]

A family vignette conveys what guerrilla statistics cannot: the desire of many Filipinos literally to embrace returning Americans. The family Eduardo Romualdez, homeless in Manila, spent several days in February 1945 scurrying from shelter to shelter, living on cookies cadged from the Japanese, and dodging American shrapnel. While heading for the ruins of the one building still standing in their neighborhood, they saw a strange white-faced soldier half a block away. Judging from the man's uniform, the father dizzily

[4] Benedict J. Kerkvliet, *The Huk Rebellion: A Study of Peasant Revolt in the Philippines* (Berkeley: University of California Press, 1977), gives Huk armed strength in Table 11, 87, and discusses effectiveness, 93–94; the overall guerrilla figure is from Smith, *Triumph*, 651. For Huk movement in general, see also Eduardo Lachica, *Huk: Philippine Agrarian Society in Revolt* (Manila: Solidaridad, 1971). The Kenpeitai estimated overall Huk troop strength at 50,000 (*Kenpei Seishi* [see chap. 9, note 2] [Tokyo, 1976], 919), an impressionistic exaggeration.

[5] On the guerrilla recognition program: Vinton Chapin, *Philippines Free Press,* May 8, 1950, p. 25. I owe the citation to Morton J. Netzorg.

[6] I have used the unpublished concept of binational restoration since before interruption of my work in 1972 I am glad to acknowledge, however, the subsequent essays touching on "bi-nationalism" by Alfred McCoy, "The Philippines: Independence without Decolonisation," in Robin Jeffrey, ed., *Asia: The Winning of Independence* (New York: St. Martin's, 1981), 23–65, esp. 50–53, and on restoration by Stephen Rosskamm Shalom, *The United States and the Philippines: A Study of Neocolonialism* (Philadelphia: Institute for the Study of Human Issues, 1981), 1–32.

guessed that the Japanese had German help, then reconsidered. "No, he can't be German," Eduardo said to his wife, "look at the way he slouches, with his rifle slung like that." Recognition dawning, Romualdez dashed at the soldier and, still moving at full speed, gave him a hug that knocked him to the ground. American! The family surrounded him and from his pockets came chocolate and cereal for the ravenous family.[7]

The Filipino ecstasy of liberation eventually subsided into a glow of reestablished security. Filipinos were relieved at being saved from their Asian invader, and glad of the victory of a power they trusted to keep its earlier promise of independence. To rid themselves of the Japanese, however, cost the Filipinos far more in lives and property than it cost the Indonesians to rid themselves of the Dutch. At least 500,000 Filipinos died as a result of battles in 1941–42 and 1944–45, and because of malnutrition, illness, or hostilities occasioned by conditions of occupation. The $500 million later legislated as a sum for rehabilitation was conceded to be far less than real losses, and aimed more at reinvigorating businesses than compensating individuals.

As for Indonesians, the total killed fighting the British in 1945 and in the Dutch police actions of 1947 and 1949, as well as the number of deaths directly attributable to the revolution, probably did not exceed 25,000. The figure may have been less. Monetary settlement produced bitter argument. Indonesia had to assume $1.3 billion worth of Dutch debts as part of the independence agreements, even though many assumed that the costs of Dutch military operations against themselves were included.[8]

In any event, the agents of Indonesian liberation were the Indonesians themselves. For Filipinos, even with guerrilla action, being rescued was an exercise largely dependent on American forces. In the policymaking that followed, the initiative was mostly American, while Filipino official and middle classes, suffering extensive damages, lives and loves lost, hope destroyed, and morale torn,

[7] Antonio Romualdez, interviews, May 9, 12, 1968.

[8] Total deaths of Filipino and Indonesian nationals are my estimates, based on a variety of sources. Takahashi Akira states that of 640,000 Japanese soldiers dispatched to the Philippines, 480,000 died (Rinjirō Sodei, ed., *Sekaishi Ni Okeru Nihon Senryō* [Tokyo: Nihon Hyōronsha, 1985], 41).

For the Indonesian-Dutch debt question, see Robert T. McMahon, *Colonialism and the Cold War: The United States and the Struggle for Indonesian Independence, 1945–1949* (Ithaca: Cornell University Press, 1981), 300–1, and George McTurnan Kahin, *Nationalism and Revolution in Indonesia* (Ithaca: Cornell University Press, 1952; reprinted, 1970), 441–43.

sought comfort in the arms of what Carlos Romulo had called "Mother America." The risk of prolonged maternal embrace is that it may stifle development. The Indonesians, by fighting for *ibu pertiwi*, the motherland, instead of succumbing to alien security, would eventually find themselves more truly independent than the Filipinos.

LIBERATION AS RESTORATION

Of the matters in General MacArthur's domain, victory over Japan came first; and after that victory, occupation statesmanship in Japan itself. But having made his first-person promise to return to the Philippines, and having returned, MacArthur was assiduously concerned about restoring order and delivering independence on schedule. Three specific questions presented themselves to him: what to do about Huk insurrection; what to do with Filipinos who collaborated with the Japanese; and what to do about the Philippine presidential election.

On the first major issue to face him, MacArthur was presented by his aide Courtney Whitney with a sharp choice. Moved by allegations of atrocities by the Huks, Whitney presented a draft proclamation to MacArthur that called on all Filipinos not in the army, Constabulary, or police to turn in their arms to the nearest American military commander. Only MacArthur's "personal leadership" could achieve that end without force, Whitney wrote, and only by his proclaiming it in a context of celebrating liberation could it be accomplished while avoiding "misunderstanding."

MacArthur answered "No. This is a matter," he wrote in his own hand, "for the Commonwealth Gov't. The present law prohibits carrying of arms without license. I do not care to enforce it. It would precipitate most violent reactions—much more blood would then be shed—than under any present guerrilla conditions—and if it becomes the white man against the Filipino—we will have another insurrection with all Filipinos finally crystallizing against us. At bottom it is political—not merely a question of law and order—and as such should not be handled by the military. These guerrillas are absolutely no menace to our armed forces."[9]

With regard to collaboration, MacArthur split Manuel Roxas away from the mass of other accused and accusable leaders who had

[9] Memo, C. W. to CinC, February 20, 1945 with holographic surcharge by "MacA," RG 4, Box 6 (MacA).

remained in Manila. On the basis of Roxas's connection with the USAFFE intelligence network, he publicized that a Loyalty Board "completely exonerated him" from any culpability in having briefly chaired the Economic Planning Board and BIBA (rice administration agency) in the puppet republic.[10] Both Roxas's collaboration with the Japanese and his American espionage connection were relatively insubstantial. Ill and ambitious, he spent part of the war in recuperative seclusion and much of it in careful maneuvering for opportunity when peacetime should come. His compadre, President Laurel, protected him from the Kenpeitai. His friend, General MacArthur, shielded him from the postwar Peoples Court. With such determination and skill, and such friends, Roxas would become president of the peacetime republic.

MacArthur not only cleared Roxas, but he accelerated the presidential elections to occur before independence (rather than after, which might have favored Osmena as incumbent), and he allowed unofficial army support of Roxas in the weeks of campaigning. MacArthur got what he wanted, a poker-playing Rotarian pragmatist, a man he "could work with," to oppose the frail and gentlemanly Osmena, whose political primacy had come in his youth, as Speaker of the Assembly and president of the Senate (1907–22).[11]

After leaving the Huk problem to the Philippine government, MacArthur ignored the collaboration issue and accelerated the presidential election in favor of Roxas. In the first action, a professional economy of motion prevailed: defeat the Japanese as the major enemy, and let Filipinos settle their own conflicts. In the latter two actions a discriminating and domineering personal will was at work. In all three a charismatic lordship asserted itself, which identified the Philippines with use of the first-person singular, and which would go on in a like way to rule Japan.

"I have returned." MacArthur's message and American presence

[10] David J. Steinberg, *Philippine Collaboration in World War II* (Ann Arbor: University of Michigan Press, 1967), 115, 146; MacArthur, press release, May 9, 1946 (HC). Roxas's own account of his behavior, "Brief Summary of the Activities of Manuel Roxas during the Japanese Occupation," September 29, 1945, appears in several manuscript draft variations (R), and is published in Mauro Garcia, ed., *Documents on the Japanese Occupation of the Philippines* (Manila: Philippine Historical Association, 1965), 238–58.

[11] For the desire of Manila Americans on MacArthur's staff for smooth return to *status quo ante*, see Charles Parsons to Quezon, draft, secret, September 14, 1943, RG 16, Box 112 (MacA). The letter does not appear in the Quezon collection, and was probably not sent. For MacArthur's actions and motivations: interviews, A.V.H. Hartendorp, November 15, 1957, and Evett D. Hester, April 4, 1958; Hernando Abaya, *Betrayal in the Philippines* (New York: A. A. Wyn, 1946).

gave the Philippines a restored but borrowed security of identity. In Freudian terms, national id accepted alien ego. Voices from Manila, however, reveal more than Viennese vocabulary.

The Philippine press in the first seven months after the liberation of Manila was content to rejoice and muse about independence: would it be seen through on time, or actually accelerated?[12] Only when Secretary of the Interior Harold Ickes claimed his jurisdictional prerogatives over insular policy was there a ruffle of protest, which did not break the prevailing mood.[13] The expressions nearest to the Indonesian pemudas were largely rhetorical: "A new, awakened and determined youth is now demanding its right to participate in the shaping of the nation it has helped to defend throughout the long night of the Japanese occupation." The demand that "our youth ... doing its share ... should get its due,"[14] was earnest enough, but it had no correlative in action.

"After three years of Japanese brutality, the inhabitants of Manila saw in every American soldier ... an angel of liberation, a deliverer from evil, a shining symbol of freedom and democracy. With smiles on their lips, with tears in their eyes, and with gratitude in their hearts, they welcomed this beautiful vision." In September 1945 the first note of hesitation appeared. Now those same soldiers' behavior with their daughters and their antics with bartenders, pimps, and prostitutes suggested that the honeymoon was over. "But all the same Filipinos want a lasting peace and friendship with the Americans. For they have the same ideals, and somehow their destinies seem to be inextricably intertwined."[15]

A UP story carried news of rioting by "native Annamites" against the French in Hanoi, which prompted Americans to ask Viet Minh leaders for "order in the interest of international goodwill." And an AP story telling of a mass rally of "10,000 nationalists" demanding

[12] Newspapers sprang up in number with liberation, consolidated, and collapsed. An outstanding guide is Shiro Saito and Alice W. Mak, *Philippine Newspapers: An International Union List*, Philippine Studies Program, Philippine Studies Occasional Paper No. 7 (University of Hawaii, 1984). Because Manila was the center of any anti-American expression, I am confident of the generalizations that follow, which are based on a relatively steady run of the *Manila Times*, and occasional issues available of eighteen other newspapers, metropolitan and provincial, available in the Library of Congress.

[13] Sec. Interior Ickes to Pres. Truman, July 17, 1945, and subsequent documents, RG 126, Box 44, Folder 4, National Archives; reactions to Ickes, *Manila Times*, September 14, 20, 23, 1945.

[14] Renato Arevalo, "Youth Does Its Share," Manila *Sunday Times*, June 24, 1945.

[15] Guillermo Ortiz, "The Honeymoon is Soon Over," *Manila Times*, September 16, 1945.

"freedom for Java" noted that "All nationalist propaganda is designed to appeal to Americans." Against other circumstances of nationalist ferment Filipinos felt a senior pride of developed status. A Philippine cabinet member revealed that the Indonesians had asked President Osmena to intercede on their behalf for "recognition of their right to be free." "Millions of oppressed peoples of Asia and Indonesia are looking up to [us] for guidance and inspiration, and . . . Filipinos should show them an example . . . of peace, unity and courage."[16]

In Java, Surabayans looked to each other for unity and courage in the face of General Christison's threat, after General Mallaby's death: unless Indonesians attacking his forces surrendered, "I intend to bring the whole weight of my sea, land and air forces and all the weapons of modern war against them until they are crushed." Side by side in the *Manila Times* with word of Christison's ultimatum was an article on full cooperation of Filipino authorities with High Commissioner Paul McNutt, who would arrive to carry out directives outlined by President Truman.[17]

In the symphony of Fil-American cooperation there was amazingly little discord. Even a paper titled *The Guerrilla* looked forward "to close and mutually protective trade relations between the Philippines and the United States," and trusted in "sympathetic" American businessmen to aid economic rehabilitation.[18] Manila journalism included little reporting on the Huks and disorder in Central Luzon, some criticism of President Osmena's leadership, and much worrying on collaboration and back-pay problems. As the shape of a new relationship with the United States began to emerge, the Tydings-McDuffie Act was seen as a historic first, and the ties developed in "the most novel and progressive experiment in colonial administration ever attempted" were hailed in renewal and prospective redefinition.[19]

A few countering notes came from the *Express* (Manila), which lamented that "we have to beg for the establishment of bases in the belief that another Pacific war might occur." A month later there appeared the sharpest editorial opinion discoverable in the first year of liberation, criticizing the Bell Bill. Its twenty-year extension of Philippine-American free trade, by "perpetuating our lopsided economy . . . producing mainly export crops giving enormous profits to

[16] *Manila Times*, September 20, 24, 1945; Manila *Sunday Times*, October 21, 1945.
[17] *Manila Times*, November 2, 1945; Christison quoted in Anderson, *Java in Revolution*, 163.
[18] *The Guerrilla*, May 8, 1945, and passim, through October 31, 1945.
[19] *The Philippine Liberty News*, November 15, 1945.

a few big corporations ... would make a mockery out of our independence.... Effectively political power would always reside in the hands of those who control the economic life of the islands. We would become in time no better than one of the banana republics in Central America."[20]

On the key elements in shaping postwar relations, bases and trade, the Philippine Commonwealth government in Washington worked toward defining a sustained bilateral relationship, and American officials familiar with the Philippines worked with them. Later Congress would enter the process and would complicate and compromise the result. At no time was there any sign of Filipino leaders seeking a complete severance along with sovereignty; and none either on the American side, although the mood of some American commentaries verged closer to it than any from Filipino sources.

The disposition of political wills resembled that of two previous crises, the First World War and the Great Depression. In both cases the Filipino leaders' rhetorical desire for independence covered a deep anxiety about its form and impact. In each instance the American forces idealistically disposed toward independence on grounds of anti-imperialism and self-determination were of less effect with Congress than those opposed to Filipino immigration and competition from protected Philippine imports, and those concerned about American strategic overextension and jeopardy with regard to Japan. Such a combination of unlike elements in 1916 produced legislation affirming eventual independence in principle, and in 1934 legislation devolving sovereignty on a twelve-year schedule.

What was different now? No Filipino, so close to a sovereignty sought "for three and a half centuries," would turn away from it. At the same time, the destruction, depletions, and exhaustions of the war made most Filipino leaders think more than ever in bilateral terms of security and restoration. Americans responsible for these matters saw themselves fulfilling a promise and clearing away a problem. The natural tendency of victorious states to strategic expansion and consolidation entered the picture, along with a curdled mixture of reconstruction policies and commercial opportunism.

ORPHAN SECURITY: THE BASES

Bases arose first in the planners' minds; and to what the planners sought there was little popular opposition. Quezon, Osmena after

[20] Manila *Express*, September 20, October 18, 1945.

Quezon's death, and Roxas, even though he became Osmena's opponent on other matters, all wanted American bases in the Philippines. Without significant objection from any quarter, they saw such bases as indispensable to the nation's future security, as possibly alleviating its budget costs for defense, and as contributing toward a new democratic era in the Pacific. The Philippines would be a favored and exemplary party within a Pax Americana, a kind of inverse Cinderella, most beloved adoptee of a benign and powerful stepmother.

In September 1943, Manuel Quezon wrote President Franklin Roosevelt his last "political testament" to the Filipino people, and asked that it be published if he died before American reoccupation. When he did die, shortly before Leyte was taken, his letter was forgotten. But his message, even without publication, seemed to be expressed in the actions of most Filipino and American leaders in the years that immediately followed. The Japanese effort "to convince the Filipino people that their salvation depends upon abandoning . . . their occidental way of life . . . would accomplish nothing less than the disappearance and destruction of the Filipino people as they are today." Geographically the Filipinos will be forever Oriental, but spiritually, "because of our culture and Christian civilization, we are with the West." Quezon repeatedly stressed that "After the lessons of the present war, one would be very blind indeed not to see that the post-war relationship between the Republic of the Philippines and the Republic of the United States should be as close, if not closer, than our relationship before the war. The security of both the United States and the Philippines, and perhaps the future peace of the Pacific, will depend very much on that relationship."[21]

The young S. P. Lopez had already envisioned new and different syntheses in the Filipino national character.[22] Future statesmen, and Lopez himself as a cultural commentator, would strive to evolve away from a relationship too close for comfort, and too special for self-respect. But Quezon's view prevailed long after his voice was gone. It stood as the consensus of experienced American hands among Filipinos, and Philippine hands among Americans, a binationalist statement of faith that weathered attacks from Filipino nationalists and American internationalists of many varieties. The elements of binationalism have since split and frayed in many

[21] Quezon to Roosevelt, October 26, 1943 (Q).
[22] See chap. 7.

ways, but the two nations are not yet uncoupled. A persistent, if possibly accursed, connecting factor has been successive revised agreements on bases.

As early as November 1943, President Quezon succeeded, through a directive from President Roosevelt, in getting the Joint Chiefs of Staff to stipulate a list of air bases that the United States would need in the Pacific and on the Asian coast. Thirty-nine areas were proposed in January 1944 to the president, who approved the findings and asked Secretary of State Hull "as a matter of high priority" to initiate negotiations for long-term or permanent bases, "at the earliest possible moment."[23] Urgencies of conducting the war delayed such action, but the United States was already clearly transforming itself strategically from a Western Hemisphere power in the early 1930s, with a standing army smaller than that of the Kingdom of Thailand, to a global power with clear trans-Pacific capabilities. Instead of being a reluctant empire incapable of defending the Philippines, it would adopt a new strategic poise in which the Philippines was of critical air and naval value in the West Pacific and East Asia.

In May of 1945, President Truman and President Osmena signed an agreement of "the fullest and closest military cooperation," determining that "military plans . . . will be closely integrated in order to insure the full and mutual protection of the United States and the Philippines." After the requisite staff work, the Joint Chiefs of Staff submitted to the secretary of state through the State-War-Navy Coordinating Committee a list of bases and facilities for negotiation.

Discussions between High Commissioner McNutt and President Roxas began in June 1946, before the Philippines became independent. The initial difficulties—a sharpness of feeling on the Philippine side to which General Eisenhower was sensitive, and which he was concerned might become "potentially recriminatory"—had to do not with the large number of bases desired, nor the long terms sought for them, but the possible presence of large numbers of American servicemen in the area of Manila. Eventually, in March 1947, agreement was reached on twenty-two military- and naval-

[23] James F. Schnabel, "The Joint Chiefs of Staff and National Policy, 1945–1947," "History of the Joint Chiefs of Staff," Historical Division, JCS, February 1979, 1: 299–301 (hereafter, JCS History); CCS 686.9, "Philippine Bases Subsequent to Independence," November 7, 1943–September 20, 1945, and CCS 680, "SWPA Base Dvlpmnt Plan," February 24, 1945, CCSJCS files, National Archives; Marshall to MacArthur, May 6, 1945, RG 4, Box 3, MacA.

base sites with ninety-nine-year leases, from which the Manila area was excluded.[24]

Subic Bay and Clark Field were the most notable inclusions. Their continued importance in American strategic planning would prolong for decades problems that may be defined as either neocolonial or postcolonial—problems of jurisdiction and behavior touching depths of racial and cultural feeling; problems of aid or rent that were critical to the evolution of politico-economic relations between the two countries; and problems of intention and use, which were critical to each nation's concepts not only of its security, but of its identity.

A BILATERAL POLITICAL ECONOMY

Paul McNutt was a friend of Douglas MacArthur, and like him a formidably self-sure personality. Taking over as high commissioner to the Philippines in September 1945, he inherited a staff that was strongly predisposed to reconstruction of bilateral relations in the same way Quezon had hoped—as close or closer than before independence. The elevated tutorial tone of official correspondence in the high commissioner's office included genuine concern about want and distress among the Filipino population, forthright response to legitimate claims for fair treatment, and recognition of their assistance against the Japanese. In addition, their "unfortunate position . . . of falling between two stools" was borne in mind; they did not always benefit from policies adopted for the welfare of American people, nor were they able always to take advantage of policies adopted for the benefit of America's allies.[25]

In the first several months of 1945, the high commissioner's office tried to infuse the White House with their own supportive and protective attitude.[26] But the eventual shape of rehabilitation, trade, and developmental policies was instead a function of private enter-

[24] *Manila Daily Bulletin*, March 11–22, 1947; JCS History, 341–46.

[25] Examples: John K. Davis to [Thomas] Finletter, July 15, 1941, RG 126, Box 44, Folder 3; Richard R. Ely, Exec. Asst. to Hi. Comm., to H. J. Slaughter, Chief, Legislative Division, Dept. Interior, September 17, 1945, RG 126, Box 44, Folder 4, NARS.

[26] "Agenda for Discussion with the President" (n.d., probably early 1945), and "Statement by the President on Administrative Policy Respecting the Philippine Islands," draft, "final version as it went to the White House," September 1945, RG 126, Box 44, Folder 4, NARS.

prise theory, neoimperial nostalgia, special-interest maneuvering, and a series of tactical choices in which McNutt was preeminent.[27]

The view that came to prevail was that only half of the actual war damage, at most, could be covered by the Rehabilitation Act, and that the rest of the money for renewal must come from private capital. Then, formulating policy on Philippine-American trade led to a complex tangle of points of view in which long-existing interests, not surprisingly, triumphed. A White House conference in November 1945 produced a compromise among McNutt, Congressman Jasper Bell, Senator Millard Tydings, and representatives of State and Interior: eight years of free trade followed by twenty-five years of gradually declining preferences. The preferences restored the Philippine economy to its prewar situation. Pegging the peso to American currency benefited Americans who exported to the Philippines and who lived there, and unrestricted convertibility and transferability of funds benefited all Americans doing business in or with the Philippines. These trade terms were guaranteed to reproduce a dependent economy. The currency terms clearly infringed on Philippine sovereignty. Such criticism from State and Treasury was ignored by Congress.[28]

Few Filipinos, however, sharply criticized either the trade or currency terms. The greatest provocation arose over the parity provision, which gave American citizens equal rights with Filipinos in ownership and use of natural resources and operation of public utilities. Doing this would require the Philippines to amend its constitution, whose relevant article required 60 percent Filipino ownership.

McNutt was the symbol, compounder, and eventual implementer of these policies. He proposed making no payments exceeding five hundred dollars under the Rehabilitation Act until the Philippines accepted the trade bill. He was also a leading proponent of inserting the parity provision into the trade legislation, on the grounds that it would attract American capital and thus complete Philippine rehabilitation, which was consciously underfunded on the grounds that private capital should do much of the job.[29]

[27] For instance: McNutt, "Suggested Amendments to S.1610," February 11, 1946, revised February 25, Legislative Branch, NARS.

[28] Shalom, *United States and the Philippines*, 36–37, 46–57. A key document is Actg. Sec. State Dean Acheson to Sen. Walter George, April 2, 1946, Legislative Branch, NARS.

[29] Shalom, *United States and the Philippines*, 37, correctly stresses McNutt's ef-

In the Senate debate on the trade bill, Robert Taft gave a rationale for this complex of arrangements that stated the situation with a clarity unconsciously grotesque. Because America was going to have military bases in the Philippines and citizens established in business there, a "permanent relationship" should be recognized, both political and economic. "The Philippines should always be an American outpost in the Pacific. The fact that they have a completely independent, autonomous government is, I think, a good thing. . . . But certainly we shall always be a big brother, if you please, to the Philippine Islands."[30] Taft's remarks sound pompous because too little adjusted from his father's turn-of-the-century Big Brotherism. Rhetoric aside, however, there was little difference in substantial intent between Taft's neoimperial blessing on the legislation, and the thrust of Quezon's last political testament.

What the Office of Strategic Services had predicted as the consequences if an early draft of the Bell bill were enacted, proved true in fact: "the Philippines will continue to be dependent upon the American market and preferential treatment in it, with that economy increasingly under the control of the already established, predominantly foreign (mainly American and Spanish) and politically powerful firms."[31] No one saw a way to create new firms or a new form of economy, and so all administrators and legislators took natural recourse to restoration, rather than invention *ab initio*.

If Secretary of the Interior Harold Ickes had prevailed upon President Truman to appoint a major investigatory study and planning commission in July 1945, a different shape of things could perhaps have been effected. But a study commission along the lines of those led by Jacob Gould Schurman (1899), or by Leonard Wood and Cameron Forbes (1921), or even by Rōyama Masamichi from Tokyo (1943), was neither in Truman's style, nor easily conceived in a late stage of prosecuting the world war. When Truman received the Bell Act from Congress, some of the departments criticized it drastically, and tried to persuade him that it was "unworthy" of the United States government. But Congress felt it had taken a "very fine and magnanimous" series of actions regarding the Philippines,

forts to tie the trade bill to the rehabilitation bill. Congressman Bell, however, had already been thinking about doing so; Ely to Hi. Comm., December 19, 1945, RG 126, NARS.

[30] *Congressional Record*, April 12, 1946, p. 3537.

[31] OSS, Research and Analysis Report No. 3269, October 5, 1945, RG 59, NARS.

and was judged "resentful" of any suggestion of doing other or more.[32] Truman signed and had done with it.

PARITY RIGHTS AS BINATIONAL SEAL

As in the United States, more so in the Philippines: the sticking point was parity. A compromise of sovereignty in the act of its bestowal naturally excited opposition. Had Osmena won the presidential election in April, it is conceivable that he could have made good on his stand of opposition to parity, because it required constitutional amendment. The effort to pass it could have died of inaction, or met with a failure of the three-fourths' margin of both houses required as a first step toward the national plebiscite that was requisite for final passage.

But Osmena lost. The signs of a defensive coalition were clear in his embracing the Democratic Alliance, a Central Luzon organization reflecting arousal to Huk energies, sympathies, and visions, in the parliamentary phase of what later would become open rebellion. For a Confucian from the Visayas, a constitutional moderate, it was not a natural affinity. It appeared necessary, however, given the initial sympathy to Roxas from MacArthur, the final sympathy from McNutt, and his increasing momentum. Even with strength in Central Luzon, Osmena only took 46 percent of the popular vote.[33] Roxas was the winner in the first of seven postwar two-party elections, each of which would have some share of fraud and violence, but all of which were openly and evenly contested in a national system of familistic-factional ties and shifting alliances.

Once elected, Roxas was faced with getting parity through a Congress that contained a Democratic Alliance bloc. Members of his Liberal party introduced motions to bar the seating of representatives and senators on the grounds that there had been fraud and terror in Central Luzon. The motions were anomalous, given the fact that collaborators with the Japanese indicted for treason were being seated, but when the vote on parity was taken, the Senate carried it 16 to 5 and the House by 68 to 18. Had the three ousted senators and eight ousted congressmen been present and voted negative, parity would have failed of the three-quarters needed for passage, and

[32] Ely to Hi. Comm., April 30, 1946, RG 126, Box 42, Folder 5, NARS.
[33] Roxas to Roy Howard, November 1, 1945, R; McNutt to Hester for Osmena, April 10, 1946, HC; Theodore Friend, *Between Two Empires* (New Haven: Yale University Press, 1965), 254–58.

Philippine-American relations would have been tossed back to Washington for redefinition.[34]

The subsequent national plebiscite on the proposed constitutional amendment was held in March 1947, and the amendment was passed overwhelmingly. Only about half the electorate cast ballots, far fewer than in the presidential election. Apathy, rather than voter alienation or intimidation, may explain the relatively low turnout; Filipino voters respond far more actively to personal contests than to issues abstractly posed. But how explain the margin of nearly 4 to 1 in favor of parity for American investors?[35] One critic of the process thinks chicanery and pressure account for the results: ballots printed only in Spanish and English; schoolteachers prohibited from serving as poll watchers because of bias against parity; polling places moved out of rural areas to minimize the Democratic Alliance vote; and opponents of parity finding it "virtually impossible" to raise funds for fear of retribution by government financial institutions and other agencies.[36] More than manipulation, however, appears in the results.

Even Manila, which is generally antigovernment and where local journalists, educated critics, and foreign observers are poised to detect coercion or dishonesty, went in favor of parity by a nearly 3 to 1 margin. Among provinces strong for the Huks and the Democratic Alliance, Pampanga and Tarlac voted overwhelmingly for parity, by 8 to 1 and 7 to 1, respectively. These results could suggest either, as one newspaper put it, "the progress of the pacification campaign waged by the department of the interior," or could imply heavy abstention or intimidation, or both. In Bulacan and Laguna, also Huk-infested, the margins were more believable, but still 2 to 1 for parity.[37]

The most significant evidence, however, may not be proportions of votes, but the mild press statement of the Democratic Alliance when all the balloting was over: "The outcome is not a green-light for an orgy of extravagant projects ... but for mature responsible planning in accordance with the deliberate and cautious attitude of the people as shown in the plebiscite. The opposition, still con-

---

[34] Shalom, *United States and the Philippines*, 52–57, is a good account, although it twice mentions the proportion "two-thirds" rather than the "three-fourths" mandated by Article 14 of the Constitution.

[35] Such is the early margin noted by the *Manila Times* on the second day after the poll (March 13, 1947): 432,932 affirmative, 115,853 negative.

[36] Shalom, *United States and the Philippines*, 58.

[37] *Manila Times*, March 12, 13, 1947.

vinced of the validity of its stand, will, precisely because of this implication conveyed as the result of the plebiscite, with more reason but without obstructionism, strive to continue in its vigilance and fight to the end that our independence is real."[38]

In the same month as the plebiscite gave Americans extraterritorial business rights in the Philippines, the bases agreement was finally signed. The Philippines was now independent mainly in the sense that it was a member of the United Nations. With sovereignty compromised, external security tied to American forces, economic development framed in a model of binational trade, and special hospitality to American investors, the degree of Philippine independence was highly limited. Filipino leaders, however, had envisioned and helped design this binational restoration, and Filipino voters had overwhelmingly approved rights for American investors. Whereas they might well have treated it as a compromise of sovereignty, or as coercive exploitation, they were willing to accept it as a seal of binationalism.

Myths of Perfection, Facts of Dependence

The phenomenon of the Philippine-American restoration may be portrayed in a strikingly different way: as a neocolonial alliance between the "leading classes" in the Philippines and the United States, detrimental to the mass of the Filipino population. In the post-1945 phase of this alliance, as before, despite "Washington qualms . . . the United States has invariably chosen to support the Philippine elite . . . because only by so doing could the United States guarantee its own economic and strategic interests."[39]

But what is an "elite"? What acknowledgment is given to the changing composition and conflicts within Philippine leadership, not to mention the same in the so-called American establishment? In order to guarantee its most selfish tangible interests, (and to express its anti-imperialism at the same time), the United States

---

[38] Ibid., March 13, 1947, 18. The foregoing analysis of the plebiscite on parity can be wildly misunderstood if not read as a summary of documented Filipino reactions at the time. A Mr. T.J.S. George, reviewing my historical essay in John Bresnan, ed., *Crisis in the Philippines*, is upset about what he sees as my "Kiplingesque monotones" and "partisan emotionalism" (*Asiaweek*, February 15, 1987, 72). I doubt that he has researched the period. As for perspective, Kipling is obviously antique, but even George Orwell (whom I admire) is now dated. The present work attempts to look at imperialism factually, including emotions as significant facts, with such understanding as is possible nearly forty years after Orwell's death.

[39] Shalom, *United States and the Philippines*, xiv, xv, 185.

could have cut completely loose from the Philippines in 1916 or 1933. The neo-Marxist critic, by neglecting felt duty, misses major motivation. And by minimizing felt affinity, he also misses the major irony that the Japanese conquest and occupation from 1941 to 1945 actually intensified the Fil-American bond on both sides.

The new military tether and economic umbilical cord of 1945–47 have produced recriminatory writing.[40] Such a tone may have its justifications, but neglects salient facts: among ordinary Filipinos, joy at the reappearance of Americans, and calling the period "the liberation" rather than "the reoccupation"; among ordinary Americans, a sense of responsibility for rehabilitation and redevelopment of a traumatized people, many of whom had fought together with them, and most of whom hoped for continuing close relations with the United States.

Critical writings that overlook these major historical phenomena depend on several suprafactual constructs to support their point of view: the myth of the revolution, the myth of absolute independence, the myth of complete liberation, and the myth of perfect equality. The utopian hunger for perfection yields easily to the myth of revolution. As long as revolution does not happen, its unpredictability, its purgative power, and its potentially unlimited use of violence make it alluring to some imaginations. But once a specific revolution does occur, traumas, terrors, miscarriages, and regressions will accompany its benefits.

Three other concepts are mythic ends for which revolution is the mythic means. Absolute independence is at best a slogan, as the early twentieth-century Filipino nationalists wittingly used it; complete liberation is a mid- and late-twentieth-century bourgeois notion of cultural transcendence, without root or flower; and perfect equity is found only in the grave, where all are at rest.[41]

---

[40] Of which two of the more intelligent examples, in addition to Shalom, are the book of Renato Constantino, elsewhere cited, and various articles by Robert B. Stauffer on Philippine political and economic developments in which multinational corporations, the World Bank, and the International Monetary Fund are the villains.

[41] Were one to make explicit the forces on which Shalom's cloistered hopes appear to depend, one would have to answer: (1) "the militant peasantry," (2) the Huks and the Democratic Alliance, (3) the statistical poor, and (4) the New People's Army (22, 32, 53–58, 145–60, 170, 173, 181–82, and passim). Each of these categories contains worthy and noble persons, as well as a share of the selfish and ignoble. But none have concreteness in the study. Luis Taruc gets only four mentions in the index, and none of the Lava family any mention at all; as later, for the 1970s, the New People's Army is mentioned but not Jose Maria Sison. The excellent studies by Eduardo Lachica and Benedict J. Kerkvliet (see note 3) are incomparably more persuasive. They do not talk

Whatever value these abstractions may have as political ideals, they are unsuitable standards for historical assessment. Looking at Indonesia, however, allows an important contrastive understanding. Different circumstances (power vacuum) and different scale (small colonizer, large colony) could produce a totally different outcome— an independent nation sealed against neocolonialism.

---

of "militant peasantry"; they know the terrain and personalities involved. They understand the systemic failures against which the Huks rebelled, and the systematic failure of the Huks themselves to export revolution effectively beyond the plains of Central Luzon. They speak in humane tones of muted tragedy or stoic objectivity, as appropriate to understanding binationalism, and with it, indifferent American dominance and thirsting Filipino dependency.

CONCLUSION

DYNAMICS OF EMPIRE

AND LIBERATION

Imperial Dynamics

Societies in the Greater East Asia Co-Prosperity Sphere, trying to give birth to national states, went through unusual trauma. They suffered great economic disruption and social dislocation, while taking the opportunity to resist both inherited social order and imposed foreign power.[1] Obviously Ho Chi Minh's Vietnam is the most extreme example of success in both, that is, success in overcoming the most considerable foreign opposition (French, followed by a foolish American surrogation), and in most fully overturning cultural traditions. In the perspective of the late twentieth century, however, Vietnam's regimented people, stagnant economy, and imperialistic army in Cambodia can hardly be considered a model of social creativity.

What should be said of the nation at the opposite end of the spectrum from Vietnam in postwar behavior? The Philippines accomplished the inverse of expelling its Western conqueror by welcoming it back. Its lassitude in challenging inherited social structure and values leads to either of two chains of thought: analysis of the failure of Huk leadership, strategy, and ideology; or reflection on the obduracy of the psychosocial system characterized by utang na loob, compadrazgo, pakikisama, and tayo-tayo.

The fragile state, spastic economy, and riven society of the Philippines forty years after "liberation" may suggest a lesson. Certain kinds of extreme passivity eventually generate ignoble conditions; these may become just as undesirable as the inhumane conditions

[1] Christopher Thorne, *The Issue of War: States, Societies, and the Far Eastern Conflict of 1941–1945* (New York: Oxford University Press, 1985), chap. 9, esp. 311–12. Thorne's perspective, embracing all of Asia, is necessarily more abstract than what I advance here.

produced by hyper-discipline. Only in 1986 did a variety of elements in the Philippines courageously reclaim initiative against the Marcos dictatorship.[2]

Let us allow that Vietnamese society might be considered "passive" in relation to direction by a new mandarinate, pseudo-technical and doctrinally severe; and that the Philippines was extraordinarily active in its resistance to the Japanese. We are nevertheless drawn to reflect on the more vital and productive relationships that existed from 1965 to 1985 among state, society, and economy in Indonesia, Malaysia, Singapore, and Thailand. All of the latter have suffered tragedies, committed errors, and continue to display their own weaknesses. But none are as rigid and exhausted as Vietnam from national and social revolution combined; none as torpid as the Philippines from xenophilia in matters of culture and from native familism regarding power.

The game of categorizing states and societies by degrees of modernity, productivity, or humanity changes with the observer and the decade. A historian, looking for some constancy in themes, may find it in the dynamics of transformation involved in the contact of imperial states with national societies. To array phenomena that have occurred within this century:

1. The Japanese rise through felt unequal status with Western empires, through triumph over the major traditional Asian power (China, 1895), then over a failing traditional Western power (Tsarist Russia, 1905), to a 3 to 5 naval ratio with England and the United States (1921), to swift attack against heavy numerical odds, and triumph over major powers (British, Dutch, American). Organizing for equality and empire enables Japan progressively and severally to defeat overlord states, each previously presumed greater than itself.

2. Indonesians welcome Japanese as liberators from the Dutch, only to feel new subjection and severe repression. Here more than elsewhere in the Southern Area, Japan promoted the mythic story of the heroic boy Momotaro, who with the aid of a monkey, dog, and pheasant, defeats the evil demons. Japan, of course, is Momotaro, Indonesia the monkey, the Dutch the

---

[2] I have examined the meaning of those events in "The 'Yellow Revolution': Its Mixed Historical Legacy," in Carl H. Lande, ed., *Rebuilding a Nation: Philippine Challenges and American Policy* (Washington, D.C.: Washington Institute Press, 1987), 69–86; "Revolution in the Philippines, 1983–1986: Forces, Sources, and Perspectives," *Philippine Studies*, vol. 35 (1987): 357–68; and "Marcos and the Fil-American Tangle, 1942–1986," paper presented to a conference of the Foreign Policy Research Institute, Philadelphia, May 30–June 2, 1987, under revision for publication.

demons. "Liberation" is indefinitely delayed (1942–44), and cooperation induced with the promise of preparation, mobilization, and common battle against return of the Allies.

3. Filipinos, on balance (1942–44), resist Japanese "liberation" as a repeal of progress under the Americans toward autonomy, and as a potential reinslavement of the nation. In like fashion, Filipinos resist Japanese "fatherhood" in the great Asian family as undesirable racially, and unsuitable culturally.

4. Indonesians revolt against lords once beaten and thereby debunked. The British and Dutch returning armies (1945) cannot quell the revolution. This is the time of the bondsman's self-ennoblement, his heroic assertion that he will be nobody's valet, but master in his own house.[3]

5. Filipinos welcome the American return as "the liberation" (1944–45), enabling the realization of the independence promised for 1946. They fight with the Americans as "brothers." This familistic attachment, which the Japanese professed but could not produce, the Americans decline even as the Filipinos thrust it upon them. Legislation and diplomacy establish a new Fil-American bond, with Filipinos subordinate.

6. The Japanese respond to General MacArthur as the new shogun, accepting feudal bondage to his conquering lordship and his dispensing of political and cultural decrees. They even temporarily attribute to him some of the imperial majesty that by defeat, and by the victors' requirement, the traditional emperor yields from his office and official myth.[4]

7. Indonesia charts its own course, while occasionally expressing affinity for Vietnam as the only other Southeast Asian nation that "fought for independence." Incipient imperialism begins

[3] There remained, of course, dispositions toward subservience. An American journalist covering the first Dutch "police action," interviewing a village headman in southern Bali, August 21, 1947, found him intrigued with American power. "Is it not true that your General MacArthur now occupies the Emperor's palace in Tokyo?" The Japanese had defeated the Dutch, he said, and the Americans defeated the Japanese. The Dutch therefore lost face and had no right to come back; whereas the Americans had presumptive rights in Indonesia of which they had not availed themselves (James Halsema to the author, December 26, 1986, quoting his journal as correspondent).

[4] A professor of anthropology at the University of Florence goes so far as to say that "In a curious metaphorical way the cryptic feminine component of the Japanese personality was taking delight in a sort of national 'rape' by the great, good, loving, just, stern, sage, strong, blue-eyed shogun—General Douglas MacArthur" (Fosco Maraini, *Tokyo* [Amsterdam: Time-Life Books, 1976], 16).

to flow in the failed vanity for "crushing Malaysia" (1962–64), and the successful expansions to displace the Dutch in Irian Jaya (1962) and the Portuguese in East Timor (1976).

8. Philippine bonding to the United States occurs in voluntary semicolonial affinity (1945–47). Having fought against Americans for independence and lost (1898–1901), and with them for independence and won (1941–42, 1944–45), powerful Filipino consensus holds that the two national destinies are historically linked. It appears more beneficial in the long run to be semi-indentured to America than to stand alone in the world.

The array suggests the importance of felt power, as distinct from "objective power," in the behavior of societies and states.[5] That distinction pertains whether the power is felt as imperial subjection by others, or as violent self-liberation from an overlord state; whether in affinitive self-subjection to a superpower, or, in the case of new national entities, the absorption and reduction of smaller powers and less organized peoples. Power so defined, desired, and expressed clearly prevails over factors of production, market oppression, wage slavery, and the like. "The means of subsistence form simply one of the data of this problem," because the preeminent problem is social relations among humans construed in terms of power.[6]

DEPENDENCE AND REPRESSION: THE JAPANESE DEMAND

Japan on the march, after 1937, built up an impressive tissue of theory of state and society, expansionary strategy, racial supremacy,

[5] In stressing the psycho-cultural aspects of power, I am not forgetting what overwhelming might in a military empire can mean. Plainly, the fighting use or the poised proximity of Soviet armies determined the outcome of events in Hungary, 1956, Czechoslovakia, 1968, and Poland, 1981–82.

[6] Simone Weil, *Oppression and Liberty*, trans. Arthur Wills and John Petri (Amherst: University of Massachusetts Press, 1973), 71. "Power, by definition, is only a means. . . . To possess a power is simply to possess means of action which exceed the very limited force that a single individual has at his disposal. But power-seeking, owing to its essential incapacity to seize hold of its object, rules out all consideration of an end, and finally comes, through an inevitable reversal, to take the place of all ends. It is this reversal of the relationship between means and end, it is this fundamental folly that accounts for all that is senseless and bloody, right through history. Human history is simply the history of the servitude which makes men—oppressors and oppressed alike—the plaything of the instruments of domination they themselves have manufactured, and thus reduces living humanity to being the chattel of inanimate chattels" (ibid., 69).

and regional economic autarchy.[7] Japan in retreat held on even more tenaciously to the theories as a defeat approached, in 1945, that would end the policies and repudiate the ideas that strung them together. In between, the imperial projection of Japanese power and culture on Southeast Asian societies produced unresolvable conflicts and unleashed extraordinary energies. Japan, as a homogeneous society built on vertical structural principles,[8] contrasts sharply with American heterogeneity and its checks-and-balances style; and Japanese totalism was mortally impatient with Philippine pluralism. The Japanese were more at home in Indonesia, partly because the Dutch also imparted vertical structure to society. "Pillariziation," however, was peculiar to the Netherlands.[9] The Dutch expressed their own columnar structure in trying to split and insulate colonial constituencies from each other; but the exigencies of war led the Japanese to mix and mobilize Indonesians in a manner contrary to classic imperial strategems, while maintaining their sense of hierarchy.

Hierarchy, rank-order, and central authority were, and are, far more pronounced in Japan than in any other industrial imperial society to affect Southeast Asia. Of none other could it be said, customarily, that "obedience . . . takes the form of total submission";[10] nor of any other that there is such a high predictability of success of power issuing from the top. All these enduring characteristics existed emphatically in 1942. They pointed to the high probability that actions taken under Japanese jurisdiction would be received as ultrarepressive by peoples of different cultures.[11]

The colonial conundrum grew more complex, and the incidence of misunderstanding rose considerably, because the Japanese also,

---

[7] John W. Dower, *War Without Mercy: Race and Power in the Pacific War* (New York: Pantheon, 1986), esp. chap. 10· "Global Policy with the Yamato Race as Nucleus."

[8] Nakane Chie, *Japanese Society* (Berkeley: University of California Press, 1972)

[9] Johann Goudsblom, *Dutch Society* (New York: Random House, 1967); Maarten Brands, "Reinventing Europe," MS, lecture series at Cornell University, 1983, third lecture, 9ff.

[10] Nakane, *Japanese Society*, 103.

[11] Ramon H. Meyers and Mark Peattie, eds., *The Japanese Colonial Empire, 1895–1945* (Princeton: Princeton University Press, 1984) is excellent on Taiwan, Korea, Southern Sakhalin, the Kwantung Leased Territory, and the Mandated Islands of Micronesia. But insofar as Japan in those circumstances shared a calligraphic tradition that softened their strangeness, or were completely overpowering in scale (Micronesia), their conquests represented different classes of situation than those discussed here.

again uniquely among major cultures, exhibit a pronounced disposition toward "dependence."[12] The analyses of Nakane Chie and Dōi Takeo merge at this point. Nakane has demonstrated that "the core of the Japanese family, ancient and modern, is the parent-child relationship, not that between husband and wife,"[13] and Dōi has shown the key operations of the verb *amaeru*, to behave self-indulgently, presuming upon a special relationship. Structure and psychology together produce an affirmative attitude toward the spirit of filial dependence. If that is perhaps the chief characteristic of the Japanese, interculturally,[14] it was also a pronounced feature of their theory of the Greater East Asia Co-Prosperity Sphere.[15]

Japanese indulgence of filial dependence, however, only faintly cloaked their idea of racial supremacy in the Southern Area. And it frontally clashed with the requirements of imperial order and efficiency. Under wartime conditions, in the end, the contradictions were constant. The Japanese exalted dependency with a paternal tone of promissory abundance; at the same time they exacted order through minatory hierarchical stricture. The mouth issued propaganda assuming unusual intimacy, and exalting mutual hopes. At the same time the hand was brandishing a whip; and applying it.

By announcing a holy war for the liberation of a billion Asians, and then gathering their resources, their food, and their labor to a seigneurial center, Japan presented conquered peoples in their "coprosperity sphere"[16] with excruciating ironies. The British, French,

---

[12] Dōi Takeo, *The Anatomy of Dependence* (Tokyo: Kodansha International, 1973). The key word, *amae*, is also translatable as "passive love."

[13] Nakane, *Japanese Society*, 128.

[14] Dōi, *Anatomy of Dependence*, 11–27. See also Dōi Takeo, *The Anatomy of Self* (Tokyo: Kodansha International, 1986), 48–58, for especially suggestive comparisons of American with Japanese psychology.

[15] In *Asian Power and Politics: The Cultural Dimensions of Authority* (Cambridge: Harvard University Press, 1985), Lucian Pye does not confront the wartime period, but takes acute note of more recent contradictions between Japanese political nurturing and succoring at the same time as being paternalizing and patronizing (e.g., 178).

[16] Rōyama Masamichi chaired a commission and edited a four-volume report on the Philippines, 1943, of which volume 4 was by Tobata Seiichi, Itō Choiji, and Sujimura Hirozō. There the practical economic theory of the sphere was laid out, as in volume 2 the political theory was applied. The latter, translated by Takéuchi Tatsuji and edited by Theodore Friend, has been published as Rōyama and Takéuchi, *The Philippine Polity: A Japanese View*, Yale University Southeast Asia Studies, Monograph Series, no. 12 (New Haven, 1967). Miwa Kimitada has examined such thinking in the light of prewar Japanese controversies over geopolitics, theory of national polity, and imperial and strategic theory: "Japanese Policies and Concepts for

and Belgians also used doctrines of state to impose costs upon their colonial subjects during both world wars, but none of them, it can be argued, did so as exactingly as the Japanese. Whatever positive bias the Japanese had to welcome dependence and to treat it tenderly was distorted by the political, logistical, and military necessities of competitive empire. And whatever inclination the conquerors had, under pressure of total war, to fall back on tangible Japanese loyalties was expressed with more and more ruthless defensive repressiveness.[17]

Such civilized restraints as higher military officers possessed tended to melt in fear of the Kenpeitai. The Japanese military police took on the functions of political intelligence and counterintelligence, propaganda and counterpropaganda. They were enabled to bypass military court procedures, and in many situations to endrun, override, or intimidate high regular army officers. The Kenpeitai's own officers gave way to expeditiousness more and more barbaric. Their kikōsaku, or "operation hades," justified executions without trial in Java. The same occurred throughout the Southern Area. Torture of suspects, often innocent, became standard in both Indonesia and the Philippines.[18] Hunger, disease, lack of medical attention, war casualties, and executions produced at an outer estimate three million dead in Java alone, which was only for nine days actually a theater of war. In the Philippines, where battle took place for six months at the beginning of the war and ten months at the end, there were probably half a million dead as a direct result of fighting, not to mention larger numbers from other causes. For all of this suffering, fairly or unfairly, the Kenpeitai became the most tangible symbol. Mysterious and yet concrete, dedicated and increasingly desperate, they became the metaphorical magnet for all that was terrible in wartime actuality, and in memories afterward.

The fact that Japanese soldiers in mid-1945 were in desperate con-

a Regional Order in Asia, 1938–1940," Sophia University, Institute of International Relations for Advanced Studies on Peace and Development in Asia, 1983.

[17] The most eloquent Japanese critic of this imperial expansion and its cruel consequences is Ienaga Saburō, *The Pacific War* (New York: Pantheon, 1978).

[18] *Kenpei Seishi* (see chap. 9, note 2), 1031–34. For selected translation, annotation, and interpretation of these Kenpei memoirs, see Barbara Gifford Shimer and Guy Hobbs, trans., *The Kenpeitai in Java and Sumatra*, introduction by Theodore Friend, Cornell Modern Indonesia Project, Translation Series, no. 65 (Ithaca, 1986). Also relevant are various documents of the Rijksinstituut voor Oorlogsdocumentatie, Amsterdam (e.g., RAPWI to NEFIS, October 3, 1945, RVO 006296); and various war crimes trials (e.g., U.S.A. vs. Akira Nagahama, JAG, Box 1457, FE 43-29, Washington National Records Center).

dition is not a matter for sympathy in the Philippines. Much of General Yamashita's army, on retreat in Luzon, was driven through hunger and jeopardy to near barbarity. Repressive force become mortal menace. Some Japanese were reduced to eating their own kind—an occasion, in retrospect, for terrible pathos.[19] For the ordinary Filipino, however, the retreating army was only the last and worst of the terrors of the Japanese invaders.

The Japanese in Indonesia never had to fight the Allies, but in merely preparing to do so they were calculating and merciless. Just after Terauchi moved his Nanpō headquarters to Manila, the Seventh Field Army staff made a basic decision. As a corollary of regional policy, the staff bore responsibility for maintaining stability and acquiring resources in all of what is now Indonesia, Malaysia, and Singapore. On May 19, 1944, they formally defined a policy "to maintain the natives' standard of living *at the lowest possible level*." The policy may be understood in the light of an expected attack, which took place at Leyte five months later. But it must be evaluated in its effect throughout the region, and especially in crowded Java, during another fifteen months of occupation. The stark language of the policy unmistakably suggests the barest minimum level to sustain life. It conveys no sympathy for the people whose lands were invaded and whose food was being taken. It evokes the old samurai saying, "Ikasazu, korosazu": "Don't let them live, don't let them die."[20]

CO-OPTATION AND REVOLT:
INDONESIAN RESPONSE TO THE JAPANESE

Hatta, negotiating for independence in 1949, was characteristically cool and subtle: "The Indonesian-Dutch conflict is mainly [a] psychological matter, which originates in colonial history." He stressed that it was "complicated by the psychological conflict of the last four years."[21] Hatta's words point toward the Dutch style of imperial dominance as the key to understanding Indonesian response to

[19] For a fictional account, in Leyte, see Ooka Shōhei, *Fires on the Plain*, trans. Ivan Morris (New York: Knopf, 1957).

[20] Bōeichō Bōeikenkyūjo Senshibu (Japanese Defense Agency, War History Division), *Nanpō no Gunsei* (Military Administration in the Southern Area) (Tokyo: Chōun Shimbunsha, 1985), 30–31. For exacting translation of the passage (emphasis added), I am grateful to Barbara Gifford Shimer, who consulted three other informed persons in Tokyo, and provided the samurai axiom.

[21] Deliar Noer, ed., *Mohammed Hatta: Portrait of a Patriot* (The Hague: Mouton, 1972), 509.

the Japanese in 1942, and then to the Dutch in 1945. Hollanders nourished dependence with horticultural care. They also exercised repression with the calculating instincts of hydraulic engineers. They were stiff, scrupulous, exacting, unyielding; they intended to endure.

Indonesians, on the whole, were not barbarously treated; but a North Sea hierarchism, merged with South Pacific traditions of ceremonial subordination, left little latitude for self-enfranchisement. Indonesian striving for nationhood has been amply documented; but its course is neither a straight line nor smooth.[22] The beginnings took the ostensible form of a furtherance of cultural dignity, followed by expression of an Islamic element in native pride, before erupting in premature social rebellion against colonial injustice. The names of Tjipto Mangunkusumo, Haji Omar Said Tjokroaminoto, and Musso and Alimin suggest the sequence in the first quarter of the twentieth century. Only the latter pair stated their aims in Marxist terms, but there was a masked rage present previously among the lower priyayi of Budi Utomo, and messianic unrest within Sarekat Islam, before the communist uprisings of 1926–27.[23]

The Dutch were no happier to find bourgeois nationalism arising in the 1930s than they had been earlier to see surges of Islam and of communism. They cracked down severely. The effect of their surveillance, control, and punishments in the Indies before the Pacific war is graphically measured by two acts of self-abasement: Sukarno's failed plea in 1933 to be released from jail in return for a lifelong abjuring of politics;[24] and Soetardjo's supplicant farewell visit to the governor general a few years later.[25] Soetardjo is best remembered for his petition for self-government within a Dutch commonwealth, and Sukarno, of course, emerged as the focal leader of the

[22] R. C. Kwantes, ed., *De Ontwikkeling van de Nationalistische Beweging in Nederlandsch-Indie, 1917–1942* (Development of the Nationalist Movement in the Netherlands Indies), 4 vols. (Groningen: Wolters–Noordhoff/Bouma's Boekhuis, 1975–1982).

[23] Akira Nagazumi, *The Dawn of Indonesian Nationalism: The Early Years of the Budi Utomo* (Tokyo: Institute of Developing Economies, 1972); Bernhard Dahm, *The History of Indonesia in the Twentieth Century* (London, Praeger, 1971); Merle Rickleffs, *History of Indonesia* (Bloomington: University of Indiana Press, 1981).

[24] John Ingleson, *Road to Exile: The Indonesian Nationalist Movement, 1927–1934* (Singapore: Heinemann, 1977), 218–22; Kwantes, *Nationalistische Beweging*, 4: 37–50.

[25] S. L. van der Wal, ed., *Herinneringen van Jhr. Mr. B.C. de Jonge* (Groningen: Walters-Noordhoff, 1968), 387–88; passages translated for me by Margaret Broekhuysen.

revolution. In the period of Netherlandish supremacy, however, Dutch leaders took an aloof satisfaction in the prisoner's cringing and the petitioner's fawning.

Into such a political climate burst the Japanese, proclaiming Asian liberation, allowing the flying of the Indonesian flag, speaking of their older brother–younger brother relationship with Indonesians. The spectacle of the Dutch in swift surrender was a revelation. The white man, long suspected of being not infallible, was now proven not invincible. The opportunities were clear: to raise the colonial ceiling on employment, to remove the colonial censor on expression, and to advance native initiative within the framework of a nation-state.

The Japanese as occupiers, however, steadily adjusted expectations downward and inspired new hatreds. The supposedly sacred war revealed its unholy side. "Liberation" became renewed subjugation. The Indonesian flag and national anthem were disallowed. The Rising Sun and the saikeirei, bowing toward the emperor, were the dominating symbols instead. The Japanese discriminated among their "Asian brothers" on a basis of strategic necessity or economic convenience. Indonesians were not invited to the Greater East Asia Conference of November 1943. Omission made them question if they were in the family at all; and even if included, moved them to wonder if they were not the youngest and least favored child of an arbitrary and demanding father.

When Japanese surrender produced a sudden power vacuum in Indonesia, and paralysis of Japanese will, Indonesian nationalists proclaimed the independence promised them. The radical elements who carried off Sukarno and Hatta to Rengasdenklok in a shortsighted kidnapping may or may not have delayed the actual proclamation. Almost certainly they could not have produced a freer, more powerful Indonesia by provoking an immediate clash of arms with the Japanese.[26] Sukarno, Hatta, and others knew that skill and more patience were required. They had to get as many Japanese weapons as peaceably as possible; to organize a government to which Indonesians could rally; and to prepare for the Allied return.

Indonesian circumstances differed critically from those in Hanoi with regard to positioning and timing. If Ho Chi Minh with eighty

[26] B. M. Diah and Adam Malik (interviews, November 28, 29, 1983), however, both contradict Hatta's view that the pemuda kidnappers delayed the proclamation of independence rather than strengthening the resolve behind it (for which latter view, see *Bung Hatta's Answers*, interviews with Dr. Z. Yasni, translated by Rochmuljati Hamzah [Singapore: Gunung Agung, 1981], 119).

rifles could declare a revolution, organize a government, and eventually succeed, why not Sukarno? The answer, of course, is not only that they were different men, of different beliefs and styles, but that Java differed from North Vietnam in political culture and geostrategic opportunity.

Was the diplomatic style pursued during the revolution by Sukarno, Hatta, Sjahrir, and others lacking in bravado, or infected by colonialized debilities of character? If so, it would have to be conceded by critics holding such opinions that Indonesia won its independence far sooner than did Vietnam (1949 rather than 1954); obtained its framework of union far sooner still (1949 rather than 1975); and has demonstrated, partly as a factor of such independence and union, far greater momentum in economic and social development than Vietnam has yet begun to show.

In the closing months of 1945, a newborn Indonesian government faced a thinly staffed Netherlands Indies Civil Administration. A spirited but unevenly trained and untested Indonesian army awaited the return of Dutch troops. A shocked and aroused people groped toward its new identity as an Indonesian nation. The will of the people was critical, and was now dramatically revealed. As the new national government and the old imperial one shadowboxed, and mutually tested their weakness,[27] and before Dutch troops even arrived, the future was foretold in Surabaya. Admiral Shibata saw "a group of young officers of the Indonesian revolutionary army wearing Japanese uniforms . . . and looking very important with their Japanese swords. . . . They behaved in exactly the same way as the Japanese army had done ever since the Manchurian incident." The swagger of militant enthusiasm is the same everywhere. "They were crazed with the desire for *merdeka*."[28] British troops, surrogate imperial forces for the Dutch, clashed with the people of the city, lightly armed but mightily motivated. The ferocity of their battle, in November 1945, made clear that a life-and-death struggle impended.

[27] On the confused emergence of an Indonesian National Army (not so named until February 1946), see Ulf Sundhaussen, *The Road to Power: Indonesian Military Politics, 1945–1967* (Kuala Lumpur: Oxford University Press, 1982), 1–12. On its Japanese-trained core of officers, see Nugroho Notosusanto, "The PETA Army in Indonesia," in William H. Newell, ed., *Japan in Asia* (Singapore: Singapore University Press, 1981), 32–45.

[28] Shibata Yaichiro, "Surabaya After the Surrender," in Anthony Reid and Oki Akira, eds., *The Japanese Experience in Indonesia: Selected Memoirs of 1942–1945*, Southeast Asia Series, no. 72 (Athens: Ohio University Center for International Studies, 1986), 367.

This mortal confrontation was not only literal, but symbolic. As Hegel had spoken of the ultimate clash between lord and bondsman, now several thousand Indonesian fatalities proved the willingness of the bondsman to die. The Dutch never faced their foe as frontally, or calamitously, as the British did in that event. Surabaya overshadowed all other battles of the revolution. The Dutch suffered relatively few casualties in their two "police actions," certainly fewer than the Japanese suffered trying to keep order until the Dutch returned.[29]

Deadly showdowns produce "absolute fear" in both sides. The matter may be decided by which has the more nearly absolute courage. Allied soldiers, brave as they were, did not have the motivation of Surabayans, other Javanese, and Indonesians of many kinds, to fight for homeland. They were at the end of a war, but the Indonesians were at a beginning. The availability of arms was an indispensable factor accompanying the will to fight. Where once 40,000 Dutch troops had easily kept peace and order, now 145,000 could not put the empire back together again.

Indonesians had seen the Dutch lord beaten and humiliated by the Japanese; had seen the Japanese liberator become another onerous lord; had then seen the Japanese themselves stricken in defeat. Now they had no more tolerance of lords, or respect for them. The Indonesian owed respect to none but the lord within himself. Hegel's translator, like Freud's, calls that entity "Ego."[30] Chairil Anwar, as poet, gave "Aku,'" the first-person singular, new force and bite in the Indonesian language. Understood and objectified selves now shared in the national identity of a people prepared to join the constellation of nations. Such selves were ready to shed blood to remain new beings.

[29] See chap. 10. For that matter, Indonesian casualties in the revolution were far fewer than those suffered by the Sukarno-Hatta republic against the Dar'ul Islam rebellion: Karl Jackson, *Traditional Authority, Islam, and Rebellion: A Study of Indonesian Political Behavior* (Berkeley: University of California Press, 1980); also C. Van Dijk, *Rebellion Under the Banner of Islam: The Darul Islam of Indonesia* (The Hague: Martinus Nijhoff, 1981).

[30] Hegel in the original, however, uses the term "Ich" rather than the Latin when he describes self-consciousness in its "essential nature and absolute object" (*Phänomenologie des Geistes* [1921 edition], 125, compared with Baillie translation, 231). On the problems arising from translating Freud's *Ich* as "Ego" instead of simply "I," see Bruno Bettelheim, *Freud and Man's Soul* (New York: Knopf, 1982). The matter does not become problematic in the case of Hegel so long as we understand him to be dealing with a sense of self as agent capable of action, rather than with a slice of a multiple-tiered personality.

CONCLUSION

REJECTION AND REVERSION:
FILIPINO RESPONSE TO THE JAPANESE

The Filipinos were the first colonized Asians to fight a revolution
to become a nation-state (1896–1901). They might have worn out
Spain, but they could not dislodge a United States seized with expansionistic exuberance. McKinley, as imperialist, beat Bryan, as
anti-imperialist, in the elections of 1900. Bryan's principles, however, were ascendant by 1916, when the Congress promised eventual independence to the Philippines. The first such promise in
modern history was followed by the first legislated independence
act, in 1934. Filipinos could plan for a future in pursuit of their own
chosen path of development, while Indonesians still had to conjure
with Governor General de Jonge's remark that the Dutch intended
to rule the Indies three hundred years more.[31]

Within an atmosphere shaped by turn-of-the-century progressiv-
ism and traditional American anti-imperialism, the conservative
Republican, Elihu Root, determined that insular government
should shape Philippine destiny for the Filipinos, conforming "to
their customs, their habits, and even their prejudices." By 1913, a
liberal Democrat, Francis Burton Harrison, was interpreting that
policy as governor general.[32]

Congressional policy and local practice converged in 1935 to produce a Philippine Commonwealth, autonomous in domestic affairs.
The elected president, Manuel Quezon, sought a twenty-one-gun
salute at his inaugural, but found he could only get nineteen. The
United States was still sovereign, and in control of foreign affairs.
American restraints of protocol were galling to Quezon, but Dutch
restrictions of expression upon Indonesians were so severe that he
could not even understand them. As a guest in Surabaya, Quezon
advised Indonesian nationalists to make "a hell of a lot of noise."
He did not appreciate that Sukarno, Hatta, and Sjahrir, among

[31] Prof. S. L. van der Wal, in *Tijdschrift voor Geschiedenis* (1967), 498–99, traces
this remark to a press interview by de Jonge in 1936. Bernhard Dahm analyzes the
"postmature" Indonesian revolution of 1945 in the light of the "premature" Philippine revolution in 1896, in *Emanzipationsversuche von Kolonialer Herrschaft in Su-
dostasien: Die Philippinen und Indonesien, ein Vergleich* (Attempted emancipation
from colonial rule in Southeast Asia: the Philippines and Indonesia, a comparison)
(Wiesbaden: Otto Harrossowitz, 1974).

[32] Peter Stanley, *A Nation in the Making· The Philippines and the United States,
1899–1921* (Cambridge: Harvard University Press, 1974) is the best study of the period.

– 270 –

others, were all at the time in detention for relatively modest sounds.[33]

American colonial government did not lack a police system,[34] but its light monitoring and relatively nonpolitical style were at the far end of a spectrum from the Netherlands Indies. Dutch surveillance was part of a professedly objective and apolitical system that actually included intense survey reports by the political police. Arrests were triggered by "seditious" speech, remarks that in the American colony would have been considered merely annoying, and ignored as within normal bounds. Where the Dutch restricted any nationalist they found objectionable, the Americans tried to isolate potentially violent ones by working closely with established leaders.

Quezon would not have flourished in Java, but he once cursed the Americans for not tyrannizing enough—for not giving him nationalist issues to work with. Long after the Philippines became sovereign, the American style of political and cultural assimilation continued to be felt as asphyxiation. A quarter century after Quezon's death, Benigno Aquino, Jr., said, "The United States really kills you with love. A fire starts and they smother you with foam. They kill you with Hershey bars." Aquino smiled as he spoke, but he was serious.[35]

During wartime occupation Aquino's father had been the most enthusiastic of Filipino leaders for the militant, inspiring Japanese way. But militancy was difficult for the Japanese to impart, and nearly impossible for the Filipinos to accept. Cultural history and political schedules denied it. Lieutenant General Hayashi Yoshihide, first chief of military administration, was not the only Japanese soldier to conclude that the Filipinos were the least disciplined, least cooperative, and least admirable people of all in the Greater East Asia Co-Prosperity Sphere.[36] Other, more flexible Japanese held the extremists back until the war drew closer to its end, and military necessity prevailed in almost all decisions. Overt allies

[33] Theodore Friend, *Between Two Empires: The Ordeal of the Philippines* (New Haven: Yale University Press, 1965), 170.

[34] For the rationale behind creation of the Philippine Constabulary and unbalanced enthusiasm about its effectiveness, see Dean C. Worcester, *The Philippines Past and Present* (New York: Macmillan, 1914), 1: 378–99.

[35] Interview with the author, Manila, January 19, 1968. For an analogous statement by Quezon, see Friend, *Between Two Empires*, 4.

[36] Author's interviews, Hayashi and Nakamura Koji; Tokyo, 1957; Fukushima Shintarō, ed., *Murata Shōzō: Ikō hitō-nikki* (Posthumously published Philippine diaries) (Shinjuku: Hara-shobo, 1969).

and sympathizers, such as Aguinaldo, Ricarte, and Ramos, were used to the utmost. General Mutō Akira supported Ramos's plot to assassinate Laurel, but cooler heads prevailed.[37] No contrary counsel, however, restrained Colonel Nagahama, the commander of the Kenpeitai; arrest on suspicion, torture, summary executions—all increased.

Filipino relief at the return of American troops was enormous. "Liberation," it still is called, except by those whose nationalistic consciousness finds that an indignity. To those who remember, the euphoria of rescue and reembrace with Americans remains unforgettable. Even the ways in which American investment policy and rehabilitation aid took advantage of Philippine weakness in 1946 appeared, to many, forgivable or acceptable.

How understand this reassumption of the subordinate and supplicant role? One angle of insight may come through wartime rhetoric. Executive Secretary Jorge Vargas, putty in the hands of the Japanese, publicly spoke of a Philippines happily "liberated" from "enslavement" by the imperial Japanese army. "We were the orphan of the Pacific, and fast becoming the pampered child of Asia," said Vargas. Then Japan came and offered an "independence . . . achieved by our own hands."[38] The statement was presumably contrived by Japanese propaganda writers for the presence of Premier Tōjō on the same platform, but the words contained a partial truth. American inattentive domination and indulgent neglect had helped produce a nation that the Japanese saw as both "orphan," with regard to Asian cultural roots, and "pampered child," with respect to building a new and productive Asian sphere.

Philippine reattachment to the United States through the neomercantile structure of the Bell Act of 1946 and the expansionist strategy of the bases agreement of 1947 would support a similar view in the eyes of other Asians and certain Filipinos. Some Indonesians in later years have commented not unlike the wartime Japanese: the Filipinos' culture was derivative, their Catholicism was fanatic, and their orientation to American commercial and poor cinematic values was deplorable. A contemporary Filipino critic makes similar points. His Marxism does not vitiate the analysis, which here is factually sound and emotionally apt. He ties postwar Filipino flaws to "the trauma of Japanese occupation," which "made

[37] Friend, *Between Two Empires*, 234, 244.
[38] Far Eastern Bureau, British Ministry of Information, New Deli, Fortnightly Intelligence Report No. 4, May 3, 1943, National Archives and Records Service.

the old bondage that much more desirable, and when they came at last, the victorious Americans were as gods walking the earth. MacArthur's masterly moves insured the restoration of power of the old elite conduits of American rule, and independence with strings was the reward for our blind loyalty."[39]

NOSTALGIA AND FILIALISM

Nostalgia may not propel development, but it illuminates historical unfoldings. Queen Juliana's visit to Indonesia in 1971 was the first of the Netherlands' sovereign to the former Dutch colony. She evoked among Indonesians the transpersonal feelings that such figures do: yearning for times past, gratitude and forgiveness, longing for lost maternal protection, and respect for a kind of power that is robed in ceremony and at the same time stripped of any possibility to threaten or chastise.[40] In Indonesia now the people are sovereign, but royal personhood still has deeply evocative qualities. In Java, where once a god-king was at the apex of a sacro-magical state, the concept of divine kingship will be especially slow to disappear.

The Philippine analogue is General MacArthur's famous "sentimental journey" of 1961, just three years before his death.[41] His return to Manila brought a million people into the streets. That was arguably the most emotional celebration of an individual in the independent Philippines until the visit of the Pope in 1981 and the funeral of the murdered Benigno Aquino, Jr., in 1983. MacArthur had successfully projected his ego into Philippine history as potential savior ("I shall return," 1942), and as actual savior ("I have returned," 1944). In Filipino popular feeling, he earned the attributes of defender and symbol of continuity and of conquering hero, friend

[39] Renato Constantino, *Neocolonial Identity and Counter-Consciousness: Essays on Cultural Decolonization* (White Plains, N.Y.: M. E. Sharpe, 1978), 253.

[40] Dutch accounts. *Algemeen Dagblad*, September 4, 1971; for a right-of-center summary of healing wounds, and the two peoples "finding each other again," see *Elseviers Weekblad*, September 4, 1971; for a left-of-center analysis of the timing and motivation of the visit and its likely consequences, see the three-part series in *NRC Handelsblad*, especially the initial article, August 23, 1971. Other analyses of Dutch-Indonesian relations at the time: *de Volkskrant*, August 26, September 4, 1971; *Utrechtsch Nieuwsblad*, August 21, 1971, *Leeuwarder Courant*, August 25, 1971. The royalist magazine *Vorsten* (July 1982, 32–33) published a retrospective article on the trip, in addition to an account of the return trip eleven years later (July 1982, 20–23, and August 1982, 34–39).

[41] William R. Manchester, *American Caesar: Douglas MacArthur, 1880–1964* (Boston: Little, Brown, 1978), 696, 698; Douglas MacArthur, *Reminiscences* (New York: McGraw-Hill, 1964), photographs following 376.

of the people. He may be the only man in the twentieth century to have enjoyed both the antithetical symbolic roles of imperial sovereign and of national liberator.[42]

The majestic aura surrounding Queen Juliana and General MacArthur prepares us to cast back into the wartime period at a deeper psychological level. One Dutch analyst, writing about Indonesia in Freudian terms, has pointed to the sequence of Western "father" being "killed," 1942, by the Japanese and the new Japanese "father" being "killed" in turn, 1945.[43] Eschewing Freudianism, one may prefer to look at these events in other ways, such as gang warfare among the advanced industrial countries, or competitive suicide within the modern imperial system. In any case, these years so disoriented, or so motivated, many Indonesians that they compulsively expressed a fanatical devotion to ibu pertiwi, the motherland. Long-suppressed symbols, such as Njai Loro Kidul, the Queen of the Southern Seas, took on rich and compelling meaning. Indonesians were poised to kill Dutch and to die for their country.

The language of government is thin with regard to the unconscious, and the language of analytical psychiatry is loose with regard to worldly arrangements. Where political scientists say "revolutionary conditions existed," depth psychologists might say that "readiness for the primal murder had arrived." Some of each vocabulary is necessary to suggest the critical point at which Indonesia had arrived by the last four months of 1945. Indonesians were prepared for parricide in order to take the motherland; for combat, even death, to claim their heritage and to rule themselves.

In a contrasting vein, the Philippines' Carlos Romulo wrote brilliantly in exile about "Mother America."[44] Was something not

[42] Present-day Filipino critics look back and regard 1945–46 as a time of "missed opportunities." Seeing MacArthur as radical reformer in Japan, they ask why was he merely a restorer in the Philippines? There are at least three practical answers: (1) Japan was his major military target and the Philippines only his launching site; (2) Japan as a defeated nation was subject to a new master. The Philippines, however, was a freed nation about to be, at least theoretically, its own master; it would have been unseemly and untimely to try to reshape it; (3) pressures of old friendships, not merely MacArthur's, but of many Manila Americans and leading Filipinos, constrained against change; but no such binational faction existed in Tokyo.

[43] P. M. van Wulfften Palthe, *Psychological Aspects of the Indonesian Question* (Leiden: E. J. Brill, 1949). For a different perspective: Justus M. van der Kroef, *Indonesian Social Evolution: Some Psychological Considerations* (Amsterdam: Wereld Bibliotheek, 1958).

[44] Carlos Romulo, *Mother America: A Living Story of Democracy*, and Romulo, *My Brother Americans* (Garden City: Doubleday, Doran, 1943 and 1945).

wrong here? Why not "Mother Filipinas"? Many Filipinos had the same feeling about their native land that Indonesians had about theirs. But extremely few of them were moved to kill Americans to claim their heritage and maturity. Part of the explanation must revert to the lack of an indigenous central kingdom and sacred state before the Spanish. Some of it may relate to the affinitive style of the best rule of the Spanish friars. Much of the story lies in the power politics of 1945. Independence as promised by Americans was only a year away. The obstacle to it was the Japanese. American forces were present in such numbers that to fight them for "immediate, absolute, and complete independence"—the ancient slogan of the Nacionalistas—would have been unthinkably and catastrophically foolish.

Nonetheless, the euphoria of liberation by Americans in 1944–45, the overwhelming passage of the plebiscite in 1946 amending the constitution to give Americans parity investment rights with Filipinos, the largely secure silence about the bases agreement of 1947, all suggest something distinctly other and more than power politics. As a Filipina critic has said of America, "We fell in love with your culture."[45] Maybe it was a terrible mistake, as some intercultural loves of individuals are; but as a national predilection of Filipinos it was apparently inescapable.

That attachment, as later expressed in flaming consumerism and TV-inspired hunger for upward mobility, need not be considered wholly complimentary to the United States. A strong statehood movement in the Philippines claimed six million card-carrying members as late as 1971, and it revived in the 1980s. Its leader publicly, like some of his countrymen privately, has cracked that the Philippines is a "concubine" of the United States. "Why not make it legal?"[46] Such remarks compel wonder about whether the image of the *querida*, or mistress, is not fitting. Unlike the imagined Freudian young male who wishes to commit parricide to claim adulthood, the querida makes an adult choice, or "recognizes her fate," by compromising herself. The best she can hope for is split-level domesticity. She may have the illusion that she is sovereign at home. But all the world knows, and she knows too, that when the master enters her castle, it becomes a *casa querida*.[47]

[45] Carmen Guerrero-Nakpil, cited by Theodore Friend, "Goodbye Mother America," *Asia* 15 (1969): 1–12.

[46] Bartolome Cabangbang, *Wall Street Journal*, April 19, 1983, 1.

[47] Against these indignities, one of the best protections may be the character of Corazon Aquino. As the widow of an assassinated leader, she is a focus of sanctity

CONCLUSION

MIRRORING AND MUTUAL DEPENDENCE

After Manuel Quezon escaped Corregidor in 1942 and returned by way of Australia to Washington, he paid a call on General Dwight D. Eisenhower, then deputy chief of the War Plans Division. Quezon sought to press upon Eisenhower a large emolument for his services to the Philippines Commonwealth from 1935 to 1939.

Eisenhower answered that it was *"inadvisable and even impossible for me to accept a material reward for the services performed."* He labored with all his tact and charm to make the Filipino president understand. In the end he accepted a citation instead, which had been devised to accompany the honorarium; and Quezon left without any apparent loss of face. "This latter point . . . had given me tremendous concern," Eisenhower wrote. "To refuse a gift from anyone raised in the Far East, especially if a point of ethics had to be plead, is quite apt to develop into a serious personal matter."[48]

Where Eisenhower managed to sustain friendship with Quezon while declining the gift and hewing clearly to regulations, his former commander, MacArthur, had chosen another course. On Corregidor, in January, he accepted $500,000 from Quezon as "recompense and reward." By late February the transaction had resulted in a deposit to his account at the Chase National Bank in New York.[49] Does the difference in behavior suggest why Eisenhower rose to become president of the United States, and MacArthur, despite his appetite for the apex of power, did not? Perhaps. But that is too simple, and does not explain why MacArthur chose as he did.

The temptation exists for some to think of MacArthur as enriching himself, another imperial parasite in a plantation economy.[50] But that would be tendentious to the point of being grotesque. MacArthur had deep emotional ties with the Philippines, going back to his father, who had served as military governor in 1900–1901 during the Philippine-American War. He himself had put in

in national character—a living Mater Dolorosa, Mother of Sorrows (cf. chap. 4, n. 11). As the brave woman who prevailed over Ferdinand Marcos, she is also a focus for integrity in national policy, and a potential leader of incremental disengagement from overassociation with the United States. Time will tell.

[48] Carol Morris Petillo, *Douglas MacArthur, The Philippine Years* (Bloomington: Indiana University Press, 1981), 212–13, 280n.

[49] Ibid., 208; 278–79n. Gifts to three of MacArthur's aides brought total disbursements to $640,000.

[50] Petillo draws close to arguing such a point in her earlier article, "Douglas MacArthur and Manuel Quezon: A Note on an Imperial Bond," *Pacific Historical Review*, 48 (1979), 107–17, esp. 107. She lets her exquisitely careful research prevail, however. I gratefully take up her invitation to readers to ponder the facts she has established.

four tours of duty in the Philippines, had become Quezon's close friend in the 1920s, and had made Quezon his compadre, and godfather of his only son in 1938. Between MacArthur's first, unhappy marriage and his second, happy one, he had had a Filipina mistress whom he brought to Washington while he was Chief of Staff. His first wife had wounded and inflamed him with allusions to his sexual inabilities, but the publisher, Roy Howard, well knew the MacArthur of the Philippines. He jestingly asserted of the first wife, "If he was impotent, it was just geographical, limited to one spot."[51]

In Corregidor, a terrible impotence threatened of a different sort: no guns, no planes, no troops were promised to help relieve the garrison holding out against the Japanese. In his cablegrams to Washington, MacArthur ranted for help. Quezon considered a neutralization treaty with the Japanese. Washington denied their requests. Isolated, and told to brave it out, the two men turned to each other in the bicultural terms with which each was familiar: Quezon projecting the Americanized surface style that had made him a credible colonial leader; MacArthur, receptive in some core sensitivities, presenting the values of a would-be Western frontiersman, an outsider looking for a home, and a commander relishing devotees. Quezon had little power left but through his portable treasury, and MacArthur felt indignant at being abandoned for a Europe-first strategy. The only remaining mode of self-validation that each had was the other. So Quezon conferred half a million dollars upon MacArthur for services rendered. MacArthur accepted it.

In that moment the master-servant relationship took its most inverted form in the colonial period. More even than those times when he had refused to see MacArthur in 1940, Quezon could feel his lordship as employer. More than at any instant until his wadings ashore in 1944–45, MacArthur could feel appreciation for his service to America's colony—a wave of positive feeling that seemed to flow to him more readily from the Philippines than from the United States.

The value of the transaction was far more emotional than financial. At the time it was made, neither man could be sure of surviving; oddsmakers might have quoted against both. Nothing was available to be bought by either. The cash sum gave hugely more momentum to the honor that MacArthur received; and the gift probably did not, in Quezon's mind, deplete the treasury so much as give him a transient symbolic eminence over the soldier.

[51] Petillo, *The Philippine Years*; Friend, *Between Two Empires*, 78, 160–68, 190–94; quotation from author's interview with Roy Howard, May 7, 1962, previously held confidential.

Quezon had already paid MacArthur annually as much as the former American governors general.[52] The half-million dollars in addition is a datum in a compadrazgo tie with a mutually binding utang na loob (debt of honor). But it did not purchase a particular policy, or practice, or act from MacArthur, any more than large prewar gifts to Quezon from Manila business leaders swayed him from his own caudillo impetuosity.[53] Either man could be patron, either client, in their mutual relationship; the important thing was to intensify the bond for the sake of mutual trust and dependence.

Isolation and the chance of death on Corregidor did not rob MacArthur of soldierly courage. Circumstances did, however, deprive him of what he always had in lesser supply, his civil judgment. Accepting the money was a clear offense against military regulations. Secretary of War Stimson, Secretary of the Interior Ickes, and President Roosevelt held their noses and attended to more important business.

In that instant of accepting the half-million dollars, MacArthur went beyond reflecting Filipino values, and passed through the looking glass itself. Being Filipino, however, did not suit him, except at such a moment. There would be ahead of him greater roles— as liberator of the Philippines, and as de facto emperor of Japan. For Quezon there were few great moments left. He died in the United States wracked by tubercular coughing. He was still close to his compadre, the general; but he cursed the little neoimperial lords on MacArthur's staff.[54]

"BLUE-EYED ENEMY"
and "BLUE-EYED FRIEND"

Ethology is in a still more raw speculative stage than depth psychology. Its assertions about animals—though controversial even

[52] Teodoro A. Agoncillo, *The Burden of Proof* (Mandaluyong: University of the Philippines Press, 1984), 2–8, based chiefly on Philip Dion's transcription of interview with Jorge Vargas; Petillo, *The Philippine Years*, 170, 273n.

[53] Petillo in her article argues the possibility that "notice of the completed transfer of funds influenced MacArthur's decision to evacuate the Philippine president on February 20." Her book (p. 208) juxtaposes the two events but subsequently withdraws from that and other allegations, and goes on into argumentation on *compadrazgo/utang na loob/walang hiya* (209–11). I think the latter reasoning more sound. Both Quezon and MacArthur, however, rise above any merely positivistic calculus or deterministic accounting, Philippine or American.

[54] Petillo, *The Philippine Years*, 217–20, on continuing bond; Col. Jesus A. Villamor, *They Never Surrendered* (Quezon City: Vera-Reyes, 1982), 236–37, on curses.

there—are sounder than those about humans. The wartime period, however, heaved up considerable comment upon differences in stature, features, and skin color between contending national groups, and the evidence bears some interpretation. The physical and "animal" reactions of Japanese to Malayo-Polynesians as well as to Caucasians, of Caucasians to Japanese as well as to Malayo-Polynesians, and of Malayo-Polynesians to Caucasians and to Japanese, would be a lengthy study in itself. In any relationship, differences of culture and power become easily fixed upon and exaggerated with respect to what may be physically distinct between the peoples concerned.

Most revealing for this analysis is the exhortation of the Japanese general to his troops in Southeast Asia in 1942: "With one blow you will annihilate the blue-eyed enemy and their black slaves."[55] No clearer fighting distinction between "us" and "them" could be imagined. The existing imperial power is classified as other and hostile by the epithet "blue-eyed enemy." Their colonial wards are categorized as other and lower by the epithet "black slaves." Japanese militant enthusiasm fed on racial feeling to strengthen it for defeat of Americans and Dutch, and for subjugation of Filipinos and Indonesians. The euphoria of the Japanese as victors and lords is hard now to recapture, but it was certainly heady in 1942.[56] Less than a century after humiliating Western trade incursions into Japan, and after decades of diplomatic chafing against inferior treatment, the Japanese had reversed the order of things. They were on top, in a manner far more extensive and satisfying even than their earlier victories over Manchu China and Tsarist Russia.

Imperial "blue-eyes" as an ethological datum signified competition and enmity to many Japanese. To many people in the great arc of Malayo-Polynesian ethno-culture, however, it could suggest dependence and nurture. Mannoni notes in a poem, "an absolutely typical text" of the Malagasy describing the white men, "how easily the father-*imago* came to be identified with the first colonizers":

Now the country the strangers conquered is at peace.
There are no more outlaws and the slaves have been freed.
The blue-eyed strangers are mighty indeed.

[55] ATIS Research Report 76, pt. 3, p. 5, MacA. For full initial citation, see chap. 3, note 16.

[56] For examples: Miyoshi Shunkichirō, "Jawa senryō gunsei kaikoroku" (Memoirs of the Military Administration of Occupied Java), in *Kokusai Mondai*, 61–82 (1965–67), and Imamura Hitoshi, *Imamura Taishō kaisōroku* (The memoirs of General Imamura Hitoshi) 7 vols. (Tokyo: Jiyu Ajiasha, 1960–).

The new master, however, would be mistaken to expect gratitude. "For he has done no good; he has simply introduced a change for which he bears on his shoulders the fearful responsibility: the Malagasy is pleased to see that his shoulders are so broad."[57]

When the colonizer sheds that burden, some of the people will feel betrayed, and others moved to atavism. Rebellion in Madagascar, 1947, revealed an incipient sense of abandonment at the French breaking of dependence systems, and a national desire to restore "the *ancient* pattern of dependences"—that is, upon native leaders.[58]

The desire for indigenous lords and fathers links the Malagasies to other colonial nationalist movements, such as the Indonesian. Sukarno there became the giver of modern law with his Pancasila address in 1945. In world intellectual history, the speech may be a bourgeois goulash of received ideas, but in Indonesian colonial history, it is the very moment of political liberation. Power flows at last not from the Dutch bureaucrat's pen, or the Japanese officer's sword, but from Bung Karno as the tongue of the people.

The Filipinos fit the pattern of the Malagasies and Indonesians in the sense that Quezon, Magsaysay, and Marcos, in different decades and in different ways, were national voices of destiny, more credible and more compelling than any foreign voice can be. But astonishingly, the Filipinos also contradict the pattern. Whereas the Malagasies and Indonesians accepted and then revolted against a "blue-eyed stranger" and the Japanese fought a "blue-eyed enemy," the Filipinos in some manner adopted a "blue-eyed friend."

The causes of binational and bicultural bonding reached deep into Philippine history. They included the lack of a native god-king, the Western bias of Catholicism, the concord of priests and principales,[59] the normality and even prominence of mestizo ethnicity, and the size and power of the United States, not to mention the unconscious, sloppy, acceptable prevalence of American cultural influence. The result was that long after sovereignty, Filipinos continued, on balance, to appear to prefer the constraining security of psychological dependence to the creative insecurity of psychic and cultural independence.

[57] Mannoni, *Prospero and Caliban: the Psychology of Colonization* (New York: Praeger, 1964), 162–64.

[58] Ibid., 85–88, 134–41 (quotation, 141; emphasis supplied).

[59] Alfonso Felix, Jr., introduction to Bruce Cruikshank, *Samar: 1768–1898* (Manila: Historical Conservation Society, 1985), dwells on the positive roles of priests.

AGGRANDIZEMENT AND DIMINISHMENT IN
IMPERIAL-NATIONAL DYNAMICS

Perhaps nothing so clearly illustrates Japanese inflation of their own identity, and intended reduction of others' identities, as their wartime use of the popular fable of Momotarō, or Peach Boy. The fundamental story is simple: a heroic boy adventures into strange southern lands, and with the aid of a dog, a monkey, and a pheasant, overcomes the demons there. He returns home to his doting foster parents with a cart full of treasures pulled by the dog and pheasant and pushed by the monkey. Small overcoming large is a universally appealing theme. Imperial conflict tilts the fable so that a Japanese David prevails over a number of Western Goliaths, who are each behemoth and barbarian. But the innocent young hero needs accomplices. By superior intelligence and charming generosity, he enlists the "natives" in a struggle to liberate themselves from the foreign oppressor, not to mention labors to enrich Momotarō himself.

The Japanese love of this tale took real form in Saito Takeji, a school dropout at age fourteen who went to Papua in 1931 to join a development program in New Guinea launched by the Japanese. He grew expert in cotton growing and fluent in Bahasa Indonesia. In wartime he rose to become chief secretary of the Bukanfu (naval attache's office), and was nicknamed "Flying Momotarō" and "Momotarō of the Shōwa Era."

After surrender, Saito flew to Semarang, October 14, 1945, to help rescue Japanese in danger. He was caught instead. Ironically, the young man who had delivered a eulogy at Thamrin's grave was executed by Indonesian nationalists, along with fifty other Japanese. The bodies were found near a wall, on which the slogan "Indonesia Merdeka" was written in characters of blood, in a way unmistakably Saito's.

Deeply as Momotarō's story appeals to Japanese mythic sensibilities, educated Javanese reacted with outrage to the implications of a Japanese "civilizer" on a mission in "barbarian" Java. Diminution by the Japanese was no more acceptable than belittlement by the Dutch.[60]

[60] The Saito story is from an essay by Goro Taniguchi, in Tamura Yoshio, ed., *Hiroku Daitoa senshi: Ranin-hen* (A confidential history of the Greater East Asia war: Netherlands East Indies) (Tokyo: Fujishoen, 1953), 66–71, on Javanese attitudes toward Momotarō, author's interviews, Sudarpo and others, February–March 1968. Anthony Reid, "Indonesia: From Briefcase to Samurai Sword," in Alfred W. McCoy, ed., *Southeast Asia Under Japanese Occupation*, Yale University Southeast Asia Studies, Monograph Series, no. 22 (New Haven, 1980), 24, gives an example of Acehnese ad-

Psychological, ethological, and mythological themes converge in such particulars, but they do not always play out in the same direction. The Filipino official who was willing to speak the Japanese script about his country being "the orphan of the Pacific" was one of many pleased to be readopted by "Mother America" after the war. The Filipino nationalist critic who calls urgently for more psychic and cultural autonomy in his countrymen is the same who describes most eloquently MacArthur's troops in 1945–46 as "like gods walking the earth"—gods not so much feared as adored.[61]

The rebonding of the Philippines with the United States was incomparably more a readoption by an orphan looking for a surrogate parent than the reverse. Such awe was all the more touched with pathos in that the behavior of individual American soldiers, and the policy conduct of their state, were far from godlike in any Christian way. America and Americans were self-interested, which is godlike only in the Greek sense, referring to the willful behavior of beings who make life seem larger, more replete with meaning. Exceedingly few Filipinos, in the rubble that was peace, were willing to face the deprivation implied in forced separation from the United States. If allowing readoption was America's major postwar service to the Philippines, subsequent disservices are well catalogued by Constantino.

The Dutch, by contrast, were no longer capable, after 1942, of protracted mythic ability to enhance or erode the lives of Indonesians. Pictures and texts in schoolbooks provided by the Dutch to Indonesians vastly magnified Dutch geography and global centrality. Holland's land and population, however, were small fractions of those of its colony; and the mythic function of aggrandizement was as much provided to the Dutch by Indonesia as the reverse. As the sands of imperial time ran out, Indonesia's diminishment at being a colony of the Dutch became intolerable to its people. The "gods" in this instance—British and Dutch soldiers—had to be cut down for the sake of the motherland. The only way for Indonesia to grow was to throw off Dutch command, control, and censorship, and the only way to do that was by force.

Out of the later Franco-Algerian struggle, Frantz Fanon wrote that "The first necessity is the reestablishment of the nation in order to give life to national culture in the strictly biological sense. . . . The

---

aptation of the Momotarō legend. Dower, *War Without Mercy*, 251–57, is excellent on the multiple uses of Momotarō in the Japanese war effort (see also illustration, 198).

[61] Re "orphan," see note 35 above; Constantino, *Neo-Colonial Identity*, 253.

struggle for freedom . . . aims at a fundamentally different set of relations between men. . . . After the conflict there is not only the
disappearance of colonialism but also the disappearance of the colonized man."[62] Jean-Paul Sartre adopted Fanon's psychological arguments and threatened his fellow Frenchmen that they must join
those making history, or die: "No gentleness can efface the marks
of violence; only violence itself can destroy them. The native cures
himself of colonial neurosis by thrusting out the settler through
force of arms. When his rage boils over, he rediscovers his lost in-
nocence and he comes to know himself in that he himself creates
his self."[63] In Sartre, however, there is something of the bookworm
at the blackboard, militant with chalk.

It is an odd pose, to daub oneself like Sartre, with secondhand
philosophic blood. Real blood, some Indonesians not only shed, but
drank. Surabaya pemuda slew Japanese captives and sipped their
blood from the samurai swords they had used, as an elixir of courage. Indonesian irregulars from Aceh did the same to Gurkha soldiers.[64] Stories of Javanese drinking Dutch blood are hard to find.[65]
Perhaps it was less likely to be reported, as too politically embar-
rassing. Or perhaps the Dutch were being reserved for a postcolonial
mythic role, as Gurkhas need not be, nor even Japanese. When the
Dutch queen came visiting, years later, she saw great crowds of
smiling faces. Even after ibu pertiwi triumphed, and perhaps because of it, there remained psychological room for a colonial
mother, or father, from a shed past.

[62] Frantz Fanon, *The Wretched of the Earth* (New York: Grove Press, 1966). Fanon
says that "national consciousness . . . is the most elaborate form of culture" (198). I
believe, however, that if national consciousness does produce the most elaborate
forms of *power*, the highest expressions of *culture* nonetheless seek to transcend
those forms.

[63] Ibid., Sartre's introduction, p. 18.

[64] Benedict R. O'Gorman Anderson, *Java in a Time of Revolution: Occupation and
Resistance, 1944–1945* (Ithaca: Cornell University Press, 1972), 155n; C.L.M. Pen-
ders, ed., *Mohammad Hatta, Indonesian Patriot: Memoirs* (Singapore: Gunung
Agung, 1981), 255.

The meanings of ritual cannibalism are well defined in Peggy Reeves Sanday, *Divine Hunger· Cannibalism as a Cultural System* (New York· Cambridge University
Press, 1986). Problems of subordination and equality are nicely resolved by drinking
the blood of the powerful "other," particularly if the other's warrior attributes are
desirable to ingest and add to one's own. This motivation is totally different, of
course, from the dire absence of food that drove some Japanese soldiers to eat their
own dead (see note 19 above).

[65] Abu Hanifah's blood-drinking anecdotes in *Tales of a Revolution* are one of Japanese blood, and one of "spies" whose nationality is unclear (179, 180).

CONCLUSION

Revolution involves more, and less, than violence. A British general passed a twelve-year-old Indonesian boy leaning asleep against a wall with a rifle on his shoulder. "That is revolution," he said.[66] Even if the gun were never fired, even though the boy's eyes were closed with fatigue, he acknowledged no imperial master. The boy wished to grow up a man, not a servant in his own land.

EMPIRE, LIBERTY, AND MUTUAL BONDING

Montaigne's beloved friend, Etienne de la Boétie, wrote four centuries ago in sustained astonishment at the human capacity for voluntary servitude. Tyrants prevail, and masses collude in their prevalence. Why is it? "Liberty is the only joy upon which men do not seem to insist. . . . Apparently they refuse this wonderful privilege because it is so easily acquired."[67]

The irony flattens out when we observe the superior might of imperial armies; how difficult it was in Southeast Asia to oppose Western firepower, and the technology and organization that accompanied it. Only the Japanese succeeded, by imitating. They then failed by overreaching. Out of the litter and carnage arose revolution and restoration.

As the British and Dutch attempted imperial restoration in Java, they interrogated General Yamamoto at length. They extracted from him finally that he had had the power to stop executions, and to commute sentences, and that he was responsible "for all execution carried out during [his] governor-generalship." In extenuation, Yamamoto pleaded total ignorance of any atrocities committed by the Kenpeitai, of which he only heard after the war ended. The interrogator pressed his point. "So you were Lord of life and death in Java?" Yamamoto demurred.[68]

A cheerful, able, military politician, Yamamoto made a poor Siva. In Java there was no single "Lord of life and death." The notion itself is mythic. The Japanese as invaders had collectively stolen the godlike attributes of the Dutch. Many individuals among them exercised power harshly. Yamamoto was no worse than most and better than many; not a fiend but a calculator, less a scourge than a

---

[66] *Hatta Memoirs*, 255.

[67] Etienne de la Boétie, *The Politics of Obedience: The Discourse of Voluntary Servitude*, ed. Murray Rothbard, trans. Harry Kurz, (New York: Free Life Editions, 1975), 51.

[68] Yamamoto interrogation, RVO 16898-904. Yamamoto, of course, was not a "Governor General," but he likened himself to one, and the interrogator took him up on it.

bureaucrat. If as chief of military administration he had the arms of Siva, he used them to cover his eyes and ears against things he did not wish to know. To pursue the analogy in Hindu iconography, he did not resemble Bhairava, god of dread and terror, so much as Andhaka, the blind demon ultimately defeated by Siva, his procreator.[69]

In the power vacuum—the god-vacuum?—of Japanese surrender, revolution broke out. Indonesians seized the liberty that no power was strong enough to deny them. "All of us had thought," Admiral Shibata recalled, "that the Indonesians were a docile race and were not capable of such radical and violent behavior. We were wrong. Even now I believe that once the Indonesians started to riot, there was nothing we could have done to stop them."[70]

How explain the contrasting behavior of the Filipinos vis-à-vis Americans? An argument from the power circumstances in 1945 and the independence scheduled for 1946 will not suffice. The presence of American forces, the imminent realization of American promises, cannot explain Filipino behavior during the previous three and a half years of Japanese occupation. The Filipino president of the Historical Conservation Society sees this as testimony to the feelings of a population "colonized with love" and remembering its colonial past with kindness. In both the Spanish and the American periods, despite phases of violence and individual failings, "the general policy was one of loving assimilation."[71]

If those daring remarks be true, there still remains plenty of room to observe the shallow qualities of American restoration policy. Senator Robert Taft, with a patrician lordliness like his father's, said that the United States "shall always be a big brother" to the "Philippine Islands." But Taft was answered even before he spoke. While dying of tuberculosis in 1944, Manuel Quezon expressed his resentment of the Manila Americans and neoimperialists on MacArthur's staff. "Tell our people," he said privately to one who would live to return, " . . . that those *hijos de putas* will not get away with making fools of them. . . . *Puneta!* They think we're *their little brown brothers*. The condescending bastards."[72]

---

[69] Pictorial and thematic evocations abound in the richly suggestive books by Stella Kramrisch: *The Presence of Siva* (Princeton: Princeton University Press, 1981), e.g., 374–83; and *Manifestations of Shiva* (Philadelphia Museum of Art, 1981), 30–39.

[70] Reid and Oki, eds., *Japanese Experience in Indonesia*, 372.

[71] Quotations from Alfonso Felix, Jr., to the author, August 19, 1985.

[72] Taft in *Congressional Record*, April 12, 1946, p. 3537; Quezon in Villamor, *They Never Surrendered*, 236.

CONCLUSION

Binational restoration and three more decades of ambiguity moved a Filipina critic to write: "Those who survived Japanese hate did not survive American love. Both were equally deadly; the latter more so because sought and longed for."[73] The sting and meaning of that remark would require another book to analyze. Only partly do the worlds of love and power interpenetrate. Only in narratives of the gods are they identical.

To return to the language of power: Indonesian revolt and Filipino reversion were the measures of two different styles of repression, Dutch and American, when displaced by a third, that of the Japanese. The stakes were sovereignty. When a presumptive social revolution appeared to threaten the struggle for sovereignty, as at Madiun in 1948, or to displace a newly won sovereignty, as through the postwar Huks in Central Luzon, it was crushed by the national leadership. Sovereignty always has a blood cost. Acephalous organisms do not evolve; neither do states without leaders. All leadership contains an element of lordship, and of the sword. To master one's own people may become as difficult and deadly as to master another.

In time the hotels and statues of the Marcos regime came to recall the monuments of the Sukarno regime. Indonesia conquered and colonized weak neighbors in Irian Jaya and Timor. It policed itself in a style reminiscent of the Dutch, and occasionally the Japanese, with regard to Marxist cells and Islamic radicals. Under martial law the Philippines drew on Indonesian examples of authoritarian government, militarized bureaucracy, and police surveillance, while Indonesia proceeded in part from precolonial archetypes of rule and repression.

After the master-servant relationships of the Western neo-mercantile empires departed, the phenomenon of lord and bondsman clearly remained. Partly it was an internalized mirroring of the imperial afterimage; increasingly it expressed indigenous cultural archetypes. Latent traditions emerged even as modern socioeconomic development progressed.

In the long-term future, ways in which the cultures of Java and Luzon will manifest and revitalize themselves—and by extension, Indonesia and the Philippines—are largely unpredictable. The particular forms of internal lordship and bondage that have prevailed in the early postcolonial decades may soften in some ways, harden

[73] Carmen Guerrero-Nakpil, *A Question of Identity*, quoted by Cristina Pantoja Hidalgo, *The Manila Review* 1, no. 1a (1975), 109.

in others.[74] But it is clear that only in an epochal sense can colonizer and colonized ever be "completely cured."[75] The error is to think that a mode of healing can be final. What happens? Relationships become so altered, vectors so varied, and identities so transformed, that we speak of a new era.

But we can not simply eject power from human systems, and inject love, let alone substitute the qualities of individual love. "When force changes hands it still remains a relation of stronger to weaker, a relation of dominance. It can go on changing hands indefinitely, without a single term of the relationship being eliminated."[76] History is inescapable, and with it the changing identities of the dominant and dependent. To reverse roles is to transpose positions, but not to banish imbalances from the human condition.

An inescapable part of the phenomenology of the spirit is to be completed in another than oneself. In an age past, the colonized needed the colonizer as model and antithesis, just as the colonizer needed the colonized as admirer and servant. In whatever terms may illuminate the discourse of the future, in whatever subtle dialectic may be produced by new processes of global differentiation of energies, the terms lord and bondsman will be anachronistic. The colors of the eyes of the imperial enemy will change, and so will the colors of skin of the subjugated, but the fact of dominance and the appetite for liberation will persist. Even so, on both sides of relationships defined by a difference in power, and even amid inevitable striving, folly, and bloody error, a tragic faith must include a hope for crucial acts of benevolence—the hope that in each the insight that completion inheres in the other may lead to apt forms and moments of love, redeeming bits of time from the carnage of history.

[74] Soedjatmoko to the author, August 21, 1985, stresses that the de-Westernization of institutions in the last thirty years may come to appear irrelevant, in fifty or a hundred years, to the creation of new indigenous institutions.

[75] Albert Memmi, *The Colonizer and the Colonized* (Boston: Beacon Press, 1965), mandates a cure, but without a prescription; quotation, 147.

[76] Simone Weil, "Fragments, London 1943," in *Oppression and Liberty*, 158.

THE SOURCES

A BIBLIOGRAPHIC ESSAY

The selective brief assessments that follow are arranged under categorical headings appropriate to this study. Many works cited in footnotes are not listed here; but some works not elsewhere cited are here included, because of their influence on my thinking or their possible significance to others.

My paper for the Woodrow Wilson International Center for Scholars includes a historiographical appendix on major books about insular Southeast Asia during and after the Second World War (East Asia Program, Occasional Paper No. 19, June 1984, pp. 52–70).

Published Analytical and Interpretative Work

Perspective

For strengthening an ontological understanding of history, I am indebted to the writings of Eric Voegelin. The most accessible introduction to his work is *Anamnesis*, trans. and ed. Gerhart Niemeyer (Notre Dame, Ind.: University of Notre Dame Press, 1978). Wolfgang J. Mommsen's *Theories of Imperialism*, trans. P. S. Falla (Chicago: University of Chicago Press, 1982) is a terse and penetrating survey of the late nineteenth century to the present. Reinhold Niebuhr, *The Structure of Nations and Empires* (New York: Charles Scribner's Sons, 1959) is still valuable for tracing community and the anatomy of dominion from Egyptian to modern times.

Orlando Patterson's *Slavery and Social Death: A Comparative Study* (Cambridge: Harvard University Press, 1982), and *Slavery, Bondage and Dependency in Southeast Asia*, ed. Anthony Reid (New York: St. Martin's Press, 1983), astutely treat degrees of human "thingness," alienation, and caste degradation. Each is sensitive to cross-cultural settings; and Patterson has a splendid command of institutional dialectics.

Shlomo Avineri's introduction to *Karl Marx on Colonialism and*

Modernization (Garden City, N.Y.: Doubleday, 1968) stresses the transformations seen and foreseen by Marx, in a Hegelian tradition of understanding dialectical energies in social development. Of Marx's exaggerated explanatory stress on economics, and his under-appreciation of the complexity of the forms of power and domi-nance, Simone Weil is a brilliant critic in *Oppression and Liberty*, trans. Arthur Wills and John Petrie (Amherst: University of Massa-chusetts Press, 1973).

In understanding Hegel on lordship and bondage I have found par-ticularly helpful George Armstrong Kelly, *Hegel's Retreat from Eleusis* (Princeton: Princeton University Press, 1978), and Judith Shklar, *Freedom and Independence: A Study of Hegel's Phenome-nology of Mind* (Cambridge: Harvard University Press, 1976). The most useful text is G.W.F. Hegel, *The Phenomenology of Mind*, trans. and ed. J. B. Baillie, George Lichtheim, intro. (New York: Har-per and Row, 1967).

The literature on ethology and sociobiology is diffuse in theory and hot with dispute. While useful insights arise in Konrad Lorenz, *On Aggression* (New York: Harcourt Brace & World, 1966), the im-plications of the two fields for the study of humans are skeptically assessed in Ashley Montagu et al., *Man and Aggression*, 2d ed. (New York: Oxford University Press, 1973), and Montagu et al., *So-ciobiology Examined* (New York: Oxford University Press, 1980).

On the psycho-cultural and psycho-political phenomena of colo-nialism, three studies from the French context are, in ascending or-der of value: Frantz Fanon, *The Wretched of the Earth*, trans. Con-stance Farrington (New York: Grove Press, 1966); Albert Memmi, *The Colonizer and the Colonized* (Boston: Beacon Press, 1967); and O. Mannoni, *Prospero and Caliban*, trans. Pamela Powesland (New York: Praeger, 1968). Philip Mason developed thoughts both contra-puntal with and contradictory to those of Mannoni, using a range of examples from English colonial experience and images from English literature, in *Prospero's Magic* (London: Oxford University Press, 1962).

For explicit psychological interpretations with a doctrinal base, P. M. van Wulfften Palthe, *Psychological Aspects of the Indonesian Problem* (Leiden: E. J. Brill, 1949), offers a Freudian inspection, and Justus M. van der Kroef, *Indonesian Social Evolution: Some Psy-chological Considerations* (Amsterdam: C.P.J. van der Pelt, 1958), tenders a Jungian outlook. Both are provocative. To understand a wide range of political, economic, and military phenomena, how-ever, requires more empiricism in taste and more eclecticism in theory than theirs.

Of the relevant literature on revolution, I have found most valuable Chalmers Johnson, *Revolutionary Change*, 2d ed. (Stanford: Stanford University Press, 1982); Theda Skocpol, *States and Social Revolutions: A Comparative Analysis of France, Russia, and China* (Cambridge, 1979); and Mark Hagopian, *The Phenomenon of Revolution* (New York: Dodd, Mead, 1974). Except for Robert A. Kann, *The Problem of Restoration: A Study in Comparative Political History* (Berkeley: University of California Press, 1968), there is little systematic work on that subject. I have brought such readings to bear in my paper, "Revolution and Restoration: Indonesia and the Philippines as Paired Opposites, 1945–1949," presented to the Ninth Conference of the International Association of Historians of Asia, Manila, November 1983.

International History and Comparative Method

Ernest May, "Writing Contemporary International History," *Diplomatic History* 8 (1984): 103–13, states the problems and sets a high tone. I agree with the spirit of Raymond Grew, "The Case for Comparing Histories," *The American Historical Review* 85, no. 4 (1980): 763–78, and with the perspective supplied by Soedjatmoko in his critique, "Eurocentrism in the Global Context," an address (December 16, 1982) given at the Free University of Amsterdam, MS available through U.N. University, Tokyo.

Illuminating in comparative method is the essay by Robin Winks, "Imperialism," in C. Vann Woodward, ed., *The Comparative Approach to American History* (New York: Basic Books, 1968). Two classic examples of bilateral comparison, now dated, are J. S. Furnivall, *Colonial Policy and Practice* (New York: New York University Press, 1956) on Burma and the Netherlands East Indies; and Rupert Emerson, *Malaysia* (New York: Macmillan, 1937), which also uses the Indies for comparison. Clifford Geertz, *Islam Observed: Religious Development in Morocco and Indonesia* (New Haven: Yale University Press, 1968), is stimulating, and suggests the need for analogous work on Philippine Catholicism.

Bernhard Dahm compares the Philippines prior to 1898, and its "premature revolution" (*die aufgezwungene Revolution*), with Indonesia prior to 1942, and its "retarded revolution" (*die verzogerte Revolution*), in *Emanzipationsversuche von Kolonialer Herrschaft in Südostasien: Die Philippinen und Indonesien, ein Vergleich* (Attempted emancipation from colonial rule in Southeast Asia: the Philippines and Indonesia, a comparison) (Wiesbaden: Otto Harrassowitz, 1974). Michael Adas, *Prophets of Rebellion: Millennarian*

Protest Movements Against the European Colonial Order (Chapel Hill: University of North Carolina Press, 1979), is worth noting for the breadth of its five examples (including Indonesia and Burma), and for the definitions and discoveries flowing from its structure.

Modern Southeast Asian History

The best text is David Joel Steinberg et al., *In Search of Southeast Asia*, rev. ed. (Honolulu: University of Hawaii Press, 1987). A sophisticated view of the field is represented by O. W. Wolters, *History, Culture and Region in Southeast Asian Perspectives* (Singapore: Institute of Southeast Asian Studies, 1982). The state of Southeast Asian studies is brightly represented in Anthony Reid and David Marr, eds., *Perceptions of the Past in Southeast Asia* (Singapore: Heinemann, 1979), and in David K. Wyatt and Alexander Woodside, eds., *Moral Order and the Question of Change: Essays on Southeast Asian Thought,* Yale University Southeast Asia Studies, Monograph Series, no. 24 (New Haven, 1982). Requirements for further progress in the field are presented in Ronald Morse, ed., *Southeast Asian Studies: Options for the Future* (Washington, D.C.: University Press of America, 1984).

Modern Indonesian and Philippine History

Continuity and Change in Southeast Asia: Collected Journal Articles of Harry J. Benda, Yale University Southeast Asia Studies, Monograph Series, no. 18 (New Haven, 1972) is still excellent for Indonesian specifics. Once useful short histories by J. D. Legge, *Indonesia* (1965), and O. D. Corpuz, *The Philippines* (1966), both published in Englewood Cliffs, N.J., by Prentice-Hall, are now succeeded by Bernhard Dahm, *The History of Indonesia in the Twentieth Century* (London and New York: Praeger, 1971); Merle Rickleffs, *History of Indonesia* (Bloomington: Indiana University Press, 1981); Renato Constantino, *A History of the Philippines* (New York: Monthly Review Press, 1975); and David J. Steinberg, *The Philippines: A Singular and a Plural Place* (Boulder, Colo.: Westview, 1982). John A. Larkin, "Philippine History Reconsidered: A Socioeconomic Perspective," *American Historical Review* 87, no. 3 (1982): 595–628, is a basic historiographical essay. For understanding social change in twentieth-century Java, two recent works stand together with an older one: Koentjaraningrat, *Javanese Culture* (Singapore: Oxford University Press, 1985); Sartono Kartodirdjo, *Modern Indonesia: Tradition and Transformation* (Yogyakarta:

Gadjah Mada University Press, 1984); and Selosoemardjan, *Social Changes in Jogjakarta* (Ithaca: Cornell University Press, 1962).

Two collaborative volumes treat key phenomena region-wide: Alfred W. McCoy, ed., *Southeast Asia under Japanese Occupation*, Yale University Southeast Asia Studies, Monograph Series, no. 22 (New Haven, 1980) and Robin Jeffrey, ed., *Asia—The Winning of Independence* (New York: St. Martin's Press, 1981). I look at the wartime period through current regional perspective in "Filipin Shinseiken no Sentaku: Kenishugi no Saikōchiku wa Kanōka?" (Choices before the new Philippine regime: can authority be reestablished?), trans. Miwa Kimitada, *Chūō Kōron*, September 1986, 213–22.

On the occupation and revolution in Indonesia: Benedict R. O'G. Anderson, *Java in a Time of Revolution: Occupation and Resistance, 1944–1946* (Ithaca: Cornell University Press, 1972) is excellent; George S. Kanahele's Ph.D. dissertation, "The Japanese Occupation of Indonesia: Prelude to Independence," Cornell University, 1967, touches events throughout the archipelago; Bernhard Dahm, *Sukarno and the Struggle for Indonesian Independence* (Ithaca: Cornell University Press, 1969), and Harry J. Benda, *The Crescent and the Rising Sun: Indonesian Islam Under the Japanese Occupation, 1942–1945* (The Hague and Bandung: W. van Hoeve, 1958) are authorities in their domains. Lev Mikhailovich Demin, *Iaponskaia Occupatsiia Indonezii* (The Japanese occupation of the Philippines) (Moscow, 1963) features the triumph of "national democratic anti-fascist forces" over Japanese and Western imperialism. Similar historic forces are frustrated in G. I. Levinson, *Die Philippinen gestern und heute* (The Philippines yesterday and today) (Berlin: Akademie-Verlag, 1966), translated by Willy Steltner from two Russian volumes published in Moscow in 1958 and 1959. Anthony Reid, *The Indonesian National Revolution, 1945–1950* (Hawthorn: Longman Australia, 1974) is a provocative short synthesis. George McT. Kahin, *Nationalism and Revolution in Indonesia*, 2d ed. (Ithaca: Cornell University Press, 1970) is a pioneer work still valuable for detail. Audrey R. Kahin, ed., *Regional Dynamics of the Indonesian Revolution* (Honolulu: University of Hawaii Press, 1985) carries authoritative study into local specifics.

For contributing and competitive currents of revolution see Sartono Kartodirdjo, "Agrarian Radicalism in Java: Its Setting and Development," in Claire Holt, ed., *Culture and Politics in Indonesia* (Ithaca: Cornell University Press, 1972), 71–125; Soe Hok-gie, "Simpang kiri dari sebuah djalan" (The left fork in the road), M.A. thesis, University of Indonesia, 1969; Karl D. Jackson, *Traditional*

Authority, Islam, and Rebellion (Berkeley: University of California Press, 1980); and C. Van Dijk, *Rebellion Under the Banner of Islam: The Darul Islam in Indonesia* (The Hague: Martinus Nijhoff, 1981).

On the occupation and restoration in the Philippines: Teodoro Agoncillo, *The Fateful Years: Japan's Adventure in the Philippines, 1941–1945*, 2 vols. (Quezon City: R. P. Garcia, 1965) is a comprehensive narrative; David Joel Steinberg, *Philippine Collaboration in World War II* (Ann Arbor: University of Michigan Press, 1967) is acute; and the reliable articles of Grant Goodman on Philippine-Japanese relations are too many to list here.

Stephen Rosskamm Shalom, *The United States and the Philippines: A Study of Neocolonialism* (Philadelphia: Institute for the Study of Human Issues, 1981) is closely researched, but much more may be learned about the Philippines from Reynaldo Ileto, *Pasyon and Revolution: Popular Movements in the Philippines, 1840–1910* (Quezon City: Ateneo de Manila, 1979); David Sturtevant, *Popular Uprisings in the Philippines, 1840–1940* (Ithaca: Cornell University Press, 1976); Benedict J. Kerkvliet, *The Huk Rebellion: A Study of Peasant Revolt in the Philippines* (Berkeley: University of California Press, 1977); and Eduardo Lachica, *Huk: Philippine Agrarian Society in Revolt* (Manila: Solidaridad, 1971).

Biographies and personal writings of major figures include: J. D. Legge, *Sukarno: A Political Biography*, 2d ed. (Boston and Sydney: Allen and Unwin, 1984), which is balanced, and a necessary corrective to *Sukarno: An Autobiography*, as told to Cindy Adams (Indianapolis: Bobbs-Merrill, 1965). M. S. Kapitsa and N. P. Maletin, *Sukarno: Politicheskaia biographiia* (Sukarno: a political biography) (Moscow: Mysl, 1980) pictures a Third World revolutionary leader with some petit-bourgeois failings. My paper, " 'Menjadi Banteng': Sukarno's Wartime Rhetoric and Its Aims, 1942–1945" (delivered to the Association for Asian Studies' regional meeting, Philadelphia, October 1983) covers a subject only swiftly treated in this book. A memoir edited by C.L.M. Penders, *Mohammad Hatta: Indonesian Patriot* (Singapore: Gunung Agung, 1981), is useful, taken together with Deliar Noer, ed., *Portrait of a Patriot: Selected Writings by Mohammad Hatta* (The Hague: Mouton, 1971) and *Bung Hatta's Answers* (Singapore: Gunung Agung, 1981), containing interviews with Dr. Z. Yasni. Sjahrir is well expressed through his philosophic letters and terse reminiscences in *Out of Exile*, trans. Charles Wolf (New York: John Day, 1949), and by *Our Struggle*, trans. Benedict R. O'G. Anderson, Cornell Modern Indonesia Project Publications, no. 44 (Ithaca, 1968).

Filipino wartime and restoration leaders are represented and defended in: Teodoro A. Agoncillo, *The Burden of Proof: the Vargas-Laurel Collaboration Case; with Jorge B. Vargas' 'Sugamo Diary'* (Quezon City: University of the Philippines Press, 1984); [Jose Lansang, ed.] *War Memoirs of Dr. Jose P. Laurel* (Manila: Laurel Memorial Foundation, 1962); Armando J. Malay, *Occupied Philippines: The Role of Jorge B. Vargas During the Japanese Occupation* (Manila: Filipiniana Book Guild, 1967); and in Malay's introduction to *Memoirs of General Artemio Ricarte* (Manila: National Heroes Commission, 1963); Claro M. Recto, *Three Years of Enemy Occupation: The Issue of Political Collaboration* (Manila: People's Publishers, 1946); and Marcial Lichauco, *Roxas* (Manila: n.p., 1952).

Japanese Expansion, Imperial Policy, and Their Consequences

Kawashima Shin'ichi has compiled *Tōnan Ajia Hōbun Shiryō Mokuroku* (Bibliography on Southeast Asian materials in the Japanese language, 1946–1983) (Tokyo: Japan Orientalist Librarians Group, 1985), an excellent starting point. Harry Wray and Hilary Conroy, eds., *Japan Examined: Perspectives on Modern Japanese History* (Honolulu: University of Hawaii Press, 1983) contains numerous relevant contributions and bibliographic leads on important themes. Akira Iriye, *Power and Culture: The Japanese–American War, 1941–1945* (Cambridge: Harvard University Press, 1981) is a lucid study of war objectives, concrete and symbolic, with a valuable bibliography. John W. Dower, *War Without Mercy: Race and Power in the Pacific War* (New York: Pantheon Books, 1986) is excellent on ethnopsychological demonism. Christopher Thorne brings earlier studies to comprehensive focus in *The Issue of War: States, Societies and the Far Eastern Conflict of 1941–1945* (New York: Oxford University Press, 1985).

Of a number of books justifying Japan's motives and conduct in the Second World War, Hattori Takushirō, *Dai Tōa sensō zenshi* (Complete history of the Greater East Asian War) (Tokyo: Masu Shobō, 1953) is a detailed account of military courage. Tsunoda Jun, *Taiheiyō sensō e no michi* (The Road to the Pacific War), 8 vols. (Tokyo: Asahi Shinbunsha, 1962–63) contains contributions that seek to shift guilt and responsibility from Japan; and Ueyama Shumpei, *Dai Tōa sensō no imi* (The meaning of the Greater East Asian War) (Tokyo: Chūō Kōronsha, 1964), sorts interpretations under a prevailing tone of nostalgia. Kojima Noboru's biography of

General Yamashita Tomoyuki, *Shisetsu Yamashita Tomoyuki* (Tokyo: Bungei Shunju, 1979) is a more recent vehicle for such review.

Ienaga Saburō, *The Pacific War, 1931–1945: A Critical Perspective on Japan's Role in World War II* (New York: Pantheon, 1978) eloquently establishes an interpretative tone contrary to that of those defending the war. Imai Seiichi et al., *Taiheiyō sensō-shi*, 5 vols. (Tokyo: Aoki Shoten, 1972–1973) finds occupation policies "blatantly imperialistic" (4;182). Kamiyama Shumpei, *Daitōa sensō no isan* (Tokyo: Chūō Kōronsha, 1972) asserts that it was "more a war for colonial reorganization than a war for colonial liberation" (75–76).

Nanpō no Gunsei (Military administration in the Southern Area) (Tokyo: Chōun Shimbunsha, 1985) is an authoritative collection of documents, essays, and tables with a chronology and bibliography, edited by the War History Division of the Japanese Defense Agency. Among useful works on a more specific level are: Historical Documents Section of the Defense Agency, *Hitō Kōryaku sakusen* (Strategy for invasion of the Philippines) (Tokyo: Chōun Shimbunsha, 1966); and Saka Kuniyasu, ed., *Hitōsen to sono sensō saiban* (The war in the Philippines and the war trials) (Tokyo: Tōchōsha, 1967).

Ramon H. Myers and Mark R. Peattie, eds., *The Japanese Colonial Empire, 1895–1945* (Princeton: Princeton University Press, 1984) concentrates on Korea, Taiwan, Kwantung, and Micronesia. Although it does not touch Southeast Asia, its global and historical perspectives are superb. Other studies contributing to the missing part of the picture are: Josef Silverstein, ed., *Southeast Asia in World War II*, Yale University Southeast Asia Studies (New Haven, 1966); Grant K. Goodman, ed., *Imperial Japan and Asia: A Reassessment* (New York: Columbia University, East Asian Institute, 1967); Joyce C. Lebra, *Japanese-Trained Armies in Southeast Asia* (New York: Columbia University Press, 1977); and William H. Newell, ed., *Japan in Asia* (Singapore: Singapore University Press, 1981).

L.E.L. Sluimers, *Samurai, Pemuda, und Sakdalista: Die Japaner und der Radikalismus in Indonesien und der Philippinen, 1941–1945* (Samurai, pemuda and sakdalista: the Japanese and radicalism in Indonesia and the Philippines, 1941–1945) (Amsterdam: University of Amsterdam, Anthropology/Sociology Center, 1972) contains interesting comparisons of Japanese tactical efforts to "spiritualize" nonestablishment persons and groups. Barbara Gifford Shimer, Guy Hobbs, and I collaborated on, and they translated, *The Kenpeitai in Java and Sumatra*, Cornell Modern Indonesia Project, Translation Series, no. 65 (Ithaca, 1986).

A richly textured study of the Japanese advance on and presence in Indonesia is Gōto Ken'ichi, *Shōwaki Nippon to Indonesia* (Japan and Indonesia in the Showa Era) (Tokyo: Keisō Shobō, 1986). In a comprehensive collection, Rinjirō Sodei, ed., *Sekaishi Ni Okeru Nihon Senryō* (The Allied occupation of Japan in world history) (Tokyo: Nihon Hyōronsha, 1985), there occur essays on the Philippines by Renato Constantino and Grant Goodman, as well as Takahashi Akira's "Philippine Occupation," which considers that "one of the most dreadful" of all occupations.

Japanese memoirs are a rich and increasingly accessible source. An invaluable starting point, well edited by Anthony Reid and Oki Akira, is *The Japanese Experience in Indonesia: Selected Memoirs of 1942–1945*, Southeast Asia Series, no. 72 (Athens: Ohio University Center for International Studies, 1986). The most significant memoirs of top level military administrators are Yamamoto Moichirō's *Kaisōroku* (Memoirs) (Tokyo: Yamamoto Akiko, 1978), and *Watakushi no Indonesia* (My recollections of Indonesia) (Tokyo: Indonesia Kyokai, 1979), neither of which are included in Reid and Oki; and Utsunomiya Naotaka's "Minami Jūjisei O Nozomitsutsu" (Looking at the Southern Cross), an excerpt on the Philippines in *Shiryosho Nanpō no Gunsei*, 500–516, from his 1982 autobiography.

Ōshima Kazuko has translated for me in full the Javanese parts of *Imamura Hitoshi Taishō Kaisōroku* (The reminiscences of General Imamura Hitoshi) 7 vols. to date (Tokyo: Jiyū Ajiasha, 1960–); some of his recollections, written in Dutch jails, are translated as "A Tapir in Prison," RVO 002460. Ōshima also translated the recollections of Miyoshi Shunkichirō, written on shipboard, 1945, and published in their most complete form as "Jawa senryō gunsei kaikoroku" (Memoirs of the military administration of occupied Java) in *Kokusai Mondai* 61–82 (April 1965–January 1967). Other memoirs include Machida Keiichi, *Tatakau Bunka Butai* (Cultural Fighting Squad) (Tokyo: Harashobō, 1967), an account by the chief of propaganda in Java; and Tamura Yoshio, ed., *Hiroku Daitōa senshi: Ranin-hen* (A confidential history of the Greater East Asian War— Netherlands East Indies) (Tokyo: Fujishoen, 1953), by journalistic observers. Nakamura Hiroshi's forty-three pages of recollections (RVO 04833) are coy and exhibitionistic, but still useful.

Fukushima Shintarō, ed., *Murata Shōzō: Ikō hitō-nikki* (Posthumous Philippine diaries) (Shinjuku: Hara-shobō, 1969) is the most complete published version of what the wartime Japanese ambassador wrote. Briefer, and more subject to diplomatic editing, is Ito Takeo, ed., *Murata Shōzō Tsuisōroku* (Osaka: Isaja Shosen Kabushiki-gaisha, 1959). Selections from Takéuchi Tatsuji's "Manila Diary," translated by himself, appear in Theodore Friend, ed., *The Philippine Polity: A Japanese View*, Yale University Southeast Asia Studies (New Haven, 1968), 209–85. Morton J. Netzorg is working on a revised edition of *The Philippines in World War II and to Independence (December 8, 1941–July 4, 1946): An Annotated Bibliography*, Cornell University Southeast Asia Program, Data Paper no. 105 (Ithaca, 1977).

Dutch Colonialism

Hubertus Johannes van Mook, *Past and Future in the Netherlands Indies* (New York: Netherlands Information Bureau, 1945) expresses Dutch views and intentions in the spring before Hiroshima, peace, and revolution. His *Indonesië, Nederland en de wereld* (Indonesia, Netherlands, and the world) (Batavia: De Brug Opbouw, 1949), and *The Stakes of Democracy in Southeast Asia* (New York: Norton, 1950) reassessed the situation. Henri Baudet and I. J. Brugmans, eds., *Balans van Beleid* (Assen: van Gorcum, 1961) collects informed analysis and nostalgic justification, mainly by former colonial officials. Baudet's "The Netherlands After the Loss of Empire," *Journal of Contemporary History* 4 (1969): 127–40 describes an economically vigorous, politically reoriented Netherlands that has finally achieved a postcolonial outlook. *Between People and Statistics: Essays on Modern Indonesian History Presented to P. Creutzberg* (The Hague: Martinus Nijhoff, 1979) contains a number of fine essays, mostly by Dutch nationals, written from a postcolonial perspective.

American Colonialism

John Bresnan, ed., *Crisis in the Philippines: The Marcos Era and Beyond* (Princeton: Princeton University Press, 1986) contains valuable essays on the whole range of the Philippine-American relationship. Peter Stanley et al., *Reappraising an Empire* (Cambridge: Harvard University Council on East Asian Studies, 1984) has useful specialized articles. Theodore Friend, *Between Two Empires* (New Haven: Yale University Press, 1965) is still central for understanding the period 1929–41.

For an Indian nationalist angle, Usha Mahajani is interesting: *Philippine Nationalism, External Challenge and Filipino Response, 1565–1946* (St. Lucia: University of Queensland Press, 1971). Antonio Molina, *Historia de Filipinas*, 2 vols. (Madrid: Instituto de Cooperacion Iberoamericana, 1984), looks at the American and Japanese periods dispassionately from a Hispano-Catholic perspective. Nick Joaquin, *The Aquinos of Tarlac* (Manila: Cacho Hermanos, 1983), is provocative throughout on the "anti-sajonista" (anti-Saxon) currents in twentieth-century Philippine history.

Published Documentary Sources

The Netherlands Historical Society established a Publications Committee for Netherlands Indies Historical Sources, 1900–1942, which produced twelve volumes, dense with information and rich in editorial apparatus, between 1963 and 1982. The first four volumes were edited by Professor S. L. van der Wal: *Het onderwijsbeleid in Nederlands-Indië, 1900–1940* (Educational policy in the Netherlands East Indies, 1900–1940); *De volksraad en de staatkundige ontwikkeling van Nederlands-Indië* (The Volksraad and the political development of the Netherlands Indies), in two volumes, covering 1891–1926 (vol. 1) and 1927–1942 (vol. 2); and *De opkomst van de nationalistische beweging in Nederlands-Indië* (The rise of the nationalist movement in the Netherlands East Indies). All four were published in Groningen by Wolters in 1963, 1964, 1965, and 1967.

The next four volumes, edited by Piet Creutzberg, are titled *Het ekonomisch belied in Nederlandsch-Indië* (Economic Policy in the Netherlands East Indies) and were published in Groningen by Tjeenk Willink in 1972, 1974, and 1975. The final four volumes, edited by Drs. R. C. Kwantes, *De ontwikkeling van de nationalistische beweging in Nederlandsch-Indië* (Development of the nationalist movement in the Netherland-Indies), cover 1917–1923 (vol. 1), 1923–1928 (vol. 2), 1928–1933 (vol. 3), and 1933–1942 (vol. 4). Volume 1 (1975) was published in Groningen by Tjeenk Willink; volumes 2 (1978), 3 (1981), and 4 (1982) were published in that city by Wolters-Nordhoff.

By government commission, Professor van der Wal also edited, from 1969 until his death, the series entitled *Officiële Beschieden Betreffende de Nederlands-Indonesische Betrekkingen 1945–1950* (Official documents concerning Netherlands-Indonesia relations, 1945–1950) (The Hague: Martinus Nijhoff, 1971–79). The eight volumes thus far published cover August 10, 1945 to May 20, 1947.

No such American effort exists for the Philippines, although in the regular Department of State series, *Foreign Relations of the United States*, Philippine problems appear with increasing frequency beginning in the late 1930s. University Publications of

America (1987) has produced thirty-five microfilm reels and a printed guide on *Confidential U.S. State Department Central Files, The Philippine Republic: Internal and Foreign Affairs, 1945–1949.*

For the Netherlands East Indies, the most useful sources of prewar statistical data are: *Jaarcijfers voor het Koninkrijk der Nederlanden, Kolonien* (Statistical annual of the kingdom of the Netherlands, the colonies) (The Hague: Central Bureau voor de statistiek, 1888–1923); and *Statistisch Jaaroverzicht voor Nederlandsch-Indië* (Statistical abstract for the Netherlands East Indies) (Weltevreden: Statistisch kantoor van het Department van Landbouw, nijverheid en handel, 1922–29). Thereafter, the "Statistisch Jaaroverzicht" appeared as the second part of the preexisting *Indisch Verslag* [Indies report] *1931–1941* (The Hague: Algemene Landsdrukkerij, 1932–42). (The "Statistisch Jaaroverzicht" covers phenomena of the year before the publication of the *Indisch Verslag*, e.g., *Indisch Verslag,* 1931, pt. 2, "Statistisch Jaaroverzicht 1930"). Before 1931, the *Indisch Verslag* was part of the *Verslag van bestuur en staat van Nederlandsch-Indië, Suriname en Curacao, 1924–1930* (The Hague, 1925–31), itself a continuation of the *Koloniaal Verslag, 1866–1923.* The *Verslag van bestuur en staat* and its precursors were published as a part of the *Handelingen van de Staten Generaal* and also separately, usually without indication of publisher.

The nearest equivalents published for the Philippines are the *Annual Report[s] of the Governor General.* Unpublished statistics and information survive in quantity in Bureau of Insular Affairs files, in the National Archives.

Parliamentary debates for the Netherlands Indies are reproduced in *Handelingen van de Volksraad* (1918–1940/41) and for the Philippines in *Diario de Sesiones de la Legislatura Filipina* and its predecessors.

Intentional burning of records, as well as some wartime destruction, have made it hard to reassemble documentary sequences on wartime Japanese policy in Southeast Asia. Joyce C. Lebra's *Japan's Greater East Asia Co-Prosperity Sphere in World War II: Selected Readings and Documents* (Kuala Lumpur: Oxford University Press, 1975) contains some leading documents and assessments and a useful bibliographic note. Harry J. Benda, James K. Irikura, and Kōichi Kishi, eds., *Japanese Military Administration in Indonesia: Selected Documents,* Yale University Southeast Asia Studies (New Haven, 1965) provides a more reliable research tool than does Nishijima Shigetada, Kishi Kōichi et al., *The Japanese Military Administration in Indonesia* (translation of *Indonesia ni Okeru Nihon*

Gunsei no Kenkyū, 1959) (Washington, D.C.: Joint Publications Research Service, 1963). Frank H. Trager, ed., *Burma: Japanese Military Administration: Selected Documents 1941–1945* (Philadelphia: University of Pennsylvania Press, 1971) allows comparisons. There is no such collection of Japanese documents on the Philippines, but Mauro Garcia has collected and edited materials reflecting many of the critical Filipino policy responses: *Documents on the Japanese Occupation of the Philippines* (Manila: Philippine Historical Association, 1965).

NEWSPAPERS AND PERIODICALS

The *Official Gazette* in the Philippines ran from January to October 14, 1943, under the imprint of the Philippine Executive Commission; thereafter, until July 1944, under that of the Republic of the Philippines. The *Philippine Review,* monthly from March 1943 through December 1944, published articles by Filipinos praising Japanese spirit and arguing for reorientation of Philippine culture. The Manila *Tribune,* the only daily paper sanctioned in the capital during the occupation, ran until February 1945.

Taniguchi Gorō, in Tamura, *Hiroku Daitōa senshi,* 125–30, describes the relationship of journalism to military administration in Indonesia, and conflicts on propaganda and censorship policy. *Kan Pō (Berita Pemerintah)* was the biweekly official gazette. Nomura Hideo, ed., *Jawa Nenkan* (Java Yearbook) (Jakarta: Jawa Shimbunsha, July 1944) gives tables of organization and other useful data. *Jawa Shimbun,* a daily for the Japanese, ran until October 1945, and *Shinjawa,* a monthly, published political and cultural articles in 1944 and 1945.

In Bahasa Indonesia, *Keboedajaan Timoer* was a cultural annual analogous in content to *The Philippine Review,* and *Djawa Baroe* was a popular biweekly. The Japanese controlled editorial policy in the leading daily paper, *Asia Raya* (Jakarta), which is available on microfilm in the Echols Collection, Cornell University Library, and in the Library of Congress. Newspapers in other cities reflected that policy but conveyed some regional flavor: *Sinar Baru* (Semarang), *Tjahaja* (Bandung), *Pewarta Perniagaan* (Surabaya), *Suara Asia* (Surabaya), and *Sinar Matahari* (Ambon); I am indebted to George Kanahele for providing me typed extracts of key articles from these five papers. A variety of "liberation" newspapers and journals blossomed in Manila after February 1945 (unsystematically covered by the Library of Congress), and revolutionary publications in Java after August 1945 (many available in the Echols Collection at Cornell). Shiro Saito and Alice W. Mak have compiled a comprehensive guide in *Philippine Newspapers: an International Union List* (Honolulu: Center for Asian and Pacific Studies, University of Hawaii, 1984).

Manuscript Sources

THE PHILIPPINES

Through the kindness of Rafael Salas, then executive secretary to the president, I obtained access to the Malacanang Bodega, Records Division, Malacanang Park, across the Pasig River from the Presidential Palace. The records contained approximately 230 volumes on the period of the Executive Commission (January 1942–October 1944), 170 volumes on the wartime republic (October 1943–December 1944), and a smaller number on the period from February 1945 to July 1946. The guide to the filing system had disappeared, and more than half the volumes lacked identifying covers on the spine. The volumes, however, were topically discrete (e.g., Executive Orders, Government Corporations, Rice, Constabulary, Kalibapi), and their documents usually in rough chronological or topical order.

The Laurel Memorial Museum at the Lyceum of the Philippines contains almost all documents relating to the long public life, legal and political, of Jose P. Laurel; they include wartime correspondence, memos, and clippings, materials prepared for the treason trials in the People's Court, and the original of his prison memoir. The "Addresses, Speeches, Messages and Statements of His Excellency, Jose P. Laurel, October 14, 1943, to December 31, 1944," are informally collected in a single volume, whose contents correlate with and partially supplement the *Official Gazette*.

The National Library contains the Quezon collection, now well organized and protected (cf. Friend, *Between Two Empires*, 291), with some Osmena materials for 1944–45. More germane to this study is the collection of Manuel Roxas, located in the same room, with abundant and revealing material on wartime economic and food problems, guerrilla and treason questions, postwar ties with the United States, and the Huk rebellion.

The files of the People's Court that remained in the Department of Justice Building on Padre Faura included summaries of investigations, administrative records of the progress of cases, and records of the solicitor general. Some bundles of evidence in the cases of Laurel, Sergio Osmena, Jr., Vicente Madrigal, and others survived.

INDONESIA

I visited the Arsip Nasional (Indonesian National Archives) but have to cite Robert Van Niel's groundbreaking work, *A Survey of Historical Source Materials in Java and Manila* (Honolulu: University of Hawaii Press, 1970), for its paucity of material and its erratic coverage. In the Dalam Negeri (Department of Internal Affairs) Van Niel found scattered material of Japanese and Dutch origin, 1942–49, but none of Indonesian provenance.

The Museum Pusat, Jakarta (Jakarta Museum) contains wartime books and periodicals. The oral history project recently begun at the National Archives in Jakarta promises to enrich the field for future researchers, although most of the principals of the wartime years were deceased before the project began.

JAPAN

In the Documentation Office of the Gaimushō (Ministry of Foreign Affairs) a large, blue-bound volume documents Philippine independence and the treaty of alliance with Japan (September–October 1943). After the destruction of records at surrender, the Gaimushō reconstructed this sequence from its own files and those of the Daitōashō (Greater East Asia Ministry) and the Rikugunshō (War Ministry). With the advice of Mr. Nagaoka Shinjuru of the Gaimushō, and the generous aid of the late Prof. Nagazumi Akira, I selected for translation the major items, which Mr. Ōshima Shōtarō rendered in excellent English.

Japanese scholars have taken an inspired step by forming (April 1986) a Forum for Research Materials on the Japanese Occupation of Indonesia. Stimulated by the leadership of Nagazumi Akira, Gotō Ken'ichi, and Nakamura Mitsuo, the international cooperation of the forum is promising for the field.

THE UNITED STATES

In the files of the Bureau of Insular Affairs, Interior Section, National Archives, Washington, are voluminous files, well preserved and cross-indexed, on all aspects of Philippine life up through the Commonwealth period. In the Military Reference Section are extensive files on the wartime and immediate postwar periods, covering surrender, internment, guerrilla unit claims and recognition, and USAFFE general correspondence.

The MacArthur Archives, MacArthur Memorial, Norfolk, Virginia contain eighteen record groups, chiefly covering 1929–64. Of these, portions of RG 3 (GHQ, SWPAO), 4 (GHQ, USAFPAC), 5 (GHQ, SCAP), 10 (General MacArthur's private correspondence), and 16 (Gen. Courtney Whitney's personal papers, 1942–45) are relevant to this study.

The Washington National Records Center in Suitland, Maryland contains files of SCAP and the office of the judge advocate general. For the Manila war crimes trials, there survive transcripts, interrogations, prosecution and defense documents, and records of judgment. Morton P. Netzorg generously provided me with xerox copies of ATIS-ADVATIS material (Allied intelligence research reports and translations of Japanese publications) from the University of Maryland Library, upon which collections Frank Joseph Shulman produces excellent bibliographic guides.

THE NETHERLANDS

Nugroho Notosusanto, "Sumber² sedjarah Indonesia pada Rijksinstituut voor Oorlogsdocumentatie, Amsterdam," *Inti Sari* (Jakarta), February 1968, 74–88, surveys materials at the Royal Institute of War Documentation in Amsterdam. The Indies Collection there contains a variety of interrogations of and statements by Japanese, and a few fugitive sources of Indonesian origin. Anderson (*Java in a Time of Revolution*, 471–73) lists a good many of these; Dahm (*Sukarno and the Struggle for Indonesian Independence*, 354–55) gives a smaller number; and Kanahele ("Japanese Occupation of Indonesia," 326–28) provides still others. One may order them by microfilm, but there is no substitute for file-by-file research in the collection itself. Much of the RVO material is in English, the common language of Allied investigators and prosecutors.

For voluminous sequences in Dutch in other archives, Evert H. van den Broek undertook inquiry for me on selected questions, especially on political surveillance and intelligence. The major sources were: Archief van het voormalig Ministerie van Koloniën (Archive of the former Ministry of Colonies), for the years 1900–49, in the Ministerie van Binnenlandse Zaken (Ministry of the Interior) in the Hague; the Algemeen Rijksarchief (General National Archive), also in the Hague, for the Collectie J. P. Graaf van Limburg Stirum and the Collectie Th. B. Pleyte; and the International Instituut voor Sociale Geschiedenis (International Institute for Social History) in Amsterdam, for the Collectie J. E. Stokvis.

BIBLIOGRAPHIC ESSAY

PHOTOGRAPHS

The major public sources for photographs in this book are:

For 1898–1941:
The National Archives and Records Service, Washington, D.C.
Koninklijk Instituut voor Taal-, Land en Volkenkunde, Leiden.

For 1941–1945:
Audio-Visual Branch, Office of Chief of Information, Department of
  the Army, Pentagon, Washington, D.C.
MacArthur Memorial, Norfolk, Virginia
People's Court Records, Department of Justice, Manila
Rijksinstituut voor Oorlogsdocumentatie, Amsterdam.

I have also benefited greatly from the private collection of Niels
A. Douwes Dekker, of Huizen, N.H., Netherlands, which contains
materials from the whole era covered by this book, including some
particularly rare photographs of the Indonesian revolution.

INTERVIEWS AND CORRESPONDENCE

The passage of a few decades allows one to learn from participants
and critics much that the documentary record does not or cannot
convey, as well as to check personal memories against the written
record. A few of my interviews were undertaken as early as 1957–
58, and have not been fully expressed in scholarship until now. The
great majority of interviews were conducted between 1967 and
1972. Fourteen were conducted in Tokyo, Manila, and (mainly) Jakarta late in 1983. Specific dates of interviews appear in footnotes
when cited. In many cases the conversation and/or correspondence
contributed more to my perspective than to any citable fact or assertion. That neither lessens my debt to those individuals nor im-
plicates them in my mistakes.

In Japanese names, the family name precedes the given name. In
Indonesian cases, I have tried to use the name by which the person
is best known. Titles, if military, are those from the Second World
War; otherwise they reflect the highest position of the person relevant to this study. Mr. is the Dutch equivalent of J.D. Drs. (*docto-
randus*) is the Dutch term for a person preparing for a doctor's degree. A considerable number of persons on the following list are
now deceased. The initials "vdB" indicate three interviews conducted by Evert van den Broek on my behalf. An asterisk indicates
two or more interviews, conducted by myself, and sometimes suggests an open conversation over a period of years.

Kol. Abdul Kadir Widjojoatmodjo
Emilio Abello
Eleuterio Adevoso
Teodoro A. Agoncillo
Alwi St. Osman, S.H.
Sen. Benigno Aquino, Jr.*
Adm. Arudji Kartawınata
Dr. Bahder Djohan*
Judge Jose S. Bautista
Prof. Dr. R. F. Beerling
Prof. Dr. C. C. Berg
Ramon Binamira
Dr. Boentaran Martoatmodjo
Judge Fortunato V. Borromeo
Prof. Dr. M. C. Brands*
Drs. R. deBruin
Juan Collas, Sr.
B. M. Diah
Niels A. Douwes Dekker*
Drs. P. Dronkers
Att'y, Alfonso Felix, Jr.
Fujita Ichirō
Fukushima Shintarō*
Judge Angel Gamboa
Goenawan Mohamad
Gonzalo Gonzalez
Carmen Guerrero-Nakpil
Hamamoto Masakatsu*
Prof. Dr. Harsja Bachtiar
Dr. Moh. Hatta*
Gen. Hayashi Yoshihide
Drs. Hazil
G. H. de Heer
G. K. de Heer*
Dr. W. Hoven
Dr. P.J.A. Idenburg (vdB)
Prof. Ishida Takeshi*
Ishikawa Kin-ichi*
Iwa Kusuma Sumantri, S.H.
Mr. J. A. Jonkman
H. A. Joustra
Karkono Partokusumo

Prof. R. H. Kasman Singodimedjo
Prof. Kataoka Tetsuya
Gen. Kemal Idris
Dr. B. Kharmawan*
Kihara Jitaro
Kishı Kōichi*
Dr. J.A.C. de Kock van Leeuwen
Mr. P. J. Koets
Jose Lansang*
Pres. Jose P. Laurel*
Dr. Lıe Tek Tjeng
Commander Lıwayway
Drs. Elsbeth Locher-Scholten
Adm. Maeda Tadashi
H.E. Adam Malik
Margono Djojohadikusumo
Prof. Maruyama Masao
Prof. Miwa Kimitada
Miyoshi Shunkichirō*
Mochtar Lubis
Nagaoka Shinjuru
Prof. Nagazumi Akira*
Nakamura Kōji
H. E. Mohammad Natsir
Amb. Felino Neri
Robert Nieuwenhuis
Nıshijima Shigetada
Moh. Toha Nishimura
K.R.T. Notojudo
Gen. Drs. Nugroho Notosusanto*
Hernando Ocampo
Pres. Sergio Osmena, Sr.*
Col. Ohta Kaneshirō*
Rev. Dr. Mr. Jac. Ozinga
Prof. Dr. G. F. Pijper
Prof. Dr. J. M. Pluvier
P. A. van der Poel* (vdB)
B.P.H. Poeroebojo
A.M.W. Pranarka
Carlos Quirıno*
Sen. Claro M. Recto*
Antonio Romualdez*

Moh. Jusuf Ronodipuro*
Rosihan Anwar
Sixto Roxas*
Prof. Rōyama Masamichi
Dr. Ruslan Abdulgani
Moh. Said Reksohadiprodjo*
Dr. Ali Sastroamidjojo
Satyawati Suleiman
Mr. E.L.C. Schiff
Dr. Selosoemardjan
Hassan Shadily*
Shimizu Hitoshi*
Shiohara Tamozu
H.E. Sjafruddin Prawiranegara
Prof. Dr. Slamet Imam Santoso*
Dr. L.A.L. Sluimers
Soebadio Sastrosatomo
Soedjatmoko*
Mr. R. Soedjono
Drs. Soeroto*
Mr. Ahmed Subardjo*
Sudarpo Sastrosartomo*
Mr. Sudiro
Mr. Sumanang

Dr. Sumitro Djojohadikusumo
Prof. Sunario, S.H.
Drs. Moh. Amir Sutaarga*
Suzuki Keizō
Prof. Takéuchi Tatsuji*
Arturo V. Tanco, Jr.
Taniguchi Gorō
Luis Taruc*
Prof. Dr. Jac. P. Thijsse
Prof. Dr. J. Tinbergen
Harry Tjan Silahi
Anwar Tjokroaminoto
Harsono Tjokroaminoto*
Dr. Leandro Tormo Sanz
H. Usmar Ismael
Col. Utsunomiya Naotaka
Gen. Basilio Valdez
Amb. Jorge Vargas*
H.J.A. Vermijs* (vdB)
Gen. Wachi Takagi*
Jusuf Wanandi
Prof. Dr. W. H. Wertheim
Gen. Yamamoto Moichirō*
Capt. Yanagawa Motoshige

INDEX

INDEX

LIBRARY OF CONGRESS
Library of Congress Cataloging-in-Publication Data

Friend, Theodore.
The blue-eyed enemy: Japan against the West in Java and Luzon,
1942–1945 / Theodore Friend.
p.   cm.
Bibliography: p.   Includes index.
ISBN 0–691–05524–6 (alk. paper)
1. Indonesia—History—Japanese occupation, 1942–1945
2. Philippines—History—Japanese occupation, 1942–1945. I. Title.
DS643.5.F75 1988
959.8'022—dc19

88–2480
CIP

CPSIA information can be obtained
at www.ICGtesting.com
Printed in the USA
BVHW011842280620
582516BV00007B/387